No Win, No Fe
No Worries

C000173949

Conditional and Contingency
Fees Explained

Revised Reprint
November 1999

No Win, No Fee
No Worries

Conditional and Contingency Fees Explained

Revised Reprint
November 1999

Kerry Underwood
Solicitor

CLT Professional Publishing Ltd
A Division of Central Law Training Ltd

About the First Edition

What the Judges said

"Kerry Underwood could justifiably claim to be the leading practitioner in the new field of conditional and contingency fees. Now he has written a full and readable guide which should be on every lawyer's desk. The reader will find all the hard facts on the subject together with plenty of practical guidance as well as being stimulated by some of the author's controversial opinions; for example, he believes that "the day will come when experts will work on a no win – no fee basis in the same way as solicitors", a forecast which would currently be rejected by a large majority of lawyers, experts and judges."

Sir Michael Davies
Former High Court Judge and Founding Chairman
of the Expert Witness Institute

"... this is an excellent book and is highly recommended
.... highly practical .... thought-provoking .... very readable .... an invaluable tool."

District Judge Craig Osborne
Civil Justice Quarterly

What the Press said

"The profession's leading advocate of conditional fee agreements".
The Guardian

"Underwood, a leading authority on CFA's doesn't mince his words".
The Independent

"highly accessible to the lay reader"
Gregor Stewart, Producer BBC Radio 4

"Just brilliant. Epic."

St Albans and Harpenden Review

"This is a brilliant book.

Kerry Underwood has been developing his ideas for a good while and he knows that a commitment to the concept of conditional fees is essential against a background of the most fast-moving review of the civil justice system in our lifetime.

The best advice I can give is to buy a copy of this book, read it, consider it and then implement just about every suggestion that it contains.

This book is essential reading for all litigators."
Jonathan Ripman, Law Society's Managing for Success.

"One of England's leading legal thinkers".

Watford Observer

"As Maria Callas was to opera so Kerry Underwood is to conditional fees.

This enjoyable book is incisive, witty and passionate ..... the overall experience is compelling..... stimulating and challenging..... studded with down-to-earth tips and comments"
Bill Montague, Law Society's Litigation Funding Magazine

"comprehensive, practical and highly readable .... warmly commended".
Expert Witness Institute Newsletter

"practitioners would do well to follow his advice".
The Legal Executive Journal

What the lawyers said:

"From the outset Kerry Underwood has viewed conditional fees as a positive business opportunity for firms. This book, showing his approach and innovative ideas will help the confidence of other practitioners, now facing the real new world of conditional fees".
Michael Napier, Deputy Vice President of the Law Society

"Kerry Underwood's book is a compulsive contribution to the debate on how best to make a success of conditional and contingency fees."
Tony Girling, Past President of the Law Society

"Excellent book, excellent read, plenty of thought provoking stuff!
Andrew Foden, Solicitor

"Excellent"

Luke Clements

"The best £28 I have spent!"
Derek Wilcock, Solicitor

"…. extraordinary book …. should be compulsory not just for litigators but practice managers, senior partners …."

Tim Beasley, Solicitor

"extremely useful"

Laurence Ross, Solicitor

"extremely impressed"

Stephen Blower, Solicitor

"practical tips presented in an easy to read manner by a lawyer who clearly practises in the real world."

Chris Ward, Managing Director, Abbey Legal Protection Ltd.

© Kerry Underwood 1999

Published by
CLT Professional Publishing Ltd
Part of the Central Law Group
31–33 Stonehills House
Welwyn Garden City
Hertfordshire
AL8 6PU

ISBN 1 85811 132 3

Typeset by Jane Conway

Printed in Great Britain

Contents

Chapters

Appendices

Acts, Regulations etc

Model Conditional and Contingency Fee Agreements

Precedent Letters and Forms

Law Reports and miscellaneous documents

Dedication

To my Mother
and
To my Father, who landed on D-Day
and
To Clare

Thanks to

Fiona Bawdon
Peter Brown
Mark Carine
Luke Clements
Cozen and O'Connor, Los Angeles
Louis Doyle
Tony Girling
Andrew Griffin
Michael Napier
Clare Ranger
Mark S. Roth
Mark Solon
Cathy Tribe
Chris Ward
The Staff of the Tropikist Hotel, Tobago

Introduction

Take a simple idea that is attractive to clients and beneficial to solicitors, get the Law Society to prepare all the documents you need, get insurance to back the scheme and you have a successful conditional fee scheme and everyone lives happily ever after.

Well not quite. We are after all dealing with lawyers here. I am one. I know what they are like. Most lawyers will find endless reasons *not* to do anything new. They invent complications and objections and confuse matters unnecessarily. I have heard more nonsense from lawyers about conditional fees than any other legal topic. Fortunately the courts are taking a more positive and common sense view.

If solicitors were operating profitably in a stable and unchanging world I could understand (if not accept) a reluctance to change or embrace anything new. A solicitor in the 1950's or 1960's had little need to worry about the future.

All that has changed. The dismantling of the Legal Aid system and the collapse of conveyancing fees have combined to make life tough for all but the largest firms of solicitors, and even they are under threat from the influx of American law firms.

The further changes to Legal Aid proposed by the Government and to Civil Justice brought in by the Civil Procedure Rules 1998 on April 26th 1999 alter radically the way civil litigation cases are run and remunerated.

So far the main impact of conditional fees has been in plaintiff personal injury work, but all that will change as conditional fees have now been extended to all civil litigation (except, at the moment, family work) and as Legal Aid is withdrawn from personal injury work[†].

Plaintiff personal injury lawyers can still make an acceptable living from the costs received from the defendant's insurers in the successful cases. That is all about to change. Once the fixed costs regime proposed in Woolf comes into play solicitors will have to utilize Part 36 offers and obtain a success fee in order to get a proper fee.

[†] The Government's intentions are clear. In the debate on the extension of Conditional Fee Agreements to all civil work the then Parliamentary Secretary said that they were "extraordinarily attractive" to the public. Speaking in Parliament on 2 November 1999 the Lord Chancellor said that lawyers "cannot go on living their lives being paid by the hour on a taxi meter" and said that people would know when the reforms were working "when you hear the squealing of lawyers". Don't say that you have not been warned.

Conditional fees or even better contingency fees, offer a clear, fair and regulated way of operating profitably.

This book looks at the difference between conditional and contingency fees and how they work in practice. It does *not* consider individual areas of work recently opened up to conditional fees by the 1998 Order and by the Access to Justice Act 1999. That consideration must await a future edition. Significantly major commercial firms such as Linklaters are now offering to work on a conditional fee basis.

I will not mourn the death of the hourly rate. It rewards inefficiency and punishes those with skill, speed and good judgment. The classic example is the lawyer who "dabbles" in personal injury work, *i.e.* does not know what he is doing. He takes a long time, undersettles but racks up more hours and gets a higher fee than the specialist who identifies the issues and receives a prompt and proper settlement. In the former case the defendant's insurers are happy to pay the solicitor a bit over the top on costs because they have saved more than that in damages. The same principle applies in any area of work.

In his formidable exposure of the current system Sir Peter Middleton in his *Review of Civil Justice and Legal Aid* says:

> Payment calculated after the event on the basis of an hourly rate for all work done offers the greatest rewards to the least efficient providers.

Many years ago a solicitor friend and I both applied for jobs in Hong Kong. I was a criminal lawyer and he was a family lawyer and there was an advert for both jobs. We both applied for both jobs. I went to the criminal interview first and did reasonably well but told my friend all of the questions. As a family lawyer he coasted through the criminal interview. The reverse happened with the family job. Aware of the questions to be asked I sailed through.

Thus we got offered each other's jobs.

Those concerned for the people of South China will be pleased to know that in the end we did not go. But the truth is that on hourly rates it would have made little difference to our profitability and value to our firms or indeed anything except of course the fate of the literally ill-advised clients.

Conditional fees, contingency fees and fixed fees are a tremendous opportunity for solicitors who are prepared to back their judgment, and if you are not prepared to back your judgment why on earth should your clients do so?

Some lawyers, especially barristers and some members of the judiciary, have expressed the view that conditional fees are wrong in principle, *i.e.* it is wrong that a lawyer should have a financial interest in the outcome of a case.

This argument is open to attack on a number of fronts. Firstly anyone doing civil legal aid work under a certificate granted in the last four years is operating under a conditional fee scheme. This is because civil legal aid rates were cut to £65 per hour for certificates granted from 25th February 1994. So if a solicitor fails to win he gets £65 per hour. However if he wins and recovers costs from the other side he will recover around £120 per hour on a County Court between the parties taxation and significantly more in the High Court. So in a civil legal aid case a solicitor stands to gain approaching double the costs if he wins. Thus in hundreds of thousands of cases solicitors already have a significant financial interest in the outcome.

It is ironic that so much attention has been paid to the success fee in conditional fee cases when at the same time virtually nothing has been said about the success fee in legal aid cases. Yet this is almost always much higher but is paid by the client's *opponent* and not the client out of damages.

Furthermore straightforward contingency fees – taking a percentage share – have long been permissible in non-contentious proceedings, which somewhat curiously include Employment Tribunal proceedings. No one is seriously suggesting that these developments have led to a lowering of professional standards in these cases or civil legal aid cases.

Virtually all plaintiff personal injury solicitors have operated on an unofficial conditional fee basis since the beginning of time or at least since the invention of the concept of negligence. True most of them have not taken a share of the damages if they have won but they have proceeded on the tacit understanding with the client that no charge would be made unless the case reached a successful conclusion, in which case the defendant's insurers would pay.

This scheme has a variety of euphemisms, "prospective funding", "speculative funding", "delayed billing" and so on. It was the only way most non-legally aided clients could embark upon personal injury litigation. It has very recently been sanctioned by the Court of Appeal in *Thai Trading Co. (a Firm)* v *Taylor, The Times* 6th March 1998.

The introduction of conditional fees allows us to come out of the closet and market and advertise "no win – no fee" arrangements.

Furthermore because it is now out in the open our clients can insure the other side's costs and their own disbursements (but *not* their own Counsel's fees) in the event of losing. In return solicitors can take a share of the damages.

Thus everyone with a worthwhile case has access to the courts, the consequences of losing are insured against and the solicitor gets an extra fee. Everyone is happy. There are no downsides in personal injury work yet few solicitors are operating "no win – no fee" arrangements. Those who have a significant number of conditional fee agreements signed – say over 50 – are very enthusiastic about the scheme, have done very well out of it and have happy clients.

I believe it is a fear of change, combined with the apparent, rather than real, complexities of the assessment of risk and the calculation of the success fee, that has prevented solicitors undertaking conditional fee work.

Conditional fees are here to stay. The Woolf Report strongly supports them and the proposed fast-track fixed costs regime goes hand-in-hand with conditional fees. I have quoted the Middleton review above. The Law Society said in *Scales of Justice,* its July 1997 submission to the Middleton Review:

> Conditional fees should be extended to all non-family cases where litigants are claiming money

although it points out the need for affordable insurance to cover the opponent's costs in the event of losing. The Consumers Association supports them[†]. The Lord Chancellor loves them.

In this book I hope to demonstrate that there is nothing difficult or risky about operating on a conditional fee basis in many areas of civil litigation work. I have concentrated on those areas of work where conditional or contingency fees have been permitted since 1995 primarily personal injury work, including Criminal Injury Compensation Authority claims and Employment Tribunal work, and insolvency. Conditional fees in such cases are indeed simple, attractive to clients and profitable to solicitors.

They will be even more attractive when the success fee is recoverable from the other side and the conditional fee client keeps all of her money.

The tyranny of the hourly rate and blank cheque justice (or lack of it) are on the way out.

Breaking out of the manacles of the hourly rate will set you and your clients free: you have nothing to lose but your overdrafts.

---

† Law Society's Gazette, 14 April 1999, Lord Irvine said "What I would like to hear solicitors acknowledging is that the extension of conditional fees is good for legal business. Because if it is true, and I have no doubt that it is, that millions are brought into access to justice for the first time that means more business for lawyers and more litigation".

Table of Statutes and Materials

Table of Cases

Glossary

ACAS	Advisory Conciliation and Arbitration Service. Statutory body charged with mediating in Employment Tribunal cases.
Access to Justice	The formal title of the Woolf Report.
ADR	Alternative Dispute Resolution or Appropriate Dispute Resolution. A form of mediation. As with ACAS, the idea is to promote settlement without the expense and trauma of litigation and court hearings.
APIL	Association of Personal Injury Lawyers.
AVMA	Action for Victims of Medical Accidents.
Basic Costs *Base Costs*	The amount the client is contractually obliged to pay to his or her solicitor part of which is recovered from an unsuccessful opponent in the event of a win. The element recovered is known as "inter-partes" costs, or "between the party" costs.
Blank Cheque Arrangement	The traditional and still most common way for a client to pay a lawyer's fees – an hourly rate is agreed but neither the lawyer nor the client knows how many hours will be spent and indeed normally neither will have control over the amount required. Thus the client is effectively giving his lawyer a "blank cheque".
Cap	An agreement to limit the success fee by reference to damages recovered, e.g. agreeing to limit the success fee charged to the winning client to say, 25% of damages.
Champerty	Aggravated Maintenance whereby a third party provides assistance to a party in return for a promise of a share in the proceeds or subject matter of the action.

Conditional fee	A creature of statute. A form of contingency fee but subject to additional conditions laid down by Parliament. In return for agreeing to charge no fee in the event of losing, the lawyer is entitled to charge an additional fee over and above his or her normal fee, in the event of a win. The distinguishing feature of conditional fees as opposed to straightforward contingency fees is that the lawyers success fee is calculated by reference to their ordinary fees and not damages. However the imposition of a cap on that additional fee effectively transforms conditional fees into contingency fees.
Contingency fee	An arrangement whereby the lawyer's fee is expressed as a percentage of damages and is thus governed by the amount recovered and not the amount of work done. The precise opposite of the blank cheque arrangement. Common in the United States.
Costs following the event	See Cost-shifting.
Cost-shifting	Rule whereby the losing party in litigation pays the winning party's costs, or more generally, a percentage of them. Sometimes wrongly known as "indemnity" which has a different meaning in English law. Also known as "loser pays" or "costs following the event" or "two-way rule".
Delayed Billing	See Prospective Funding.
Double Damages	Concept that in difficult and expensive areas, such as medical negligence, damages be doubled to give lawyers an incentive to take such cases on a no win no fee basis.
Even Cost Volume	The assumption, wholly erroneous, that the work done in a lost case is the same as the work done in a successful case. This is an assumption often made by non-lawyers and has heavily distorted research and commentary on conditional fees.
Indemnity Costs	See Basic/Base Costs.

Indemnity Principle	Extremely complicated principle which expressed simply means that the losing party is only liable for legal costs which the winning party has agreed to pay their lawyers. This has traditionally been interpreted as making no win no fee agreements unenforceable as the law does not distinguish between a win and a loss. Thus in the event of a loss the client had agreed to pay his lawyer nothing, so under the indemnity principle, even if the client wins and had agreed to pay his lawyer in the event of a win, he can recover nothing from the other side. Has always encouraged solicitors to increase fees to justify recovery from the other side. Probably the worst single feature of the civil justice system in England and Wales as it prevents lawyers acting for clients of modest means. Under attack by almost everyone including the Court of Appeal. Section 31 Access to Justice Act 1999 gives power for its abolition by Rules of Court.
Inter-partes costs	Costs recovered by a winning party from a losing party. In the new language known as "between the party costs".
Loser pays	Rule whereby the losing party in litigation pays the winning party's costs, or more generally a percentage of them. Sometimes wrongly known as "indemnity" which has a different meaning in English law. Also known as "cost-shifting", "costs following the event" or "two-way rule".
Maintenance	Improper financial assistance by one person to another in prosecuting or defending proceedings in which the person rendering the assistance has no legitimate interest.
Multi-party Actions	Defined as cases where there are ten or more people bringing a claim.
No Fault Liability	Payment of compensation in certain cases, e.g. medical negligence, whether or not anyone was actually at fault. The perceived benefit is that an individual injured whilst undergoing medical treatment obtains compensation to meet their needs without needing to prove that the doctor or surgeon was negligent.

No-way rule	Rule whereby the court generally makes no order for costs, ie. each party pays their own costs, win or lose. In contingency fee cases this means a losing party has no liability for costs, either to his own lawyers or to the winner's lawyers. System in operation in the United States.
One-way rule	Rule whereby one party only is potentially liable for the other side's costs and one party is immune. Suggested solution to medical negligence cases, ie. a winning Plaintiff recovers costs from the Defendant but each party bears their own costs if the Defendant wins – suggested and rejected in British Columbia, Canada.
PIBA	Personal Injury Bar Association.
Pro bono work	Work which is free to the consumer and for which the lawyer receives no fee. More correctly work "for the public good". Done by almost every lawyer who has ever been born.
Prospective Funding	Very common and long standing practice whereby solicitors agree to take on a case on the basis that they will win the case and recover costs from the other side. Thus the solicitor does not expect to ever actually charge the client legal costs and the client never expects to pay. A long standing unofficial form of conditional fee work and recognised as such and sanctioned by the Court of Appeal in the Thai Trading Case, The Times, 6th March 1998. Put on a statutory footing by Access to Justice Act 1999.
Running up the hours	Maximizing time spent on a case to increase costs which are traditionally paid according to hours spent on the file rather than progress made in the case.
Small Claims	A more informal procedure in the County Court in which costs do not follow the event, i.e. each party is liable for their own lawyer's fees and cannot recover them from the other side. Currently applies to Personal Injury and Housing cases worth under £1,000 and other cases worth less than £5,000.

Solicitor and own client costs	See Basic/Base Costs.
Speculative Funding	See Prospective Funding.
Standard Costs	See Inter-Partes Costs.
Success Fee	The additional fee, over and above ordinary fees charged by a successful lawyer in a conditional fee case.
Taxation	Procedure whereby the party paying costs, either to the other side or to their own lawyers, can have the lawyer's bill checked by a Judge who has power to alter the bill and to reduce the charges. Known as "assessment" in the new language.
Thai Trading v Taylor	1998 Court of Appeal decision sanctioning no win – no fee deals in all litigation to the extent of allowing a solicitor to charge nothing in the event of defeat but full charges in the event of a win. Does *not* sanction extra fees over and above ordinary fees to reflect risk of losing and receiving nothing.
Thai Trading Agreement	An agreement between solicitor and client following the principles set out in the *Thai Trading* case.
Uplift	The percentage by which a lawyer increases his normal fee in the event of a win in a conditional fee case.
Woolf Report	Detailed report prepared by Lord Woolf, a Court of Appeal Judge, proposing revolutionary changes in civil justice procedure for England and Wales. Partly came into effect in April 1999. Key features include much speedier court process and fixed costs for the vast majority of cases and thus the abolition of the hourly rate, in such cases.

Sources And References

Books

Achieving Civil Justice		Roger Smith Legal Action Group
Agent Orange on Trial	1987	P. Schuck Hansard University Press
Conditional Fees	A Survival Guide	Michael Napier and Fiona Bawdon The Law Society
Guide to the Professional Conduct of Solicitors	Eighth Edition	The Law Society
The Price of Success	Lawyers, Clients and Conditional Fees	Stella Yarrow Policy Studies Institute

Other Sources

A new contingency?	31 March 1998	Michael Cook, The Times
A Proposal by the Law Society to link Legal Aid and Conditional Fees	December 1997	The Law Society
Access to Justice	Draft Civil Proceedings Rules July 1996	Lord Woolf HMSO

Access to Justice Proposed New Procedures for the Specialist jurisdictions of the High Court	A Consultation Paper December 1997	Lord Chancellor's Department
Access to Justice	Final Report July 1996	Lord Woolf HMSO
Access to Justice	"The Way Forward" October 1996	Lord Chancellor's Department
Access to Justice with Conditional Fees	Consultation Paper March 1998	Lord Chancellor's Department
Access to Justice	Interim Report June 1995	Lord Woolf HMSO
Access to Justice The Small Claims Procedure	A Consultation Paper November 1997	Lord Chancellor's Department
Access to Justice: Labour's Proposals for reforming the civil justice system	1995	The Labour Party
Access to Justice: A comment and some proposals	1995	Liberal Democrats Lawyers Association
Access to Justice – Civil Fees		Lord Chancellor's Department
Affording Civil Litigation	March 1998 Report to the Law Society	Professor Joanne Shapland and others The Institute for the Study of the Legal Profession University of Sheffield
An Approach to Non-Contentious Costs		The Law Society
Bond Solon Expert Witness Society	1997	Bond Solon

Civil Procedure Rules Judgements and Orders	A Consultation Paper 1997	Lord Chancellor's Department
Civil Procedure Rules Security for Costs	A Consultation Paper 1997	Lord Chancellor's Department
Civil Procedure Rules Service of Court Process Abroad	A Consultation Paper 1997	Lord Chancellor's Department
Civil Procedure Rules Transitional Arrangements	A Consulation Paper 1998	Lord Chancellor's Department
Conditional Fee Agreements	The Consumer View	Ashley Holmes Consumers Association
Conditional Fees and Payments Into Court: A Problem Solved	30 May 1997	Kerry Underwood Solicitors Journal
Conditional Fees and the Public	10 November 1995	Kerry Underwood New Law Journal
Conditional Fees Business Case	8 April 1998	KPMG for Lord Chancellor's Department
Conditional Fees Speech to the Policy Studies Institute	23 September 1997	Geoff Hoon M.P. Parliamentary Secretary Lord Chancellor's Department
Consultation Paper on Proposed New Court Rules	1997	Lord Chancellor's Department
Contentious Costs		The Law Society
Contingency Fees in Industrial Tribunals	18 October 1996	Kerry Underwood Solicitors Journal
Council on Tribunal's Annual Report 1996/97	16 December 1997	HMSO
Court Service Annual Reports		HMSO

Ensuring Justice? The Law Society's Response to the Government's Consultation Paper "Access to Justice with Conditional Fees"	April 1998	The Law Society
Health and Safety Statistics	1996/1997	Health and Safety Commission Government Statistical Service
House of Lords debate on Conditional Fee Agreements Order 1995	12 June 1995	Hansard
How to Profit from Conditional Fees	6 September 1996	Kerry Underwood Solicitors Journal
The Indemnity Principle	7 May 1998	The Law Society's Gazette
The Indemnity Principle following *Thai Trading* v *Taylor*	20 March 1998 New Law Journal	Peter Hurst, the Chief Taxing Master
Interest in Country Court Judgement Debts under £5,000 which include a claim for interest under the Late Payment of Commercial Debts (Interest) Legislation	A Consultation Paper 1997	Lord Chancellor's Department
Judicial Case Management The Fast Track and Multi-Track	An Access to Justice Working Paper July 1997	Lord Chancellor's Department
Judicial Statistics Annual Reports		HMSO
Legal Aid – Targeting the Need	Consultation Paper 1995	Lord Chancellor's Department
Legal Aid Board Annual Reports		Legal Aid Board

Legal Aid and Civil Justice Reforms Statement at an Adjournment Debate in the House of Lords	9 December 1997	Lord Irvine of Lairg The Lord Chancellor
No win, no fee? No contest....	August 1995	Kerry Underwood Legal Aid News
No win, no fee sets the standard	27 August 1996	Kerry Underwood The Lawyer
Non Contentious Costs		The Law Society
Paper on Presentation of Policy Studies Institute Report on Conditional Fees	September 1997	Daniel Brennan Q.C. Bar Council
Proposed New Procedures for Multi-Party Situations	A Lord Chancellor's Department Consultation Paper 1997	Lord Chancellor's Department
Proposed New Procedures for Clinical Negligence	A Consultation Paper 1997	Lord Chancellor's Department
Recovery of Social Security Benefits and Payments into Court	A Consultation Paper 1998	Lord Chancellor's Department
Reform of Civil Justice and Legal Aid The Government's Proposed Changes Parliamentary Brief	December 1997	The Law Society
Reforming the civil advice and assistance scheme	April 1998	Legal Aid Board
Report of the 74th Annual Conference of the Labour Party, Blackpool 1975	1975	The Labour Party

Review of the Legal Aid and Civil Justice Reforms	1997	Sir Peter Middleton Lord Chancellor's Department
Road Accidents Great Britain The Casualty Report	1996	Department of the Environment, Transport and the Regions Government Statistical Service
Scales of Justice The Law Society's Submission to Sir Peter Middleton's Review of the Legal Aid and Civil Justice Reforms	July 1997	The Law Society
Shaping the Future New Directions in Legal Services	1995	Legal Action Group Editor: Roger Smith
Speech to the Law Society Conference on Legal Aid and Civil Justice	20 April 1998	Geoff Hoon M.P. Parliamentary Secretary Lord Chancellor's Department
Striking the Balance	The Future of Legal Aid in England and Wales June 1996	Lord Chancellor's Department
Survey of Litigation Costs Report for the Woolf Inquiry	1996	H. Genn HMSO
The Effectiveness of Representation at Tribunals	1989	H. Genn and Y.Genn Lord Chancellor's Department
The Funding of Personal Injury Litigation	1994	S. Fennell University of Sheffield
Time at the Bar	1995 Page 314	Kerry Underwood The Litigator

Additional Sources and References

Access to Justice Act Explanatory Notes	July 1999	
Access to Justice Bill	2 December 1998	Hansard
Second Reading	14 December 1998	(cols. 1107–1127 & 1140–1201)
The Committee Stage	19 January 1999	(cols. 475–575)
	21 January 1999	(cols. 701–752 & 771–792)
	26 January 1999	(cols. 876–935 & 951–1008)
	28 January 1999	(cols. 1137–1193 & 1210–1278)
The Report Stage	11 February 1999	(cols. 329–384 & 390–456)
	16 February 1999	(cols. 551–571, 580–619 & 627–672)
The Third Reading	16 March 1999	(cols. 611–628 & 646–693)
House of Commons	17 March 1999	
Second Reading	14 April 1999	(cols. 230–332)
Standing	27 April to	(cols. 230–332)
Committee E 8 sittings	13 May 1999	
Report Stage	22 June 1999	(cols. 980–1079)
Third Reading	22 June 1999	(cols. 980–1079)
House of Lords considered amendments made by the Commons	14 July 1999	(cols. 398–538)
The Commons considered Lords' reasons for disagreement and proposed alternative amendments	21 July 1999	(cols. 1201–1243)
The Lords considered and approved these	16 July 1999	(cols. 1295–1312)
Royal Assent	27 July 1999	
Access to Justice Bill Explanatory Notes	3rd December 1998	House of Lords
Bond Solon Expert Witness Survey	1998	Bond Solon

Calculating Success	May 1999	Kerry Underwood Litigation Funding
Conditional Fees: Sharing the Risks of Litigation Consultation Paper	September 1999	Lord Chancellor's Department
Conditional Fees in Practice: 1	29 October 1999	Kerry Underwood Solicitors Journal
Conditional Fees in Practice: 2	5 November 1999	Kerry Underwood Solicitors Journal
Conditional Fees in Practice: 3	12 November 1999	Kerry Underwood Solicitors Journal
Conditional Fees in Practice: 4	19 November 1999	Kerry Underwood Solicitors Journal
Draft Code of Guidance for Experts under the Civil Procedure Rules 1999	September 1999	Lord Chancellor's Department
Draft Code of Guidance for Experts: for consultation	September 1999	Lord Chancellor's Department
Draft Conditional Fee Agreements Order 1998	28 July 1999	Parliamentary Debates House of Commons Official Report
Expert Warning	4 November 1998	Law Society Gazette
Guide to the Professional Conduct of Solicitors	August 1999	The Law Society
Income Tax and Contingency/ Conditional Fees	29 October 1999	Kerry Underwood New Law Journal
Inland Revenue Press Release	22nd December 1997	
Inland Revenue Tax Bulletin	December 1998	

Litigation Funding	Volume 1 March 1999	The Law Society
Litigation Funding	Volume 2 May 1999	The Law Society
Litigation Funding	Volume 3 July 1999	The Law Society
Litigation Funding	Volume 4 Sept 1999	The Law Society
Litigation Funding	Volume 5 November 1999	The Law Society
Modernising Justice	2 December 1998	Government White Paper
Revenue Note thereon re: barristers	22nd December 1997	
Speech to the AGM of the Motor Accident Solicitors' Society	15 October 1999	David Lock MP Parliamentary Secretary, Lord Chancellor's Dept
Taking Advantage of New Tax Regulations	30 July 1999	Hew Tittensor Geoff Everett New Law Journal Expert Witness Supplement
Tax Treatment of Partnerships	20 January 1999	Law Society's Gazette

December 1999 Update – Introduction

Since the publication of the first print of the First Edition last year there have been significant developments in litigation funding generally and conditional and contingency fees in particular.

The new chapter at the beginning of this book sets out developments and also comments upon the original text where appropriate.

The original text remains unaltered.

Appendices have been updated.

The main areas that the update chapter deals with are:

- The Conditional Fee Agreements Order 1998
- The Access to Justice Act 1999
- Experts and No win – no fee work
- Counsel
- Income Tax on No win – no fee work.

A major new publication – *Litigation Funding* – is now on the market[†].

Thanks to all of you who have written to me about the book and to those who wrote the reviews – all favourable but some more so than others!

Keep the comments coming and thanks for making the First Edition a sell-out so quickly.

Kerry Underwood
Bovingdon,
Hertfordshire.

December 1999

---

† It deals exclusively with conditional and contingency fees and is published six times a year, at a cost of £175.00 for the year 2000. It is available from Law Society Publishing – telephone 0171 320 5876, fax 0171 404 1124.

The Access to Justice Act is unlikely to be brought into effect before April 2000. The latest Lord Chancellor's Department Consultation Paper on "Conditional Fees: Sharing the Risks of Litigation" appears at Appendix 31.

Conditional Fees Extended to All Civil Work

Conditional fees have been extended to *all civil work* except family work.

This has been achieved by Parliament approving The Conditional Fee Agreements Order 1998, Statutory Instrument 1998 No. 1860 which was made on 29th July 1998 and came into effect on 30th July 1998.

It revokes the Conditional Fee Agreements Order 1995 (Statutory Instrument 1995/1674).

The new Order appears at Appendix 2 of this revised reprint and replaces the 1995 Order which appeared at Appendix 2 of the first print.

The key is Article 3 which states:

Specified Proceedings

3. (1) All proceedings specified for the purposes of section 58(3) of the Act (conditional fee agreements in respect of specified proceedings not to be unenforceable).

   (2) Proceedings specified in paragraph (1) shall be specified proceedings notwithstanding that they are concluded without the commencement of court proceedings.

The whole of section 58 Courts and Legal Services Act 1990 appears at Appendix 1 as in the first print.

The regime for increasing costs – the so-called "success fee" – remains exactly the same as before with a maximum permitted increase on *solicitor and own client* costs of 100%. No distinction is made between different kinds of proceedings. The heaviest commercial case involving millions of pounds costs, let alone damages, is subject to precisely the same scheme as a "rear end shunt" road traffic accident resulting in minor whiplash injuries.

This scheme and its interplay with the cap is considered in detail in Chapter 3 "The Success Fee and The Cap – Myth and Reality".

The Law Society Working Party on Conditional Fees is in the process of producing a generic Conditional Fee Agreement capable of being adapted to all types of civil work.

In the meantime the various specimen agreements in this book, covering non-personal injury matters, should assist solicitors. An agreement for non-personal injury work is at Appendix 30.

Family Work

Family work remains excluded, but probably not for long. The current exclusion is achieved by a combination of Sections 58(1) and 58(10) of the Courts and Legal Services Act 1990.

Section 58(1) reads:

> In this section "a conditional fee agreement" means an agreement in writing between a person providing advocacy or litigation services and his client which:
> (a) does not relate to proceedings of a kind mentioned in subsection (10).

Subsection (10) then lists, and thus excludes, all family jurisdictions, and all criminal proceedings.

In the Lord Chancellor's introduction to the Government's White Paper, Modernising Justice, 2nd December 1998, Lord Irvine says:

> We will extend conditional fees to cover cases about the division of matrimonial property.

Paragraph 1.17 of the White Paper reads:

> We have already extended the opportunity for lawyers to charge on a "no win – no fee" basis in civil cases; and will do the same for some types of family cases as well.

and at Paragraph 2.43:

> Where they are allowed conditional fees have already greatly extended access to justice. With conditional fees, people can take good cases in the certain knowledge that they will not be left out of pocket if they lose (except by the amount of any insurance premium). In July 1998, following consultation, the Government extended the benefits of conditional fees to all types of civil cases, except family proceedings. This was as far as we could go under the present law. In future we intend to allow conditional fees in some types of family case as well. Conditional fees are not appropriate in cases about the care of children or domestic violence. On the other hand, they offer a potentially attractive option in cases about the division of matrimonial property. We see no reason to prevent people from

choosing to fund those cases by a conditional fee, rather than having to pay their lawyer, win or lose.

Clause 27 of the Access to Justice Bill proposed to do just that by amending Section 58 Courts and Legal Services Act 1990 and restricting the *exclusions* as follows:

58A – (1)
The proceedings which cannot be the subject of an enforceable conditional fee agreement are:
(a) criminal proceedings; and
(b) family proceedings relating (in whole or in part) to a matter which is neither a financial matter nor a matter concerning property.

In the event this was withdrawn and thus did not appear in the Access to Justice Act 1999 which is discussed below.

However there is no logical basis for the continued exclusion of purely financial matters in family cases and in any event such exclusion is likely to be in breach of the Human Rights Act 1998 when it is brought in, on 2nd October 2000.

Thus family lawyers would be well-advised to familiarise themselves with conditional fees.

Criminal Work

Section 27 of the Access to Justice Act 1999 – not in force at the time of writing – introduces a new Section 58 of the Courts and Legal Services Act 1990 and when in force will be the statutory authority for conditional fee agreements which, as opposed to contingency fee agreements, are entirely creatures of statute.

The new section 58A lists the prohibited areas, that is those matters "which cannot be the subject of an enforceable conditional fee agreement".

These are broadly the same as the old section 58(10) – still in force at present – and as we have seen maintains the bar on family proceedings, and on criminal proceedings but in the latter case with one important exception.

This is that proceedings under section 82 of the Environmental Protection Act 1990 will be allowed to be prosecuted, and presumably defended, under a conditional fee agreement. Section 82 cases are statutory nuisance cases and this is the criminal provision relating to housing disrepair cases.

Its significance is the recognition by Parliament that certain criminal cases are suitable for no win – no fee agreements in the broadest sense.

The structure of the new provisions is discussed below but section 82 cases are part of a new statutory breed – cases which may be done on a no win – no fee basis *but where no success fee is allowed*.

These have been commonly known as Thai Trading Agreements, and thus are now put on a statutory basis ending any question of their legality.

Thai Trading Agreements questioned – the Hughes decision

The full judgment of the Court of Appeal in the Thai Trading Case appears at Appendix 24 of this book (page 330). This case apparently allowed solicitors to work on a "no win – no fee" basis, but without charging a success fee, in all civil matters.

However at page 168 of this book under the heading "Solicitors Practice Rules" I said

> In spite of the Court of Appeal's decision the Law Society has reminded solicitors... that Thai Trading agreements still amount to a contingency fee as defined in Practice Rule 8 of the Solicitors' Practice Rules and solicitors taking on such cases are in breach of Practice Rule 8 even though the Court of Appeal has said that it is positively in the public interest to have lawyers acting in this way.

> The Law Society has now re-examined this rule which, as Lord Justice Millett pointed out, is based on a perception of public policy which is now wrong. It is to be amended to allow contingency fee agreements where permitted under Statute or common law.

In *Hughes* v *Kingston upon Hull City Council*, The Times 9th December 1998 the Divisional Court (Lord Justice Rose and Mr Justice Mitchell) held that the Thai Trading decision was undermined by the fact that the decision of the House of Lords in *Swain* v *The Law Society* [1983] 1 AC 598 was not cited to it.

The Solicitors' Practice Rules 1990 made under the provisions of section 31 Solicitors Act 1974 have the force of law. Rule 8 prohibited solicitors entering into a contingency fee arrangement in contentious work and thus renders such arrangement unenforceable, both as against the client and, under the indemnity principle, any losing party.

In *Swain* v *The Law Society* Lord Diplock said that the Solicitors Act 1974 imposed a number of statutory duties in relation to solicitors whether they are members of the Society or not.... It also conferred upon the Council of the Society ... the power to make rules and regulations having the effect of subordinate legislation under the Act.

Lord Brightman said in *Swain* that the Solicitors' Practice Rules "have the force of a statute".

Swain was an appeal from a magistrates' court to the Divisional Court in a criminal matter and, apparently, the Divisional Court is technically superior to the Court of Appeal and free not to follow the Court of Appeal decision in *Thai Trading*.

This is the case even though the Divisional court in this case comprised a Court of Appeal judge and a High Court judge whereas in *Thai Trading* there was a full three judge Court of Appeal.

Strictly this decision is obiter as it is dealing with a contingency fee agreement in criminal proceedings. It is distinguishable because Parliament has specifically legislated for contingency fees in civil cases – conditional fees being a form of contingency fee – and specifically prohibited then in criminal cases (Section 58(1) and 58(10) Courts and Legal Services Act 1990).

The decision is also, in my view, plain wrong. In the event of conflicting Acts of Parliament the latter is deemed to have repealed the former. Contingency fee agreements *are* lawful in civil cases – Parliament has said so in Section 58 Courts and Legal Services Act 1990 and that Act must be taken to have impliedly repealed any section of the Solicitors Act 1974, and any secondary legislation made thereunder.

The logic of the Divisional Court's decision is that the Law Society could, *today,* prohibit conditional fees, relying on its powers under the Solicitors Act. Who needs Parliament when you have the Law Society!

And what about the "purposive approach" always adopted in relation to European Law?

I have no argument with the end decision in this case as Parliament has clearly set itself against contingency fees in criminal proceedings but I do take issue with the Divisional Court's attempt to undermine the Thai Trading decision.

The Law Society itself questions the Divisional Court's decision. Claire Morgan a policy executive in the solicitors remuneration team of the Law Society's Policy Directorate, writing in the Law Society's Gazette calls the decision "surprising" and says

Practice rule 8 deals with professional conduct between a solicitor and the Law Society, not the contractual position between a solicitor and client.

The Law Society had thought that *Swain* did not decide that the practice rules override a private contract between a solicitor and client, and that the decision in Thai Trading was based on such a contract and public policy and that, even though a solicitor may be in breach of the practice rules, this does not override the contractual position. If this view is right, the question arises as to whether the line taken in Hughes is correct.

The Law Society's Gazette – hardly a radical publication – refers to "the unruly tendency of our higher courts to declare to be black what another court called white six months earlier."

Rule 8 has now been amended to allow Thai Trading agreements. (See Law Society Gazette 13 January 1999).

In the Access to Justice Act Parliament has reversed the *Hughes* decision and the old Rule 8 but that Act is not yet in force and so the amended Rule 8 governs such agreements.

The great advantage of Thai Trading agreements has been in acting for defendants where, in the event of a win there is no monetary award to "cap". To say "£170.00 per hour if we win – nothing if we lose" is very attractive to defendants and makes them much more willing to instruct solicitors.

Access to Justice Act 1999

This Act received Royal Assent on 27th July 1999 but none of its important provisions have been brought into force and no date has yet been set for their introduction.

The Act revolutionizes legal funding and its full effect is beyond the scope of this update.

As far as no win – no fee agreements are concerned the key effects are:-

- Thai Trading Agreements put upon a statutory basis (Section 27)
- Premium for insuring against loss becomes recoverable from the losing party (Section 29)
- success fee becomes recoverable from the losing party. (new Section 58A(6) Courts and Legal Services Act 1990 inserted by Section 27)
- power to abolish the indemnity principle (Section 31).

The provisions are extremely complicated and I do my best to analyze them.

Access to Justice Act 1999

The New Section 58

Section 27

This section introduces a new Section 58 of the Courts and Legal Services Act 1990 and is the statutory authority for conditional fee agreements, although as at the time of writing it has not yet been brought into force.

It is the only primary statutory provision and should be read and understood. It is set out in Appendix 6.

Section 58(1) retains the provision that a conditional fee agreement must satisfy all the technical requirements of this section so as to render it "not ..... unenforceable".

Specifically any other conditional fee agreement "shall be unenforceable".

This is a new provision. Previously this matter was left open but this clause categorically makes any conditional fee agreement that does not comply with this section "unenforceable". Under the old Section 58(6) only those agreements where the maximum permitted percentage increase over normal fees (the "success fee") was exceeded were specifically unenforceable.

Section 58(3) sets out the conditions which must be fulfilled to stop the conditional fee agreement being unenforceable, and is a mixture of the old Section 58 and the Conditional Fee Agreements Regulations 1995 (S.I. 1995 No. 1675).

Section 58(4) only applies to conditional fee agreements containing a success fee provision and as well as dealing with that success fee it provides that

(a) it must relate to proceedings of a description specified by the Order made by the Lord Chancellor.

Thus the structure of the new provisions is that conditional fee agreements with no success fee – commonly known as Thai Trading agreements – may be used and be enforceable in any proceedings unless specifically prohibited.

Broadly the prohibited proceedings are family and crime, but see below.

Conditional fee agreements *with* a success fee can only be used in *specified* proceedings. Thus one is exclusive and one inclusive. In time this is likely to become important. There are now three potential categories of work as far as conditional fees are concerned:-

1. Totally prohibited.
2. Thai Trading agreements, that is no win – no fee but no success fee.
3. Conditional fee agreements with a success fee.

An example of category 2 is proceedings under Section 82 Environmental Protection Act 1990 which are criminal proceedings. These are not prescribed but are specifically excluded from the prohibited list.

The section also allows for different maximum percentage success fees in different types of proceedings but before making such variable orders the Lord Chancellor must consult with the "usual suspects", that is:-

(a) the designated judges
(b) the General Council of the Bar
(c) the Law Society
(d) such other bodies as he considers appropriate.
(Section 58A(5)).

Section 58(A) lists the prohibited areas, that is those matters "which cannot be the subject of an enforceable conditional fee agreement".

Section 58A(3) refers back to Section 58(3)(c) which states:-

58(3) The following conditions are applicable to every conditional fee
    agreement –
    (a) –
    (b) –
    (c) it must comply with such requirements (if any) as may be
        prescribed by the Lord Chancellor.

Section 58(A)(3)(b) then provides that those requirements

may be different for different descriptions of conditional fee agreements
(and, in particular, may be different for those which provide for a success
fee and those which do not).

Thus the Lord Chancellor is empowered to introduce a more relaxed set of requirements for conditional fee agreements which provide for no uplift. Such agreements are generally known as Thai Trading agreements.

The Lord Chancellor is also empowered to apply different rules to different descriptions of conditional fee agreements.

Thus the rules may be different for, say, claimants in personal injury cases as compared to defendants in such cases or different for claimants in personal injury cases as compared with claimants in say contract disputes.

The Government's intentions are made clear in Paragraph 121 of the Explanatory Note published when the Access to Justice Bill was introduced into the House of Lords on 2nd December 1998 (the note was published on 3rd December 1998) in discussing Clause 27 which became Section 27:–

> This clause replaces the existing Section 58 of the Courts and Legal Services Act 1990 with two new sections: Section 58 and 58A. The provisions of the new Section 58 seek to take into statute law the decisions in the Thai Trading and Bevan Ashford cases described in paragraph 46 above. It does this by making all agreements to work for less than normal fees subject to the provisions of the new sections. It goes on to draw a distinction between agreements which do, and do not, provide for enhanced fees and to make particular provisions in respect of agreements which include provision for enhanced fees. It also allows the Lord Chancellor to prescribe different requirements for the two categories of agreement.

The Explanatory Note to the Act states:

> "133. New section 58 also draws a distinction between agreements which do, and do not, provide for an additional success fee to be paid. It empowers the Lord Chancellor to define the proceedings in which such fees are to be permitted and to prescribe their maximum size. New section 58(6) allows for success fees to be recovered in costs from the losing party in the case..."

Section 58A(4) extends the application of the whole of Section 58 by defining "proceedings" to include "any sort of proceedings for resolving disputes (and not just proceedings in a court) whether commenced or contemplated".

"Advisory services" and "litigation services" related to this wider definition of proceedings are covered.

Thus conditional fee agreements are now specifically allowed in all tribunal proceedings which clearly come within this wider definition.

As stated above any other conditional fee agreement "shall be unenforceable".

Thus on the face of it *contingency* fee agreements which have always been allowed in non-contentious work, are now prohibited in tribunals and for pre-issue work in other civil matters. All tribunal work (except in the Employment Appeal Tribunal and the Lands Tribunal) has always been classed as "non-contentious" as has pre-issue work in all other civil proceedings.

The ability to work in such fields under a *contingency,* as opposed to a *conditional,* fee agreement appears to be preserved by Section 58(5) which provides that a conditional fee agreement to which Section 57 of the Solicitors Act 1974 (non-contentious business agreements between solicitor and client) applies shall not be made unenforceable by Section 58(1).

A contingency fee agreement is of course a form of "conditional" fee agreement or to put it another way a conditional fee agreement is a species of contingency fee agreement.

Thus a contingency fee agreement in relation to non-contentious business and which complies with Section 57 of the Solicitors Act appears to be a not unenforceable agreement unregulated by Section 58 Courts and Legal Services Act. This double negative appears to leave the matter as it was under common law.

Success fee recoverable

Section 58A(6) makes the success fee recoverable and the details, which will be crucial, will be in rules of court yet to be published.

This short subsection is of course extremely important and, interestingly specifically covers tribunal proceedings as by reason of Section 58A(4) "proceedings" include matters before tribunals (see above).

Furthermore the wording of Section 58A(6) clearly differentiates between "court proceedings" and other proceedings.

> 58A(6)
> A costs order made in any proceedings may, subject in the case of court proceedings to rules of court, include provision requiring the payment of any fees payable under a conditional fee agreement which provides for a success fee.

Thus a solicitor acting in, say, an Employment Tribunal case under a conditional fee agreement may recover the success fee if she obtains an order for costs. Orders for costs are of course not usual in Employment Tribunals.

Section 58A(7) is self-explanatory

> Rules of court may make provision with respect to the assessment of any costs which include fees payable under a conditional fee agreement (including one which provides for a success fee).

This is also evidence that Parliament intends the term "conditional fee agreement" to be wider than before as it now clearly includes Thai Trading agreements and, I suggest, by virtue of Section 58(5) contingency fee agreements.

The detailed rules will be crucial to the significance of these changes but the Government has previously stated that there will be a presumption that the success fee is recoverable from the loser.

If that is the case it is hard to see why any client would ever want to instruct a solicitor on any other basis.

The Government's intention can be seen in the Explanatory Note published on 3rd December 1998 after the Bill was introduced into the House of Lords on 2nd December 1998.

> 31. It will enable the court to order a losing party to pay, in addition to normal inter partes costs, the uplift on the successful party's lawyers' fees, and in any case where a litigant seeks protective insurance against losing and facing an order for the other side's costs, any premium paid by the successful party for insurance (see paragraphs 45 and 47 below). The intention is to:–
>   - ensure that the compensation awarded to a successful party is not eroded by any uplift or premium. The party in the wrong will bear the full burden of costs;
>   - make conditional fees more attractive, in particular to defendants and to plaintiffs seeking non-monetary redress. (These litigants can rarely use conditional fees now, because they cannot rely on the prospect of recovering damages to meet the cost of the uplift and premium);
>   - discourage weak cases and encourage settlement;
>   - provide a mechanism for regulating the uplifts that solicitors charge. In future, unsuccessful litigants will be able to challenge unreasonably high uplifts when the court comes to assess costs.

and at Paragraph 122

> The new Section 58A seeks to make recoverable any enhancement to the lawyer's fees payable to the lawyer under a conditional fee from the losing party.

These statements are largely repeated in Paragraph 32 of the Explanatory Notes accompanying the Act.

What should be noted is that solicitors acting on a conditional fee basis will earn higher fees *without the money necessarily coming out of the client's damages.*

Of course we know that the market will bear a deduction of fees from damages – generally at present conditional fee clients are having 25% of their damages taken as a capped success fee.

A key, and unanswered, question is whether the Government will make it illegal for solicitors to charge a fee to their own clients in the event of a win. This raises the "Clifford Chance" question – will the major city firms be restricted to charging rates recoverable on between the parties taxation? This seems unlikely.

One possibility is that fast-track claims will be governed in this way but not multi-track claims, although the Civil Procedure Rules which came into effect on 26th April 1999 make no such provision.

Either way a sharp increase in legal fees seems certain.

Take the example of Mr Jones at Pages 34 to 36. Obviously if the losing party is to pay the success fee no-one, but no-one, is going to cap it unless forced to do so by legislation or court rules (and then we are back to the Clifford Chance question).

So option A will apply (although solicitors will want to frame a separate agreement whereby only 25% is taken *from the client*).

Thus in the example below £1,250 not £2,000 will be charged to the client.

The table on Page 34 will now look like this

A   No cap

	£
Base costs	6,000
Success fee	6,000
	12,000
Less received from other side	10,000 +
Balance actually charged to client	2,000
Damages	5,000
Money to client	3,000

+ comprised – between the parties	4,000
100% success fee on base costs	6,000
	10,000

This is good news for Mr Jones whose damages have moved from minus £3,000 to plus £3,000, an improvement of £6,000 entirely funded by the defendant's insurers.

The defendant's costs exposure has increased from £4,000 (40 hours at £100 per hour) to £10,000 (original between the parties costs £4,000 plus *success fee on base costs*), an additional 150% or to put it another way two and a half times their previous exposure.

Based on between the parties costs being two-thirds of base, or solicitor and own client, costs and assuming a maximum 100% success fee *the losing defendant's exposure will always be two and a half times what it is now.*

Far be it from me to protect defendants' insurers but........

Schedule 15 of the Access to Justice Act 1999 deals with repeals and revocations but does not mention The Conditional Fee Agreements Order 1998 (Statutory Instrument 1998 No 1860) which revoked The Conditional Fee Agreements Order 1995 nor The Conditional Fee Agreements Regulations 1995 although clearly the Act does affect both Statutory Instruments.

It is presumed that they will be dealt with when the detailed Regulations and Orders are made.

In the meantime note that Sections 27–31 have not yet been brought into force and the old law remains.

The Government had intended to bring in the changes in October 1999 (paragraph 304 of the explanatory note) but it now seems unlikely that the changes will be in before April 2000.

Section 28 deals with litigation funding agreements and is likely to be relevant to any conditional Legal Aid Fund but is beyond the scope of this chapter but the areas of work covered are the non-prohibited area. The Lord Chancellor is empowered to add further prohibited areas to Litigation Funding Agreements, but not to conditional fees.

Insurance premia

Section 29 makes conditional fees insurance premia recoverable from the loser but it is not clear from the wording of the section whether the premia recoverable relate only to insurance in respect of the opponent's costs or to the client's own costs as well:-

> 29. Where in any proceedings a costs order is made in favour of any party who has taken out an insurance policy against the risk of incurring a liability in those proceedings, the costs payable to him may, subject in the case of court proceedings to rules of court, include costs in respect of the premia of the policy.

Thus in principle the insurance premium becomes recoverable but note the qualified nature of this section containing the discretionary "may" rather than the mandatory "shall" and making it subject to the rules of court.

It is arguable that the "risk of incurring a liability in those proceedings" covers the risk of a costs liability to one's own solicitor.

Support for this wide interpretation can be found at Paragraph 47 of the Explanatory Note to the Bill.

> There are also available insurance policies which can be taken out when someone is contemplating litigation to cover the costs of the other party and the client's own costs (including, if not a conditional fee case, the client's solicitor's fees) if the case is lost. Some of them were developed to support the use of conditional fee agreements but others are used to meet lawyer's fees charged in the more traditional way. For the same reasons that the success fee under a conditional fee is being made recoverable, it is also proposed to make any premium paid for protective insurance recoverable too.

and at Paragraph 124, describing what became Section 29:-

> This clause makes provision to allow the court to include in any costs it may award against the losing party, any premium paid for an insurance policy against the need to meet legal costs. It is not limited to insurance policies taken out alongside a conditional fee agreement.

This is largely repeated in Paragraph 48 of the Explanatory Notes to the Act.

It could be argued that it covers insurance against paying *damages* as well as that is arguably a "liability in those proceedings".

Whether the terms of this section will effectively be retrospective allowing premia incurred now to be recoverable of the case is concluded after the section is brought into effect is not known and will depend on the detailed rules of court which have not yet been published.

In ordinary personal injury cases the amounts involved are relatively modest, typically under £350, but in medical negligence cases they run into thousands of pounds.

In commercial cases, already permissible under the 1998 Order, the premium may run into tens of thousands of pounds and thus this question needs to be addressed as soon as possible.

Section 30 deals with external funders such as trade unions *etc* and allows them to fund members' cases and recover the costs thereof.

Indemnity Principle

Section 31 allows for Rules of Court to be made to abolish the indemnity principle.

> 31. In section 51 of the Supreme Court Act 1981 (costs), in subsection (2) (rules regulating matters relating to costs), insert at the end

or for securing that the amount awarded to a party in respect of the costs to be paid by him to such representations is not limited to what would have been payable by him to them if he had not been awarded costs.

Thank you Parliament, but not before time.

I have long campaigned for this change. See chapter 16.

Contingency/Conditional Fees and Income Tax

There are very significant tax advantages in working on a no win – no fee basis.

The Finance Act 1998 abolished the cash basis of income taxation for the professions and thus solicitors and barristers will have to pay income tax on a realistic assessment of work in progress rather than paying income tax in the tax year in which the money is received.

In any event new firms have been taxed on the work in progress basis for some time giving the old established firms an unfair tax advantage over young firms. All firms will now have to calculate their profits for tax on a "true and fair" basis.

(Note that there are different rules for barristers. Section 43 Finance Act 1998 allows barristers to compute their profits for tax purposes on a cash basis for periods of account ending not more than 7 years after they first commence in practice.)

These rules came into effect on 6 April 1999 and thus apply to the first accounts year starting after that date. So for a business with a 30th April 1999 year end the new rules have been in operation since 1st May 1999 and will apply to the accounts for the year ending 30th April 2000.

Thus in this example the transitional arrangements would mean that all work done but not paid for, whether billed or not, would have to be brought into the accounts and tax paid on it. This would result in huge tax bills for some firms and thus this catch-up charge is spread over a ten year period starting with the tax year 1999/2000 with the first payment of tax on this charge being made on 31st January 2001.

For a very useful article dealing with this change, but not conditional or contingency fees, see "Taking advantage of new tax regulations" by Hew Tittensor and Geoff Everett, New Law Journal Expert Witness Supplement 30 July 1999.

For young firms of solicitors this makes no difference as that is the way they are taxed anyway.

The question arises as to what work in progress exists in a conditional or contingency fee case.

The Inland Revenue's very clear answer is "None" which is very good news for all those doing no win – no fee work.

Thus all firms will receive very significant tax advantages by working on a conditional or contingency fee basis as no tax is payable until the case is successfully concluded – at which point the fee should be received anyway.

Thus the old firms effectively remain on a cash basis and younger firms effectively move from a work-in-progress basis to a cash basis.

On a work-in-progress basis not all such work is taxed. A detailed explanation is beyond the scope of this chapter but for example partners' work is not included and staff time is at the cost to the business rather than the charging rate to the client.

Cost to the business will include the gross salary of the fee-earner and *may* include other direct costs such as secretarial support, rent and occupancy costs – in other words a share of the overheads. (See paragraphs 25–29 Inland Revenue Guidance Note – "Withdrawal of Cash Basis").

Let us take an assistant solicitor doing claimant personal injury work. She has 150 files which will eventually, over a period of time, be billed out at £300,000. She is on average half way through the work and it thus has a billable value of £150,000.00.

As a rough and ready measure we will discount that by two-thirds leaving a cost price of £50,000.

Tax at 40% on £50,000 = £20,000.

This would be the basis of the catch-up charge spread over 10 years but thereafter the new work will be taxed in real time, that is each year.

So if the solicitor is doing £150,000 worth of work a year and half is unbilled at the end of the year £75,000 is potentially taxable.

Applying the two-thirds reduction tax will be charged on £25,000. 40% of £25,000 = £10,000.

Or take a new solicitor. She takes all the new personal injury work and at the end of the first year has billed nothing but has done £100,000 worth of work.

Applying the two thirds discount, tax will be charged on £34,000. 40% on £34,000 = £13,600.

This is very rough and ready but the Inland Revenue in its guidance note gives an extremely detailed example of assistant solicitors' unbilled work of £135,000 having a net realisable value of £39,692 (a reduction of 70.6% compared with my 66.66%) with a consequent tax liability, at 40% of £15,876.80. (Annex D Example 3).

If all work on conditional fee basis = Nil.

The tax saving will depend upon the type of work. In employment, with a very rapid turnover, there will be less work in progress carried over but in personal injury, where most conditional fee work has been done to date, the savings will be great because the work has a very slow turnover, often measured in years rather than weeks.

So why am I so confident that no tax is payable until the case is concluded?

Because the Inland Revenue say so. This whole area is dealt with in a Guidance Note prepared by the Tax Faculty of the Institute of Chartered Accountants and agreed by the Inland Revenue. It appeared in the Inland Revenue's Tax Bulletin of December 1998 at pages 606–615.

Work-in-progress has to be valued at the lower cost or "net realisable value" (NRV) and I have dealt in very broad terms with what this means for a non-conditional fee practice.

Paragraph 36 of the Guidance Note says:-

> As with other judgements, the estimate of the net realisable value of work-in-progress should be made on the basis of the information available at the time the accounts are drawn up. Thus, where work is done on a speculative or contingency basis ("no win, no fee"), but it is clear at the time the accounts are drawn up that the case has been won and that the firm will at least recover its costs, work-in-progress on the contract should be valued at cost. Where, however, the contingency has not been satisfied at that time, so that there is still a reasonable chance that the firm will recover nothing, the net realisable value of work-in-progress is likely to be nil. Paragraph 49 also gives guidance on the recognition of income and contingent fee cases.

"But", I hear you say, "this requires "a reasonable chance that the firm will recover nothing" and that cannot be true in a field where most cases are won".

Well Paragraph 49 puts it beyond doubt.

> Paragraph 36 above discussed the treatment of contingent events in relation to work-in-progress. In the case of income recognition, the Revenue have told us that they accept that income need not be recognised for a job which depends on a contingency until that contingency is satisfied. For example, a lawyer who took on a case on a "no win, no fee" basis need not recognise the fee until the case is won; only then is the condition met which is necessary to earn the fee. In addition, the Revenue accept that, for this purpose, it is open to the professional to deal with a large number of similar cases either in the aggregate or to look at each one separately. Under the

former approach it might be possible to say that a certain percentage will yield a fee and to recognise income accordingly.

Under the latter approach there is no certainty that any particular case will yield a fee and so no income need be recognised for any of them until the contingency is satisfied in each case.

The situation is the same for barristers. In a Revenue note for barristers, accompanying its Press Release of 22 December 1997, the Inland Revenue said

Conditional fee cases

No fees need to be brought into your accounts (and subjected to income tax) until the case has been won. The amount of the fee, if any, would remain uncertain until the case was won.

Thus conditional and contingency fee cases *delay* (but do not get rid of) income tax liability and will thus assist cash flow as far as income tax is concerned. This helps to offset the clear cashflow disadvantages of conditional and contingency fees discussed in chapter 17.

Although work in progress is nil for income tax purposes banks and prospective partners will readily understand that conditional fee files do have a real work-in-progress value and thus it is possible to have the best of both worlds – work-in-progress with a genuine saleable or borrowing value but upon which no tax is paid.

Experts

Experts are still very firmly in dinosaur land and as a result risk becoming extinct.

Suddenly everyone is in favour of conditional fees – Judges, Governments, journalists – but not experts, and even the Law Society is opposed to experts working on a contingency fee basis.

I say in chapter 17 "I believe the day will come when experts will work on a no win – no fee basis in the same way as solicitors *i.e.* if a case is lost they charge nothing but if it is won they charge an enhanced fee".

I stick by that – but clearly it will take a while and in the meantime the Civil Procedure Rules 1998 (The Woolf Reforms) and the abolition of Legal Aid (Part 1 Access to Justice Act 1999) are likely to lead to a sharp reduction in the use of experts, a view shared by Mark Solon of Bond Solon (see below).

The Law Society Council for whom even dinosaurs are unduly modernistic, has now instructed solicitors not to engage in contingency fee arrangements with experts.

The 8th edition of the Law Society's "Guide to Professional Conduct", August 1999, states as 21.11.(page 378–379):-

> A solicitor must not make or offer to make payments to a witness contingent upon the nature of the evidence given or upon the outcome of a case.

and at 21.11.4:-

> The court has disapproved of arrangements whereby expert witnesses are instructed to provide a report on a contingency basis. It is possible (subject to prior agreement, see 20.01, p.363) to delay paying an expert until the case has concluded, but the fee must not be calculated dependant upon the outcome.

Thus, bizarrely, no distinction is made between witnesses of fact and expert witnesses.

The Expert's Protocol under the Civil Procedure Rules 1998 has been abandoned for the time being and a Draft Code of Guidance for experts under the Civil Procedure Rules 1998 has been published. A consultation paper was issued at the same time and the consultation period ended on 11th October 1999. Once approved by the Vice-Chancellor the code will be converted into a Practice Direction under the Civil Procedure Rules and will be amended from time to time as case law on Part 35 of those Rules develops.

Paragraph 4 reads:-

> 4. Payments contingent upon the nature of the expert evidence given in legal proceedings, or upon the outcome of a case, must not be offered or accepted, because to do otherwise might contravene the expert's overriding duty to the court.

The consultation paper at Paragraph 2 asks:-

> Is the absolute prohibition in paragraph 4 relating to contingency fee arrangements correct? Should the paragraph refer specifically to the Law Society's instruction to solicitors not to engage in such arrangements?

So, there it is – legal establishment hostility to experts working on contingency fees.

Whither (or maybe wither!) the Civil Procedure Rules.

Specifically the overriding objective?

Part 1.1 reads:

> (1) These Rules are a new procedural code with the overriding objective of enabling the court to deal with cases justly.
>
> (2) Dealing with a case justly includes, so far as is practicable –

(a) ensuring that the parties are on an equal footing; *etc*

Quite clearly those of limited means are to be under a very serious disadvantage in civil proceedings as they will be unable to hire experts. They will simply be unable to take the risk of having to pay, win or lose, an expert's fee that they cannot afford.

How does the Court then ensure "that the parties are on an equal footing".

The Law Society Guidance and the Draft Code of Guidance are almost certainly in breach of Article 6 of the Human Rights Convention which appears as Schedule 1 of the Human Rights Act 1998, and which will come into force on 2nd October 2000.

Article 6 provides a right to a fair trial. The Law Society is denying that right to millions of people of limited means who, with the abolition of legal aid probably in April 2000, will be unable to afford to engage an expert.

An early Human Rights Act challenge is expected in relation to this topic and to the remaining restrictions on contingency fees.

Any lawyer who has a case that they think is appropriate for such a challenge is welcome to contact me for assistance.

The great guru of expert witnesses, Mark Solon, solicitor and director of expert witness training company, Bond Solon, regards expert witnesses as the Achilles' heel in the Woolf Reforms and said that a Bond Solon survey of 482 experts showed that 79% did not think that they should be allowed to work on a conditional fee basis, while 67% said that they would not do so even if allowed.

Mark Solon said that the combined effect of conditional fees and the Civil Procedure Rules, with the control of excessive expert fees, would lead to a recession for experts. (Law Society Gazette 4 November 1998).

Writing in "Litigation Funding" November 1999 Mark Solon says:-

> Experts are generally professional people. They can be relied on to act professionally. Solicitors and barristers are paid by one side but do not fight cases to win at all costs. If an expert believes in the case, he can maintain his prime duty to the court. Anyway how can there be a problem with a conditional fee for quantum?

But what to do in the meantime?

Bring it in house and do it yourself *on a conditional fee basis*, charge a success fee if you win and, when Section 27 Access to Justice Act 1999 is implemented recover the success fee from the other side!

Bye-bye experts!

Example

Donald Dinosaur is a solicitor. He has a personal injury case involving someone who may or may not work again and will need some nursing care. None of the reports will make the slightest difference to the issue of liability. They go to quantum only.

He instructs:-

Employment Consultant	£800.00
Care Consultant	£800.00
Accountant	£3,000.00
Total	£4,600.00

These fees are for *reports alone*. If the experts have to attend trial the cost will go through the roof.

Case won

Potential costs for the solicitor on this work	Nil

Case lost

Potential loss to client	£4,600.00

In contrast solicitor, Melinda Modernist prepares all of this information herself and attaches to the Schedule of Special Damages source material and the basis of the calculations. It is an impressive piece of work brought together in one document.

It takes her 30 hours. She is working on a no win – no fee basis.

Case won

Her between the parties costs are

30 x 130.00	£3,900.00

Her private charging rate is £195.00 per hour. It is a complicated and difficult case warranting a 100% success fee. Therefore

Success fee 30 x 195.00	£5,850.00

Total profit costs for this work	£9,750.00
Advantage over Donald Dinosaur	£9,750.00

Case lost

Potential loss to client	Nil
Advantage to client	£4,600.00

The whole issue has acquired increased importance by the decision of Accident Line Protect to withdraw from all but fast-track cases. Thus since 1st November 1999 no new multi-track cases can be taken on except on a case by case basis with a variable premium. Obviously a solicitor will not necessarily know whether a claim is a fast-track claim when the medical report is commissioned.

Furthermore the track is not just determined by value – it is determined by the likely length of trial and number of expert witnesses. It is true that most sub-£15,000 cases will be fast-tracked but the lack of certainty is a major disadvantage.

Of course medical experts will still have to be instructed although modern diagnostic techniques and technology bring the role of even medical experts into question.

As for employment consultants, accountants, care cost consultants *etc* they will adapt or be history.

Many firms of solicitors will not necessarily have the in house expertise to prepare all non-medical material but they can instruct those solicitors who do and can do so on a conditional fee basis.

In any event firms are of course free to bring specialists in as and when necessary and charge them out on an hourly basis as part of the firm's overheads, just like an assistant solicitor, or a costs draftsman.

What of course happens is that the evidence ceases to be expert evidence and becomes part of the pleadings or the skeleton argument or whatever. That has enormous advantages for everyone, except perhaps the experts.

The truth is that many "expert witnesses" are no such thing. They are solicitor's sub-contractors.

The advent of multi-disciplinary partnerships (MDPs) may solve the problem. MDPs would allow fee-sharing between linked partnerships of lawyers and non-lawyers. So for example a firm of solicitors and a firm of accountants could form an MDP for the purposes of civil litigation and could work together on a conditional fee basis, that is the accountancy input would be charged on the same basis as the legal input.

The real losers under the current rules are small high street firms. They are less likely to be able to form MDPs, will be less attractive to insurers other than Accident Line Protect, and can least afford to take the risk over from the client of paying the expert's fees in the event of defeat.

I accept that medical experts are in a different category.

In any event is it not insulting to experts to suggest that they are incapable of giving impartial evidence if their fee depends on the outcome?

They do it in the United States. Does a British cancer expert who gives evidence on a contingency fee basis in the United States suddenly become untrustworthy in a British court? Of course not.

Furthermore even if that view is not accepted what possible problem can there be in an expert giving evidence on a conditional fee basis when his or her evidence goes to quantum only?

Example

Roger Racer has a head-on collision with Susie Speedster. Each is injured and wishes to pursue a claim against the other.

Each instructs a medical expert on the basis of a fee of £500.00 if the case is won but nothing of the case is lost.

The experts' evidence is limited to quantum only and the fee is not dependent upon the quantum – in other words the experts' fees are entirely dependent upon the issue of *liability* over which they have no control.

Can anyone please tell me what is wrong with that?

Employment Tribunals

If you are not yet convinced consider this.

Legal Aid is not, and never has been, available for Employment Tribunals. Costs are not usually awarded. Thus an Applicant has to fund his or her own case with little prospect of recovering costs.

Employment Tribunals have exclusive jurisdiction over Disability Discrimination at work.

The Employment Appeal Tribunal has said that if the evidence is not agreed medical reports should be prepared and expert evidence given in such cases. (*Buxton* v *Equinox Design Ltd* [1999] IRLR 158).

Anyone can appear, with or without a fee, in Employment Tribunals.

Only solicitors are forbidden from instructing experts in the Employment Tribunal, because of Guidance Note 21.11.

Thus a trade union official, the CAB, or anyone else, including a number of cowboy operations, can instruct an expert on a no win – no fee basis. Because the Civil Procedure Rules do not apply to Employment Tribunals, the expert is free to accept such instructions.

Thus the applicant of limited means has a choice:-

- instruct a solicitor and have no expert
- have an expert but be deprived of a qualified lawyer.

That is wrong, unjust and an affront in a society that professes to allow freedom of choice.

It is also almost certainly illegal.

The Law Society should change this rule immediately.

Counsel

On page 182 I suggest a scheme whereby Counsel and his or her instructing solicitor split any success fee equally irrespective of the amount of work done. My firm is now using this method with counsel and the wording we use is:-

(1) The rate of Counsel's success fee will be 100% of Counsel's normal fees;

(2) the success fees payable to the Solicitor and Counsel (inclusive of VAT) will be capped so that their aggregate shall not exceed 25% of the aggregate of damages and interest awarded or agreed, whether recovered or not;

(3) the success fees of the Solicitor and of Counsel shall be aggregated and divided equally between them;

(4) in the event that the normal fees of the Solicitor and/or Counsel are reduced by agreement with the Client's opponent or his opponent's Solicitors or by party and party assessment, that part of the normal fees not recovered from the opponent and charged to the client, together with the success fees of the Solicitor and Counsel (inclusive of VAT), will be capped so that their aggregate shall not exceed [%] of the aggregate of damages and interest awarded or agreed, whether recovered or not;

(5) for the purpose of such calculation damages will be net of any benefits deductible under the Social Security (Recovery of Benefits) Act 1997.

Although (5) is specific to personal injury cases the clause as a whole is suitable for all types of civil work.

It preserves the guarantee to the client of taking a maximum of 25% of damages, whether by way of a success fee or the shortfall between solicitor and own client costs and inter partes costs or more usually a mixture of both.

At Appendix 28 is the whole agreement which readers are free to use. I can no longer commend the APIL/PIBA agreement which has therefore been deleted from this revised reprint, although the agreement now included is structured on the APIL/PIBA Agreement No 4.

Clinical Negligence

Legal Aid in clinical negligence (formerly medical negligence) work is now restricted to those firms with a "clinical negligence" franchise and a franchise will only be given to those firms with a member of the Law Society's Medical Negligence Panel, or the Action for Victims of Medical Accidents Panel, on their staff.

In the last financial year 3,261 solicitors' firms claimed legal aid for medical negligence work.

The number of contracted firms is expected to be between 100 and 200.

The recoverability of the conditional fee insurance premium (Section 29 Access to Justice Act 1999 – not yet in force) and the willingness of "after the event" insurers to operate on a "no win – no premium" basis will make it much easier for solicitors to pursue such claims on a conditional fee basis.

More about that in the Second Edition by which time it is hoped that the insurance premium will be recoverable.

The Future

So what is happening in practice. What are the likely practical effects of the changes made by the Access to Justice Act 1999, specifically the recoverability of the insurance premium and the success fee from the losing party?

What is highly significant about the extension of conditional fees is that it is the *leading* firms in any given area that are utilizing such funding arrangements. Thus Linklaters, probably the best large firm, have indicated its willingness to do all firms of litigation on a conditional fee basis (see *Litigation Funding*, Issue 4). In defamation both Peter Carter Ruck and Partners and Stephens Innocent handle cases in this way as do Irwin Mitchell in actions against the police and Underwoods in employment law.

This news should send a shudder through those firms that have not yet got to grips with conditional fees in particular and contingency funding in general.

Far from being an alternative means of funding, conditional and contingency fees are set to be become standard in all types of civil work, with the very best lawyers offering their services in that way. It is no coincidence that this should be the case – the top lawyers in any given field have the best understanding of risk and therefore the confidence and ability to operate on a "payment by results" basis.

Much attention has been focused on the recoverability of the success fee but in many ways it is the recoverability of the insurance premium which is of greater significance. After all, we know that clients will part with a share of their damages – the market has shown that. However the insurance premium, traditionally paid at the outset and paid *win or lose* has deterred many clients, especially in the riskier areas where the premia are highest, such as medical negligence and commercial work. The recoverability of the insurance premium and the innovative policies produced by insurance companies change all that.

At present a client who pays the insurance premium and wins forfeits the premium. Combined with the success fee, even a capped one, this will make significance inroads into the damages, leaving aside the question of whether the client can actually afford the premium up front.

Example – Old World

Christina Commercial has a breach of contract claim concerning the installation and operation of equipment in a hospital. It is not clear cut by any means and the value is £100,000.00. It is thus a multi-track claim.

The solicitors are prepared to take the case on a no win – no fee basis but strongly advise that insurance be taken out against the prospect of losing. Such insurance will cover the other side's costs and her own disbursements. The premium is £15,000.00. The success fee is capped at 30%.

Options

1   Christina Commercial loses.

Cost to her – £15,000.00 (the insurance premium) Good buy.

The other side's costs and her own disbursements far exceed this sum.

2   Christina Commercial wins.

Cost to her – Insurance Premium	£15,000.00
Success fee (capped)	£30,000.00
	───────────
Total	£45,000.00
	───────────

Of course Christina Commercial gets the £100,000 damages but nearly half – 45% – has gone in payment of the irrecoverable insurance premium and success fee.

Maybe Christina Commercial, who was always reasonably confident that she would win feels that she could have got away without insurance, or would have been better off paying an hourly rate, or indeed settling the matter direct without seeing a solicitor.

Example – New World

In the new world no such considerations apply.

Options

1   Christina Commercial loses.

As before – Good buy.

2   Christina Commercial wins

Cost to her NIL

(Insurance premium recovered under Section 29 Access to Justice Act 1999. Success fee recovered under Section 27)

Affordability

At the outset Christina Commercial went through all of this and agreed that no win – no fee with insurance was the best option but simply could not afford the £15,000.00 premium. No problem.

> In a variation of the old football chant
>   "You only sing when you're winning"
> the insurance companies have come up with
>   "You only pay when you're winning".

How does this work?

In the example above Christina Commercial pays nothing up front.

She wins. She has to pay the insurance premium, plus interest, to the insurance company but the premium is recoverable so it costs her nothing except interest which of course she would have foregone anyway had she paid the premium up front.

She loses. Nothing is paid. The insurance company accepts it is part of the costs of defeat along with the other side's costs and both sides' disbursements.

Thus Christine Commercial pays nothing. win or lose.

Litigation Protection Limited and Royal Sun and Alliance are already offering policies on this basis. Thus once the Access to Justice Act is brought into force no party in civil litigation need ever pay a lawyer again, win or lose. That is an advertiser's dream. It is a client heaven. It is a solicitor's risk.

Work will simply not be available on any other basis from most clients.

As we relax by our swimming pools or in our jets, some of us fat cat conditional fee lawyers already laugh about the days when we used to charge by the hour.

Soon you will be, or you will be looking for another job!

Thank you and good night.

Elvis has left the building.

Kerry Underwood
Bovingdon
Hertfordshire

December 1999

Amendments and Corrections

Employment Tribunals

With effect from 1st August 1998 Industrial Tribunals were renamed "Employment Tribunals". Consequently throughout this book, which is a revised reprint and not a Second Edition, all references to "Industrial Tribunals" should be read as "Employment Tribunals".

On page 159, Line 6 the figure "£6,000" should read "£5,000".

On page 42 the second table, commencing Line 11, should be as follows:-

Thus		£
Case 1 – won	Fee	2,000.00
100% uplift		2,000.00
Case 2 – won	Fee	2,000.00
100% uplift		2,000.00
Case 3 – won	Fee	2,000.00
100% uplift		2,000.00
Case 4 – won	Fee	2,000.00
100% uplift		2,000.00
*Case 5 – lost	Fee	0.00
	Total	16,000.00

* (Five, not four cases are required to compare like with like. Four cases would indeed produce the shortfall of £6,000 but of course by doing the extra case the shortfall has risen to £8,000. Thus five cases, not four, produces the breakeven point.)

Thus even without taking into account, as solicitors must do, the absence of payment on account *etc, cases with a 80% prospect of success or less should be charged at 100% uplift* **not** 25% as the "Mathematical" (sic) table at Appendix 12 of "Conditional Fees – A Survival Guide" states.

Getting Started

Getting Started

Introduction

This chapter deals with only plaintiff personal injury work as that is the only significant area where conditional, as opposed to contingency, fees are allowed. Conditional fees are allowed in cases before the European Commission of Human Rights and the European Court of Human Rights but there have been few cases in either forum conducted on a conditional fee basis. Conditional fees are also allowed in insolvency cases but again take-up has been low. By contrast some 45,000 personal injury cases are believed to have been undertaken on a conditional fee basis.

You will need:

1. Someone to oversee the introduction of the Woolf Report.
2. A stock of the Law Society's Conditional Fee Agreements – currently £7.02 for a pack of ten available from the Law Society Shop (*specimen appears at Appendix 12*).
3. A stock of the Law Society's client leaflet *Personal Injury Conditional Fees Explained* available from the Law Society Shop
4. A commitment to make conditional fees work.

The Woolf Man or Woolf Woman

Working on a conditional fee basis involves a change in the way firms work – a change for the better as far as the clients are concerned. To operate successfully from the firm's point of view, it is important that all staff are involved, especially those dealing with the public: secretaries, receptionists and telephonists as well as fee earners.

The Woolf Person should be forward-looking and committed to the concept of conditional fees, and must be prepared to embrace information technology and computerised case-management systems.

One person should be in charge of conditional fees. In small and medium sized firms this will almost certainly be a fee-earner but in larger firms it could be someone from the marketing or public relations department or the Practice Manager. Whoever it is should also be responsible for implementing the Woolf Report proposals. The changes that firms need to make because of the Woolf Report are closely linked to the changes that need to be made for conditional fee work.

A detailed consideration of the Woolf Report is beyond the scope of this book but those firms that are to survive and prosper need to look to the future and start planning now. The Woolf Person as well as keeping abreast of developments in conditional fee work needs to monitor the introduction of the Woolf Report, and in particular monitor *now* the effect of fast-track fixed costs which are likely to apply to all claims worth £15,000 or less, *i.e.* the vast majority of personal injury cases, and indeed all civil cases.

When?

It is almost certain that the Woolf regime of fixed costs will apply to all cases where proceedings are issued after a certain date, probably Monday 4th October 1999. Thus whether or not the case is dealt with under the new procedure will depend on the date of *issue of proceedings* and *not* the date of the accident, breach of the contract or whatever is the reason for the claim. This is the way the increase in small claims jurisdiction from £1,000 to £3,000 was dealt with.

This is much easier and more certain for everyone. Otherwise you could have a situation where a child born on 1st January 1998 has an accident on the 1st February 1998. Time does not run out until 31st December 2118 and thus he could bring a claim in 2118 and have it dealt with under a procedure abolished 19 or 20 years earlier.

Because of the often lengthy delay in issuing proceedings in personal injury cases the effect is that some of the files you have in your filing cabinet *now* will be subject to the Woolf fixed costs regime, because proceedings will be issued *after* the due date. The Government proposes an 18 month transitional period so that even cases issued pre-Woolf will be on the fast-track by, say, Spring 2001 although at present it is not proposed to bring them within the fast-track fixed costs regime.

An Example

It is the Spring of 2000 and you have just settled the claim of Felicity Whiplash for £9,000. The matter was settled after proceedings were issued in March 2000 but before "a defence was filed "stage. The accident happened in January 1998 and you were instructed in March 1998 and the fast-track procedure under Woolf came in on 4th October 1999.

You will receive fixed costs of around £1,000.

(Moral: issue proceedings as soon as you are able.)

Start the Analysis Now

It is easy *now* to analyse the effect on a firm's costs of:

    (a)   Conditional Fees
    (b)   Woolf Report Fixed Costs.

Simply look at the last ten, twenty, fifty or whatever completed files, ascertain the damages figure and the stage that the case had reached when it settled and you have the answer.

To assist I have prepared a model Conditional Fee analysis form which appears at Appendix 22.

Staff and Staff Preparation

Ideally every member of a solicitor's firm should be familiar with the concept and basic rules relating to conditional fees and should be able to answer common questions asked by clients.

Everyone should become familiar with the Law Society leaflet *Personal Injury Conditional Fees Explained* (Appendix 17). This is not because it is a good leaflet. It isn't. However it *is* distributed to clients, Citizens Advice Bureaux etc., so will be the source of client questions.

That leaflet lists 14 questions for clients to ask their solicitors (these questions appear at the end of this chapter). In practice some of these questions would never occur to clients but for being in the leaflet and the questions relating to the success fee are particularly mischievous as you will see in Chapter 3: *The Success Fee and The Cap – Myth and Reality.*

To help I have prepared model answers for receptionists, secretaries etc to give to clients in response to telephone enquiries or someone calling into reception. I have included a Question and Answer Sheet so you can simply photocopy it. This appears at the end of this chapter.

Role Playing

It is important that all staff feel comfortable and confident about conditional fees. Staff can gain practice by someone telephoning and pretending to be a client interested in a "no win-no fee" deal and asking awkward questions, *i.e.* the ones in the Law Society's leaflet. The act of doing this a dozen times will help telephone call takers to develop a patter and a confidence that will pay dividends when it comes to the real thing. It is also a good practical way of involving staff and helps break down the barriers between lawyers and other staff and those barriers are just as destructive as the ones that exist between lawyers and their clients.

This form of exercise is very valuable in any event, irrespective of conditional fees. In most firms it is the least well paid, least trained person – often the office junior – who takes telephone calls and thus your potential new business is in the hands of the person least well-equipped to deal with it.

The same exercise should be carried out in relation to face-to-face interviews with someone playing the role of the new conditional fee client. Lawyers too need to feel comfortable about explaining conditional fees to clients.

Is it Worth the Effort?

You may now be thinking:

- This sounds like a lot of effort: is it worth it?

- I still have not got a clue about what cases I should take on let alone how I calculate the success fee and the cap etc.

To which the answers are:

- Yes.
- See next Chapter.

Conditional fees properly marketed will increase substantially your personal injury case load, increase your fees per case and prepare you and your staff for the Woolf Report revolution.

You will enjoy a more relaxed relationship with your clients.

Remember that personal injury work is the most profitable work for many firms. With the added profits of conditional fee work most firms should be able to average £2,500 to £3,000 per case. (Less when the Woolf Report comes in – but more cases, less work and quicker results.)

Therefore it is worth spending time and effort attracting, capturing and keeping personal injury work. If one client every two weeks rings off because the phone is not answered quickly enough, or decides not to come in because no-one can see them for a week, or whatever, that is £65,000 to £78,000 of work a year lost.

Of course you may prefer your staff lycra clad and prancing around the supermarket for "Make a Will Week" or having lunch with an estate agent... After all you only need around one thousand nine hundred and fifty new will clients or three hundred new conveyances a year to make up for that one personal injury client a fortnight that you do not keep.

Personally I would want a lot of money to dress up as Will Power. As to lunch with estate agents... it is, as Judges say, a matter for you.

Summary

1. Nominate someone to be in charge of Conditional Fees and Woolf Report changes.
2. Obtain Conditional Fee Agreements.
3. Obtain *Personal Injury Conditional Fees Explained* leaflets.
4. Read and understand those documents and train staff in them.
5. Distribute model answers to the questions in *Personal Injury Conditional Fees Explained*.
6. Conduct role-playing exercises with staff.
7. Analyse the effect of conditional fees on your firm, especially cashflow.
8. Analyse the effect of the Woolf Report Fixed Costs on your firm, especially profitability.
9. Estimate general damages on each and every personal injury file in the office.
10. Prepare for the withdrawal of Legal Aid.

Model Answers

Answers to the "What To Ask Your Solicitor" questions on the *Law Society Leaflet* Conditional Fees Explained

These answers try to give a clear and full answer to *each* question separately as clients tend only to ask one or two questions. No client has ever asked me how the success fee is worked out or what solicitors' basic costs are and what "success" and "win" mean. Few solicitors understand fully these concepts – fewer clients have heard of them.

It is a matter for each firm as to who fields the call but with a potential new personal injury case I think that the caller should be put through to a lawyer straightaway. This will not always be possible and it is worth having one secretary or telephonist who is particularly familiar with these questions and answers.

The answers also form the basis of information to be given at the first meeting between the lawyer and the client.

They can also form the basis of a firm's leaflet in a "Your questions answered" format but clients may find this unnecessarily confusing.

What other means of paying are available to me?

You may be able to get Legal Aid, either free or with you paying something towards it or you can pay our ordinary hourly rate. It may be that you have legal expenses insurance to cover our fees or that your trade union will pay them. The solicitor will discuss these options with you at your first meeting which is free of charge.

Am I eligible for Legal Aid?

That depends on you and your partner's income, savings and expenses. The solicitor will discuss this with you at your first meeting which is free of charge. If we think you may qualify for Legal Aid we will make the application for you at no charge. Would you like me to send you a letter and leaflets explaining Legal Aid?

Will Legal Aid be free?

No, not necessarily. This will depend on you and your partner's income, savings and expenses. We can advise you at your first meeting whether you are likely to get free Legal Aid.

Can I get insurance cover against having to pay the other side's costs if I lose?

Yes.

How good are my chances of winning my case?

We cannot tell until we have seen you and taken more details from you. Usually the solicitor can give you a good idea during your first meeting.

Is it likely that my opponent can or will pay even if I win?

Yes, they are almost certainly insured and if it is a road accident you will still get your money even if the driver was not insured.

What damages would I be likely to receive?

We cannot tell until we have seen you. Normally we can give you some idea at your first meeting.

What is the effect of winning on any benefits payments I may be receiving?

Like most things connected with benefits and the DSS this is complicated. The solicitor will discuss this with you but overall you cannot be worse off than you are now.

How is the "success fee" worked out?

The stated success fee will be 100%, but it rarely comes to anything like that. This is because we promise you that you will get at least 75% of your damages: in no circumstances will we take more than 25% of your damages and that includes VAT. We will give you a written guarantee confirming this.

What do "success" and "win" mean?

That we succeed in getting money for you.

What are solicitor's basic costs and who pays these?

You ought to be a solicitor! The basic costs are the costs you would pay as a private client without legal aid and without a "no win – no fee" agreement. In "no win – no fee" cases they form part of our total costs but of course if you do not win you pay nothing. If you do win, then the other side pay some of the basic costs and you pay some. However, this does not really matter because we promise you that you will get at least 75% of your damages; in no circumstances will we take more than 25% of your damages and that includes VAT. We will give you a written guarantee confirming this.

What expenses might I be required to pay and when?

*There is a one-off insurance premium of £95.68 in road traffic cases and £161.20 in other cases. This means that you never have to pay any legal costs. There will be other expenses as we go along such as the fee for the medical report but we will get these back from the other side if you win and the insurance will pay you back the cost of these if you lose. There is one exception. If you or we decide not to go ahead *before* the papers are sent to the court then the insurance will not cover these expenses.

We can usually tell at the first meeting if there is a chance that we will advise you not to go ahead and so you can decide whether or not to take that chance.

Although generally we expect you to pay the expenses as we go along and then get them back at the end, we can help if you genuinely cannot afford to pay them as we go along.

In any event we will always give you plenty of notice of expenses to be incurred and to make it easier we take all major credit cards.

What happens if I need a barrister?

We are specialist personal injury lawyers. We would not expect you to need a barrister. If we decide you need a barrister we will make the necessary arrangements. What we promise you is that you will get at least 75% of your damages: in no circumstances will we take

---

*   These are the Accident Line Protect Rates. If the firm is not an Accident Line member then the actual rates of the actual insurance, if any, obtained by the firm, should be inserted.

more than 25% of your damages and that includes VAT. We will give you a written guarantee confirming this.

If you decide against our advice that you want a barrister then you must bear the full cost and this is not covered by your insurance and will come out of *your* share of the damages.

How will I be kept informed about the progress of my case?

It is this firm's policy to respond promptly to telephone calls and letters and to keep you informed of all developments in your case.

Chapter 2

What Can I Do?

What Can I Do?

Introduction

The historical reluctance of lawyers to work on a contingency basis, or even acknowledge the existence of such a possibility, is demonstrated by the fact that there is still no clear guidance in the Solicitors' Practice Rules on what can and cannot be done on a contingency fee basis and how to go about working that way.

Consequently there is no attempt to regulate or advise on matters such as the appropriate percentage of damages to be charged to the client in particular areas of contingency fee work. In Industrial Tribunals where Legal Aid has never been available this has for years been a common, but almost entirely unregulated, way of working by lawyers and non-lawyers alike.

So whilst the Law Society has given clear guidance governing *conditional* fees there is virtually none for *contingency* fees. A model Conditional Fee Agreement has been prepared and is sold by the Law Society and a new Working Party has been set up to revise and improve it but nothing similar exists for contingency fees.

Similarly Parliament has spelt out the conditions upon which conditional fees work can be done, but not contingency fees.

I will look at this later in this Chapter but it is for this reason that Conditional Fees are examined first.

Conditional Fees

The starting point is that both contingency and conditional fee arrangements which are a species of contingency fees have been illegal in *contentious* work.

This has apparently been the position since the Statute of Westminster 1275 and was reinforced 699 years later by Section 59(2)(b) Solicitors Act 1974 which apparently outlawed:

> any agreement by which a solicitor retained or employed to prosecute any action, suit or other contentious proceeding, stipulates for payment only in the event of success in that action, suit or proceeding.

Trading v *Taylor* – discussed in detail in Chapter 16 – The Indemnity Principle.

What is covered?

Conditional Fees were made lawful by Section 58 of the Courts and Legal Services Act 1990, which is set out below.

Courts and Legal Services Act 1990, s.58

Conditional Fee Agreements

58–(1)
> In this section "a conditional fee agreement" means an agreement in writing between a person providing advocacy or litigation services and his client which –
> (a) does not relate to proceedings of a kind mentioned in subsection (10);
> (b) provides for that person's fees and expenses, or any part of them, to be payable only in specified circumstances;
> (c) complies with such requirements (if any) as may be prescribed by the Lord Chancellor; and
> (d) is not a contentious business agreement (as defined by section 59 of the Solicitors Act 1974)[1]

(2) Where a conditional fee agreement provides for the amount of any fees to which it applies to be increased, in specified circumstances, above the amount which would be payable if it were not a conditional fee agreement, it shall specify the percentage by which that amount is to be increased.

(3) Subject to subsection (6), a conditional fee agreement which relates to specified proceedings shall not be unenforceable by reason only of its being a conditional fee agreement.

(4) In this section "specified proceedings" means proceedings of a description specified by order made by the Lord Chancellor for the purposes of subsection (3).

(5) Any such order shall prescribe the maximum percentage for each description of specified proceedings.

(6) An agreement which falls within subsection (2) shall be unenforceable if, at the time when it is entered into, the

---
1 1974 c.47

percentage specified in the agreement exceeds the prescribed maximum permitted percentage for each description of proceedings to which it relates.

(7) Before making any order under this section the Lord Chancellor shall consult the designated judges, the General Council of the Bar, the Law Society and such other authorised bodies (if any) as he considers appropriate.

(8) Where a party to any proceedings has entered into a conditional fee agreement and a costs order is made in those proceedings in his favour, the costs payable to him shall not include any element which takes account of any percentage increase payable under the agreement.

(9) Rules of court may make provision with respect to the taxing of any costs which include fees payable under a conditional fee agreement.

(10) The proceedings mentioned in subsection (1)(a) are any criminal proceedings and any proceedings under –
   (a) the Matrimonial Causes Act 1973[2];
   (b) the Domestic Violence and Matrimonial Proceedings Act 1976[3];
   (c) the Adoption Act 1976[4];
   (d) the Domestic Proceedings and Magistrates' Courts Act 1978[5];
   (e) sections 1 and 9 of the Matrimonial Homes Act 1983[6];
   (f) Part III of the Matrimonial and Family Proceedings Act 1984[7];
   (g) Parts I, II or IV of the Children Act 1989[8]; or
   (h) the inherent jurisdiction of the High Court in relation to children.

Note that Section 58 allows for the introduction of conditional fees in *all* civil litigation except family work, and thus the Government's proposals to extend the conditional fee regime to all money claims do not require primary legislation. At the time of writing the Lord Chancellor's Department Consultation Paper *Access to Justice with Conditional Fees* has been published and the consultation period ended on 30th April 1998. There have been 233 responses. The Department's response is expected in July or August 1998.

---

2   1973 c.18
3   1976 c.50
4   1976 c.36
5   1978 c.22

6   1983 c.19
7   1984 c.42
8   1989 c.41

Areas of Work

By virtue of The Conditional Fee Agreements Order 1995 (S.I. 1995 No 1674) and The Conditional Fee Agreements Regulations 1995 (S.I. 1995 No 1675) conditional fees were introduced with effect from 5th July 1995 in limited areas of work:

(i)   personal injury including medical negligence;
(ii) insolvency;
(iii) proceedings before the European Commission of Human Rights and the European Court of Human Rights but not in the earlier stages of such proceedings in Courts in England and Wales and not in the European Court of Justice which is a totally separate body.

But note:

Medical Negligence is regarded as a species of personal injury and thus claims may be brought under Conditional Fee Agreements with exactly the same rules and regulations applying as in conventional personal injury work.

However there are practical problems peculiar to medical negligence work, particularly relating to risk, disbursements and insurance and those are covered in Chapter 7 Medical Negligence.

Children and those under a disability: Personal Injury cases, including medical negligence cases, involving children or those under a disability, may be brought using Conditional Fee Agreements with exactly the same rules and regulations applying as for adults or those not under a disability. The same applies to insolvency work and proceedings before the European Commission of Human Rights and the European Court of Human Rights.

However there are potential problems relating to the success fee and those are looked at in Chapter 9 Children and Patients.

Multi-party, or class actions: No separate rules exist and thus these actions are permissible if they fall within the category of work allowed, that is personal injury, insolvency and proceedings before the European Commission of Human Rights and the European Court of Human Rights. However specific practical considerations arise and these are dealt with in Chapter 8.

Small claims in the County Court: Although there is no liability, or entitlement, to costs and no Legal Aid such claims are governed by the ordinary law and are thus prohibited unless in the field of personal injury, or insolvency. I look at small claims in Chapter 10.

As at the time of writing the Government has made a clear commitment to extend conditional fees to all money claims but no start date has been announced and it is not known if the regulatory framework will be the same as for personal injury work, *i.e.* in relation to the success fee etc.

Conditional fees can apply to plaintiff and defendant work in personal injury cases but not to defendant work in insolvency cases. (Insolvency is dealt with in Chapter 13.)

Thus the existing scope of conditional fee work is clear, with the exception of the question of a professional negligence action arising out of a personal injury case.

A model conditional fee agreement also exists for human rights cases and this whole area is bound to increase in significance when the European Convention on Human Rights is incorporated into domestic law. Note that domestic remedies, where CFA's are *not* permitted, must be exhausted first. (Human Rights is dealt with in Chapter 14.)

Professional Negligence Mr Hurt instructs Messrs. Late and Hopeless who miss the Limitation date and so Mr Hurt instructs Messrs. Sharp and Quick to bring a negligence action against them. Can this negligence action be brought on a conditional fee basis?

The Law Society says "Yes" but the Bar Council says "No". I agree with the Bar.

The authorization for conditional fees in personal injury cases is contained in Paragraph 2(1)(a) of The Conditional Fee Agreement Order 1995 which covers:

> proceedings in which there is a claim for damages in respect of personal injuries or in respect of a person's death and "personal injuries" includes any disease and any impairment of a person's physical or mental condition.

I cannot see how that can cover professional negligence cases – they are proceedings in which one claims damages for loss of a chance, not personal injury.

The Law Society relies on assurances given by Government Ministers that the clause was intended to cover professional negligence cases but the wording of 2(1)(a) clearly does *not* cover them. If Parliament had intended to cover such claims it could easily have added a sub clause:

> proceedings for professional negligence arising out of any such claim as specified in this paragraph.

Those who say it does cover professional negligence claims point out that if a person instructs a solicitor on a conditional fee basis in a personal injury case and that solicitor is negligent then that client is deprived of his choice to pursue a remedy on a "no win-no fee" basis.

Well that is true, but the Order still prohibits it. In any event is that any more illogical than a victim of professional negligence in a personal injury case being able to proceed on a "no win-no fee" basis but a victim of professional negligence in any other area of law being deprived of that option?

With the proposed introduction of conditional fee work in all money cases this argument will soon become academic, but see further a Law Society statement "Conditional Fees" which appeared in the *Law Society's Gazette* 27th November 1996, and is reproduced at the end of this chapter.

Who can do conditional fee work?

Any firm and any of its staff and any barrister may undertake work on a conditional fee basis. You do not need to be qualified for a particular time or be on any panel or have any specialist knowledge. The category of lawyers who can undertake conditional fee work is exactly the same as work funded on any other basis.

However as we shall see later there are consequences when it comes to insuring your client against losing, as the cheapest comprehensive insurance – Accident Line Protect – is available only to firms of solicitors who have at least one member of their staff on the Law Society's Personal Injury Panel.

Contingency Fees

Rule 8 (Contingency Fees) of the Solicitors' Practice Rules 1990 states:

(1) A solicitor who is retained or employed to prosecute any action, suit or other contentious proceedings shall not enter into any arrangement to receive a contingency fee in respect of that proceeding.

(1A) Paragraph (1) of this Rule shall not apply to a conditional fee agreement relating to specified proceedings as defined in Section 58 of the Courts and Legal Services Act 1990 provided the agreement complies with all the requirements of that section and any order thereunder.

(2) Paragraph (1) of this rule shall not apply to an arrangement in respect of an action, suit or other contentious proceedings in any country other than England and Wales to the extent that a local lawyer would be permitted to receive a contingency fee in respect of that proceeding.

Paragraph (1A) was inserted to remove the restriction in so far as it related to *conditional* fee agreements which are of course a species of contingency fee. Thus the areas where solicitors may operate contingency fees in this country is defined by exclusion: they are allowed except in contentious proceedings, *i.e.* they are permissible in all *non-contentious proceedings.*

What then, in law, are non-contentious proceedings? The answer is most surprising.

Non-contentious business is defined by the Law Society (see page 26 at the end of this chapter):

1. Proceedings before all tribunals other than the Lands Tribunal and the Employment Appeal Tribunal.
2. Planning and other public enquiries.
3. Non-contentious or common form probate business.
4. Conveyancing, company acquisition and mergers, the administration of estates and trusts out of court, the preparation of wills, statements and contracts and any other work not included in the "contentious" column.
5. Work done preliminary to the proceedings included in the "contentious" column if such proceedings are *not* subsequently begun.

It will be seen that paragraph 4 of this statement (see page 26) permits contingency fees in **"any other work not included in the "contentious" column"**. Thus to establish what you can do it is necessary to look at what you *cannot* do, that is those matters classed by the Law Society as contentious namely:

1. Proceedings actually begun in the county courts, High Court, Magistrates' courts (including licensing), Crown Court and the Court of Protection.
2. Proceedings actually begun before the Lands Tribunal and the Employment Appeals Tribunal.
3. Contentious probate proceedings actually begun.
4. Proceedings on appeal to the Court of Appeal, Privy Council and House of Lords.
5. Proceedings in an arbitration.
6. Work done preliminary to proceedings covered by 1–5 above including advice, preparation and negotiations provided the proceedings are subsequently begun.

Thus contingency fees are permissible in many area of litigation which are in fact highly contentious but classed as non-contentious. Some examples are set out below

Industrial Tribunals (see Chapter 19)
Yes, you can do contingency fee work in any Industrial Tribunal case and yes, this includes advocacy and yes it can include the advocacy only when you have been advising the client under a Green Form.

Hardly a lecture, talk seminar or whatever goes by without someone telling me that I am wrong and that contingency fees in Industrial Tribunals are prohibited by the Law Society. Indeed in the 1997 survey conducted by the Policy Studies Institute 10 per cent of respondents said they would be interested in doing employment or industrial tribunal work on a conditional fee basis if they were permitted so to do. Medical Negligence was mentioned by 6 per cent even though *conditional* fees are already permitted for such cases. As the Author of that survey says:

> "These solicitors may also not have been aware that contingency fees can already be used for industrial tribunal work as with other types of non-contentious business."
>
> *The Price of Success, Lawyers, Clients and Conditional Fees,*
> Stella Yarrow, Policy Studies Institute 1997.

I do not know how this myth has grown up but perhaps it can be killed once and for all by quoting the *Law Society's Gazette* 93/37 9th October 1996 "Question of Ethics" feature:

> Q Can I do industrial tribunal work on a contingency fee basis?
>
> A Yes. The restrictions on contingency fees in practice rule 8 only apply to contentious matters. Proceedings before tribunals, other than the Lands Tribunal and the Employment Appeals Tribunal, are non-contentious and, therefore, the restrictions on contingency fees do not apply. You must, of course, ensure that your fees are fair and reasonable.

This is a major area of potential contingency fee work and a model agreement is provided at Appendix 15. It should be noted appeals to the Employment Appeal Tribunal are *not* permissible under a contingency fee arrangement, but Thai Trading agreements may be used in the EAT.

- *Other Tribunals* All other tribunal work, save in the Lands Tribunal and Employment Appeals Tribunal may be carried out on a contingency fee basis.
- *Criminal Injuries Compensation Authority Claims* Another significant area dealt with in a separate chapter, with a Model Contingency Fee Agreement provided in Appendix 14. Note also the Criminal Injuries Compensation (Overseas) Scheme for members of the Armed Forces.
- *Planning and other public enquiries*
- *Coroner's Court Work*
- *Pre-issue work in any case where proceedings are not subsequently begun*
- *Appropriate (or Alternative) Dispute Resolution ("ADR")* There are no special rules for ADR and thus one must look to the type of work which is the subject of ADR. See Chapter 10.

Foreign work

It has always been both lawful and within the Solicitors Practice Rules for an English solicitor to work on a contingency fee basis in proceedings in a country where such arrangements are lawful. Thus a solicitor in England and Wales with a client in this country who has been injured in, say, California may lawfully work on a contingency fee basis. So for example the English solicitor may agree to take say 10% of the damages with the Californian attorney taking 20%.

Rule 8(2) Solicitors Practice Rules disapplies the prohibition in Rule 1 in such cases.

Who can do contingency fee work?

In those cases where contingency fee work is permitted any firm and any of its staff may undertake such work.

The Future for Contingency Fees

Whilst there is widespread official support for extending the scope of *conditional* fees the situation is less clear as far as *contingency* fees are concerned.

The almost universal use of the 25% cap on damages in the Law Society's Model Conditional Fee Agreement – and the fact that it is generally the cap and not the percentage uplift by way of success fee which determines how much the client pays – means that conditional fees in plaintiff personal injury work are, in effect, contingency fees. However this may not be the case in other areas – it depends upon how the Regulations are drafted. If for example in contract cases a success fee uplift of only 20% was allowed, then it would be this low uplift, and not any cap, which determined how much the client paid and thus it would *not* be a contingency fee arrangement in all but name.

However given that plaintiff personal injury work is regarded as the work with least risk it seems extremely unlikely that the maximum success fee uplift will be *lower* in all other, riskier, areas of law.

As we have seen the legality or otherwise of contingency fee arrangements hinges on whether the work done is "contentious" or "non-contentious" business.

Interestingly the Government proposes to abolish the distinction. In a Consultation Papers on costs, published in the summer of 1997, contains the following statement (Part C1.2.3):

"...the new rules do not define "contentious/non-contentious business", "party", "patient", "registrar", "standard/indemnity basis", "taxed costs", or "proceedings in the Family Division".

"Parties" and "standard/indemnity basis" are defined elsewhere in the Rules *and it is considered that the other definitions do not need to be retained."* (My italics)

Thus the distinction between contentious and non-contentious business and accordingly the consequent division between what can and cannot be done on a contingency fee basis is likely to disappear.

This leaves four options:

(1) Contingency fees being banned for everything including areas where they are currently allowed.

(2) Contingency fees being permitted for everything.

(3) The terms being retained purely for the purpose of prescribing what is allowed under contingency fee arrangements.

(4) A new, clear rule allowing, but regulating, contingency fees in all civil work.

Option (1) seems extremely unlikely.

Option (4) is my preference.

Thai Trading agreements

On 27th February 1998 (Times Law Report 6th March 1998) the Court of Appeal delivered its historic judgment in *Thai Trading (A Firm)* v *Margery Taylor and Wilfred David Taylor.* I look at this case in more detail in Chapter 16 "The Indemnity Principle" and the whole case transcript is at Appendix 24.

However the effect of the judgment is that "no win – no fee" arrangements are lawful in all civil work provided that the solicitor does not seek to recover more than his ordinary profit costs and disbursements if he wins. Thus "success fees" are not permissible except where Parliament has authorized them, *i.e.* conditional fee cases. Nor are straightforward contingency fees (taking a cut of the damages) except in non-contentious work. What *is* now allowed for the first time is "speculative funding", that is agreeing to make no charge in the event of a loss but charging the normal rate in the event of a win.

Furthermore, according to the Court of Appeal, the indemnity principle is *not* broken by such agreements and thus a winning party can recover his costs from the other side even though he had contracted to pay his solicitor nothing in the event of defeat.

The Law Society has now amended Practice Rule 8 to allow solicitors to enter into contingency fee agreements where permitted under statute or common law. (*Law Society's Gazette* 10th June 1998).

Arbitrations

In *Bevan Ashford* v *Geoff Yeandle (Contractors) Limited (in liquidation)* 8 April 1998 *The Times* 23 April 1998 the Chancery Division, building on the Thai Trading case, decided that it was lawful for a "success" fee to be charged by a winning lawyer even though the case was not one to which *conditional* fees within the meaning of the 1995 Order applied.

The case involved insolvency proceedings which *are* covered by the 1995 Regulations but in an *arbitration* which took it back outside the regulations.

The Court held that proceedings before an arbitrator were *not* within the Conditional Fee legislation. However *Thai Trading* v *Taylor* had declared no win – no fee arrangements in contentious litigation lawful so there was no problem in that regard. However the barrister in the Bevan Ashford case wished to charge 50% over and above his normal fees in the event of a win and the Court specifically approved this arrangement.

Thus the significance of the case is that a success fee, over and above normal fees, is lawful in no win – no fee cases *not* covered by the Conditional Fees Order. However this case did involve insolvency proceedings and Parliament has specifically approved success fees for such cases in *court* proceedings.

In *Bevan Ashford* the Vice Chancellor, Sir Richard Scott, said in his judgment:

> "I would regard as absurd a result that upheld as lawful a conditional fee agreement for use in court proceedings but condemned as unlawful the identical conditional fee agreement for use in arbitration...
>
> it seems to me quite impossible to argue that use of that same conditional fee agreement for litigation in arbitration would be contrary to public policy...
>
> For these reasons I hold that if a conditional fee agreement relating to a particular cause of action is sanctioned for proceedings in court by section 58 of the 1990 Act and by the 1995 Order and the 1995 Regulations, the conditional fee agreement is free from any public policy objection in relation to arbitration proceedings in pursuance of that cause of action."

The 1990 Act sanctioned conditional fees in all work save criminal and family and thus it could be argued that success fees are now lawful in all civil work. On the other hand, whilst no win, no fee arrangements clearly *are* lawful in all civil work, it may be that *success fees* are only lawful in the areas covered by the 1995 Order, that is personal injury, insolvency and European Human Rights.

A court dealing with a success fee in, say, a breach of contract claim may not uphold it.

Miscellaneous

The Law Society's traditional hostility to contingency fees is shown in another, highly obscure, document. Appendix 10B the CCBE Code of Conduct for Lawyers in the EC, published in the Professional Conduct Guide reads

> 3.3.   Pactum de quota litis.
> 3.3.1. A lawyer shall not be entitled to make a pactum de quota litis.
> 3.3.2. By pactum de quota litis is meant an agreement between a lawyer and his client entered into prior to the final conclusion of a matter to which the client is a party, by virtue of which the client undertakes to pay the lawyer a share of the result regardless of whether this is represented by a sum of money or by any other benefit achieved by the client upon the conclusion of the matter.
> 3.3.3. The pactum de quota litis does not include an agreement that fees be charged in proportion to the value of a matter handled by the lawyer if this is in accordance with an officially approved fee-scale or under the control of the competent authority having jurisdiction over the lawyer.

Commentary
These provisions reflect the common position in all member states that an unregulated agreement for contingency fees is contrary to the proper administration of justice because it encourages speculative litigation and is liable to be abused. The provisions are not, however, intended to prevent the maintenance or introduction of arrangements under which lawyers are paid according to results or only if the action or matter is successful, provided that these arrangements are under sufficient regulation and control for the protection of the client and the proper administration of justice.

Perhaps the Law Society could take this garbage out when it repeals Practice Rule 8.

What Is Non-Contentious Business?

'Non Contentious business' means any business done as a solicitor which is not contentious business.   **s.87(1) Solicitors Act 1974**

Generally, any work which does not involve proceedings begun before a court in England and Wales, or an arbitrator.

Work done preliminary to proceedings is non-contentious provided proceedings are not subsequently begun. Once proceedings have begun, all prior work leading to the action automatically becomes contentious.

If solicitors in England and Wales are involved in work where proceedings are issued abroad the work will be treated as non-contentious.

Examples of Contentious and Non-Contentious Business

Contentious	*Non-Contentious*
Proceedings actually begun in the County Court, High Court, Magistrates' Court (including licensing). Crown Court and the Court of Protection.	1. Proceedings before all tribunals other than the Lands Tribunal and the Employment Appeal Tribunal.
Proceedings actually begun before the Lands Tribunal and the Employment Appeal Tribunal.	2. Planning and other public enquiries.
Contentious probate proceedings actually begun.	3. Non-Contentious or common form probate business.
Proceedings on appeal to the Court of Appeal, Privy Council and House of Lords.	4. Conveyancing, company acquisitions and mergers, the administration of estates and trusts out of court, the preparation of wills, statements and contracts, and any other work not included in the "contentious" column.
Proceedings in an arbitration under the Arbitration Act.	5. Work done preliminary to the proceedings included in the "contentious" column if such proceedings are not subsequently begun.
Work done preliminary to proceedings covered by 1–5 above including advice, preparation and negotiations provided the proceedings are subsequently begun.	6. Criminal Injuries Compensation Board.[1]

---

1. Now the Criminal Injuries Compensation Authority

Conditional fees in professional negligence cases

The availability of conditional fee agreements (CFA's) for professional negligence cases arising out of a personal injury action has been the subject of uncertainty. The Bar Council has advised barristers that CFA's are not available because a professional negligence action is one for loss of a chance, not a personal injury action. The Law Society and the Lord Chancellor's Department (LCD) believe that such professional negligence cases are within the permitted scope of conditional fees.

A personal injury action is defined in RSC Order 1, r4. In *Paterson* v *Chadwick* [1974] 2 All ER 772, it was held that an action against a former solicitor for breach of duty to prosecute a claim for personal injury is an action for personal injuries, although the cause of action lies in contract. The Bar Council, however, says that the action is for loss of a chance.

The Law Society has pressed the LCD to make the position clear in amendments to the Conditional Fee Agreements Order 1995. It is the Society's view that professional negligence proceedings arising out of a personal injury action should, as a matter of policy, be within the permitted scope. It is unlikely that any steps will be taken by the Lord Chancellor prior to a general election.

Barristers will not accept instructions on a conditional fee basis in these cases in the light of the Bar Council's advice. They are likely to advise that any conditional fee agreement entered into by the client may be invalid. Prospective clients should be advised of this before signing a CFA. Practitioners will wish to consider what option to offer in respect of payment of counsel's fees. If the solicitor is willing to take the risk and to pay counsel's fees in any event, an additional success fee may be justified. The total of all success fees must not exceed 100%.

Accident Line Protect insurance covers professional negligence cases arising out of personal injury actions. Prospective clients will wish to know whether insurance cover is available. If the negligence action is lost, but insurance cover is in place, the defendant will receive payment of costs and is unlikely to challenge the validity of the CFA. This is unlikely to be a better protection for a defendant firm and their professional indemnity insurers than if the client was legally aided or uninsured.

If it is proposed to enter into a CFA without after-the-event insurance, and the case is lost, the client will usually be ordered to pay the costs. If the client is unlikely to be able to meet the costs order, there may be an application by the opponent for an order that the solicitor should pay the costs on the basis of being either a maintainer of the action or for wasted costs.

Acting for a client who the solicitor knows is unable to afford to pay costs does not create a liability to pay the opponent's costs see Tolstoy v Aldington [1996]

2 All ER 566. There are complex arguments about whether a solicitor would be an unlawful maintainer in these circumstances and any practitioner faced with a challenge on this basis is invited to seek further advice from the Society. In the Society's view, a wasted costs order would be inappropriate. Where the LCD and the Society believes that it is permissible to enter into a CFA, can it be negligent, unreasonable or improper so to do? The point has not yet been tested.

In a winning case, there may be more prospect of a challenge to the validity of the agreement if the opponent is aware of the existence of a CFA. The unsuccessful opponent could argue that the CFA was an unlawful contingency fee arrangement and that, by operation of the public policy bar against contingency fees and the indemnity principle of costs recovery, there would be no costs liability. If this point were to arise, it would have a significant public policy element. Practitioners are urged to seek further advice from the Society if the validity of their agreement is challenged in this way.

A client might challenge the validity of the agreement on the grounds that it was an unlawful contingency fee agreement and, therefore, unenforceable. It is not clear whether this would still entitle the solicitor to charge on a *quantum meruit* basis to recover their 'basic costs'.

The Society suggests that practitioners are likely to want to advise their clients in the following terms before signing a conditional fee agreement for proceedings for professional negligence arising out of the conduct of a personal injury action:

- that solicitors may offer CFA's for this type of work;

- that Accident Line Protect insurance is available to cover the opponent's costs and the client's own disbursements, but only through firms offering Accident Line Protect insurance;

- if the services of a barrister are required, it is unlikely that a barrister will accept instructions on a conditional fee basis;

- arrangements for the financing of any barrister's fees should be discussed and dealt with appropriately in the CFA;

- if the case is successful, the opponent may raise a point of law to avoid responsibility for payment of costs if they become aware of the existence of a CFA; and

- the solicitor will not disclose any information to the opponents about the existence of a CFA without the express permission of the client.

The Success Fee and the Cap Myth and Reality

The Success Fee And The Cap Myth And Reality

Conditional fees differ from U.S. style contingency fees only in that it is not permissible to simply agree a "percentage take". The Conditional Fee Agreements Order 1995 stipulates a maximum increase of 100 per cent (the "success fee") but does not impose a percentage cap ("the cap"). However as far as the public is concerned the key consideration is the cap – *i.e.* will the solicitor guarantee to limit the percentage of damages taken in costs?

Discussions about the percentage *success fee* (as opposed to the cap), the assessment of risk and which fees form the base sum to be increased by a maximum of 100% are lost on most solicitors, let alone the public. Amongst those who have considered the success fee in detail there is a widespread but erroneous view that it is the risk of losing which is the main factor in calculating the success fee. **It is not!**

Understanding this is the key to working successfully on a conditional fee basis.

The Statutory Background

Conditional fees were made lawful by Section 58 of the Courts and Legal Services Act 1990 and that section, without using the term, created the concept of the success fee. By contrast the cap, which actually protects the client, is neither mentioned nor alluded to in the Act or the Conditional Fee Agreements Order 1995. However the Conditional Fee Agreements Regulations 1995 make it mandatory, in a Conditional Fee Agreement, to state whether or not there is a cap but impose no requirement to actually have one.

Why Parliament chose to use the concept of a "success fee" rather than the cap is a mystery but when Parliament extends the operation of conditional fees probably this autumn, 1998, it is to be hoped that the existing regulations will be replaced by a section reading:

It shall be unlawful for a solicitor to charge a client in a conditional fee case more than 25%, including Value Added Tax, of the damages actually recovered for that client.

However in the meantime we must deal with the law as it is, and the relevant parts of Section 58 read:

(2)   Where a conditional fee agreement provides for the amount of any fees to which it applies to be increased, in specified circumstances, above the amount which would be payable if it were not a conditional fee agreement, it shall specify the percentage by which that amount is to be increased.

(4)   In this section "specified proceedings" means proceedings of a description specified by order made by the Lord Chancellor for the purposes of subsection (3).

(5)   Any such order shall prescribe the maximum permitted percentage for each description of specified proceedings.

(6)   An agreement which falls within subsection (2) shall be unenforceable if, at the time when it is entered into, the percentage specified in the agreement exceeds the prescribed maximum percentage for each description of proceedings to which it relates.

(9)   Rules of court may make provision with respect to the taxing of any costs which includes fees payable under a conditional fee agreement.

Thus the scheme of the Act is to limit the amount by which the solicitor's costs can be raised, *not* to limit the percentage of damages that can be taken.

This, as we will see, in Mr Jones' example below has bizarre consequences.

The Consequences for Mr Jones

Five years later Parliament approved The Conditional Fee Agreements Order 1995. Article 3 reads:

For the purpose of Section 58(5) of the Courts and Legal Services Act 1990 the maximum permitted percentage by which fees may be increased in respect of each description of proceedings specified in article 2 is 100%.

Article 2 includes personal injury proceedings.

Thus under the scheme laid down by Parliament solicitors may double their fees, but no more, and *may ignore the consequences to the client.*

The following is a letter *not* to send even though it complies with these regulations.

Dear Mr Jones,

I am pleased that the Judge found in your favour and indeed I have already received the damages cheque for £5,000.

My Firm's costs total £6,000 of which I have recovered £4,000 from the other side.

You will recall that under the terms of the conditional fee agreement we agreed that I could increase my costs by 100% if you won. We agreed that figure because this was a risky case as shown by the fact that it went to trial.

The effect of increasing my costs by 100% is that they now total £12,000 and, as mentioned above, I have received £4,000 costs from the other side leaving a shortfall of £8,000, but I have applied the £5,000 damages and so the balance due to me from you is £3,000. To make this easy to follow I have prepared a little table.

	£
My firm's basic costs	6,000
Success fee	6,000
Total	12,000
Less costs from other side	4,000
Balance	8,000
Less damages applied to costs	5,000
Balance due to me from you	3,000

Please let me have your cheque in due course.

You will recall that for £85 we insured against you having to pay the other side's costs and our own disbursements if we lost. This means that if you had lost it would have cost you nothing but as you have won it has cost you £3,000.

Never mind. It's a funny old world.

I recall that you wanted the conditional fee scheme because you could not afford lawyer's fees. A wise decision!

I will be pleased to act for you again in the future – after your forthcoming bankruptcy has finished.

Alternatively next time you are a passenger in a bus and you get injured you might find it cheaper just to admit liability.

Yours sincerely

Some scheme. Some protection.

The Need for a Cap

Of course, as many of those involved in looking at conditional fees realised, the "success fee" concept is hopelessly flawed. One only has to look at why it is *not* used in those jurisdictions which have contingency fees. Those jurisdictions recognise that the cap is the client's protection.

Thus in The Conditional Fee Agreements Regulations 1995 Parliament made its first faltering steps towards the cap.

Thus Regulation 3:

An agreement shall state:-
(a) the particular proceedings or parts of them to which it relates (including whether it relates to any counterclaim, appeal or proceedings to enforce a judgment or order);
(b) the circumstances in which the legal representative's fees and expenses or part of them are payable;
(c) what, if any, payment is due :-
  (i) upon partial failure of the specified circumstances to occur
  (ii) irrespective of the specified circumstances occurring; and
  (iii) upon termination of the agreement for any reason;
(d) the amount payable in accordance with sub-paragraphs (b) or (c) above or the method to be used to calculate the amount payable; *and in particular whether or not the amount payable is linked by reference to the amount of any damages which may be recovered on behalf of the client.* (my italics)

Thus the Conditional Fee Agreement does *not* have to contain a cap but it *must* state whether or not there is a cap.

The rest of Regulation 3 is very difficult to follow. It is primarily concerned with what payments are due when there is not necessarily a win, *e.g.* because one or other party terminates the agreement, or because the agreement stipulates that disbursements are payable in any event. These possibilities must be covered in advance in the agreement.

However the section italicised above refers to a limit of these costs by reference to the amount of damages recovered and yet by definition there will not necessarily be any damages and yet certain payments may be due. The italicised section should be a free-standing regulation applying unequivocally to all aspects of a solicitors charges to his client.

The Law Society, to its credit, saw the reality and in its model Conditional Fee Agreement imposed a 25% cap plus VAT on damages *taken by way of a success fee,* and thus the gap between solicitor and own client costs and inter-partes costs does *not* need to be brought into either the 25% cap figure, or the maximum 100% success fee.

I strongly recommend that practitioners include **all** charges to the client including any solicitor and own client costs and VAT in the 25% cap but **not in the percentage success fee.** ("the Underwoods Method").

In Conditionalfeesspeak the full solicitor and own client costs – which *include* any costs received from the other side – are known as *"base costs"*.

The Options for Mr Jones

To make this clear let us return to poor Mr Jones and look at the three options.

A   100% success fee but no cap.
B   100% success fee but a 25% cap on success fee
C   100% success fee but a 25% cap on all fees charged to client.

The damages recovered in each case are £5,000.

A   No Cap

In the position set out in the letter to Mr Jones.

		£
Base costs		6,000
Less received from other side		4,000
Balance		2,000
Success fee (100% of basic costs)		6,000
Balance actually charged to client		8,000
Damages		5,000
Money to client	Minus	3,000

B   Cap on Success Fee only

Base costs	6,000
Less received from other side	4,000
Balance	2,000
Success fee (£6,000 but capped at 25% of £5,000)	1,250
Charged to client	3,250
Damages	5,000
Balance due to client	1,750

Actual success fee (£1,250 on £6,000) = 20.833%

Thus in B, applying the 100% success fee *and* limiting that *success fee* to 25% in accordance with the Law Society's agreement the solicitor actually takes £3,250 from the client's £5,000. I have excluded VAT for the sake of simplicity (!) but you are entitled to add that to the £3,250 and thus:

	3,250.00
VAT at 17.5%	568.75
Total costs	3,818.75
Balance to client	1,181.25
TOTAL	5,000.00

You might like to undertake an exercise to compose a letter to Mr Jones explaining that his cheque for £1,181.25 out of £5,000.00 damages really does represent 75% of his damages and that the £3,818.75 taken by you out of his £5,000.00 really is a 25% cap on the success fee.

C All Costs to Client Capped – The Underwoods Method

	£
Base costs	6,000
Less received from other side	4,000
Balance	2,000
Success fee (£6,000 but capped at 25% of £5,000)	1,250
	3,250
But total charged to client capped at 25% of damages	
Therefore charged to client	1,250
Damages	5,000
Balance due to client	3,750

Actual success fee (£1,250 charged less base costs of £2,000 = minus £750)

Minus £750 on £6,000 = Minus 12.5%

Thus in example C in order to ensure that the client gets 75% of the damages we have actually foregone part of the Base Costs as well as taking no success fee and thus there is a negative success fee.

Only the Underwoods method fully protects the client, *i.e.* guarantees that the client will get 75% of his or her damages.

In return for *always* protecting the client in this way you should also aim to achieve 25% of the damages by way of an additional fee, that is additional to the costs cheque received from the Defendant's insurers. To maximise that chance I advise always having the success fee in the agreement as 100%, unless in a particular case you wish to make no charge to the client, *e.g.* because the client is a friend, relative, minor, client who gives you a lot of work or whatever. In these cases the correct percentage is 0%, *i.e.* you will take none of the damages.

Can the Underwoods Method be Challenged?

The arguments above have been criticized on three main points:

1. In the examples given I have always used the maximum 100% success fee which is precisely what others say should

not be done. A lower figure will produce different and less objectionable results.

2. These are artificially created situations to produce the results I want. Anyone can do that. It proves nothing.

3. In any event, like it or not, the law requires us to assess the risk and put in a percentage success fee based on the assessment.

Objection 1 can be dealt with by looking at the examples again. It will be seen that the Underwoods method has produced a negative success fee. Thus all risk assessment to arrive at a percentage success fee would have been a waste of time. Thus the insertion of 10% or 20% or 50% rather than 100% would have made not one penny difference to the amount to be charged to the client.

Objection 2 purports to refute this. It says "but you have created this example to suit your argument – of course it works out the way you want but in real cases this sort of thing rarely happens".

Do not take my word for it.

At Appendix 23 is a blank Conditional Fee Analysis Form. Photocopy this form. Work out what the actual success fee would have been on your last ten or twenty concluded personal injury cases, if you had been working on a conditional fee basis using the Underwoods Method.

Done that? Enough said.

For those of you too lazy, busy or confused to do this and in any event to give you a flavour of how real cases work, there is at Appendix 29 an analysis of the first 50 Conditional Fee cases which we concluded at my firm.

Objection 3 – the "we've got to do it anyway" one.

You will search the Act, Regulations and Order in vain for any regulations concerning the assessment of risk in arriving at the success fee. Reference to assessment of risk will only be found in the Rules of the Supreme Court and the County Court Rules (Appendix 4 and 5).

The success fee can be challenged on taxation under Order 62 Rule 15A of the Rules of the Supreme Court and the same provisions apply in the County Court by virtue of the County Court Rules – Order 38 Rule 21 (4A). The proposed Unified Costs Rules under Woolf maintain the same wording.

Of course the success fee can only be challenged by your client, and not by the defendant, as the success fee has no bearing on inter-partes costs. It will be an ungrateful duplicitous client (but we all have the odd one) who having agreed a 75% – 25% split all along then tries to get out of paying the full 25% by challenging the success fee.

In any event the risk of losing, and thus not getting any fee, is only one of the factors to be taken into account by the District Judge or Taxing Master in considering whether the success fee is too high. Order 62 Rule 15A Paragraph 12(5) reads:

> On taxation to which this rule applies:
> (a) Where the client applies for taxation of the basic costs, the basic costs shall be taxed on an indemnity basis as if the solicitor and his client had not entered into a conditional fee agreement and rule 15(2) shall apply to the taxation of the base costs;
> (b) Where the client applies for a taxation of a percentage increase, the percentage increase may be reduced where it is disproportionate having regard to all relevant factors including:-
> (i) the risk that the circumstances in which the fees or expenses would be payable might not occur;
> (ii) the disadvantages relating to the absence of payments on account;
> (iii) whether the amount which might be payable under the conditional fee agreement is limited to a certain proportion of any damages recovered by the client;
> (iv) whether there is a conditional fee agreement between the solicitor and counsel.

Thus 12(5)(a) allows the client to challenge the base costs and 12(5)(b) allows the client to challenge the percentage increase but there is no power to challenge the cap, *i.e.* the client cannot say "I agreed 25% of damages but now I think it should only be 20%". It is not confined to lost cases. The "risk" element is part of one of four factors to be taken into account. Paragraph 12(5)(b)(i) covers cases where a client has a good case but part way through decides not to go ahead. In fact this is a greater risk than losing. Although in these circumstances the standard conditional fee agreement allows the solicitor to charge the client base costs, *i.e.* solicitor and own client costs, in reality the solicitor is likely to get very little or nothing at all. The solicitor will have taken no money on account and there will be no fund of damages from which to take costs.

Crucially Paragraph 12(5)(b)(iii) allows the fact that a cap is in place to justify a higher percentage success fee.

If you follow the Underwoods method not only are you applying a 25% cap to the success fee *but to the whole of the costs taken from the client* be it success fee or the balance of base costs not recovered from the other side.

This is much greater protection than the Law Society's Model Conditional Fee Agreement gives and warrants a higher success fee. Furthermore if you make the 25% *include* VAT this reduces the actual cap to 21.28% which again gives greater protection to the client than the Law Society's Model Conditional Fee Agreement.

Example

	£
Damages	10,000.00
25% taken from client	2,500.00
Splitting the VAT:	
(2,500.00 ÷ 47) x 40	2,127.66
VAT thereon at 17.5%	372.34
Total	2,500.00

Provides a net figure of 21.2766%, say 21.28%, of damages.

The sole purpose of the taxing rule is to protect the client. It is hard to see how any District Judge or Taxing Master in the land could find that the Underwoods method fails to do this.

In practice of course, we have seen it is very rare that the actual success fee will be charged at anything like the 100% even though that figure is in the agreement. This is because:

(a) the 25% cap will nearly always "bite" and thus determine the percentage success fee payable; and

(b) the base fee to which the success fee applies is the *solicitor and own client* costs and *not* the inter-partes costs

Proposed New Rules of Court

In the summer of 1997 the Lord Chancellor's Department issued a consultation paper containing proposed unified costs rules to replace Order 62 of the Rules of the Supreme Court and Order 38 of the County Court Rules and to take into account the recommendations relating to costs made in Lord Woolf's report *Access to Justice*.

An analysis of the wholesale changes proposed is beyond the scope of this book but:

- the consultation paper's commentary on the changes in relation to Conditional Fee Agreements appears at Appendix 6.
- The new Rule C2.10 "Costs payable to a solicitor by his own client" appears at Appendix 7.
- The new Rule C2.11 "Conditional Fees" appears at Appendix 8.

It will be seen that only minor changes are proposed in relation to conditional fees.

Order 62 Rule 15A(4) expressly states that where the client applies for taxation of the percentage increase he may give reasons why it should be reduced and what he believes it should be. This is to be discarded as it is considered that a client may do this anyway and without the need for an express provision to that effect.

The other difference is that the proposed Rules make it clear that "costs" in this context means *all* fees, charges, disbursements and other expenses charged by the solicitor under the conditional fee agreement. In the commentary the Lord Chancellor's Department state that clarification is needed because conditional fee agreements often refer separately to fees, costs and disbursements.

It should be noted that although Rule C2.10(1)(b) says that the rule does not apply to Conditional Fee Agreements Rule C2.11(4)(b) says that Rule C2.10 *is* to be applied to taxation of the base costs where challenged by the client.

Why The Standard Model Is Wrong Even On Its Own Terms

The assumption that two winning cases each with a 50% uplift make up for each losing case is fundamentally flawed.

The theoretical model looks like this:

Traditional method of funding		£
Case 1 – won	Fee	4,000
Case 2 – won	Fee	4,000
Case 3 – lost	Fee	4,000
Total Fees		12,000

Conditional Fee Method of Funding £

Case 1 – won	Fee	4,000
50% uplift		2,000
Case 2 – won	Fee	4,000
50% uplift		2,000
Case 3 – lost	Fee	0
		12,000

The flaw is that this assumes what is known as *even cost volume,* that is that the work done, and therefore the fees calculated on an hourly rate, are the same whether the case is won or lost. This is fundamentally misconceived.

As Daniel Brennan QC said, in his paper to the Policy Studies Institute Conference on 23rd September 1997,

> The principle underlying calculation of a success fee is that the lawyer breaks even. In a series of three cases, each of which has a two-thirds prospect of success, the lawyer should choose a success fee (before adjustment for delayed receipt, disbursements and other expenses and costs) of 50%. The principle is that the lawyer will lose one case of the three, and that the 50% uplift on the other cases will recompense him for the lost fees in the third case. The system implies equal cost volume across the series. If the costs on the losing cases are higher than the costs on the winning cases, then the lawyer is out of pocket.
>
> The assumption of even cost volume across such a series is wrong.

It certainly is. Cases are almost always won by settlement. It is estimated that only 1% of personal injury cases won by Plaintiffs are won at trial. Trial costs always form a very substantial part of any case. Even a case settled at the doors of the court will involve substantially less that one that goes ahead to trial.

Thus the average costs in a case lost are far higher than the average costs in a case that is won.

A much more likely scenario is this:

Traditional method of Funding £

Case 1 – won	Fee	2,000
Case 2 – won	Fee	2,000
Case 3 – lost	Fee	8,000
		12,000

Conditional Fee method of Funding		£
Case 1 – won	Fee	2,000
50% uplift		1,000
Case 2 – won	Fee	2,000
50% uplift		1,000
Case 3 – lost	Fee	0
Total		6,000
Shortfall		6,000

What this shows is that a 100% uplift is needed on **three** winning cases to make up for **each** losing case.

Thus		£
Case 1 – won	Fee	2,000
100% uplift		2,000
Case 2 – won	Fee	2,000
100% uplift		2,000
Case 3 – won	Fee	2,000
100% uplift		2,000
Case 4 – lost	Fee	0
Total		12,000

Thus even without taking into account, as solicitors must do, the absence of payment on account etc, *cases with a 75% prospect of success or less should be charged at 100% uplift* **not** *33%* as the "Mathematical" table at Appendix 12 of the Law Society's text *Conditional Fees – A Survival Guide* states. The authors of that book, Michael Napier and Fiona Bawdon make this very point themselves (page 92, paragraph 3):

> Of course, this calculation is complicated in practice by the fact that the costs incurred in each case-and so the amount of financial risk being run each time by the firm- would not be identical. For example, you take on two 50/50 cases, with a success fee of 100 per cent in each case (as set out in the table). If you went on to win the case where the costs are, say, £100,000 and lost the one where they were, say, £5,000, you would be rather better off than if it had been the other way around.

Most commentators, including the Policy Studies Institute in *The Price of Success* have misunderstood this fundamental point. This renders meaningless the Policy Studies Institute's findings that the success fee being charged is, on average, too high.

The Cap:
Percentage Of What?

The Cap:
Percentage Of What?

Introduction

In the world of conditional fees the amount of debate is in inverse proportion to the topic's importance. Thus the *success fee* – largely irrelevant in practice – is discussed endlessly, *the cap* – very important – is discussed much less and the question of what *damages* form the capped fund – absolutely crucial – is almost never mentioned.

In this chapter this topic is examined, together with the different ways of treating different heads of damages.

Unlike the success fee, the *cap* is determined by reference to *damages* and not *costs*.

The Policy Studies Institute research[1] shows that 97% of solicitors' firms are, voluntarily, imposing a cap on the percentage of damages to be taken. The cap may be on just the *success fee* as per the Law Society Model Conditional Fee Agreement or on *all* costs to be taken from the client which is the Underwoods Method. (For a discussion on these issues see Chapter 3 *The Success Fee and the Cap – Myth and Reality*).

For the purposes of this chapter it does not matter. I will assume a 25% cap throughout.

What Damages?

The question then arises as to what damages form the fund upon which the cap bites, or to put it another way when is it reasonable for a solicitor to take a share and when should the client get the damages without deduction?

This is less simple than it first appears, and solicitors are free to reach whatever agreement they want with their clients. The cap is voluntary and the way any cap operates is thus entirely unregulated.

---

[1] *The Price of Success: Lawyers, Clients and Conditional Fees*, Stella Yarrow, 1997, Page 63.

General Damages

These are damages for pain, suffering and loss of amenity and are not directly related to financial loss. They thus represent a direct financial *gain* to the client and should always form part of the fund from which the solicitor takes a share.

Since October 1997 general damages have been "ring-fenced" from recovery of benefits by the Compensation Recovery Unit of the Department of Social Security. Thus the problems previously caused by a situation where a Plaintiff's *general* damages have already suffered a deduction to recover benefits no longer exist.

Special Damages

Special damages are direct financial compensation to a client for actual financial loss suffered, for example loss of earnings, the cost of medical treatment etc. and thus represent money actually spent or lost by the client.

To that extent special damages are different in principle to general damages in that general damages represent pure "profit" to the client albeit by way of not very generous compensation for pain and suffering. Different considerations apply to different areas of special damages:

Compensation Recovery Unit Payments (CRU)

Where a client has received state benefits and gets special damages in respect of a related loss then the Department of Social Security (DSS) will recoup those payments direct from the Defendants' insurers without the Plaintiff ever seeing the money. The whole question of CRU, and what special damages fall to be taken into consideration, is complicated and is dealt with as an annex to this Chapter at page 53.

In practice what will happen is that a "CRU Statement" is obtained settlement reached and the defendant insurers will pay over the *net* balance to the solicitor or client.

Thus:

	£
Agreed overall settlement	10,000
Recouped benefit paid to CRU	4,000
Balance received by Plaintiff	6,000

Should the 25% apply to the gross sum or the net sum?

Virtually everyone agrees that it should apply to the net sum only. In many cases it would not be worthwhile the client going ahead if he has to repay 25% of his benefits.

	£
For example	
Agreed overall settlement	28,000
Recouped benefits under CRU	21,000
Balance received by Plaintiff	7,000
25% of gross figure taken	7,000
Balance to client	0

The Law Society Model Conditional Fee Agreement reflects the view that nothing should be taken from CRU payments. At 3(k) it says:

> The total of our success fee and any barrister's uplift (see condition 6) is capped – it will not be more than 25% of damages recovered. This calculation excludes any money your opponent pays to the DSS in repayment of any benefits you receive.

My clear advice is to exclude CRU payments from the damages fund.

Special Damages to date of Settlement

Much of this heading is likely to have been dealt with by excluding CRU payments and thus effectively excluding much of a loss of earnings claim from the fund. But what about medical expenses, prescriptions, extra fares, damaged clothing, car repairs and all of the other losses and expenses flowing from any routine accident?

The Law Society's Model Conditional Fee Agreement *includes* such items in the fund – not specifically but by the fact that the only *exclusion* is for CRU payments (see above).

My view is that where a client has incurred specific expenses they should be excluded from the fund. This accords with clients' concepts of fairness. Often an injured party is only interested in recovering their actual expenses and are pleasantly surprised to learn about general damages. This is a matter for each individual firm but put yourself in your client's shoes. How happy would you be at losing 25% of money actually spent? The sums are often trivial and it is not worth tarnishing the concept of the cap.

A further practical point arises. Even if a solicitor does not take a percentage of special damages it is in the *solicitor's* interest to have the claim as high as possible because

(a) it triggers higher scale costs (on claims of £3,000 or more)
(b) Once Woolf fixed costs come in the higher the claim the higher the *fixed costs from the other side* (Woolf fixed costs being a form of contingency fee).
(c) it may keep the claim above an increased "small claims" (*i.e.* "no costs") jurisdiction, although whether it has this effect is open to debate.

The two key areas here are recovery of damages for the client's own property (*e.g.* a car) and for loss of earnings. Clearly there is absolutely no point in the client pursuing the damages claim in respect of his car if he is to lose 25% to the solicitor and the alternative is to recover the whole lot from his own comprehensive insurance. Likewise someone who has actually been paid whilst off sick will not wish to pursue a claim on his *employer's* behalf only to lose 25% of it to the solicitor as opposed to keeping it all if he does nothing.

Under the Woolf regime this concept of maximising the notional claim will make a substantial difference to solicitors fixed costs *from the other side* and it will increase the power of a Plaintiff's offer to settle (a reverse payment-in) if the proposed penal interest rates apply to a claim including the cost of a car and loss of earnings.

I am trying to keep this book simple but events will soon overtake us all. Rather than taking a cut of special damages I see solicitors offering to *reduce* the percentage take of *general* damages in return for handling the property damages claim free of deduction and keeping the case out of the dreaded "small claims" jurisdiction.

In summary my advice is to exclude pre-settlement special damages from the fund but please see "overall offers" below.

Future Specials

(i) *Future Care Costs*

These should be excluded. To take a percentage of future care costs is wrong and leaves a client who is by definition in need of care potentially unable to get that care because a solicitor has taken a quarter of the money required to pay for it.

Thus, client aged 50, life expectancy a further 10 years. Future care award £100,000

	£
Award	100,000
Solicitors share	25,000
Balance	75,000

Result – no care for last two and a half years.

Nothing is more calculated to damage the image of the profession and the concept of "no win – no fee". You can imagine the headlines:

"Old cripple in gutter. Solicitor buys yacht with proceeds".

Don't touch it.

(ii) *Future Loss of Earnings*

I reserve the right to take a percentage of loss of future earnings. The figure is often a guess. Furthermore there is an element of double recovery in that future benefits are not recouped under CRU. I see no reason why a solicitor who uses his skill to maximize this highly speculative area of a clients claim should not receive a percentage.

Also many claims with high future loss are somewhat speculative claims where 25% of general damages, often quite small even in large loss of earnings claims, would be insufficient incentive to take the claim on.

In return for guaranteeing not to touch "ordinary" specials and not to touch future care it seems to be a reasonable balance to include future loss of earnings in the fund.

Structured Settlements

Structured settlements are very rare – usually involving settlements of over £500,000 – but the problem of applying the cap to structured settlements is one of the main reasons given by the then Lord Chancellor, Lord MacKay, for regulating solicitors fees by way of the success fee and not the cap. Thus they are one of the main reasons we are lumbered with the success fee and the whole concept of conditional fees instead of contingency fees. See *Hansard*, House of Lords, 12 June 1995, Page 1584.

> On the subject of the cap, I have taken the view that it is extremely difficult to apply a cap generally by regulation. I instance the case of the structured settlement. Your Lordships will know that a structured settlement is one in which a capital sum is payable immediately, with income payments made over a period. As an illustration, it would be difficult to apply a cap of 25% of the damages unless one gave the lawyer a pension. That would be an unworkable arrangement.

My advice is that the fund should be the lump sum only, which will always be large, and not the subsequent income payments which are likely to be substantially for future care. The fund will be further reduced by CRU payments etc. as discussed elsewhere in this chapter.

I realise that this may appear to give solicitors an incentive to avoid structured settlements and that structured settlements are considered desirable. I believe solicitors can be trusted in these cases to act in the best interests of this client as required by the Solicitors' Practice Rules. If this is considered insufficient then I suggest a statutory limit of say £20,000 to be charged to a client out of damages, whether by success fee or basic costs, in all personal injury cases conditional fee or otherwise. This would not affect the sum received from the other side in costs.

It seems a shame that the almost universal practical application of the cap cannot be made statutory because of fears about its suitability in a tiny number of cases.

Interest

It is reasonable, in my view, to take 25% of any interest received be it in relation to general or special damages, and be it "ordinary" interest or "extra" interest earnt on a reverse payment-in, that is, a Plaintiff's offer to settle.

Overall Offers

Overall offers, that is where the defendant offers a global sum not split into general damages and special damages, can cause some problems. An overall offer of £30,000 is made. The solicitor thinks that the offer is £20,000 general damages and £10,000 for a highly speculative special damages schedule whereas the client may feel that his £25,000 special damages claim is entirely reasonable and the insurers have been a bit mean by only giving general damages of £5,000.

The difference in who gets what is considerable:

Solicitor's view	£
Offer	30,000
Less special damages	10,000
Balance	20,000
25% of £20,000 to solicitor	5,000
Balance to client	25,000

Client's view	
Offer	30,000
Less special damages	25,000
Balance	5,000
25% of £5,000 to solicitor	1,250
Balance to client	28,750

This becomes even more of a problem when Defendant's insurers make an overall offer *to include costs*. Here there is endless scope for misunderstandings between solicitor and client. Most lay people find it hard to understand that one side's costs alone can be higher than the damages claimed.

Whether or not you are acting under a conditional fee agreement try explaining to a client that an offer of £8,000 inclusive of costs is probably calculated on the basis of £4,000 damages and £4,000 costs.

This is likely to become an increasing problem as defendants' insurers and their solicitors become more sophisticated in dealing with the conditional fee plaintiff.

To overcome this problem general damages should be evaluated and reviewed as new evidence, say a fresh medical report, comes in.

A full advice, supported by case law, should be prepared on the quantum of general damages and sent to the client.

This is good practice in any event and minimises, but does not eliminate, the scope for genuine solicitor – client misunderstandings.

Interim Damages

Obtaining an interim payment is *not* a win and the 25% should not be levied on interim damages, although they will of course form part of the fund at the end of the day. Note the definition of "win" at 3(m) of the Law Society's Model Conditional Fee Agreement:

> The case is finally decided in your favour, whether by a court decision or an agreement to pay you damages. "Finally" means that your opponent:
>
> - is not allowed to appeal against the court decision; or
> - has not appealed in time.

Interim damages can be useful for paying disbursements already incurred and funding payments on account of disbursements and this is acceptable.

The Law Society's Model Conditional Fee Agreement at 3(g) states:

> *Interim Damages*
> Money that a court says your opponent must pay while waiting for a settlement or the court's final decision. Out of this money we may require you to pay our remaining disbursements and a reasonable amount for our future disbursements.

In Practice

Rather than over-complicate matters at this stage I stick to the Law Society's Model Conditional Fee Agreement and then give the client the pleasant surprise of not levying on special damages.

Thus:

> *Dear Mrs Green*
>   *I have received payment of your special damages totalling £321. You will recall that special damages are those monies actually spent or lost by you as a result of your accident. I enclose a copy of the schedule we prepared to remind you of those items.*

> *Under the terms of the Conditional Fee Agreement signed by us I am entitled to deduct a maximum of 25% of these damages as a success fee. However as this is money you have actually paid out or lost I do not propose to make any such charge and enclose my firm's cheque in the whole sum of £321.*
> *Yours etc*

This preserves your options in the more difficult "overall offer" cases.

The Future

As time goes by and more work is done on a conditional fee basis, both by solicitors and unregulated claims assessors, it may be desirable to advertise the fact that the 25% applies to general and future damages only. The client is likely to prefer this to 20% of everything being advertised by competitors. At the moment to do so is likely to confuse clients but you should be sure in your own mind what you wish to do in each case.

This is a potentially difficult and very important area that is almost entirely overlooked in any debate about conditional fees.

Annex: The Cap : Percentage Of What?

The New Compensation Recovery Scheme
Social Security (Recovery Of Benefits) Act 1997

The Changes

1.1 The pre-October 1997 system was laid down in the Social Security Act 1989 and then in part IV of the Social Security Act 1992 and the Social Security (Recoupment) Regulations 1990, which deal with claims for personal injuries where the accident or injury occurred, or the disease was diagnosed, on or after *1st January 1989*

1.2 Benefits received in the relevant period five years from the first payment of benefits as a result of the accident or settlement of the claim whichever is earlier had to be paid back from *any* compensation received by the Plaintiff.

1.3 **Relevant period**
This was defined in Section 81(1) of the 1992 Act:

> All benefits received, or likely to be received during the relevant period of five years beginning with the date on which the victim first claimed a relevant benefit in consequence of the disease, or, in any other case the period of 5 years immediately following the day on which the accident or injury in question occurred; but where before the end of that period the compensator makes a compensation payment in final discharge of any claim made by or in respect of the victim and arising out of the accident, injury or disease, the relevant period shall end on the date on which that payment is made whether or not any subsequent payment falls to be made in respect only of taxed costs.

1.4 **Relevant benefits**
This was defined in Section 81(1) and prescribed under the Regulations made thereunder:

(a) attendance allowance
(b) disablement benefit
(c) family credit
(d) income support

(e)   invalidity pension and allowance
(f)   mobility allowance
(g)   benefits payable under schemes made under the Old Cases Act
(h)   reduced earnings allowance
(i)   retirement allowance
(j)   severe disablement allowance
(k)   sickness benefit
(l)   statutory sick pay
(m) unemployment benefit
(ma) disability living allowance
(mb) disability working allowance
(n)   an increase in any of the benefits mentioned above payable in accordance with the Social Security Act 1975 to 1989 or the Old Cases Act or with any regulation, order in Council, order or scheme made thereunder

1.5   **Points to note under pre-October 1997 System**

1.5.1 Under Section 85 of the 1992 Act only relevant benefits paid *in consequence of the accident injury or disease in respect of which the compensation payment is made* fell to be deducted. Thus if the victim would have been entitled to the benefit even if he had *not* suffered the accident injury or disease no deduction was required.

1.5.2 *Payments not exceeding £2,500 were not subject to deduction under the pre-October 1997 System.*

1.5.3 The rules are not restricted to court awards – they include voluntary payments and out of court settlements and payments made by the Motor Insurers Bureau. In addition, payments in to court are deemed to be compensation payments.

The New Scheme

2.0   Social Security (Recovery Of Benefits) Act 1997

This came into force in October 1997.

2.1 Benefits are no longer be recoverable from the *whole* of the claim. The following are recoverable against *loss of earnings only* during the relevant period:

- Disability Working Allowance
- Disablement pension and gratuity
- Incapacity Benefit
- Income Support
- Invalidity pension and allowance
- Jobseeker's allowance
- Reduced earnings allowance
- Severe disablement allowance
- Sickness benefit
- Unemployment benefit

The Relevant Period remains five years or earlier settlement.

2.2 Recoverable against the *costs of care* only during the relevant period
- Attendance allowance
- Care component of disability living allowance

2.3 Recoverable against *compensation for loss of mobility* during the relevant period:
- Mobility allowance
- Mobility component of disability living allowance

Thus General Damages are now preserved free from any deduction.

2.4 The small payments exemption of £2,500 no longer applies.

2.5.1 The compensator pays to the Department of Social Security the full amount of the listed benefits whether or not the Plaintiff claims them in his claim *against* the Defendant.

2.5.2 Questions regarding whether the benefits are payable *otherwise* than in respect of the accident can be referred to a Medical Appeals Tribunal as set up under Section 50 of the Social Security Administration Act 1992.

This tribunal has the power to confirm the amounts rates and periods in the certificate or order the Department of Social Security to issue a fresh certificate varied as the Tribunal thinks fit.

There is an appeal from the Medical Appeals Tribunal to the Social Security Commissioners.

2.5.3 There is provision under Section 16 of the Act for Regulations to be made governing the status of Payments in to Court in relation to the Recovery of Benefits.

All of the provisions apply retrospectively and also catch pre-1989 cases which have not yet settled.

2.6 **Effect On Plaintiffs**

Plaintiffs claiming only General Damages are better off under the new law as their damages will remain untouched. For those with enough Special Damages to cover the recoupment the position is no different.

However the abolition of the £2,500 Exemption means that the claims where nuisance payments were made by "Compensators" no longer arise.

2.7 **Effect On Defendants**

The *whole* of the recoverable benefits have to be repaid to the Department of Social Security ie no more paying £2,500 and letting the state pick up the balance. This applies whether or not the Plaintiff has claimed the heads of damage. Thus if there are care benefits the Defendant has to repay them whether or not the Plaintiff has made a claim for that item.

Costs Insurance – Accident Line Protect

Costs Insurance – Accident Line Protect

Introduction

Any solicitor can carry out "no win-no fee" work for any client in personal injury work but if the losing client has to pay several thousand pounds costs to the defendant's insurers the benefits of the scheme may not be too apparent.

Thus whilst the cap is the key protection for the winning client, costs insurance is the key for the *losing* client.

The good news is that tailor made insurance approved by the Law Society is available at a low premium – the bad news is that this particular insurance is only available to firms who have a member of the Law Society's Personal Injury Panel on their staff, and are members of Accident Line. This Chapter deals with this specific insurance – known as Accident Line Protect, which covers Plaintiff personal injury work only.

However the proposals to extend conditional fees to all money claims and the Woolf Report proposals concerning fixed costs mean that many other insurers are likely to come into the market. In any event the "loser pays costs" rule – rare outside the United Kingdom and Commonwealth jurisdictions is likely to come under further attack, and this will affect the whole concept of costs insurance.

Accident Line Protect

This is the tailor-made Law Society approved insurance.

Brokers:	J & H Marsh and McLennan (UK) Ltd
Insurer:	Lexington Insurance Company
Insurer's Agent:	Abbey Legal Protection Limited

Accident Line Protect is only available to members of the Law Society Accident Line which in turn is only open to firms of solicitors which have partners or employees who are members of the

Law Society's Personal Injury Panel. Thus no panel member – no Law Society approved insurance.

Mixed cases are covered, provided there is a personal injury element. Thus a client claims for the value of his written-off car and injuries sustained in the accident. Both elements are covered unless separate court orders are made for the different aspects of the claim. Thus for the policy to cover a failed claim it is necessary for both parts to fail under the personal injury claim. The only exception is when the mix involves a libel or slander claim, in which case the defamation element is *never* covered.

This insurance is often, but wrongly, referred to as after-the-event-insurance. It is no such thing and an understanding of what is being insured is important particularly as conditional fees become available in other, less predictable, work.

The event insured is *not* the accident, it is the prospect of *losing the case,* which is a *future* event. For reasons set out below this is of little relevance with Accident Line Protect which covers Plaintiff personal injury work and excludes medical negligence, but in the future all litigators will have to get used to assessing risk and the consequences of losing, say, a building dispute case. Then there will be variable risks and variable insurance premia. That is for the future but understanding risk and insurance will become increasingly important for solicitors. Can we at least make a start by dropping the misleading "after the event" tag? One might as well refer to life insurance (really death insurance but that is a less marketable phrase) as "after the event" of birth: after all you cannot die if you have not lived.

This is not mere pedantry. We need to prepare our clients for the day when they will buy often quite expensive legal insurance on a case by case basis. Getting the concept right now would be a help.

Exclusions

1. Cases in which proceedings have already been issued *unless* previously handled under a Legal Aid Certificate which is being withdrawn for purely financial reasons;
2. Cases earlier conducted under any other Legal Fees Insurance arrangement;
3. Medical negligence actions
    Medical negligence is defined as "allegations of professional negligence or breach of duty arising from

conventional or alternative medical or dental treatment or therapy or failure to treat, resulting in personal injury;"

4. Pharmaceutical or drug related actions;
5. Tobacco related actions;
6. Small claims arbitrations where there is no liability for the opponent's costs. At present the small claims limit in personal injury claims is £1,000. However in all other cases the small claims limit is £3,000 with a proposal to increase it to £5,000 and the lower personal injury figure is subject to review;
7. Libel or slander actions and/or any mental or other effect of libel or slander;
8. Claims not *brought* in England or Wales. (Thus cases brought in Scotland are *not* covered);
9. Claims arising out of accidents occurring outside the European Union *whether or not the proceedings are commenced in England and Wales.*

    Easy to slip up on this one – the countries of the European Union are (at June 1998)

    Austria
    Belgium
    Denmark
    Finland
    France
    Germany
    Greece
    Ireland
    Italy
    Luxembourg
    Netherlands
    Portugal
    Spain
    Sweden
    United Kingdom.

Note

The list of exclusions applies only to the Accident Line Protect Insurance, *not* Conditional Fee Agreements. Thus it is permissible (but not necessarily advisable!) to undertake on a conditional fee basis a small claims case arising out of medical negligence in Mexico.

In practice there are a number of cases worth taking on under a conditional fee basis but which are in the excluded category for insurance, *e.g.* holiday accidents in Turkey (outside the European Union) or small claims cases. This will become much more of an issue if the personal injury small claims limit is raised to include far more cases.

Although not covered under Accident Line Protect, applications for insurance will be considered on an individual basis by Abbey Legal Protection Limited in respect of holiday accidents outside the European Union.

Accident Line members do not have to join Accident Line Protect but if they do so they must insure *all* relevant conditional fee cases and not just those where the solicitor perceives a risk of losing and they must *all* be insured with Accident Line Protect, even if other insurers offer a better deal in an individual case. There is no commission payable to the solicitor. There is no excess. There is no joining fee.

Objections to the Scheme

There are theoretical objections to this scheme:

(1) It is restricted to firms of solicitors employing Personal Injury Panel Members;
(2) It forces all eligible conditional fee clients to insure;
(3) The standard premium within each category of accident (Road Traffic and other) means that clients with strong cases are subsidising the riskier cases;
(4) It limits competition – it makes it difficult for other insurers to break into the market and this in turn is, ultimately, against the best interests of clients.

To a free marketeer there is merit in all of these objections, but the proof of the pudding is in the eating. What Accident Line Protect has done is to give peace of mind at a very low premium, to tens of thousands of personal injury Plaintiffs, *many of whom would never have pursued their case but for Accident Line Protect.*

The premium is £95.68 per case for Road Traffic Accidents and £161.20 per case for all other eligible personal injury cases. These figures include Insurance Premium Tax at the June 1998 level of 4%. (Prior to 1st October 1997 the premium was £85.00 per case irrespective of the type of accident. The new price structure reflects the higher risk of losing non-Road Traffic Accident claims, and the increases imposed by the Government, *i.e.* increased insurance premium tax and greatly increased court fees, which are of course always paid in a losing case because by definition proceedings have then been issued.)

This gives cover of £100,000, with no excess, against the other side's costs. It also covers the losing Plaintiff's own disbursements provided that proceedings have been issued. The *total* cover including the other side's costs and the client's own disbursements, is limited to £100,000.

Once proceedings are issued the insurance "picks up" the pre-issue disbursements such as the police report fee and medical report fee, provided that they were incurred *after* the insurance was taken out. The *total* cover is limited to £100,000. In practice it is extremely rare that the limit will cause problems. Most solicitors will go their entire practising lives without dealing with a case where the other side's inter partes costs and the client's own disbursements combined exceed £100,000.

Counsel's fees, like agency fees, are treated as legal costs, not disbursements, and thus are not recoverable; the Woolf report takes the same view. This has significant implications for the way solicitors should work in the future (see Chapter 16 *Disbursements* and Chapter 22 *Future Shock*).

The Importance of Using the Scheme

Of course it would be impossible to provide such comprehensive cover at such a low premium if clients and solicitors were able to pick and choose which cases to insure and if solicitors with little experience of personal injury work were allowed to assess whether or not a case should be taken on on a conditional fee basis in the first place. Sharing the risk in return for a common benefit is how insurance started.

This is at the root of the Underwoods Cap – standardize the legal fees by way of a cap and protect everyone.

My advice is clear:

- Get on the Law Society's Personal Injury Panel;
- Use Accident Line Protect Insurance.

Getting onto the Law Society's Personal Injury Panel

Solicitors get very upset about specialist panels, unless of course they are on one, but the Groucho Marx principle applies: "I would not want to join a club which would have me as a member". What is the point of being a member of a specialist panel unless it is genuinely specialist and recognised as such? It would achieve nothing. It would *not* give access to cheap insurance because the premium would inevitably rise if the Panel was thrown wide open. It is one thing for clients with strong cases to subsidise those with weak cases; it is another matter for competently advised clients to subsidise incompetently advised clients.

It has been said that you cannot buck the market. Well, look at the market. Most other insurers offer a product at a much higher price for a fraction of the cover. It you can't beat it, join it!

At Appendix 29 are the criteria for admission to the Personal Injury Panel. There is a certain amount of flexibility; those who are unable to comply with the caseload requirements but have comparable civil litigation experience and a good personal injury library and good office and case management may succeed.

If getting on to the Panel is still a real problem then consider recruiting a Panel Member. Membership is personal to the solicitor and travels with him or her. If you "go for it" with conditional fees you will soon need another solicitor anyway. Work towards getting more than one solicitor on the Panel. People leave, become ill etc, and it is unwise to have the whole of a successful conditional fee based practice dependent upon one *individual's* membership, particularly as I have just advised you to poach them!

Use Accident Line Protect Insurance

Membership of the Personal Injury Panel triggers potential membership of Accident Line and indeed the Law Society invites all Personal Injury Panel members to join Accident Line.

However Accident Line is a scheme in its own right and existed before Conditional Fees were introduced. Its rules are a helpful guide to good practice in personal injury cases and I commend them.

Accident Line Protect Insurance in Practice

Once you are on the Personal Injury Panel and signed up with Accident Line you register with Accident Line Protect. There is no joining fee. You then receive a loose-leaf user manual with your own Practice Reference Number. The manual is clear and simple to use and runs to just 39 pages including the entire text of the Law Society's Conditional Fee Agreement and the policy wording.

You also receive a pad of insurance certificates with carbonless copies. Once you sign a conditional fee agreement you issue the certificate to the client and each month send the premium reports and the premia to J & H Marsh & McLennan (UK) Ltd on a premium report form.

Thus you decide whether or not to take the case on under the Conditional Fee Scheme and if you do so you issue the insurance certificate. You do *not* need to apply for the insurance or fill out a proposal form, or obtain prior approval form the Insurer *except* for clients:

1.   involved in a possible multi-party action (defined as a case where it is possible ten or more people will have the same cause of action from the same incident.);
2.   involved in an action for damages in a Personal Injury claim where there is no impairment to their physical condition (*i.e.* mental/psychiatric claims) and there is "no cause of action" recognised by English Law;
3.   who have secondary actions involving medical negligence arising from treatment of the original injury;
4.   involved in an action where proceedings have been issued;
5.   involved in an action previously covered by a Legal Aid Certificate (and this will only be considered where the certificate has been withdrawn purely for financial reasons);
6.   involved in an action previously conducted under the cover of any other form of Legal Expenses Insurance;
7.   who intend to appeal against a court decision;
8.   whose action is or was earlier handled by any other solicitor under a Conditional Fee Agreement.

All of these situations are self-explanatory except (2) which I do not understand – if there is no cause of action then there is no cause of action – but the insurers have put it in so I pass it on.

In any of these eight circumstances, a simple referral from must be completed. You must provide an estimate of the client's damages on the initial Premium report form.

Get used to doing this now in *all civil litigation*. When the Woolf Report proposals are implemented (probably October 1999) it will be essential to do this in **every case** upon issue so that the court can allocate the case to the appropriate "track".

Furthermore with the introduction of fixed costs and the Plaintiff's offers to settle *pre-issue* and penal interest against defendant's who refuse such offers, it will be crucial to make an early assessment of damages. Those solicitors who do so will have significantly more work, greater profits and higher damages. With conditional fees higher damages equals higher costs. *Early assessment of damages is crucial.*

Reporting

Claims Status Reports

Each quarter you complete and submit to Abbey Legal Protection Limited a Claims Status Report. This is done by reference to key milestones which have a lettered code. This quarterly report details

- the stage the case has reached;
- the injury status;
- a costs estimate (to allow the insurers to estimate the potential costs of the defendant).

Priority Reports

This must be submitted immediately if one of the following positions is reached:

- The case is won or settled in the client's favour;
- The case is closed and there is to be no claim on Accident Line Protect;
- The insured is now unlikely to win;
- A payment into court is to be rejected;
- A final offer is to be rejected;
- Discontinuance;

- The action has become multi-party;
- The insured has elected for Legal Aid;
- There is an allegation of negligence/error/omission or a dispute which may lead to Arbitration under Accident Line Protect insurance;
- There is to be an Appeal against the decision of the court.

The monthly premium and quarterly claim status reports can be computerised and the package is available from Abbey Legal Protection for £99. I strongly recommend this.

Payments into Court

One important decision needs to be made in relation to Accident Line Protect insurance and it concerns payments into court, or rather what happens when a Plaintiff fails to beat the payment in. There is an option to vary the Law Society's Model Conditional Fee Agreement which triggers off much greater costs protection for the client dealing with a payment into court, *but this only applies if the variation is made at the outset*, that is when the Conditional Fee Agreement is signed.

This is a crucial area which is dealt with in detail in the next chapter. It is sufficient to note at this stage that if you adopt the Underwoods Payment In Scheme *your conditional fee client enjoys much greater costs protection even than a legally-aided client with a nil contribution.*

General

This type of insurance does not fall within the Financial Services Act 1986 and thus Law Society authorization for investment business is not required in order to sell costs insurance.

Remember that Accident Line Protect does not cover medical negligence actions, pharmaceutical, drug or tobacco related actions and small claim arbitrations are excluded from the scheme, as is any accident outside the European Union, and any case brought outside England and Wales.

Special Problems

1. *Counterclaims*

    Counterclaims whether being brought by defendants or defended by Plaintiffs are *not* generally covered, but in many instances these will be dealt with by your client's insurers *e.g.* in road traffic accident your client's motor insurers will deal with the claim.

    Counterclaims *are* covered if costs are all dealt with in one action and there is no split order on costs.

2. *Appeals*

    (a) The costs of an appeal by the defendant against a decision in your client's favour *are* covered;

    (b) The costs of an appeal by your client may be covered by Accident Line Protect Insurance but only with prior approval by the Insurer's agent – although you are allowed to conduct appeals on a conditional fee basis without restriction.

    If your client is a losing *defendant* the insurance is likely to be approved for an appeal but a proposed appeal by a losing Plaintiff will attract far great scrutiny from Accident Line Protect.

3. *Interlocutory Judgements*

    If the client *wins* but has had a costs award made against him at an interlocutory hearing these costs are *not* insured and come out of damages.

Cancellations

A. The client loses insurance protection and is liable for *all* of both sides' costs (depending on the final outcome of the case) if:

   (1) the cancellation is caused by the client having breached his responsibilities;

   (2) the cancellation is because the client has, against your advice, refused to settle;

   (3) the client cancels.

B. Provided court proceedings have been issued the insurers will pay the other side's costs and the client's own disbursements if cancellation is because the solicitor now believes the case will not succeed *and* this is through no fault of the client.

If court proceedings have *not* been started at this stage then the insurers pay nothing but the client has no liability either *except for his own disbursements incurred to that stage.*

C.   If, through no fault of the client, cancellation is because the insurer now believes the case will not succeed but the solicitor disagrees, the issue will be resolved by arbitration. If the arbitrator agrees with the solicitor the policy is reinstated. If the arbitrator agrees with the insurer then the insurer will pay the other sides cost and the client's own disbursements if proceedings have been issued. If proceedings have *not* been issued then, as always, the client is responsible for his own disbursements.

Arbitration

Any dispute between the *solicitor and the insurer* is to be determined by a single arbitrator appointed by the Law Society in the absence of agreement. The losing party pays both side's costs (No win – no fee not available here!).

Any dispute between the *client and the insurer* is referred to arbitration as above. However if the dispute is over the prospects of success then the *insurer* will always pay the costs, win or lose.

Changing Solicitors

If a client sacks his solicitor the insurance automatically ends. Whether Accident Line Protect Insurance will be issued to cover the case with a *new* solicitor is at the discretion of the insurers. Prior approval is required.

Legal Aid

A client may switch from Legal Aid to Accident Line Protect but only with the prior approval of the insurer, which will only be given if the reason for any *withdrawal* of Legal Aid relates to the client's finances and **not** the merits of the case.

A client may switch from Accident Line Protect to Legal Aid although Legal Aid may well be refused on the grounds that another method of funding is available.

In any event the insurer will only be liable for costs and disbursements incurred during the period of cover.

Private Funding

If proceedings have been issued the case is not eligible for inclusion in the "Accident Line Protect" insurance scheme.

Any case, however old and however long it pre-dates the advent of conditional fees may be switched to a conditional fee funding arrangement, but the insurance may not be available in certain cases – as explained earlier.

Chapter 6

Risk? What Risk?

Risk Assessment in Personal Injury cases, excluding Medical Negligence

There is nothing complicated, difficult or unusual about risk assessment in personal injury cases. In fact it is very much easier than in any other type of litigation. All personal injury solicitors have been assessing risk for years, either for the purposes of completing a legal aid application form or in order to decide whether to take the case on a "speculative funding" basis, *i.e.* without money up front, without interim billing and on the assumption that the case is a winner and costs will be recovered from the defendants insurers at the end of the day.

That judgment will not change simply because solicitors can now lawfully and openly enter into conditional fee agreements. The *legal* considerations are unchanged; the chance of the client succeeding in any given case remains unaltered.

In any event a high percentage of personal injury cases taken on by solicitors are won by the Plaintiff. Legal Aid Board records show that in 1994 and 1995 Plaintiff success rates, *in legally-aided cases* were as follows:

Road Traffic Accident	90.6%
Accidents at Work	77.2%
Other Accidents	81.39%
Medical Negligence	49.1%

For various reasons the Legal Aid Board's figures are likely to understate significantly the prospect of success. For example in very clear cases, or cases where the Defendant's insurers have admitted liability, there is little point in wasting time and effort in applying for Legal Aid.

Furthermore the cases with the highest rate of success – Road Traffic cases – are also the most common and therefore to "average the averages" with other accidents and accidents at work does not produce a true picture of a typical solicitor's personal injury workload.

S Fennell in *The Funding of Personal Injury Litigation* (page 24 (1994) University of Sheffield, quoted in Stella Yarrow's *The Price of Success* p.41 puts it at 94% in cases handled by members of the Association of Personal Injury Lawyers and other personal injury specialists. This includes all non-medical negligence work, not just road traffic accidents.

My experience at my firm and my questioning of hundreds of personal injury solicitors suggests that the success rate for Plaintiffs in non-medical personal injury cases is at least 95% and I will use that figure.

"Success" is defined as a money settlement or order in favour of the Plaintiff even if heavily discounted for reasons relating to liability or contributory negligence and, pre October 1997, including "nuisance" payments, of £2,500 in cases where there was a high Compensation Recovery Unit statement.

If risk assessment is so difficult ask yourself how long you take to decide which box to tick in the Legal Aid Application Form – you know – the one where you have to give the prospects of success.

Does it take you:

(a) Less than 30 seconds?
(b) 30 seconds to a minute?
(c) Over a minute?

Or ask yourself what percentage of Plaintiff personal injury cases you lose

(a) 1% ?
(b) 2% ?
(c) 3% ?

Look at your old files and find out.

Furthermore do you ever lose a case unexpectedly? (I did – my own.) Or do you correctly identify the doubtful ones?

What Risks are You Taking?

Risk *assessment* is different from risk *taking*, i.e. deliberately taking on a doubtful case because if your client does win the general damages will be high and so will your 25% share.

In a given individual case there is a risk of *losing* but over a spread of cases your chance of *losing out* is non-existent. The extra cases and extra fees per case on the "winners" will more than make up for the costs of work done on the "losers". There are simply not enough losable cases around for any firm doing a significant amount of conditional fee work to lose out.

In any event when did you last actually charge a losing private client Plaintiff in a personal injury case? So what are you losing by "coming out" and operating on a conditional fee basis?

£65 per hour in Legal Aid cases I hear you answer. That is true at present – a case lost on Legal Aid pays £65 per hour whereas a case lost on a "no win-no fee" basis pays nothing. However this misses the point. You can still take such cases on a Legal Aid basis. *Conditional fee work is in addition to Legal Aid work not instead of it.*

In any event, Legal Aid looks likely to be withdrawn from all personal injury work except medical negligence under the proposals contained in the Government's Consultation Paper "Access to Justice with Conditional Fees" (March 1998).

Furthermore the true cost of a "lost" case is *not* the fees you would have earnt had you won – it is the cost of overheads applicable to that case. Thus if lost cases represents 2% of all cases and say 8% of all work (because lost cases are by definition, likely to have gone to trial and thus involve disproportionately more work than the average) the actual cost is 8% of overheads *not* the potential "selling" price of the work.

Thus if a Department's overheads are £100,000 the "loss" is £8,000 *not* the actual selling costs. It is crucial to look at the overall picture on conditional fee work, *i.e.* the extra cases, the benefits of economy of scale, the taking of a share of the damages etc, and not just the unsuccessful work done for nothing.

Of course the risk to the *client* is nil, provided he takes out the insurance against losing. Save for a one-off insurance premium of £95.68 in Road Traffic cases or £161.20 in other cases, the client cannot be worse off than if he had never embarked upon the litigation and that is the great attraction to clients of the "no win-no fee" arrangements.

None of this applies to Medical Negligence cases which I deal with in the next chapter.

Chapter 7

Medical Negligence

Medical Negligence

Introduction

Medical negligence cases are a form of personal injury work and thus may be carried out under Conditional Fee Agreements in exactly the same way as ordinary personal injury work. The same statutory and regulatory framework applies.

However there are practical problems peculiar to medical negligence work and those problems, and potential solutions, are the subject of this chapter.

Risk

The chances of a Plaintiff losing a medical negligence case are very much higher than the chances of a Plaintiff losing an ordinary personal injury case. Detailed figures are hard to come by and those that exist are not entirely consistent with one another.

Legal Aid Board records show that in 1994 and 1995 success rates, *in legally-aided cases* were as follows:

Road Traffic Accident	90.6%
Accidents at Work	77.2%
Other Accidents	81.39%
Medical Negligence	49.1%

Because of the cost and risk involved a very much higher percentage of Medical Negligence cases are funded by Legal Aid than other types of personal injury work. Thus the figure for Medical Negligence is likely to be accurate overall and I will work on the basis that such cases have a 50% chance of success.

For various reasons the Legal Aid Board's figures for the other areas are likely to understate significantly the prospect of success. For example in very clear cases, or cases where the Defendant's insurers have admitted liability there is little point in wasting time and effort in applying for Legal Aid.

Furthermore the cases with the highest rate of success, Road Traffic cases, are also the most common and therefore to "average the averages" with other accidents and accidents at work does not produce a true picture of a typical solicitor's personal injury workload.

S Fennell in *The Funding of Personal Injury Litigation* (page 24 (1994) University of Sheffield, quoted in Stella Yarrow's *The Price of Success* p.41 puts it at 94% in cases handled by members of the Association of Personal Injury Lawyers and other personal injury specialists. This includes all non-medical negligence work, not just road traffic accidents.

My experience at my firm and my questioning of hundreds of personal injury solicitors suggests that the success rate for Plaintiffs in non-medical personal injury cases is at least 95% and I will use that figure.

"Success" is defined as a money settlement or order in favour of the Plaintiff even if heavily discounted for reasons relating to liability or contributory negligence and, pre October 1997, including "nuisance" payments, of £2,500 in cases where there was a high Compensation Recovery Unit statement.

Assuming these figures are broadly correct then the chance of winning a medical negligence case is about half that of winning an "ordinary" personal injury case. However in assessing risk to a solicitor's practice it is the risk of *losing* not the chance of winning that matters. You may think that these are two sides of the same coin and in a sense they are *but the risk of losing a medical negligence case is 10 times as great as that of losing a personal injury case*, **not** *twice as great*.

Comparing Two Partners

Two partners each have 100 files, one partner's workload is exclusively plaintiff medical negligence and the other partner's workload is exclusively non-medical negligence personal injury.

Partner 1 (Medical Negligence)
50% chance
            winners 50   losers 50

Partner 2
95% chance
            winners 95   losers 5

Ratio of winners to winners = 1:1.9
Ratio of losers to losers = 10:1

This is a crucial fact about assessing risk in different areas of work as opposed to assessing risk in each individual case in a particular area of work. However good you and your firm are you will never achieve the same success rate in medical negligence cases as even an average or well below average personal injury lawyer in a poor firm.

Should you Take the Work?

Having said all of that my whole approach to conditional fees is "the more the merrier". The benefits are that they are attractive to clients and allow the solicitor to increase workload and efficiency and thus maximise costs *and* give access to justice. Eliminating losers does *not* increase the actual number of winners, just the *percentage* of winners.

Discrimination cases in Industrial Tribunals have a much lower success rate than even medical negligence but my firm takes those on. Fifty-fifty, after all, is not a bad rate so why my unusual caution about medical negligence cases? One major difference between Industrial Tribunal cases and medical negligence cases is that in the former there are, generally, no inter-partes costs whereas in the latter costs follow the event.

Because of the "costs following the event" rule it is wise to insure against the risk of losing and paying the other side's costs even in the low-risk area of "ordinary" personal injury work and the whole question of this insurance is dealt with in Chapter 5 *Costs Insurance – Accident Line Protect*. Because of the ten-times greater risk in medical negligence cases it is essential to insure and therein lies the problem.

Insurance

No cheap or even moderately priced insurance is available for medical negligence cases and it is very unwise to advise a client to proceed in such a case without insurance. The much greater cost of the insurance compared to ordinary personal injury work reflects the much greater risk of losing and the fact that costs in medical negligence cases are far higher than in ordinary cases.

Abbey Legal Protection Limited, the Agents for Accident Line Protect, do now provide an insurance policy for medical negligence cases undertaken on a conditional fee basis. Like the ordinary Accident Line Protect Insurance it provides a minimum indemnity of £100,000 and this can be increased upon request. Solicitors should be wary of some other policies which only offer such insurance in bands of say £10,000. This is often insufficient and there is then a risk that those insurers will not extend the cover when the limit is reached.

The Abbey Legal Protection insurance can be taken out at each stage of a case with different payments. The stages and premia are as follows:

Stage One   *Premium £1,300*

From date of agreement to 14 days after defence filed. The agreement will usually be entered into *after* experts reports have been obtained on liability but the cover is retrospective and will cover the original disbursements incurred in investigating the claims **before** the insurance was effected.

Stage Two   *Premium £2,600*

From 14 days after defence filed up to and including exchange of witness statements and setting down.

Stage Three   *Premium £4,056*

From setting down up to and including trial.

The premium structure needs a little explanation. Stage 2 and Stage 3 payments are on top of the previous payments not inclusive of them.

Thus a Plaintiff takes Stage One insurance and then Stage Two insurance and the claim then ends, and thus Stage Three insurance is not needed. The total cost of the insurance is £3,900 calculated as follows:

	£
Stage One	1,300
Stage Two	2,600
	3,900

not £2,600.

It will be seen that the total cost of insurance of a case that goes the whole way is £7,956:

	£
Stage One	1,300
Stage Two	2,600
Stage Three	4,056
	7,956

Note also that the premia quoted for Stages Two and Three are dependent upon the previous stages having already been purchased. Thus if a client wishes to join at a later stage, for example because of withdrawal of Legal Aid due to a change in means, he will be allowed to do so but will be quoted an individual premium. Applicants who apply to join midway through a claim will have their claim subject to greater scrutiny – the inference being that the further into a case the Plaintiff is looking for cover the greater his perceived prospect of defeat.

All figures are correct to June 1998.

Other Points

Panel membership

The insurance is only available to firms with a Law Society Medical Negligence Panel member albeit the fee-earner actually responsible for the file need not be a panel member but should be subject to the supervision of a panel member.

This is a major restriction as at 1st June 1998 there were only 140 solicitors on the Medical Negligence Panel (up from 64 in 1995 and 113 in 1996 and 122 in 1997) (see *Law Society's Gazette* 28th May 1998, Page 1). Some of those are primarily defence lawyers. Many firms have several members. Only 97 firms have solicitors on the

Panel. Karen Mackay, the Law Society's head of legal aid policy, speaking in response to the Legal Aid Board's proposal to limit legally-aided medical negligence work to firms with a medical negligence franchise, which in turn would be limited to firms with a member of either the Law Society's or the Action for Victims of Medical Accident's (AVMA) medical negligence panel, said

> We do not know to what extent there will be adequate access across the country... there needs to be time for people to come onto the panel. A shortage of solicitors could lead to "cherry-picking" of the best cases.
>
> (*Law Society Gazette*, 28th May 1998, page 1)

Thus there is insufficient national coverage. It is to be hoped that the Law Society's criteria for joining the panel, particularly in relation to the number of high value cases, will be relaxed.

The criteria for joining the Medical Negligence Panel are:

The Applicant must:

- have been a qualified solicitor or Legal Executive for at least three years,
- hold a current practising certificate,
- have a basic grounding in Personal Injury as well as Medical Negligence,
- have run at least 36 medical negligence cases over the last three years and have had at least 3 set down and ready for trial,
- at least one where the award has been approved by the court where the Plaintiff is under a disability,
- and either two of maximum severity or at least four where the value exceeded £100,000,
- have attended one major conference on medical negligence and one medical course for lawyers devoted specifically to enhancing the lawyer's understanding of medicine generally. These courses must have been attended during the previous three years.
- have satisfactory office procedures for monitoring and supervision.

Ian Walker, President of the Association of Personal Injury Lawyers (APIL), has said that he does not accept that the Law Society and AVMA panels are the only measures of specialisation and that APIL is considering introducing its own panel. (*Law Society's Gazette* 28th May 1998).

In 1996/7 the number of Legal Aid certificates issued for medical negligence work was around 11,500. (Source: *Ensuring Justice?* – Law Society April 1998).

Experts' Reports

The insurance will not be granted without sight of expert reports unless the evidence is overwhelmingly in favour of the Plaintiff.

The Premium as a Disbursement

In future, but at a date as yet unspecified, a successful plaintiff will be able to recover the insurance premium as a disbursement from the unsuccessful defendant.

Disbursements

Many clients will be unable to afford the insurance premium and if Legal Aid is ultimately abolished for all money claims, as has been suggested, then a whole new section of the community, with no hope of funding the disbursements, will need representation.

If the cases were likely to win there would be a solution – the solicitor could fund the disbursements knowing he would get them back at the end of the case (see Chapter 16 *Disbursements*). This would then be a cash-flow problem rather than a profitability problem, and one which solicitors are going to have to deal with in ordinary personal injury cases.

However as we have seen there is no such likelihood of success.

Case Assessment

None of this would matter if a competent solicitor could typically assess the case at no direct cost to him or her and thus weed out the losers and increase the success rate and thus lower the risk of funding disbursements which, in the event of a loss are irrecoverable. However this is simply not the case and this is because of the law relating to medical negligence which is beyond the scope of this book.

Suffice to say that a solicitor is likely to have to spend around £1,000 out of his or her own pocket on expert's reports before even being able to assess the case and put it to the insurers for consideration. This is of course quite apart from all of the legal work done for nothing.

If the insurer accepts the case then the cost of those disbursements is covered, win or lose, but the lowest premium is £1,300 – and where is that going to come from? Why, the solicitor of course and that is *not* recoverable in the event of a loss.

Will Solicitors Undertake Medical Negligence Work?

My advice, on a commercial basis, is that conditional fee medical negligence work should not be touched with a bargepole, unless the client funds, upfront, all of the disbursements. If you limit your cases accordingly, you are unlikely to carry out sufficient work to qualify for the medical negligence panel, and are thus unlikely to get insurance.

The risk of losing is one thing, *lending* money on disbursements is one thing but paying out in cash £1,000 or more per case knowing that in half of those cases you will not get it back is another thing altogether.

The Lord Chancellor sees it differently. In a statement to the House of Lords on 9th December 1997 he said:

> Rather than the headline grabbing £15,000 for medical negligence cases often quoted, I am told that cover has more often been provided at much lower sums – in the region of £3,000. Provided only really strong cases go forward, it is not impossible for a well-run solicitors firm to run the risk of losing money of that order in the few cases where costs are not recovered from the other side – especially given the costs they will recover, and their entitlement to a success fee, in cases that they win.

The problem with a free market is just that. Solicitors will exercise their freedom to say no. It is a characteristic of "well-run solicitors firms" that they budget and prioritise and look at what work is worth doing. Those "well-run" firms are the very ones that will pull out of medical negligence work.

Of course there are particularly pressing social and moral reasons why medical negligence work should be done but that is a separate matter and beyond the scope of this book. My task here is to advise you of what you are letting yourself in for.

Possible Solutions

There is evidence that the Lord Chancellor realises that the Government has made a mistake in proposing to abolish Legal Aid for medical negligence cases. Television pictures of brain-damaged children whose families cannot afford to seek compensation do not fit well with the notion of a caring government. However the message is somewhat mixed with the Lord Chancellor saying that the insurance is affordable really but also saying that:

> it could be that in certain types of case, and medical negligence is often the special case cited, the risks and costs cannot be borne by the lawyers. In these alternative arrangements may be necessary. I will therefore be talking to banks and financial institutions to see what arrangements can be made.
> (The Lord Chancellor to the House of Lords 9th December 1997)

It is not known how this will work – if the "banks and financial institutions" simply lend the money then nothing has changed – that's how most of us run a practice anyway. Or are they expected to *give* the money to solicitors? This seems a little unlikely. We shall see.

Retention of Legal Aid

This seems unlikely in the long run and in any event does not help the majority of the population who do not qualify, on financial grounds, for legal aid, and there is absolutely no prospect of the *financial* criteria for obtaining legal aid being relaxed significantly.

The current position (June 1998) is that Legal Aid in medical negligence cases has received a stay of execution. In its consultation paper *Access to Justice with Conditional Fees* the Government says it "does not intend to remove medical negligence now but will look to do so as the market develops and lawyers adapt to the greater use of conditional fee agreements." (Paragraph 3.16).

However it does propose to limit those solicitors who may undertake medical negligence cases under legal aid and at Paragraph 3.19 says:

> 3.19 In future, the Legal Aid Board should provide assistance in these cases through contracts under Part IV of the Legal Aid Act 1988. Contracts would be given only to solicitors who have shown that they have sufficient competence in the area. Competence might be demonstrated by membership of the Law Society Medical Negligence Panel, or of some other panel (for example, that

maintained by the Action for Victims of Medical Accidents) or by some other objectively verifiable criterion.

The full consultation paper appears at Appendix 27 and the main section dealing with medical negligence cases is at Paragraphs 3.15 to 3.21.

In its response to the consultation paper the Legal Aid Board has proposed that only firms with a medical negligence franchise be allowed to undertake such work under a legal aid certificate and that the criteria for obtaining a franchise should be as set out in 3.19 above. The Legal Aid Board proposes introducing this restriction with effect from January 1999 although those firms with a personal injury franchise could continue doing medical negligence cases until June 1999.

(See the *Law Society's Gazette*, 28th May 1998, Page 1).

Contingency Legal Aid Fund

Favoured by the Bar and the Law Society and could work if applied to all work including low-risk ordinary personal injury work but cannot work for medical negligence alone for all the reasons set out above. Its unsuitability for conditional fee work also makes it unsuitable for funding by a contingency legal aid fund.

Abolition of costs rule as against the Plaintiff only

This is the radical solution which would limit the client, and his solicitor's direct cash exposure to *his own disbursements*, and thus eliminates the need for expensive insurance. The beauty of this scheme, which I favour, is that weak cases are still weeded out because the solicitor is sharing the risk – that is he gets no fee if the case is lost – but good cases can go ahead at an affordable price.

It is argued that this is unfair on a defendant, who is at risk on costs, against a plaintiff who is not at risk on costs. However that is effectively the way the Legal Aid Scheme has worked although I accept that that is one of the criticisms of Legal Aid. Defendants in medical negligence cases are virtually always the state or an emanation thereof and thus this represents a state subsidy but only to cases where a solicitor, sharing the risk, has judged it worth proceeding with the case.

To further weed out weak cases this system could be limited to cases where the solicitor is a member of the Medical Negligence Panel, although as stated above the Panel needs to be expanded.

Abolition of costs rule – both sides

This is the same as above but the winning Plaintiff gets no costs and thus the winning Plaintiff's solicitor's fee paid entirely out of damages. Problem is that level of damages in England and Wales is not sufficiently high to make this viable. It works in other jurisdictions where there are no inter-partes costs but higher damages, notably United States.

Fixed Costs

Will probably come in with Woolf Report anyway. Benefit is that insurance premia drop sharply because exposure is both limited and certain. This benefits the "well-run solicitors firms" that the Lord Chancellor is so keen on. Efficient firms get same fee for less work compared with inefficient firms who currently get a *higher* fee because they spend more time and rack up more hours.

This argument applies to all cases: but the high risk of losing and actually having to pay costs in medical negligence cases means it has more immediate relevance here.

Double Damages

Under this system anyone who is the victim of medical negligence receives a 100% uplift on damages compared with an award for the same injury not caused by medical negligence.

This gives lawyers and clients greater motivation to take on this kind of work as although risky it would provide a higher reward for both.

Could be combined with partial or total abolition of costs rule (as above), or fixed fees.

Arguments against include that it represents a windfall for medical negligence sufferers as opposed to ordinary accident victims. True, but it is a matter of chance *to the victim* who suffers injury in hospital as to whether it is, in law, the result of negligence in which case he recovers in full, or not, in which case he gets nothing and a substantial legal bill. Which brings us to:

No Fault Liability

The real answer. Take lawyers out of it. Take the Doctors out of it. As part of society's deal with itself we agree that anyone injured as a result of medical treatment, negligent or otherwise, receives compensation paid for out of the National Health Service budget, in turn paid for out of general taxation. It would represent a tiny percentage of NHS expenditure.

At present in serious cases even a plaintiff who loses is likely to be heavily dependent upon state benefits in any event, so the true cost is even lower.

Chapter 8

Multi-Party Actions

Definitions

The court system in England and Wales has no established procedures for managing group litigation although it is widely recognised that there needs to be such a mechanism. Lord Woolf in his final report says that there is a need for a new approach in relation to court procedures, dealing with such claims. In the United States these types of matters are generally known as "class actions".

In late 1997 the Lord Chancellor's Department issued a consultation paper concerning proposed procedures in multi-party actions and listed the different types of such cases.

1. Major one-off disaster claims such as Zeebrugge and Kings Cross where causation is generally common to all cases and may not be in dispute and where the class of those affected is clearly defined from the outset. In many cases the number of people in the class will be high;

2. Product liability claims, especially those involving pharmaceutical products such as Opren and Benzodiazopene, where liability may be difficult to determine and common issues may be difficult to identify. Such claims are frequently complicated by a multiplicity of *defendants* who all manufactured similar products as well as by a multiplicity of plaintiffs;

3. Multiple claims relating to industrial diseases deriving from the same cause such as asbestosis claims, industrial deafness and vibration white finger claims;

4. Environmental cases deriving not only from specific incidents but also from damage occurring over a period of time, such as seepage from an industrial plant, or a nuclear installation, or prolonged use of chemicals in particular circumstances. Those types of claim may involve both personal injury and property damage as well as, in some cases, loss of amenity (as in the Canary Wharf case);

5. Claims relating to use or consumption of defective goods or services causing damage to property, or personal injury and/or financial loss. Examples are:

- claims by tenants of a block of flats or an estate for a landlord's failure to repair;
- shareholders against a company or its auditors for disseminating misleading information;
- residents of a neighbourhood against a public authority's decision to build a road or to permit development in their area;
- a group of package holiday customers against a tour operator;
- a group of customers who have bought defective goods;
- professional negligence claims.

Often, but not always, the claims may be individually small but together quite substantial.

The Woolf Report identified three objectives that any new system for multi-party actions should try and achieve:

1. Providing access to justice where large numbers of people have been affected by another's conduct, but individual loss is so small that it makes an individual action economically unviable;
2. providing expeditious, effective and proportionate methods of resolving cases, where individual damages are large enough to justify individual actions but where the number of claimants and the nature of the issues involved mean that the cases cannot be managed satisfactorily in accordance with normal procedure; and
3. achieving a balance between the normal rights of claimants and defendants to pursue and defend cases individually and the interests of a group of parties to litigate the action as a whole in an effective manner.

It is proposed that there be a certification procedure operated by the court and that the criteria should be:

- at least 10 potential claims by or against the same person(s);

- that the claims are in respect of, or arise out of, the same or similar circumstances;
- a substantial number of the claims give rise to common questions of fact and law; and
- the interests of justice are served by proceedings under the multi-party rules.

Claims totalling under £50,000 would start in the County Court with those totalling more than £50,000 starting in either the High Court or the County Court.

So where do conditional fees fit in in all of this?

Conditional Fees and Multi-Party Actions

In theory multi-party personal injury cases are no different from any other type of case and may be handled on a conditional fee basis just like any other case. However experience in the United States has shown that this is not necessarily so in practice.

In individual cases the interests of solicitor and client are broadly the same, that is to win the case, maximise the damages and to do so as quickly as is consistent with the demands of the case.

There is no evidence at all of clients feeling that solicitors have under-settled in order to get a quick and easy fee although it must be said that one of the few benefits of the hourly rate is that solicitors have no incentive to settle early, either at full value or less.

However in multi-party actions individuals may feel, or actually be, under pressure to settle against their will. This may be because of pressure from others in the group who are happy with the terms proposed and/or from the lawyers who may perceive a good settlement, and fee, being jeopardised by a small number of the group.

Again the considerations are no different from a legally-aided multi-party action except that there it will probably be an outside body, the Legal Aid Board, perceived as applying the pressure, not the client's own solicitor.

In the excellent Legal Action Group book *Achieving Civil Justice* Roger Smith looks at class actions in the United States and Canada and some of the problems caused. He points out that such actions inevitably subordinate the individual to the group and that decision making, even at the nominal level, is taken from individual litigants and given to the professionals, that is the lawyers and judges concerned.

Roger Smith goes on to say (page 53):

> The disempowering consequences of this move were demonstrated very clearly in the Agent Orange Litigation, when various of the campaigning veterans groups were highly dissatisfied with the settlement worked out by lawyers and the judge over the weekend before the trial was due to begin. One of the key plaintiffs expressed his dissatisfaction thus:
>
> "A reporter calls me at 7am Monday morning and tells me the case has been settled. We had no say in the settlement. Is it a lawyers' case or the clients' case? The veterans got nothing."

Multi-party or class actions, nevertheless, are likely to play an increasing part in the law and the combination of such actions and conditional fees potentially give victims a chance to seek redress where individually and without such arrangements they would have little chance.

An obvious example is lung cancer victims, who have succeeded in obtaining massive settlements in the United States. For a fictional, but highly readable, account of such United States litigation read *The Runaway Jury* by John Grisham. In this country Leigh Day & Co and Irwin Mitchell are acting for around 50 alleged victims under conditional fee agreements in suing two British tobacco companies, legal aid having been refused to the Plaintiffs.

The case does however demonstrate the need for care in multi-party actions generally. They are usually high profile with powerful and rich corporations defending a profitable commercial interest. Getting it wrong may be a disaster for the firm and not just the Plaintiffs. The potential costs risk in the British tobacco claim has been put at between £9 Million (*Daily Telegraph* 13th February 1998) and £20 Million (*Law Society's Gazette*).

In Hodgson and Others v *Imperial Tobacco Ltd and Others, The Times*, 13th February 1998, the Court of Appeal stated that the risk that a lawyer acting under a conditional fee agreement would be ordered to pay the costs of an action personally was no different from that of lawyers engaged under any other fee agreement including Legal Aid.

The Lord Chancellor's consultation paper proposes that the managing Judge, who will be dealing with the multi-party action throughout, be empowered to appoint a taxing officer to the action to attend hearings and advise on costs and costs issues.

This would presumably include the appropriate success fee in conditional fee cases and the appropriate level of any cap on damages and the fund which is capped, that is whether for example special damages or future care costs should be excluded from the fund from which the solicitor effectively takes a percentage. All of these issues, discussed elsewhere in this book, are likely to be more difficult in multi-party actions where an overall sum may be paid without reference to how much is payable to individual plaintiffs let alone a split between general damages and special damages, past and future loss etc.

Because of these and other problems discussed above The Woolf Report proposes that multi-party settlements should be approved by the court and Lord Woolf regarded this as particularly important where the defendant offers a lump sum settlement.

Lord Woolf regards such approval as necessary because:

- It ensures that lawyers do not benefit themselves whilst obtaining minimal benefit for their clients, or, alternatively profiting from the vulnerability of commercially sensitive defendants;
- all members of the group would be bound, although they might be only indirectly represented;
- a lump sum settlement must be fair although it explicitly does not try to match individual loss exactly.

The Lord Chancellor's consultation paper takes the same view.

In summary considerable care is required in dealing with multi-party actions on a conditional fee basis and they are probably only suitable for firms of solicitors who have experience of handling multi-party actions funded by other means or who have considerable experience of conditional fee cases, that is have handled one hundred or more.

Any conditional fee agreement in such cases is likely to be subject to regulation by the court quite apart from the taxation procedure.

Chapter 9

Children And Patients

Even though Legal Aid is much more widely available for children – because they almost always qualify on financial grounds whereas most adults do not so qualify – it is also the case that 6% of the conditional fee cases in the Policy Studies Institute study were brought on behalf of a person under a disability. Thus this is a significant market and will become much more so if Legal Aid is abolished for all ordinary personal injury work, whether or not legal aid remains available for medical negligence work.

The law, rules and regulations applying to Conditional Fee Agreements apply to children and those under a disability ("patients") in exactly the same way as they apply to everyone else.

Traditionally however solicitors have not taken any of a child or patient's damages by way of costs. Thus in legal aid cases the solicitor normally settles for what he can get from the other side – inter partes costs – and makes no claim for solicitor and own client costs on top, or to put it another way gets *standard* and not *indemnity* costs, or *inter-partes* and not *basic costs*.

There is no practical problem if a solicitor is happy to act on this basis – the success fee is simply inserted at 0%, that is there will be no uplift on the hourly rate and thus no success fee.

Of course there will still be a gap between the rate in the agreement – say between £150 and £170 per hour – and the amount recovered from the other side on taxation which is generally around £120 per hour including mark-up.

Inserting into the conditional fee agreement a clause limiting costs to those received from the other side risks the agreement falling foul of the remnants of the indemnity principle (see Chapter 16 *The Indemnity Principle*), even though at the end of the day the court generally expects solicitors not to "charge the gap" between inter-partes costs and solicitor and own client costs.

Thus solicitors are caught between the devil and the deep blue sea, that is the convention that a child loses none of his or her damages and potential breach of the indemnity rule.

A solicitor is free to waive the gap between the two rates but then some of the marketing effect is lost if the solicitor cannot be upfront about it and some clients, or rather their parents, may not go ahead without an assurance that the damages will be untouched.

This is another reason why the indemnity principle should be abolished. However in the meantime the best way of proceeding is to maintain the usual hourly rate in the conditional fee agreement but write a separate letter guaranteeing that no money will be taken from damages. This is still no guarantee of staying within the indemnity principle but at least the agreement on the face of it complies. The Next Friend should sign the agreement.

If a child is nearly 18 years of age it may be better to place the matter on hold until he or she attains majority at age 18. The considerations are the same as exist at present in relation to Legal Aid applications. If a child obtains majority during the case then the original agreement – a 0% success fee – remains binding. Solicitors are free, by agreement with the Next Friend, to reserve the right to amend the agreement should this happen, so as to provide a success fee. The disadvantage with this is that it gives the solicitor an incentive to delay the case. A better view is to take the rough with the smooth and accept a 0% success fee in these cases – and with luck a young client who will be your firm's client for life.

But what if the case is inherently risky and a solicitor is not prepared to take it on without the prospect of a success fee? Unfortunately there are no Rules, Regulations or Law Society guidance on this difficult area.

However in relation to patients the Court of Protection issued a Master's Direction on 14th July 1995 which states that if solicitors wish to enter into a Conditional Fee Agreement with a patient then the matter should be referred to the Master, effectively for permission. Presumably where the Court of Protection has approved such an agreement on behalf of a patient the Court, when it later considers whether or not to approve settlement, is unlikely to depart from its previous approval. The Master's Direction is at Appendix 25.

Clear new rules dealing with conditional fee agreements and those under a disability would be welcome. This problem is recognised in the Lord Chancellors Department's consultation paper on costs, but at present remains unsolved.

In discussing the proposed new costs rule (At Appendix 6 of this book) the paper, pointing out that it is substantially the same as the existing Order 62 rule 16 of the Rules of the Supreme Court says:

Views are invited on how this rule might be amended to encourage greater use of conditional fee agreements where the claimant is a child or patient. It has been suggested that at present such agreements are not used as frequently as they might be because solicitors are nervous that their success fee will be reduced or disallowed altogether. This arises mainly because of the common practice whereby, in order to ensure that the solicitor does not recover more from his client that the client recovers from the other side, costs between the solicitor and the child or patient are taxed on the standard basis, rather than the indemnity basis. The Conditional Fee Agreement uplift cannot be recovered from the other party and solicitors fear that it might not be allowed in taxation.

This seems undesirable because it means children and patients cannot enjoy the benefits of conditional fee agreements in the same way as other litigants. The risk of abuse is, it is submitted, minimal and would be outweighed by the general advantage of making conditional fees more readily available in these cases.

The paper then goes on to suggest that the answer is to enable solicitors, prior to issuing proceedings, to obtain a binding approval of the court to the terms of a conditional fee agreement which could not subsequently be subject to taxation.

This seems a good idea and could also be applied to multi-party actions (see Chapter 8). It also means that the position is being judged at the time that the solicitor is *taking the risk* and not retrospectively when, by definition, the case has been won. (There are no arguments about the success fee in lost cases!)

Although the taxation rules require the Taxing Officer to look at the position as it "reasonably appeared to the solicitor when the conditional fee agreement was entered into" this is easier said than done. Taxing Officers will rarely see the "losers" or those abandoned part way through and even when they do, they are unlikely to know that the Plaintiff was working on a conditional fee basis.

At present, in practice, acting for a child or patient under a Conditional Fee Agreement is much the same as acting privately or under a Legal Aid Certificate.

It is of course the position that any settlement of any such case, including the question of costs, requires the approval of the Court.

Note that in the case of *Cook (a minor suing by his father and next friend) v Burton*, Kingston upon Hull County Court ordered Scale 1 costs in favour of the infant Plaintiff in a personal injury claim settled for £750 (ie within the Small Claims limit even for personal injury claims) on the grounds that it was appropriate for the action to be referred to a trial under Order 19 Rule 3(2)(d) by reason of "circumstances of the parties", the circumstances being that the Plaintiff was a person under a disability, in this case a minor.

Chapter 10

Small Claims – Small Chapter

This chapter looks at *all* small claims, not just those in personal injury matters.

"Small" Claims are defined as claims worth less than £3,000 with the exception of personal injury work where they are defined as claims worth less than £1,000. However the Government has announced its intention to increase the small claims limit to £5,000, probably from April 1999, except for personal injury claims where the limit will remain £1,000 for the time being.

The significance of small claims is that:

(a)   *costs do not follow the event; and
(b)   legal aid is not generally available for such claims.

Thus they are particularly suited to being funded on a contingency fee basis as the client is at no risk of paying the opponent's costs and by the same token must fund his lawyer's fees out of his own pocket as costs are not recoverable from the other side. It also follows that the indemnity principle is not a problem.

Conditional fee arrangements are of course permissible in *personal injury* cases within the small claims jurisdiction as the legislation and Regulations governing conditional fees do not differentiate between small claims and ordinary claims. The defining point as far as conditional fees are concerned is the *type* of claim not its *value*.

However, like beef on the bone, straightforward contingency fee agreements in small claims are unlawful even though no-one at all believes they would do any harm.

Their illegality stems from the fact that *any* proceedings commenced in the county court are, by definition, contentious and therefore may not be funded on a contingency fee basis (see Chapter 2, page 26 – Classification of contentious and non-contentious work).

Footnote: However in Cook (a minor suing by his father and next friend) v Burton Kingston upon Hull County Court ordered Scale 1 costs in favour of the infant Plaintiff in a personal injury claim settled for £750 (ie within the Small Claims limit even for personal injury claims), on the grounds that it was appropriate for the action to be referred to a trial under Order 19 Rule 3(2)(d) by reason of "circumstances of the parties", the circumstances being that the Plaintiff was a person under a disability, in this case a minor.

These comments must now be read in the light of the Court of Appeal's decision in *Thai Trading Co. (A Firm)* v *Taylor* the report of which appears at Appendix 24.

This effectively means that Defendants who can pay for legal representation are at an advantage over Plaintiffs who are not allowed to instruct solicitors on a no win – no fee basis and cannot get legal aid because it is prohibited for such work.

The "small" claims limit is likely to rise rapidly. When it is increased to £5,000 the limit will be five times what it was until 8th January 1995. Furthermore under the Woolf Report fast-track all claims under £15,000 may be heard by a Circuit Judge or a District Judge with the plan being that eventually all such claims will be heard by District Judges. At that point there will be little difference between the procedure followed in a small claim and that in a fast-track claim.

Solicitors will then be used to fixed costs from the other side on fast-track claims and will have learnt how to work more efficiently and also that to survive they need to take an additional fee from their own client, which is almost bound to be a conditional or contingency fee.

At that point it is likely that all claims under £15,000 will be "small" claims. It is worth remembering that the "costs follow the event" rule is rare outside Commonwealth jurisdictions.

When conditional fees are extended to all civil work then there will be no problem – but until then plaintiff solicitors will have to find a way of allowing plaintiffs to bring small claims, especially as there is no legal aid.

Contingency fees are the perfect answer, but I repeat the health warning above – they are currently unlawful.

Just out of interest there is at the end of this chapter a model contingency fee agreement for small claims cases. This is so that you have it ready should the law change.

Remember that mere possession of a small claims contingency fee agreement is not an offence but you must not use it.

The distribution of claims issued in 1996 that were referred to small claims arbitration was as follows:

Value of claim	Number of cases
Under £1,000	64,875
£1,000 – £3,000	16,545
£3,000 – £5,000	1,175
£5,000 – £10,000	220
£10,000 – £15,000	35
TOTAL	82,850

The analysis of the claims valued between £1,000 and £3,000 is:

Type of claim	Number of cases
Personal Injury	185
Debt	12,475
Non-possession housing disputes	440
Negligence other than personal injury	1,945
Other	1,470
TOTAL	16,515*

*Discrepancy of 30. Source Law Society's Gazette 14th January 1998 quoting Lord Chancellor's Department statistics.

CONTINGENCY FEE AGREEMENT

FOR SMALL CLAIMS UNDER ARBITRATION PROCEDURE

This agreement is a legally binding contract between you and   solicitors.

Agreement Date

We, the legal representative   You, the client

What is covered by this agreement

- Your county court claim relating to your action against
- Any enforcement proceedings

What is not covered by this agreement

- Any counterclaim against you
- Any appeal you make or any appeal made by your opponent.

Paying Us

If you win the case you pay us 33% of your damages plus any disbursements. This figure includes VAT at the standard rate, currently 17.5%.

If you lose the case you do not pay us anything, except disbursements.

N.B. Disbursements are payments we make on your behalf to others involved in the case. We will notify you of disbursements incurred as we go along. We would expect the only disbursements to be travelling and subsistence expenses incurred in attending the arbitration hearing [and the cost of a medical report.] [expert report].

If you end the agreement before the case is won or lost, you are liable to pay our costs at the rate of £170 per hour with letters and telephone calls charged at £17 each unless they last for ten minutes or longer in which case they will be charged at the appropriate proportion of the hourly rate. All of these figures attract VAT at the standard rate of 17.5%.

For what happens if we end the agreement before the case is won or lost, please refer to paragraph 5.

1. Our responsibilities

We must always act in your best interests in pursuing your claim for damages and obtaining for you the best possible results, subject to our duty to the court; we must explain to you the risks and benefits of taking legal action; we must give you our best advice about whether to accept any offer of settlement.

2. Your responsibilities

You must give us clear instructions which allow us to do our work properly; you must not ask us to work in an improper or unreasonable way; you must not deliberately mislead us; you must co-operate with us when asked; you must go to the arbitration hearing when asked; you must pay for disbursements as the case goes on.

3. What happens if you win

If you win (which means that your case is decided in your favour whether by a court or an agreement to pay you damages) you pay us 33% of any damages plus any disbursements. You agree that we may receive the damages your opponent has to pay. If your opponent refuses to accept our receipt, you will pay the cheque you receive into a joint bank account in your name and ours. Out of the money you agree to let us take 33% of the damages plus any outstanding disbursements. You take the rest.

If your opponent fails to pay any damages owed to you we have the right to take recovery action in your name to enforce a judgement, order or agreement. The costs of this action are payable by you to us in addition to 33% of the damages.

4. What happens if you lose

If you lose you do not have to pay us anything, except our disbursements.

5. What happens when the agreement ends before the case itself ends

You can end the agreement at any time. You are then liable to pay us our costs incurred up to the date you end the agreement calculated at the hourly rate.

We can end the agreement if you do not keep to your responsibilities in condition 2. You are then liable to pay us our costs incurred up to the date the agreement ends calculated at the hourly rate.

We can end the agreement if we believe that you are unlikely to win and you disagree with us. You do not have to pay us anything.

We can end the agreement if you reject our opinion about making a settlement with your opponent. You are then liable to pay us our costs incurred up to the date the agreement ends calculated on the hourly rate (unless your damages are 20% more than the offer we advised you to accept in which case you do not have to pay us anything).

6. What happens after the agreement ends

After the agreement ends we will apply to have our name removed from the record of the court proceedings in which we are acting. We have the right to preserve our lien over any property of yours in our possession unless any money owed to us under this agreement is paid in full.

7. Costs

County Courts have the power to award costs in limited circumstances. If we recover costs on your behalf they belong to us. In other words, if you win, you will pay us 33% of your damages whether or not we also recover any costs from your opponent.

If you lose and you are ordered to pay costs to your opponent, then those costs will be payable by you.

The County Court Rules 1981, Ord 19, r. 6 states

(1) *"No solicitors' charges (nor costs allowed to a litigant in person in lieu thereof) shall be allowed as between party and party in respect of any proceedings referred to arbitration under rule 2 (3), except–*

   a *the costs which were stated on the summons or which would have been stated on the summons if the claim had been for a liquidated sum:*

   b *the costs of enforcing the award, and*

   c *further costs as the arbitrator may direct where there has been unreasonable conduct on the part of the opposite party in relation to the proceedings or the claim therein.*

Signed for the legal representative

Signed by the client

Payments Into Court

Payments Into Court

A Problem Solved

One of the most difficult aspects of personal injury work is advising a client whether or not to accept a payment-in to court. Often the choice is between under-settling but ensuring the client gets something or pressing on and risking all of the client's damages. The general rule is, of course, that if a plaintiff fails at trial to beat a payment-in then that plaintiff pays both sides' costs from the date of the payment-in. In many cases, especially relatively modest claims, these costs are greater than the damages and thus the plaintiff gets nothing. By definition where there has been a failure to beat a payment-in, the matter has gone to trial, and therefore the costs will always be substantial. Even if the solicitor is confident about beating the payment-in the client is often not convinced. After all it is the client's damages that are at stake.

The advent of conditional fees, backed by Accident Line Protect Insurance, changes all this: *provided the Law Society's Model Conditional Fee agreement is amended at the outset,* and allows the solicitor to back his or her judgment without gambling the client's damages.

So are you ready to gamble your costs rather than your client's damages?

Failure to Beat the Payment-in

There are two options in the context of a failure to beat the payment-in.

The damages wipe-out option

Treat the court award as a "win"(!) and claim the base costs (but not the success fee) for post-payment in work in which case the costs insurance will *not* cover the Defendant's costs from the date of payment-in except in so far as they exceed damages, *i.e.* the costs insurance will only kick in if the client is left with nothing from the case *and* costs are still due to the other side.

The ring-fenced damages option

The plaintiff's solicitor waives *all* post-payment in fees, both base costs and any success fee thereon. In return Accident Line Protect picks up the Defendant's costs payable by the Plaintiff, *i.e. the Plaintiff's damages are preserved intact.*

Most surprisingly the Law Society Model Conditional Fee Agreement opts for the first alternative: the damages wipe-out choice. This leaves the solicitor with a success fee for effectively losing and will generally leave the client with nothing.

The patently fairer option is the ring-fenced damages option. It reflects reality: *failure* to beat a payment-in, rejected on a solicitor's advice, is indeed a *failure*, not a success. Furthermore by guaranteeing that the client will keep the damages awarded, albeit the same as or less than the payment-in, both solicitor and client are relieved of one of the most stressful aspects of personal injury work – *i.e.* worrying about the final result after rejecting a payment-in.

Ring-fencing of damages represents a major and largely unrealised advantage of the Conditional Fee Scheme over Legal Aid, even non-contributory Legal Aid.

Example
Bill and Ben are identical twins who suffer identical injuries in the same accident. Both qualify for free Legal Aid.

Bill accepts Legal Aid but Ben chooses the conditional fee scheme backed by Accident Line Protect Insurance. £4,000 is paid into Court in respect of each of them but on their solicitor's advice the payments in are rejected.

At court each is awarded £3,000. Legally-aided Bill's own solicitor's post-payment in costs come out of his damages under the statutory charge as do the other side's post-payment in costs. Bill gets nothing. Ben receives at least £2,250 under the Underwood's Cap Scheme.

	£
Damages	3,000
Less success fee capped at	
25%	750
	2,250

Of course if the payment-in was beaten or accepted then legally-aided Bill would have been better off.

Thus the assumption made by many commentators that a client is *always* better off with non-contributory Legal Aid is not necessarily true. As for contributory Legal Aid the greater the contribution the more the balance tilts in favour of a conditional fee agreement.

If you wish to adopt the ring-fence option it is necessary to amend condition 3(1) of the Law Society's Conditional Fee Agreement which, as drawn, is the damages wipe-out option.

The *amended* version should read:

> It may be that your opponent makes a payment-in to Court which you reject and, on our advice, the case goes ahead to trial where you recover damages that are less than that payment-in to Court. If so, you do not have to pay any of the basic costs or success fee for the work done after the date we receive notice of the payment-in.

I commend the amended version which is made possible by the insurers who in the interest of fairness are exposing themselves to a greater risk for no extra premium.

It is probable that the Law Society's Revised Model Conditional Fee Agreement, which is likely to be available in late 1998, will include the "amended" version as standard.

The Underwoods Payment-in Scheme

You may think it fair to match the insurers generosity by lowering the capped success fee in such cases so as to leave the client no worse off than if they had *accepted* the payment-in. This is the Underwoods Payment-In Scheme.

Ben's example:
Calculation had payment-in been accepted

	£
Damages	4,000
Less success fee capped	
at 25%	1,000
To client	3,000

Therefore as the Court award is £3,000 *nothing* would be taken by way of a success fee, so as to leave Ben with the £3,000 he would have got if he had accepted the payment-in.

Another Example:

	£
Payment-in	10,000
Court awards	9,000

Calculation had payment-in been accepted	
Damages	10,000
Less success fee capped	
at 25%	2,500
To client	7,500

Therefore success fee on	9,000	
limited to	1,500	(16.66%)
to keep sum to client at	7,500	

To always forego the success fee entirely when there is a failure to beat the payment-in goes too far, in the example given above the Plaintiff would be *better off* failing to beat the payment-in as he would get £9,000 clear rather than £7,500:

being	10,000
less 25%	2,500
	7,500

Because the Underwoods Payment-In Scheme means that you are prepared to forego up to the full 25% capped success fee it gives the client a 25% *comfort zone on payments in.* It is important to remember that this situation only arises if the *solicitor* has got it wrong, i.e. if the client has rejected the payment-in on the solicitor's advice.

Examples:

All assuming a rejected payment-in of £10,000 of which the client *would* have got 75%, that is £7,500

	£	
Court award	9,000	(10% less than payment-in)
Agreed sum to client	7,500	
Therefore success fee capped at	1,500	(16.66%)
Court award	8,000	(20% less than payment-in)
Agreed sum to client	7,500	
Therefore success fee capped at	500	(6.25%)
Court award	7,500	(25% less than payment-in)
Agreed sum to client	7,500	
Therefore success fee capped at	0	(0.00%)
Court award	7,000	(30% less than payment-in)
No success fee		

Client loss: £500 but this is only 6.66% below rejected payment-in net figure of 7,500.00 because solicitor foregoes the whole of his success fee. It is important to remember that this situation only arises if the *solicitor* has got it wrong, that is if the client has rejected the payment in on the solicitor's advice.

My view is that it is unnecessarily confusing to go through all of this with the client at the beginning. It is necessary to make the amendment to the Law Society's Model Conditional Fee Agreement and to explain why but it is not necessary to explain the Underwoods Payment-In Scheme until a payment-in actually occurs.

This is because as a solicitor you are making a concession to the client over and above that required by the agreement and therefore this does not have to be dealt with at the beginning. Furthermore it enables you to use actual figures based on the actual payment-in and not hypothetical figures. At Appendix 21 is a model letter advising a client concerning a payment-in.

Remember that the situation does *not* arise if you are advising *acceptance* of the payment-in. If the client takes the advice and accepts the payment-in then there is no problem.

If the client rejects the advice then under paragraph 8(c) of the Law Society's Model Conditional Fee agreement the solicitor is free to end the agreement and make the client pay the basic costs and disbursements, there and then *and* the success fee if the client goes on to win the case. The success fee would be charged in the usual way, that is by reference to an uplift in costs, capped by reference to damages. However if the client fails to beat the payment-in the Underwoods Payment-In Scheme concession should *not* be made as it was the client's choice, acting against the solicitor's advice, to carry on.

Thus if there has been a payment-in of £10,000 rejected *against* the solicitors advice and the court awards £8,000 the calculation would be:

	£
Court award	8,000
Less success fee capped at 25%	2,000
Balance to client	6,000

If the client goes on to get an award or settlement 20% or more than the offer or payment-in which the solicitor advised him to *accept* then the client is deemed to have been right to reject the advice and thus no success fee is payable.

This can have curious effects. Thus a payment-in of £10,000 is rejected *against* the solicitors advice:

	£	
Court award	11,900	
Therefore success fee charged (capped at 25%)	2,975	
Balance to client	8,925	
Court award	12,000	(20% above rejected payment-in)
Therefore no success fee	0	
Balance to client	12,000	

Thus an extra £100 awarded at court leaves the client with an extra £3,075.

A Sliding Scale?

I prefer a sliding scale whereby the solicitor's fees (capped at 25% of damages) are reduced by precisely the percentage by which any award or settlement exceeds the amount the solicitor advised the client to accept. Thus if the client achieved 5% more then then the solicitors capped success fee is reduced by 5% to 20%.

Example A:

	£
Payment-in	10,000
Rejected against the solicitor's advice	
Court award (5% higher)	10,500
Therefore success fee charged	
(capped at 20%)	2,100
Balance to client	8,400

Example B:

Payment-in	10,000
Rejected against the solicitor's advice	
Client achieves 10% more. Thus :	
Court award	11,000
Therefore success fee charged	
(capped at 15%)	1,650
Balance to client	9,350
and so on.	

This is not particularly complicated and avoids small differences in the Court award or settlement making a very substantial difference to the amount actually received by the solicitor and client respectively.

The Future

At the time of writing, the Law Society's Model Conditional Fee Agreement is being reviewed by a Law Society Working Party. It is almost certain that the existing "damages wipe-out option" will be replaced by the ring-fenced damages option as standard. It is unlikely that the Underwoods Payment-In Scheme will be adopted as standard.

Second Opinions

The Law Society's Model Conditional Fee Agreement states:

> If you ask us to get a second opinion from a specialist legal representative outside our firm, we will do so. You pay the cost of a second opinion.

Firms who have more than one lawyer doing personal injury work may consider it good practice always to obtain an internal second opinion on whether or not to advise acceptance or rejection of a payment-in to court.

Chapter 12

Appropriate (Or Alternate) Dispute Resolution ("ADR")

ADR and No Win No Fee

There are no special rules for ADR and thus one must look to the type of work which is the subject of ADR. Thus in a personal injury claim where a conditional fee agreement has been signed the solicitor may charge his normal success fee if the matter is resolved through ADR.

In Industrial Tribunal claims, which are very often resolved by a form of ADR – namely conciliation through ACAS – a solicitor may charge a straightforward contingency fee in a case settled by ADR or conciliation.

However in, say, an ordinary breach of contract case in a county court the usual rules apply and no conditional or contingency fee can be charged, however the matter is resolved. This statement needs to be read in the light of the decision of the Court of Appeal in *Thai Trading Co. (A Firm)* v *Taylor* which is at Appendix 24.

The abolition of the Indemnity Rule and the extension of contingency fees to all civil work would give a big boost to ADR as the need to charge on an hourly rate gives solicitors a major disincentive to settle early, one of the main advantages of ADR. As Judge Peter Agnes of the Middlesex County Court, Cambridge, Massachusetts, stated as quoted in *Achieving Civil Justice*, Legal Action Group, editor Roger Smith (page 48):

> lawyers.... fear that ADR involvement early in a case will lessen the costs that can be obtained from clients. They are concerned about what will happen to the practice of law.

Significantly in Industrial Tribunal cases, where contingency fees are allowed and the indemnity rule is irrelevant (in the general absence of inter-partes costs orders), a great number of cases are settled by ADR through ACAS.

In a contingency fee system lawyers have an incentive to settle early since a fee of say £1,000 (being 25% of £4,000) earnt after 10 hours' work is worth more than after 30 hours' work. The client is financially no worse off and is better off in that the matter is resolved earlier with less worry and stress. A purely adversarial system maintains billable hours for lawyers whereas a contingency fee scheme encourages early use of ADR.

As Carrie Menkel-Meadow says in *Aiding Civil Justice* page 103, "Lawyers must be re-educated so that they are perceived as true problem solvers. To do this, co-operative behaviour must be reinforced by economic reward." She also points out that in the United States there is evidence that clients who are strong enough to control the fee structure, such as large corporations, are now reversing fee patterns and rewarding early settlement with bonuses and penalising trials by paying reduced hourly fees.

Such arrangements are of course impractical with the English indemnity rule where own lawyer costs must be kept high so as not to restrict recovery from the other side in the event of victory.

Example:
A client agrees with his solicitor that the first ten hours work will be charged at £200 per hour, the second ten at £150, the third ten hours' work at £100 per hour and all work thereafter at £50 per hour. The matter goes to trial and takes 40 hours.

The solicitors fees are:	
10 x £200	2,000
10 x £150	1,500
10 x £100	1,000
10 x £50	500
	5,000

However on taxation he achieves £120 per hour to be paid by the other side but the indemnity rule applies to hours 21 to 30 and 31 to 40 in the following way:

The first 10 hours x £120	1,200
second 10 hours x £120	1,200
third 10 hours (indemnity rule applies)	1,000
fourth 10 hours (indemnity rule applies)	500
	3,900

However on a traditional basis with the solicitor charging say £125 per hour the client's outlay is:

40 hours at £125 per hour	5,000

But the recovery from the Defendant is much higher

40 hours at, £120 per hour	4,800

Of course where the lawyer gets a higher rate early on he has greater incentive to settle and it saves the defendant money as well as fewer hours are run up and therefore the defendant pays less. The defendant also has a saving in management time and his own lawyers' fees.

It is well recognised that the earlier dispute resolution is undertaken the more likely it is to succeed. The longer litigation continues, the more entrenched the parties become in their positions. However the ban on contingency fees and the preservation of the indemnity rule and the hourly rate punishes the lawyer who seeks ADR early on and succeeds in resolving the matter, saving judicial time, client stress etc.

Thus a change in the law is required before conditional and/or contingency fees can play a significant part in ADR.

It is understood that the Government is looking at the Indemnity Rule which will, in any event, have to be modified in order to implement the Woolf Report fixed costs regime in fast-track cases.

The Indemnity Rule is also under heavy and frequent attacks in the Courts but the principle of not being able to recover more from an opponent than you are liable to pay your own solicitor, for each part of the litigation, remains.

Insolvency

Insolvency

Maintenance, champerty and conditional fee agreements in insolvency matters

Introduction

This chapter considers how an office-holder might fund litigation. In insolvency practice the question of funding is often a difficult one, particularly where assets are sparse, even with the most cast iron of potential causes of action.

Insolvency proceedings invariably involve the appointment of a licensed insolvency practitioner by the company, the court or a creditor, in circumstances where the exposure of creditors is at risk or where the company seeks to rehabilitate itself. In either case, the use of company assets to fund an action necessarily reduces the funds available to the company and creditors, although the action itself may of course recoup further monies.

As in other areas of conditional fee work the lot of the insolvency practitioner is made unnecessarily difficult by the principles of maintenance and champerty. The courts have applied these well-established concepts in the name of public policy and the interests of justice in striking down and rendering unenforceable agreements between plaintiffs and third parties prepared to fund litigation.

Note, however the momentous decision of the Court of Appeal in *Thai Trading Co (a Firm)* v *Taylor, The Times* 6th March 1998 sweeping away all the case law concerning contingency fees and querying the Solicitors Practice Rules purporting to outlaw contingency fees. This revolutionary, and extremely welcome, decision allows no win – no fee arrangements in all work but does *not* generally allow a success fee, *i.e.* an extra fee over and above the solicitor's ordinary fee, for winning. The Court of Appeal said that legislation was "needed to authorise the increase in the lawyer's reward over and above his ordinary profit costs".

What it allows is a solicitor to agree not to charge a fee in the event of a defeat but to charge the normal amount in the event of a win. This decision appears as Appendix 24 to this book. Of course *conditional* fees, with an extra charge for winning *are* allowed in insolvency matters and this is examined later on.

The Court of Appeal also said that such an agreement does not break the indemnity rule and thus a client who has agreed a no win – no fee deal with his or her solicitor *can* recover costs from the other side.

Following the decision of the Chancery Division of the High Court in *Bevan Ashford (a firm)* v *Geoff Yeandle (Contractors) Limited* (in liquidation), *The Times* 23rd April 1998, it is clear that insolvency matters before an Arbitrator, as opposed to a court, may be dealt with on a conditional fee style basis, with a success fee for winning, even though such proceedings are not within Section 58(3) of the Courts and Legal Services Act 1990 and thus are not covered by conditional fee arrangements[1].

Maintenance and Champerty

Maintenance

The Law Commission, in its report which led to the abolition of maintenance as a crime, described the concept as, "the procurement by direct or indirect financial assistance of any person to institute or carry on or defend civil proceedings without legal justification" – put another way,

> maintenance is the improper rendering of financial assistance by one person to another in prosecuting or defending proceedings in which the person rendering the assistance has no legitimate interest.

These definitions do not prevent a legitimate or proper agreement for support where the party providing the support "has a legitimate and genuine interest in the result of it and the circumstances are such as reasonably to warrant his giving his support" (*Trendtex Trading Corp* v *Credit Suisse* [1982] AC 679 per Lord Denning). Thus the provision of a "fighting fund" by creditors, or the funding of a receiver's action by a debenture holder, will not amount to maintenance.

---

1   *This chapter draws on articles in Insolvency by Louis Doyle, Barrister and published by CLT.*

Champerty

Champerty is a form of aggravated maintenance whereby a third party provides assistance to a Plaintiff in consideration for a promise to the third party (*i.e* the maintainer) for a share in the proceeds or subject matter of the action.

Thus, in *Grovewood Holdings Plc v Capel & Co Limited* [1994] 4 All ER 417 it was held that a sale of a beneficial interest in net recoveries of a liquidator's action (as opposed to the sale of the entire cause of action) was champertous on the basis that the consideration provided by the maintainer was an agreement to meet costs. This decision is considered further below.

"Insolvency exceptions" to the rules on maintenance and champerty

The Insolvency Act 1986 provides both trustees-in-bankruptcy and liquidators with powers to sell or dispose of any property of a bankrupt or company in liquidation. These exceptions, in effect, amount to an implied statutory exception to the rule on maintenance to the extent that a bare cause of action (which by definition comprises property in the bankruptcy or liquidation), is disposed of outright for an agreed sum, as a consequence of which the purchaser agrees to become substituted as a party to the proceedings. (See *Kitson v Hardwick* (1872) LR 7 CP and *Seear v Lawson* (1880) 15 ChD 426, CA (assignment of bare cause of action by trustee-in-bankruptcy) and *Re Parkgate Wagon Works Company* (1881) 17 ChD 234, CA (assignment of bare cause of action by liquidator).)

The Courts have been prepared to extend the implied statutory exception to arrangements whereby the consideration provided by the purchaser of the cause of action is a share of any proceeds arising from it, the residual proceeds falling into the bankrupt or insolvent estate. (*Guy v Churchill* (1880) 40 ChD 481 and *Ramsey v Hartley* (1977) 1 WLR (assignment by trustee-in-bankruptcy) and *Bang & Olufsen v Ton Systeme Ltd* (1993, unreported) (assignment by liquidator).)

There is no bar to an assignment being made to a bankrupt personally, in which case the assignee will – subject to the merits of the case – almost certainly qualify for legal aid and thereby avoid any application against the assignee for security for costs. However legal aid for such cases is likely to be abolished in the near future.

Limitations on the insolvency exceptions to maintenance and champerty

Recent developments in the courts indicate that, broadly speaking, there are two circumstances in which an assignment of a cause of action by an office-holder might be susceptible to attack on the basis that it does not constitute one of the above established exceptions. The first is where the assignment is set aside by the court as an invalid exercise of the office-holder's power of sale on the application of any person who is aggrieved as provided for in section 168.

The second is where the agreement for funding, whilst apparently sound on the face of it, is found to be defective. Two decisions – that of Lightman J in Grovewood and the later decision of Robert Walker J in *Re Oasis Merchandising Services Limited* [1995] BCC 911 highlight these difficulties and warn the practitioner against treating lightly the nature of the interest or asset assigned. The position remains far from clear in the light of these decisions. These limitations are now considered in turn.

Invalid exercise of office-holder's power of sale

In a liquidation a person who is aggrieved may apply to the court for an order confirming, reversing or modifying the act or decision of the liquidator complained of. In *Re Edennote Limited, Tottenham Hotspur Plc v Ryman* [1995] BCC 389, Vinelott J expressed the view that the court could exercise the power,

> "not only if it can be shown that the exercise of the power is utterly unreasonable – that it went beyond what any reasonable person properly instructed could consider proper – but also if it is shown that the person exercising the power, although acting in good faith, took into account considerations which he ought not to have taken into account or failed to take into account considerations which he ought to have taken into account".

The facts in the Edennote case provide an example of the exercise by the court of its power under section 167, although the Edennote decision turns on its particular facts and can be distinguished.

Edennote

In Edennote the liquidator sold the benefit of a right of action to his co-plaintiff Mr Terry Venables for £7,000 plus 10% of the net proceeds arising from the action. The defendant, Tottenham Hotspur, applied to the court complaining that they had offered £75,000 to the liquidator to compromise the matter. In evidence the liquidator pointed to the fact that he had been under pressure to give security for costs in the claim against Tottenham Hotspur and that his legal advisers had advised him that a sale of the right of action might not have been possible if security had been given, the liquidator apparently "adopting" the action by giving security. (Vinelott J accepted this view as incorrect on the basis of the Court of Appeal's decision in *Freightex Limited* v *International Express Company Limited* (unreported, 1982) which held that a sale or assignment is possible after security has been given).

Pressurised by time the liquidator had sold out to Mr Venables without exploring the possibility of a settlement with Tottenham Hotspur, something which the learned judge considered should have been done "at the very least".

In the circumstances Vinelott J was prepared to set aside the assignment and to replace the liquidator although the removal has subsequently been overturned by the Court of Appeal. Notably, the judge considered that the court would only interfere with the sale by an office-holder in very exceptional circumstances, such as arose in this case, and that it was insufficient for the liquidator in the case merely to establish that he had acted in good faith. The special circumstances which arise in this case, which the judge considered should have been plainly obvious, were the "nuisance value" acquired by the co-plaintiff on the sale and the liquidator's failure to explore the possibility of a settlement with Tottenham Hotspur.

The Edennote decision has been substantively affirmed by the Court of Appeal – although the Court reversed the decision of Vinelott J at first instance to remove the liquidator from office.

The special facts in Edennote distinguished the decision from the general position whereby a defendant will be unable to challenge an assignment or sale which does not itself contravene the rules of maintenance and champerty by instead challenging the decision to sell by the office-holder.

This position has been affirmed most recently by two decisions of the Court of Appeal, namely *Norglen Limited* v *Reeds Rains Prudential Limited* and *Mayhew-Lewis* v *Westminster Scaffolding*

Group Plc (The Times, 6 December 1995). (The cases were unconnected but were listed together.)

Norglen

In *Norglen* the Court of Appeal reversed a decision of first instance and permitted the assignment of a cause of action by a liquidator to directors and share-holders on the basis that net proceeds would be applied in settling the liquidator's claims and costs, any balance being divided between the company and the assignees. Irrespective of the fact that the assignees would qualify for legal aid and avoid an application for security for costs (which the company in liquidation could not resist), together with an argument that the liquidator had failed in his duties of independence and skill and care in investigating the directors (whose conduct allegedly gave rise to the action assigned in the first place), an allegation of misconduct against the liquidator for allegedly misleading creditors into believing that there were no assets in the liquidation, and the apparent adamance of the liquidator in assigning, in the face of strong opposition from the liquidation committee, the Court of Appeal refused to interfere with the assignment.

The Court expressed the view that it did not fall to it to consider retrospectively the merits of the decision of an office-holder in the context of the liquidation as a whole; neither could criticism of the directors and the liquidator, even if severe, have the effect of undermining what in substance had been a valid assignment.

Mayhew-Lewis

The court took a similar view in *Mayhew-Lewis* where joint administrative receivers had assigned the right of action to a director (who was also a personal guarantor to the debenture holder) for a nominal consideration only. As in *Norglen* the court took the view that the assignee had a genuine and significant interest in the proceeds and could not be viewed as a nominal plaintiff. (This had been the principal ground upon which the assignment had failed at first instance, the assignment being viewed as no more than a sham arrangement.)

The matter of legal aid in both cases was considered to be an insufficient ground on which to refuse to substitute the assignee as plaintiff in either action.

The approach of the courts

The cases in this area suggest that office-holders are in a strong position and that the courts will not interfere ordinarily with their decisions other than where the applicant is capable of substantiating special factors of the type present in the Edennote case. Nevertheless, an office-holder should consider the views of all parties, particularly creditors in any creditors' committee, before assigning. Equally, the possibility of a settlement should always be investigated properly before an assignment is made. The removal and replacement of a liquidator, at least at first instance in *Edennote*, will usually bring with it considerable professional embarrassment notwithstanding the judge's acceptance in that case of the good faith and the integrity of the departing office-holder.

Judicial restrictions on the assignment of certain types of action

In two recent decisions the court has reviewed and struck down two arrangements which, for the practitioner, must be seen as crossing the boundaries of legal acceptability. Notably, the funding arrangements in both cases were sophisticated and subtle. Practitioners are therefore well advised to avoid needlessly complex arrangements where more straightforward terms can be agreed on. This is particularly so in relation to the party who will adopt conduct of the action and as regards the fruits of the litigation assigned.

Grovewood Holdings

In the Grovewood case the company had a possible claim against its directors. Having failed to obtain funding from creditors and shareholders, the liquidator entered into an agreement – a "sponsorship arrangement" – with a third party sponsor. The arrangement provided that the action continued in the name of the sponsor without being subject to any inference or control by the liquidator. (The action had been commenced by the liquidator's solicitors prior to the liquidation when the solicitors had acted for the company itself.)

The agreement also provided that if the action was successful any recoveries would be applied to discharging costs (including those accrued prior to the liquidation), any balance being shared equally between the sponsor and the company in liquidation. The sponsor also agreed that it would be liable for any insufficiency in recoveries in meeting costs, including costs awarded in favour of the defendants. Furthermore, the liquidator's solicitors agreed to defer invoicing the sponsor until the litigation was concluded. The sponsorship agreement was approved by the creditors' committee. Lightman J refused to uphold the arrangement.

It seems that the principal flaw in the funding arrangement, which distinguished it from earlier cases permitting the sale or assignment of a bare cause of action as discussed above, was that it had not puported to sell or assign the cause of action itself rather, the funding arrangement constituted a sale of a beneficial interest in the net proceeds arising in consideration for the sponsor agreeing to meet the cost of the action. On this basis Lightman J considered this arrangement to be champertous in that, coupled with the loss of control referred to further below, the payment of costs in return for an interest in net proceeds was incapable of falling within one of the established "insolvency exceptions" discussed previously.

The decision recognises that the statutory powers of an office-holder, and specifically sections 165 and 166 in the case of a liquidator, whereby an office-holder may sell a cause of action on terms obliging the assignee by way of consideration to pay over a share of recoveries, in effect shelters such arrangements from attack on grounds of maintenance or champerty. However, the judgment holds that there is no basis in principle or authority for extending the statutory exceptions applicable to bare causes of action to sales of the fruits of litigation. Furthermore, it would appear immaterial as to how well-intentioned the parties might have been in entering into such an arrangement.

The Judge was also apparently influenced by the fact that the arrangement purported to surrender control of the proceedings to a third party whilst the carriage of those proceedings remained in the name of the company. This constituted an abuse of the liquidator's fiduciary power which the judge found both objectionable in principle and unsupported by authority. In reaching this finding it is not clear whether the Judge was making reference to the court's general power of supervision under section 167 in striking out the arrangement, or whether, as seems more likely, the loss of control itself took the arrangement beyond the implied statutory exceptions.

Neither is any reference made in the judgment to the decision of Knox J in *Re Ayala Holdings Limited* (May 1993, unreported) which held that an action under section 127 is incapable of assignment.

The *Grovewood* decision has come in for considerable criticism, not least because of the very technical distinction it draws between the assignment of a bare cause of action and the assignment of an interest in net proceeds.

On the other hand, the "loss of control" point is a significant one and it remains that Lightman J's objection to the surrender of control accords with the long-established public policy principle whereby the courts will not sanction arrangements allowing the sponsor to interfere with the conduct of the litigation. That principle should be viewed by practitioners and advisers as outweighing any benefit which might accrue to an individual office-holder seeking to improve the position of general creditors by way of a funding arrangement which surrenders control.

Re Oasis Merchandising

The Grovewood decision was referred to by Robert Walker J in the Oasis case. In *Oasis* the liquidator entered into a sponsorship agreement with an unconnected third party who agreed to provide funding for the continuation of a wrongful trading claim against directors in return for a equitable assignment of the fruits of the action. The sponsorship agreement provided that the wrongful trading claim would continue in the name of the liquidator. (Although this point was drawn expressly in the agreement, no substitution of plaintiff would have been possible since an action under s 214 falls solely to a liquidator: see s 214(1).)

However, the agreement provided that the assignee would control the proceedings subject to the concurrence and co-operation of the liquidator. The agreement also provided that the assignee would provide funding for the litigation in consideration for an equitable assignment of the fruits of the action together with an indemnity by way of reimbursement for any expenditure in funding which would be taken from recoveries. Any net balance remaining would be divided between the assignee and the liquidator.

The sponsorship agreement had been sanctioned by the creditors' committee and apparently by the Registrar of companies – although it is not clear why any such sanction should have been thought necessary.

Robert Walker J identified the three methods of disposing of the prospect of benefiting from current or future litigation against a third party:

1.   the sale of an item of property including a debt;
2.   the assignment of a bare cause of action; and
3.   the sale of part of the net proceeds arising.

On (1) the judge said that the sale of a debt by a liquidator (or trustee-in-bankruptcy, or receiver) did not give rise to champerty problems.

Under (2), the assignment of a bare cause of action, the assignment does give rise to problems but these are overcome by the implied statutory exceptions discussed above, whereby liquidators and trustees-in-bankruptcy may assign free of the usual restrictions on maintenance and champerty.

(3) apparently caught equitable assignments of net recoveries which had been considered champertous by Lightman J in the Grovewood case.

Robert Walker J expressed disagreement with Lightman J in holding that an equitable assignment of net recoveries was champertous but his comments on this point are obiter.

In particular, the judge considered that Lightman J's analysis had been misguided in that what was really at issue in the Grovewood case was not whether the scope of the statutory power should be extended to sales of net proceeds of litigation, but whether it was already sufficiently wide to be interpreted as extending to such sales on a proper construction.

Although the judge declined to give a view, he was clearly attracted by the conclusion that a sale (as opposed to any other arrangement) would fall within the statutory exception, even a sale of net proceeds as in *Grovewood*.

Nevertheless Robert Walker J's view is merely obiter and the view of Lightman J in *Grovewood* constitutes a clearer statement of law. Furthermore, Lightman J's view finds support from comments made obiter by Vinelott J in the Edennote case, in which the judge expressed the view that "...the rules of champerty [do] apply to a sale of proceeds leaving the action vested in the liquidator".

Unhappily, despite this support, the judgment in *Oasis* makes no reference to the Edennote decision. Practitioners may find this conclusion a difficult one to stomach, particularly in view of the greater flexibility in pursuing actions which a Grovewood-type arrangement would provide.

Before considering the particular issues in Oasis as they related to section 214 proceedings, it is worth noting the view of Robert Walker J on the effect of a loss of control over proceedings where a sale or assignment is effected by way of equitable assignment as in Grovewood. The judge considered that,

> "it is still open to debate whether a partial loss of control under an equitable assignment (eg where the company remains as plaintiff, as in Grovewood, as opposed to an assignment which is both legal and equitable, so that the assignee is substituted as plaintiff) of the fruits of an action is objectionable".

In light of Lightman J's views expressed in the Grovewood case, and the existing authorities, even a partial loss of control on an equitable assignment will render an arrangement champertous on public policy grounds. The point, nevertheless, remains unclear and requires specific judicial clarification.

Special considerations in funding arrangements for wrongful trading and other "office-holder exclusive" rights of action

The comments of Robert Walker J in *Oasis* alluded to difficulties with the reasoning in *Grovewood*. These observations were not central to the reason for the failure of the arrangement in *Oasis*. These are now considered. Note that these considerations relate specifically to the nature of an action under section 214, and in particular the fact that it is within the exclusive domain of a liquidator.

These observations are equally applicable to other rights of action under the legislation which fall exclusively to office-holders. These will include:

- fraudulent trading;
- transactions-at-undervalue;
- preferences (*Re M C Bacon Limited (No.2)* [1990] BCC 430 per Millett J);
- avoidances of floating charges under section 245;

- actions under section 127 for invalid dispositions (*Re Ayala Holdings Limited* (May 1993, unreported) per Knox J).

On the other hand, it is unclear whether these considerations will apply to a liquidator's claim in misfeasance proceedings since these are in effect a summary remedy for breach of duty owed to the company, which notwithstanding the liquidation, would have been available to the company itself. One possibility might be to pursue a claim by way of misfeasance proceedings as an alternative to a wrongful trading claim as opposed to any of the other aforementioned actions to which misfeasance proceedings alone do not substantively lend themselves.

The difficulty with this approach is that it may be that misfeasance proceedings fall subject to the following considerations merely by the fact that they are taken by a liquidator, albeit that they are also actionable at the instance of a creditor or contributory (subject to leave: see s 212(5)). Furthermore, any arrangement for funding which is seen to be contrived is unlikely to attract the support of the court, particularly in view of the views expressed in the *Grovewood* and *Oasis* cases.

The difficulties in Oasis

The principal reason why Robert Walker J struck down the sponsorship agreement in Oasis related to its subject matter. The judge considered that a liquidator's claim under section 214 did not constitute an existing asset of the company and, therefore, could not be the subject of a sale by the office-holder. One objection to this view might be that a section 214 action *does* constitute an asset of the company on the basis of the very broad definition of "property" in the Insolvency Act 1986 (s 436), which extends to,

> "money, goods, things in action, land and every description of property wherever situated and also obligations and every description of interest, whether present or future or vested or contingent arising out of or incidental to, property".

This objection is transparent however when one considers that a claim for wrongful trading is something which arises only in liquidation and which is actionable only by the liquidator, albeit for the benefit of the company itself.

Robert Walker J's view, which concurred with that of Knox J in the unreported *Re Ayala Holdings* case, was that rights of action which are conferred by statute upon office-holders as officers of the court cannot be viewed as saleable because they arise as an incident of the office-holder taking office and cannot therefore be viewed as a company asset. Furthermore, the conferring by statute of rights of action on an office-holder, and in particular a liquidator, was coupled with the court's power of supervision over a liquidator which arises under section 167(3).

Robert Walker J found it inconceivable that such supervisory controls could have been put in place by Parliament only for the liquidator to find himself at liberty to assign his exclusive rights of action to a third party assignee who himself would be subject to the court's statutory supervisory powers, although it is probably arguable that the third party would fall subject in any case to the court's inherent jurisdiction in view of the supervisory powers under section 167.

Robert Walker J was also dismissive of the sponsorship agreement in view of the special nature of a wrongful trading claim. This was identified by the judge as including a public or penal element which distinguished the claim from other proceedings in the normal course of civil litigation.

In this regard wrongful trading should be distinguished from the causes of action listed at the start of this section which, save for fraudulent trading, do not involve any public or penal element. The judge's view, which on this point was obiter, was that even a partial loss of control in the conduct of the proceedings by the liquidator rendered the agreement objectionable on public policy grounds.

Conclusions on the funding of an action

The following conclusions may be drawn from the above discussion. At the outset, however, it may be worth making a number of observations. First, conditional fee agreements, which are considered in the next section, may avoid any potential difficulties in the minefield of maintenance and champerty.

Secondly, as identified by Robert Walker J in the *Oasis* decision, the sale or assignment of a debt or the assignment of a bare cause of action are unlikely to give rise to problems in maintenance or champerty. Practitioners may therefore wish to consider these more straightforward forms of funding and avoid the potential complexities of assigning net recoveries or portions thereof, particularly in view of Lightman J's objections to such sales in the

Grovewood case (notwithstanding the later criticisms of Robert Walker J).

Thirdly, certain rights of action, notably wrongful trading, are troublesome for reasons identified at the end of the last section.

Certainly legal assignments of such actions are objectionable in that they require the substitution of the assignee as plaintiff, which by virtue of the statutorily defined nature of the action, is impossible and objectionable. Even an equitable assignment of the fruits of such an action is objectionable not only because of any loss of control of the action involved, but also because the assignment is both objectionable in principle and potentially no more than a sham arrangement. These observations are further qualified by the following:

1. An assignment or sale of an action will be susceptible to an attack on maintenance grounds if the purchaser or assignee cannot be shown to have an actual or contingent interest in the subject matter of the litigation. The giving of financial assistance to an office-holder by a third party will be equally susceptible to a charge of champerty where no legal justification for the financing of the action by the third party can be shown. The courts have persistently refused on grounds of public policy, to sanction the mere dealing in rights of action or the speculative sponsorship of claims by unconnected third parties.
2. The cases do not appear to undermine arrangements whereby parties financing actions agree to deferred payment and/or a percentage of net recoveries.
3. A liquidator should consider the attitude of parties who may wish to challenge any funding agreement by making an application to court as a person aggrieved under section 168.

The first instance decision in the Edennote case highlights that even where the rules on maintenance and champerty are not contravened, the court may resort to the removal of the office-holder if it considers that he has failed to act reasonably – albeit in good faith.

The liquidator's primary concern will be with the attitude of creditors and any creditors' committee, although the sanction of neither should be viewed as guaranteeing the validity of any funding arrangement.

4. The decision in the Oasis case provides that a liquidator's right of action under section 214 for wrongful trading is not capable of sale as an asset of the company.

Neither can a wrongful trading claim be funded under an agreement where the assignee obtains some degree of control over the action, although Robert Walker J suggested that it remains debatable whether a partial loss of control under an equitable assignment of the fruits of the action is objectionable. It is because of the partial loss of control by the liquidator in the conduct of proceedings. Similar considerations will apply to other rights of action conferred on office-holders by statute.

5. In other non-statutorily based litigation claims there appears to be no objection to the sale or assignment of a bare cause of action.

Again, the potential difficulties lie in funding arrangements which seek to assign or sell the fruits of litigation which are coupled with a loss of control by the liquidator, or which instead of constituting the sale of a cause of action, amount to a beneficial interest in net recoveries in return for an agreement to meet costs.

This was the point that Lightman J found objectionable in the Grovewood case – in which the judge had not been prepared to concede a submission that the office-holder's statutory right of sale should be extended. There is conflicting judicial statement on this point in light of the subsequent obiter statements of Robert Walker J and the comments of Vinelott J in Edennote which provides that, "the rule of champerty [does] apply to a sale of proceeds leaving the action vested in the liquidator".

The above difficulties may be overcome by the use of conditional fee agreements.

Conditional Fee Agreements

As we have seen in Chapter 2 *What Can I do?* the law on conditional fee agreements is contained in the Conditional Fee Agreements Order 1995 (SI 1995/1674) and Conditional Fee

Agreements Regulations (SI 1995/1675) made under the Courts and Legal Services Act 1990 Section 58. (See Appendices 2, 3 and 1). These regulations came into effect on 5 July 1995 and permit conditional fee agreements to be entered into in certain specified proceedings, including insolvency proceedings. (The others are personal injury and human rights cases.)

The practical use of conditional fee agreements in insolvency litigation is very much at the infant stage and it remains to be seen how much the law will be put into practice. One cynical view might be that those lawyers who advise office-holders already operate on the basis of an informal conditional fee arrangement, in that certain cases will not involve the recovery of sufficient assets to meet outstanding professional costs whereas others may well produce a surplus – justifying an uplift in fees.

Whilst the reaction of the insolvency profession to the advent of conditional fee agreements in England and Wales (and Scotland) may have been unenergetic in practice, it remains a fact that forms of conditional fee agreements have been seen to operate in practice in other common law jurisdictions such as Australia.

In which insolvency proceedings are conditional fee agreements available?

The Conditional Fee Agreements Order extends to the following insolvency proceedings:

1. Proceedings in England and Wales by a company which is being wound up in England, Wales or Scotland (although note that conditional fee agreements are not available to provisional liquidators);
2. Proceedings by a company in respect of which an administration order is in force;
3. Proceedings in England and Wales by a person acting in the capacity of liquidator of a company which is being wound up in England, Wales or Scotland or as trustee of a bankrupt's estate;
4. Proceedings by a person acting in the capacity of an administrator.

Notably, the 1995 Order does not extend conditional fee agreements to receiverships, voluntary arrangements or deeds of arrangement. Neither can a conditional fee agreement be used for the defence of any proceedings.

Prescribed form of conditional fee agreement

Section 58 of the 1990 Act and the Regulations prescribe certain matters which must be stated in the agreement. Failure to comply with these requirements renders an agreement void and unenforceable. The practical consequence of unenforceability will be that an office-holder may have to meet the costs of a successful defendant personally without recourse to the client who would otherwise be liable under the agreement for those costs and any other disbursements, including counsel's fees.

A model form agreement has been produced by the Insolvency Lawyers' Association. This is reproduced as an Appendix to this Chapter.

Notwithstanding the reference to personal injury cases the Law Society model form for such work covers the prescribed requirements set out in this section and provides an indication of those matters which will usually be an issue for insolvency practitioners and their legal advisers. Those matters are considered in a separate section below.

Detailed consideration of the law, Regulations and Orders governing conditional fees are found elsewhere in this book. The law relating to conditional fees in insolvency proceedings is exactly the same as that for personal injury, although practical matters are different, for example it is very unlikely that an insolvency office-holder will qualify for legal aid.

Security for costs

Notwithstanding a conditional fee agreement the court may still order a plaintiff to give security for costs under Companies Act 1985 section 726. It may be that the disclosure of an adequate insurance policy would provide a defence to the application, although care should be taken that such disclosure does not breach the terms of the policy itself, thereby rendering the cover void.

Costs payable in any event

A solicitor will need to agree expressly those costs payable in any event. These might include disbursements, court and expert witness fees, travel expenses and third party costs of enforcement such as bailiff's fees. Ordinarily counsel's fees will be payable in any event although there is nothing precluding a barrister entering into a conditional fee agreement with a solicitor in the course of insolvency litigation. This includes matters in an arbitration (*Bevan Ashford* v *Geoff Yeandle (Contractors) Limited (in liquidation)*).

Equally the conditional fee agreement should make provision for own costs becoming payable in any event, such as where an office-holder or, say, a liquidation committee wishes to terminate the conditional fee agreement. Insurance cover is available for costs payable in any event although the terms of the policy should always be checked.

Attacks on conditional fee agreements

The Conditional Fee Agreements Order 1995 only exempts conditional fee agreements from attack under the law of maintenance and champerty on the grounds that they are conditional fee agreements. In other words the general rules on maintenance and champerty as discussed previously continue to apply. Neither does the order shelter an agreement from challenge on other grounds.

These include the equitable ground that the legal representative has been guilty of abuse of confidence by failing to make the fullest disclosure, or has taken advantage of the client by improperly advising the client to enter into the conditional fee agreement in the first place, or has fixed an excessive fee uplift. Alternatively, a common law attack may be founded on the allegation that the legal representative has been negligent in his risk assessment.

Conclusions and risk assessment

As we have seen conditional fees have been very successful in personal injury cases although it is clear that risk assessment is far easier to gauge there than in insolvency litigation. The above account identifies that legal advisers run real risks by adopting conditional fee agreements as a matter of course and by failing to make a reasonable risk assessment at the outset.

If anything, conditional fee agreements are probably of most practical use in cases of relatively low risk where there appears to be a strong probability of recovery. Conversely, highly speculative litigation, particularly that brought about at the insistence of vexatious and/or aggrieved creditors, may be less suited to conditional fee arrangements.

In all cases the agreement should be designed to cover those possibilities which are foreseeable at the outset and consideration should be given to variation as what may well be an unpredictable action is proceeded with. Perhaps most importantly, the agreement should make adequate provision for irrecoverable costs and disbursements and costs which are payable in any event.

Legal representatives may also wish to consider protecting themselves, particularly where significant sums are at stake, by advising the client to seek independent legal advice as to the terms of the conditional fee agreement proposed and to go back to the independent adviser at subsequent critical stages, most notably as to a proposed settlement or appeal.

Case Notes

Camdex International Ltd v Bank of Zambia
The Times, 8 April 1996, Hobhouse LJ, Court of Appeal

Assignment of debt to an assignee, who intends to sue for the recovery of the debt held enforceable under English Law.

The case involved an appeal by B against a judgment in favour of the plaintiff, C, who was the assignee of a bona fide debt owed by B. C applied for summary judgment in seeking to recover the debts which had fallen due under agreements with the assignor, CBK. B accepted that the debt was owed to CBK but argued that the assignment to C was unenforceable. B's argument was that to sue on an assigned debt involved maintenance or champerty which was contrary to the public policy provisions contained in the Criminal Law Act 1967 section 14(2).

Hobhouse LJ dismissed the appeal, holding that maintenance and champerty necessarily involve the support of litigation by a party who can show no legitimate interest in the action.

Of itself the assignment of B's debt was not invalid for maintenance or champerty merely because litigation to recover the debt was envisaged. In reaching this decision the Court considered the decisions in *Re Trepca Mines Ltd (No.2)* [1963] Ch 199, *Laurent v Sale* [1963] 1 WLR 829 and *Trendtex Trading Corp* v *Credit Suisse* [1982] AC 679. (See separate case note below).

The judge went on to note that it was important that the court and litigants were able to recognise cases where a champertous intention was lurking behind the assignment of a debt since this could raise public policy objections. In the present case, however, the debt was nothing more than a bona fide purchase by C of the debt which was valid under the Law of Property Act 1925 section 136. As such, there was no objection to the assignment and C's application for summary judgment was enforceable.

Trendtex Trading Corpn. v Credit Suisse [1982] AC 679

Assignment of chose in action held not to be champertous. The plaintiff company successfully claimed damages against a bank which had defaulted by refusing to honour its letter of credit. An appeal to the House of Lords was pending, however. The plaintiff company had been financed throughout the action by the defendant company to whom it owed a large sum of money.

The defendant threatened to put the plaintiff into liquidation unless it assigned the benefit of its chose in action against the bank to the defendant. A purported agreement to that effect was signed in Geneva, to be governed by Swiss law. The defendant then assigned the right of action to an undisclosed third party for $1 Million. The defendant then negotiated with the bank who agreed to pay $8 Million damages. This sum was then paid over to the third party.

The plaintiff brought an action in England, inter alia, to set aside the Geneva agreement.

The questions for the court were:

(1) whether the agreement was valid or invalid. If the latter, the exclusive jurisdiction clause fell with it;
(2) If the agreement was valid, whether the proceedings should continue in England because there was no process compelling discovery of documents in Switzerland.

Held: (1) the crime and the tort of maintenance and champerty had been abolished by the Criminal Law Act 1967, although by s 14(2) the abolition did not affect any rule of law as to cases in which a contract was to be treated as contrary to public policy or otherwise illegal.

It was therefore now legal to assign an impersonal right to litigate provided that the circumstances reasonably warranted it. The defendant had a genuine pre-existing financial interest in maintaining the plaintiff's solvency, as it had financed the transaction which had given rise to the cause of action and was a creditor for large sums arising out of the transaction. The assignment was therefore valid.

(2) The exclusive jurisdiction clause had to be given effect unless it was unreasonable and unjust.

Both the plaintiff and the defendant were Swiss corporations and all the transactions had taken place in Switzerland. Further, there was no reason to suppose that justice could not be done in Switzerland notwithstanding that there was no process compelling discovery of documents there. Accordingly the action to set aside the agreement would be stayed.

MODEL CONDITIONAL FEE AGREEMENT

Conditional Fee Agreement

Table of Contents

THE AGREEMENT is made on   [   ]

BETWEEN

(1)   [   ] (the "Client")

(2)   [   ] (the "Firm")

IT IS HEREBY AGREED

as follows:

1.   **Interpretation**

1.1   In this Agreement :
      "Appeal" means any appeal to either the Court of Appeal or House of Lords from a decision of a lower court, or to a Judge from the decision of a Registrar or Master, in relation to the Claim.

"Basic Costs" means the fees of the Firm for the work done by the Firm for the Client in relation to the Claim on an hourly basis from [ ]. The hourly rates as of the date of this Agreement and subject to review on [ ] of each subsequent year are:

(i)   Partner £[ ];
(ii)   Assistant Solicitor £[ ];
(iii) Trainee Solicitor £[ ];
(iv)   Legal Executive £[ ];
(v)   Paralegal £[ ].

"Claim" means [   ].

"Counterclaim" means any claim by the Defendant(s) against the Client (whenever and however arising) which the Defendant(s) join(s) in any legal proceeding in the County or High Court undertaken by the Client pursuant to the Claim.

"Court Action" means any legal proceedings undertaken in the County or High Court and any Appeal by the Defendant(s) in respect of the Claim.

"Defendant(s)" means [   ].

"Disbursements" means payments that the Firm makes or is liable to make on behalf of the Client to third parties in respect of this Claim. These include, but are not limited to:

(i)   court fees;
(ii)   counsel's fees;
(iii) any expert's (including any foreign lawyer's) fees;
(iv)   any fees and expenses of document management consultants and costs draftsmen;
(v)   travelling expenses;
(vi)   photocopying charges;
(vii) communication charges;
(viii) other internal disbursements;
(ix)   the costs of obtaining any opinion from another firm of solicitors or counsel as to prospects of success or our conduct of the matter.

"Settlement" means a legally enforceable agreement between the Client and the Defendant(s) or third party whereby the Client accepts any sum paid into Court by the Defendant(s) in or towards the satisfaction of the Claim or agrees to cease any legal proceedings against the Defendant(s) in return for such acceptance or for consideration either:

(i)   during the duration of this Agreement; or
(ii)   after the Agreement has come to an end where the sum so accepted or the consideration is less than [120%] of the amount recommended as a reasonable settlement by the Firm while the Agreement was still in force.

"Success Fee" means [ ] % of the Basic Costs.

1.2 Any reference in this Agreement to the Conditional Fee Agreement Regulations 1995 or other legislation will be construed as a reference to the legislation as may from time to time be amended or re-enacted.

2. What is Covered by the Agreement

2.1 The Claim.

2.2 Any Appeal by the Defendant(s).

3. What is not Covered by the Agreement

3.1 Any Counterclaim against the Client.

3.2 Any Appeal that the Client wishes to undertake.

4. Payment of Fees to the Firm

4.1 *Limitation of the Firm's Fees*

Any payment of the Success Fee by the Client to the Firm as set out in Clause 4 will be limited to a maximum of 25% of the total recoveries arising out of the Claim from a Court Action or a Settlement.

4.2 *Successful Action*

4.2.1 If the Client finally wins the Court Action or agrees a Settlement with the Defendant(s), then he will be liable to pay to the Firm:
(i)   the Basic Costs;
(ii)   the Success Fee;
(iii) any unpaid Disbursements.

4.2.2 A Court Action is finally won when the Defendant(s) are not allowed to appeal against the decision of a Court Action or have not appealed in time permitted by the Rules of the Supreme Court then in force.

4.3 *Unsuccessful Action*

4.3.1 If the Client loses the Court Action, then the Client will be liable to pay to the Firm:
(i)   any unpaid Disbursements;
(ii)   the Defendant's(') costs and disbursements as set out in Clause 5.

4.3.2 A Court Action is lost when the Court has dismissed the Claim or the Client on the Firm's advice has stopped the Court Action.

4.4 *Termination of the Agreement by the Client*

If the Client terminates the Agreement for any reason as set out in Clause 8, then the Client will pay to the Firm:
(i)   any unpaid Disbursements;
(ii)   the Basic Costs;
that the firm has incurred or is entitled to under this Agreement as at the date that the client notifies the firm of the termination, and

(iii) the Success Fee if the Client subsequently wins the Court Action or enters into a Settlement.

4.5 *Termination of the Agreement by the Firm*

4.5.1 *Client failure to comply with responsibilities*

If the Firm terminates the Agreement for any reason set out in Clause 9.1.1, the Firm may require the Client to pay:
(i) the Basic Costs;
(ii) any unpaid Disbursements;
that the Firm has incurred or is entitled to under this Agreement as at the date the Firm notified the Client of the termination, and
(iii) the Success Fee if the Client subsequently wins a Court Action or enters into a Settlement.

4.5.2 *Third Party recoveries*

If the Firm terminates the Agreement for any reason set out in Clause 9.1.2, the Firm may require the Client to pay:
(i) the Basic Costs;
(ii) any unpaid Disbursements;
that the Firm has incurred or is entitled to under this Agreement as at the date the firm notified the Client of the termination, and
(iii) the Success Fee if the Client subsequently wins the Court action or enters into a Settlement.

4.5.3 *Disagreement as to likelihood of success*

If the Firm terminates the Agreement for any reason as set out in Clause 9.1.3, the Firm may require the Client to pay:
(i) any unpaid Disbursements;
that the Firm has incurred as at the date the Firm notified the Client of the termination.

4.5.4 *Disagreement as to the Firm Opinion to settle*

If the Firm terminates the Agreement for any reason as set out in Clause 9.1.4, the Firm may require the Client to pay:
(i) the Basic Costs;
(ii) any unpaid Disbursements;
that the Firm has incurred or is entitled to under this Agreement as at the date the Firm notified the Client of the termination, and
(iii) the Success Fee if the Client:

(a) subsequently wins the Court Action and recovers, or stands to recover an amount less than 120% of the settlement sum recommended by the Firm but not accepted by the Client; or

(b) subsequently enters into a Settlement.

4.5.5 *Disagreement as to choice of barrister*

If the Firm terminates the Agreement for any reason as set out in Clause 9.1.5, the Firm may require the Client to pay:
(i)   the Basic Costs;
(ii)   any unpaid Disbursements;

that the Firm has incurred or is entitled to under this Agreement as at the date the Firm notified the Client of the termination, and
(iii) the Success Fee if the Client subsequently wins a Court Action or enters into a Settlement.

4.6   *Costs recovered*

4.6.1 The Client may be entitled to the payment by the Defendant(s) of some of the Firm's Basic Costs and Disbursements if the Client obtains a judgment or settlement in his favour.

4.6.2 If costs are recovered at the end of the Court Action, interest can be recovered in certain circumstances from the Defendant(s). The Firm will be entitled to such interest but will account to the Client for the proportionate amount attributable to Disbursements paid on account by the Client.

4.6.3 The Firm may take in the Client's name such recovery action as may be necessary to enforce a judgment order or agreement against the Defendant(s). The costs of that action will be Basic Costs and this Agreement will apply to it.

4.7   *VAT*

The Client agrees to pay to the Firm VAT (currently 17.5%) on the total of Basic Costs, the Success Fee and Disbursements (where applicable) at the time when those amounts become payable under this Agreement.

5.   **The Defendant's(') Costs if the Client loses the Court Action, a Counterclaim or Appeal by the Defendant(s)**

5.1   If the Client loses the Court Action, a Counterclaim or an Appeal by the Defendant(s), or does not accept a payment into Court by the Defendant(s) for a sum greater than an ultimate judgment in the Client's favour, the Client may become liable to pay the Defendant's(') legal costs and disbursements as agreed between the parties or as established by the Court on a taxation of costs.

5.2   The Client may also be liable to pay to the Defendant(s) a sum being either damages or the amount of the Counterclaim.

6.   **The Firm's Responsibilities**

6.1   The Firm will:
(i)   always act in the Client's best interests in pursuing the Claim, subject to its duty to the Court and its professional obligations and duties;

(ii) subject to Clause 6.1(i), assist the Client in obtaining insurance in respect of Clause 5.1;

(iii) give the Client its best advice about whether to accept any offer of settlement;

(iv) explain to the Client the risks and benefits of taking any legal action;

(v) give the Client the best information possible about the likely costs of the case.

7. The Client's Responsibilities

7.1 The Client will:

(i) give the Firm full instructions so that the Firm is able to do its work properly;

(ii) co-operate fully with the Firm in pursuing the Claim;

(iii) pay to the Firm any Disbursements incurred or to be incurred by the Firm, as follows:

(a) Disbursements invoiced by the Firm to the Client on a quarterly basis; or

(b) in the event of Disbursements exceeding, [£   ] within any three-month period, as invoiced by the Firm at any time during that quarter; or

(c) in the event of any single Disbursement exceeding, [£   ], the Firm reserves the right to require the Client to pay this Disbursement in advance of the Firm incurring that Disbursement.

(iv) If the Client owes any money to the Firm for the period of one month after the due date, interest will be payable at the rate of [   ]% per annum.

7.2 The Client will not:

(i) deliberately mislead the Firm in relation to any matters in connection with the Claim;

(ii) ask the Firm to work in any improper or unreasonable way.

8. Termination of the Agreement by the Client

8.1 The Client will be entitled to terminate this Agreement if notice is given to the Firm in writing that the Client wishes to terminate this Agreement.

8.2 If the Agreement is terminated under Clause 8.1 the Firm will be entitled to retain a lien on all papers, documents, money or other property held on the Client's behalf until all money due under Clause 4.4 is paid or until the Firm receives a satisfactory undertaking from any solicitor subsequently instructed by the Client as to payment of the Firm's Basic Costs, Success Fee and Disbursements, on conclusion of the matter.

9. Termination of the Agreement by the firm

9.1 The Firm will be entitled to terminate the Agreement by notice in writing given to the Client on the following grounds:

9.1.1 if the Client fails to comply with his responsibilities set out in Clause 7;

9.1.2 If the Client receives funds or indemnities from any third parties in connection with the Claim or any costs in relation to it which total a sum equal to or exceeding [£   ];

9.1.3 if the Firm advises the Client that a Court Action is unlikely to be won by the Client but the Client disagrees with the advice and indicates that he wishes to continue;

9.1.4 if the Firm advises the Client that it is in the Client's best interests to make a Settlement and the Client indicates that he wishes to continue;

9.1.5 if the Firm recommends to the Client that it should instruct (a) particular barrister(s) to act on behalf of the Client in pursuing the Claim or that the services of a forensic expert or a particular forensic expert be obtained in connection with the Claim or that any interlocutory or final order or judgment of the Court should be appealed against and the Client rejects this recommendation.

9.2 If the Agreement is terminated under Clause 9.1 the Firm will be entitled to retain a lien on all papers, documents, money or other property held on the Client's behalf until all money due under Clause 4.5 is paid or until the Firm receives a satisfactory undertaking from any solicitor subsequently instructed by you as to payment of the Firm's Basic Costs, Success Fee and Disbursements, on conclusion of the matter.

10. **Removal from Record of a Court Action**

If the Agreement is terminated in accordance with either Clause 8 or 9 then the Client shall file, or ensure that his new solicitors file, in Court a notice of change of solicitors forthwith, failing which the Firm will apply to the Court to have its name removed from the record of the Court Action.

11. **Counsel**

11.1 The Firm may recommend (a) barrister(s) who in its opinion is best able to act on behalf of the Client in respect of the Claim.

11.2 Subject to Clauses 4.5.5 and 9.1.5 the Client is entitled to reject the above recommendation.

11.3 When counsel is instructed on the Client's behalf the Firm will, if so instructed by the Client, seek to instruct counsel on the basis of a conditional fee agreement on similar terms as to success as are contained in this Agreement.

11.4 If counsel is not instructed on a conditional fee basis, his or her fees will be payable as Disbursements.

12. **Insurance in Respect of Clause 5.1**

12.1 The Firm has informed the Client of the availability of insurance to cover the liability referred to in Clause 5.1 above and the Client acknowledges that he is aware of such insurance.

12.2 The insurance referred to in Clause 12.1 does not form part of this Agreement.

13. **Mediation**

In the event of any dispute between the Client and the Firm relating to or arising out of this Agreement, the parties agree that:
(i)   either party may refer that dispute to an independent mediator to be appointed by the Centre for Dispute Resolution ("CEDR");
(ii)   they will co-operate with the appointed mediator in the resolution of the dispute; and
(iii) if the mediator concludes within 30 days of the dispute being referred to him that the dispute has not been resolved and is not likely to be resolved, the parties are at liberty to pursue their traditional legal remedies in respect of that dispute.

14. **Explanatory Matters**

14.1 The Firm pursuant to Regulation 4 of the Conditional Fees Regulations 1995 draws to the Client's attention the following matters:

(i)   *Legal Aid*

The Firm has informed the Client that Legal Aid is not available in respect of the Claim.

(ii)   Liability to pay the Firm's costs and expenses

This has been explained by the Firm to the Client as set out in Clause 4.

(iii) *Liability to pay the Defendant's(') costs and expenses*

This has been explained by the Firm to the Client as set out in Clause 5. The availability of insurance to cover these costs and expenses has also been explained in Clause 12.

(iv)   *Taxation of the firm's costs*

The Firm has informed the Client of his right under Order 62 Rule 15A of The Rules of the Supreme Court to have the Firm's fees taxed.

14.2 The client acknowledges that the matters referred to in Clause 12.1 have been drawn to his attention.

15. **Notices**

15.1 Any notice required to be given under the Agreement will be in writing and deemed to be received as follows:
(i)   Fax: on the date when sent;
(ii)   Letter: when left at the other party's address as set out in this Agreement or if sent by 1st Class post two days after being sent in the post postage prepaid.

16. Law and Jurisdiction

16.1 This Agreement will be governed by, and will be construed in accordance with the law of England and Wales.

16.2 The Parties to the Agreement irrevocably submit to the jurisdiction of the courts of England and Wales.

Human Rights Cases

Human Rights Cases

As we have seen in Chapter 2 *What Can I Do?* Conditional Fees are allowed in proceedings before the European Commission of Human Rights and the European Court of Human Rights but not in the earlier stages of such proceedings in courts in England and Wales and not in the European Court of Justice (which is a totally separate body).

The Regulations and Order governing Conditional Fees in Human Rights cases are exactly the same as those governing personal injury and insolvency work and are found in the Conditional Fee Agreements Order 1995 (Statutory Instrument 1995 No.1674) Appendix 2 and the Conditional Fee Agreements Regulations 1995 (Statutory Instrument 1995 No.1675) Appendix 3.

Prior to proceedings being brought before the European Commission of Human Rights or the European Court of Human Rights domestic remedies, that is remedies in the courts of England and Wales, must be exhausted first and at present conditional fee arrangements are not permitted before domestic courts in human rights matters. This severely limits the effect of the Regulations and Order allowing conditional fees in human rights cases but the position is likely to change in the near future and human rights cases are likely to become more common. This is for a number of reasons.

Firstly the Lord Chancellor's Department Consultation Paper *Access to Justice with Conditional Fees* (March 1998) proposes the extension of conditional fees to all civil work except family work and if those proposals are implemented then conditional fees *will* be available in human rights cases before domestic courts.

Secondly the Court of Appeal has decided in the case of *Thai Trading Co.* v *Taylor* (*The Times* 6th March 1998) that there is nothing unlawful in a solicitor acting on a no win – no fee basis in any civil case provided that the solicitor did not seek to recover more than his ordinary profit costs and disbursements if he won. At the time of writing the precise significance of this case is disputed but there is little doubt that by 1999 conditional fees and/or contingency fees will be permissible in human rights cases in this country.

Furthermore the adoption of the European Convention on Human Rights into the domestic law of the United Kingdom is likely to make human rights cases more common.

I set out below, with thanks to its creator Luke Clements, a Conditional Fee Agreement suitable for use in human rights cases.

CONDITIONAL FEE AGREEMENT

(Human Rights Cases)

The Agreement is a legally binding contract between you and your legal representative. The Law Society Conditions are part of the Agreement. Before you sign, please read everything carefully. Please also read the *Conditional Fees Explained*, a Law Society leaflet which we have given you.

For an explanation of words like 'our disbursements', 'basic costs', 'win' and 'lose', see condition 3 of the Law Society Conditions.

Agreement Date

We, the legal representative   **You, the client**

What is covered by this agreement

• Your application to and representation before the European Commission and Court of Human Rights and correspondence (if required) with the Committee of Ministers.

Paying us

If you win the case, you are liable to pay our disbursements, basic costs and a success fee. You may be able to recover our disbursements and basic costs from the United Kingdom Government, your opponent. For full details, see conditions 4 and 6.

If you lose the case, you pay our disbursements only including any travel and accommodation expenses we have incurred on your behalf. For full details, see conditions 3(f) and 5.

If you end the Agreement before the case is won or lost, you pay our disbursements and basic costs. If you go on to win the case, you pay a success fee. For full details, see condition 7.

If we end the Agreement before the case is won or lost, see condition 7 for full details.

Basic costs

These are for work done from now until the review date.

Our hourly rates are:

The hourly rates are the same as would be charged if the work was done under a non-conditional fee agreement.

LAW SOCIETY CONDITIONS

1. Our responsibilities

We must:

- always act in your best interests in pursuing your complaint and obtaining for you the best possible result, subject to our duty to the European Commission and Court of Human Rights;

- explain to you the risks and benefits of taking legal action;

- give you our best advice about whether to accept any offer of settlement;

- at the outset, give you the best information possible about the likely costs of your case.

2. Your responsibilities

You must:

- give us instructions that allow us to do our work properly;

- not ask us to work in an improper or unreasonable way;

- not deliberately mislead us;

- co-operate with us when asked;

- do everything reasonable within your power to obtain Council of Europe Legal Aid;

- pay for disbursements as the case goes on, if the pay-as-you-go option is included in the agreement.

3. Explanation of words used

(a) Advocacy

Appearing for you at Commission and Court hearings and in any friendly settlement negotiations.

(b) Basic Costs

Our costs for legal work. You pay them, and a success fee, if you win.

Basic costs are worked out in line with the Agreement. But we will review the rates in the Agreement on the review date and on each anniversary of the review date. We will not increase the rates by more than the rise in the Retail Prices Index.

(c) Case

Your complaint to the European Commission and Court of Human Rights.

(d) Damages

Money that the Court says your opponent must pay or the Committee of Ministers requires your opponent to pay (or money that your opponent agrees to pay) in settlement of the case.

(e) Our disbursements

Payments we make on your behalf to others involved in the case. These may be:

- Court fees;

- Experts' fees;

- Travelling expenses;

- Hotel and other subsistence expenses;

Fees for Barristers may also be counted as our disbursements (see condition 6).

You have to pay all our disbursements, whether you win or lose. There are three exceptions to this:

- If you win, we may be able to recover on your behalf the money for our disbursements from our opponent;

- If you lose, we are liable to pay the fees of any Barrister who does not have a conditional fee agreement with us and whose fees you have not been paying on account;

- You may be entitled to Council of Europe Legal Aid which may meet some of the disbursements.

(f) Lien

Our right to keep all papers, documents, money or other property held on your behalf until all money due to us is paid. A lien may be applied after the Agreement ends.

(g) Lose

The Commission has declared your complaint to be wholly inadmissible or the Court or Committee of Ministers has found no violation of any Article of the European Convention on Human Rights (or any protocol thereto) or you have withdrawn the complaint on our advice.

(h) Opponent

The United Kingdom Government.

(i) Success fee

The percentage of basic costs that we add to your bill if you win the case. It cannot be more than 100% of the basic costs. It is paid out of your damages.

The percentage reflects:

- our opinion of the level of risk we are taking – if you lose, we will not earn anything;

- the fact that we are not receiving our basic costs in advance;

- the fact that we may not be receiving our disbursements in advance.

The total of our success fee and any Barrister's uplift fee (see condition 6) is capped – it will not be more than 25% of damages recovered.

(j) Win

The case is finally decided in your favour, whether by the Court or the Committee of Ministers or by agreement and in this results in your opponent making payment towards your basic costs and disbursements.

4. What happens if you win?

If you win, you are liable to pay our disbursements, basic costs and the success fee. The court or Committee of Ministers will decide how much (if anything) you can recover; or this will be specified by the agreement. If the amount allowed does not cover all our work, you pay the difference.

You, not your opponent, pay the success fee.

You agree that we may receive any damages and the costs your opponent pays. If your opponent refuses to accept our receipt, you will pay the cheque you receive from your opponent into a joint bank account in your name and ours. Out of the money, you agree to let us take the balance of the basic costs, success fee, remaining disbursements and VAT. You take the rest.

We are allowed to keep any interest your opponent pays on the costs.

Payment for advocates is explained in condition 6.

5. What happens if you lose?

If you lose, you do not have to pay any basic costs or success fee. You do have to pay us for our disbursements.

Payment for advocacy is dealt with in condition 6.

6. Payment for advocacy

The cost of advocacy and any other work by us, or by any Solicitor agent on our behalf, forms part of our basic costs.

Barristers who have a conditional fee agreement with us

If you win, their fee is our disbursement which can be recovered from your opponent. You must pay the Barrister's uplift fee shown in the separate conditional fee agreement we make with the Barrister. We will discuss the

Barrister's uplift fee with you before we instruct him or her. If you lose, you pay nothing.

Barristers who do not have a conditional fee agreement with us

If you lose and you have not been paying the Barrister's fees on account, we are liable to pay them. Because of this, we add an extra success fee if you win. This extra success fee is not added if you have been paying the Barrister's fees on account. If you win, you are liable to pay the Barrister's fees. See 'Success fee' in the Agreement.

Other points concerning Barristers

- If you choose a Barrister we do not recommend, we may decide not to seek a conditional fee agreement with him or her. The points in the previous paragraph will then apply.

- If we ask a Barrister to provide advice or to draft documents, the fees will be treated as set out in this condition.

- If you reject our advice to use a Barrister, you may not compel us to provide advocacy ourselves. Following our refusal to provide advocacy, we can end the Agreement if you still reject our advice to use a Barrister.

7. What happens when the Agreement ends before the case itself ends?

Paying us if you end the agreement

You can end the Agreement at any time. We then have the right to decide whether you must:

- pay the basic costs and our disbursements when we ask for them or;

- pay the basic costs, our disbursements and success fee if you go on to win the case.

Paying us if we end the Agreement

(a) We can end the agreement if you do not keep to your responsibilities in condition 2 and we then have the right to decide whether you must:

  - pay the basic costs and our disbursements when we ask for them or;

  - pay the basic costs, our disbursements and success fee if you go on to win the case.

(b) We can end the Agreement if we believe you are unlikely to win but you disagree with us. If this happens, you will only have to pay our disbursements.

(c) We can end the Agreement if you reject our opinion about making a settlement with your opponent. You must then:

  - pay the basic costs and our disbursements;

- pay the success fee if you go on to win the case (unless your damages or settlement are at least 20% more than the offer we advised you to accept).

If you ask us to get a second opinion or further opinion from a specialist legal representative outside our Firm, we will do so. You pay the costs of a second or further opinion.

8. What happens after the Agreement ends

After the Agreement ends, we will apply to have our name removed from the record of the Commission or Court or Committee of Ministers.

We have the right to preserve our lien unless another solicitor working for you undertakes to pay us what we are owed including a success fee if you win.

Success Fee

This is:

- [ ] % of the basic costs plus;

- [ ] % of the basic costs if an extra success fee is payable under condition 6.

The total of the success fee and any Barrister's uplift fee (see condition 6) will not be more than 25% of the damages or settlement you win.

Value Added Tax (VAT)

We add VAT, at the rate (now [ ] %) that applied when the work is done, to the total of the basic costs and success fee.

Our disbursements

Pay-as-you-go option

You agree to pay our disbursements now and as the case goes on.

Variation

Show any variation on paying our disbursements which would alter the details under "Paying us" about or in condition 3 (f).

Extra conditions

The following conditions are part of the Agreement.

Signatures

Signed for the legal representative

Signed by the client

Chapter 15

Conditional And Contingency Fees Compared

As we have seen in Chapter 3 *The Success Fee and the Cap – Myth and Reality* for all practical purposes there is no difference between conditional fees and contingency fees except for the way they are spelt. The Lord Chancellor's 1989 Green Paper which paved the way for the Courts and Legal Services Act 1990, even used the term "contingency fees".

The notional difference is that a *contingency fee* is a straightforward percentage of the damages. A *conditional fee* is a fee increased by a success fee added to the solicitor's notional normal fee had he *not* been working on a conditional fee basis. This notional fee is calculated by the traditional method of applying an hourly rate and then increasing it by a maximum of 100%. However solicitors may, but do not have to, limit such extra fee, or indeed all of their fees, by reference to a cap on the percentage of *damages* taken, effectively a contingency fee.

Thus in a *conditional fee* case the solicitor must charge no more than double his normal fee in any circumstances even if that fee is capped whereas in a *contingency fee* case the sum charged is governed *only* by the damages won and notions of "normal fees", "hourly rates" *etc.* are irrelevant.

In theory the "double normal costs" restriction on the success fee in conditional fee cases could make a significant difference. In practice it is of virtually no effect because of the almost universal use of the cap and the fact that the *lower* of the two figures is almost always the one reached by a *cap* on damages and *not* that obtained by imposing a 100% maximum increase on "normal" costs. Examples are given in Chapter 3 *The Success Fee and the Cap – Myth and Reality.*

The central features of both schemes are that the client only pays his lawyer in the event of a win, so the fee is *contingent* or *conditional* upon the result, and in practice that payment is a percentage fixed in advance of the result.

It is *not* the case that a solicitor who wins thereby always charges more than he or she would have under the "traditional" hourly rate system. In low-value Industrial Tribunal and Criminal Injuries Compensation Authority cases, where costs are not recoverable from an opponent, the fee is very often much lower than if charged on an hourly rate.

Thus, ironically, the heavy regulation of *conditional* fees gives little protection to the client whereas the apparent free-for all of *contingency* fees does give that protection.

Sir Peter Middleton, one of the few people in or out of the legal profession who appear to understand this, said in his review of the programmes for reviewing the civil justice system and the legal aid scheme (Autumn 1997) (Paragraph 5.50):

> I also think that the time is now ripe to reconsider whether contingency fees – where the fee is a proportion of the amount recovered rather than an uplift to the normal bill – should also be permitted. There is no essential difference in principle between conditional fees and contingency fees. Indeed, in some ways the latter may be preferable. Contingency fees create an incentive to achieve the best possible result for the client, not just a simple win, and they reward a cost-effective approach in a way that conditional fees, where the lawyers' remuneration is still based on an hourly bill, do not.

In spite of the British press' perception of it, the contingency fee system works well in the United States, and of course in many other countries around the world. United States cases attract attention because of the apparently massive awards but this is a feature of jury awards *not* contingency fees. In Britain, in libel cases where contingency fees are not permitted but juries decide damages, similarly huge awards are made.

It is the British "sign a blank cheque" system of hourly rates, rewarding inefficiency and delay which has failed its clients and which has led to the proposed virtual abolition of legal aid in civil litigation.

As Sir Peter Middleton says at paragraph 1.10 of his report:

> The sharing of risk deserves particular comment. The resolution of a dispute is inevitably a risky business. Those involved need to have as much knowledge as possible about the risks they are taking – the likely costs and benefits, the probability of success, and the way these change at different stages in the case. It is in my view the responsibility of the professionals in the system – especially the lawyers – to give this advice explicitly. The more they share the financial consequences of this judgment the more accurate it is likely to be.

In a classic denouncement of the current system he says, at paragraph 3.11:

> "Payment calculated after the event on the basis of an hourly rate for all work done offers the greatest rewards to the least efficient providers".

and at paragraph 2.11 that solicitors should

> "develop more efficient working practices rather than maximising the amount of work they do and charge for, as the current system motivates them to do."

For those reasons my view is that the conditional fee scheme should be scrapped and replaced with a contingency fee scheme regulated, unlike conditional fees, by a statutory cap on the percentage of damages a lawyer may charge by way of *any* fee, not just the extra "success" fee.

There is an increasing body of opinion that contingency fees will in fact become standard. Peter Hurst, Chief Master of the Supreme Court Taxing Office has said

> There is no doubt that following the judgment in *Thai Trading* the Law Society will alter its Professional Practice Rules to reflect the laws it has now been explained. Thus contingent fee agreements will inevitably become commonplace.
>
> The likelihood is that conditional fee agreements will gradually become redundant and give way almost entirely to contingent fee agreements.
>
> (*New Law Journal*, 20 March 1998)

His Honour Judge Cook, Editor of *Cook on Costs,* said

> It is ironic that at a time when the Lord Chancellor is considering extending the provisions for conditional fee agreements the Court of Appeal should demonstrate and confirm that they are not necessary.
>
> (*The Times*, 31 March 1998)

However the wholesale adoption of contingency fees is unlikely to happen immediately and in the next chapter I look at the problems still thrown up by the archaic indemnity principle – we all hoped that we had left champerty and maintenance behind forever when we left law school. It will be a barred entail next, which for the non-lawyers amongst you is something to do with land and *not* a type of wading bird.

The Indemnity Principle

The Indemnity Principle

Introduction

In Chapter 2 I have set out what can and cannot be done by way of conditional fee agreements and contingency fee agreements respectively, *i.e.* what is lawful and what is unlawful. So for example acting on a contingency fee in a breach of contract case where proceedings have been issued was always considered illegal; it was a breach of Section 59 Solicitors Act 1974 and a breach of the Solicitors Practice Rules. The Thai Trading case has changed all that.

However just because it is legal and permissible to act on a contingency/conditional fee basis does not altogether get rid of the indemnity principle – that is the rule that a losing party's liability for costs is limited to the amount the winning party has agreed to pay his or her own solicitor. This principle applies to all work, not just that done on a contingency basis.

Thus the solicitor agrees to work for £90 per hour inclusive of markup and wins the case. The "going" rate in the local county court on inter-partes taxation is £80 per hour plus, typically 50% markup, that is £120 per hour. By virtue of the indemnity principle the solicitor is entitled to only £90 per hour, the contractual sum he is entitled to charge his client. This rule (absurd, unjust and a disincentive to solicitors to offer their services at affordable prices) remains in place but has been subject to exceptions.

Conditional Fees

The inter play between conditional fees and the indemnity principle is complicated and unclear. The generally held view is that in lawful conditional fee cases the indemnity principle is abrogated but the authority for this view is unclear as indeed is the bar on contingency fees, stemming from common law, public policy considerations and the doctrines of maintenance and champerty. The Court of Appeal has overturned the ban on contingency fees but as at the time of writing Rule 8 of the Solicitors Practice Rules is to be amended to allow contingency fee arrangements where permitted under statute or common law. (*Law Society's Gazette* 10th June 1998)

The basis of the argument appears to be that in passing Section 58(8) of the Courts and Legal Services Act 1990 and the Conditional Fees Regulations and Order thereunder Parliament has impliedly repealed any statute or common law principle preventing recovery of costs because of the indemnity principle. Section 58 clearly removes the restriction on a solicitor enforcing the agreement *against his own client* and only then provided that the Regulations and Order are followed precisely.

This is achieved by Section 58(3):

> Subject to subsection (6), a conditional fee agreement which relates to specified proceedings shall not be unenforceable by reason only of its being a conditional fee agreement.

Section 58(6) makes unenforceable any agreement where the uplift on normal fees exceeds the prescribed maximum currently 100%.

It is Section 58(8) which appears to impliedly abolish the indemnity principle in conditional fee cases as it acknowledges that a party to such an agreement may recover costs from the other side (my italics):

> Where a party to any proceedings has entered into a conditional fee agreement *and a costs order is made in those proceedings in his favour* the costs payable to him shall not include any element which takes account of any percentage increase payable under the agreement.

Thus a defendant does not have to pay extra to a conditional fee client to cover the solicitor's success fee although the Lord Chancellor's consultation paper *Access to Justice with Conditional Fees* proposes that the success fee becomes recoverable from the defendant, something I believe is wrong.

There is a theoretical problem when the solicitor agrees a damages-related cap of say 25% governing *all* of the client's liability to costs, not just the success fee. Clearly this is desirable as it gives the client complete protection and guarantees him at least 75% of the damages.

However it is arguable that the indemnity principle applies to stop full recovery of costs from the other side. Take the three examples in Chapter 3 *The Success Fee and the Cap: Myth and Reality*. In examples A and B there is no problem as in example A there is no cap and in example B the cap is on the success fee only, ie the solicitor reserve the right to charge at his full hourly rate come what may and *add* a capped success fee. The solicitors's own client hourly rate should be higher than the inter-partes rate.

The potential problem occurs in example C where the solicitor promises to take a maximum of 25% of the damages come what may – in that case £1,250 being a quarter of £6,000. Arguably, because of the indemnity rule the solicitor's recovery of costs, from the other is thus limited to £1,250, being the maximum his client would have to pay.

The counter-argument to this is that Regulation 3(d) of The Conditional Fee Agreements Regulations 1995 makes it mandatory for a Conditional Fee Agreement to state whether or not there is a cap on fees to be charge by reference to damages and the agreement must state that in relation to *all* fees that may be payable by the client and *not* just the success fee.

The relevant sections of Regulation 3 read:

> An agreement shall state –
> (b) the circumstances in which the legal representative's fees and expenses or part of them are payable:
> (c) what, if any, payment is due -
>   (i)   upon partial failure of the specified circumstances to occur;
>   (ii) irrespective of the specified circumstances occurring; and
>   (iii) upon termination of the agreement for any reason.
> (d) the amount payable in accordance with sub-paragraphs (b) or (c) above or the method to be used to calculate the amount payable; and in particular whether or not the amount payable is limited by reference to the amount of any damages which may be recovered on behalf of the client."

Thus Parliament having envisaged a cap on *all* charges, not just the success fee, must have intended to disapply the indemnity principle in such cases. Solicitors do not have to impose a cap either on the success fee or on all fees but they must state whether or not there is such a cap.

Ironically, example C – the Underwoods Method – set out on page 36 satisfies Regulation 3 but, theoretically, runs a risk of falling foul of the indemnity principle.

When civil legal aid rates for new certificates were cut to £65 per hour on 25th February 1994 it was recognised that this caused a problem with the indemnity rule as a *winning* solicitor at that time would recover about £100 per hour costs from the other side on taxation (about £120 per hour in 1998) but only £65 per hour if he lost. In accordance with common law rules on the face of it the other side's liability was similarly limited to £65 per hour. The Legal Aid in Civil Proceedings (Remuneration) Regulations 1994 amounted to a breach in the Indemnity Principle sanctioned by Parliament and it is arguable that this is also the case with conditional fees.

It is also arguable that as the apparent statutory bar on contingency arrangements in contentious business (Section 59(2) Solicitors Act 1974) stems from public policy consideration it must be deemed to have been impliedly repealed by Section 58 of the Courts and Legal Services Act 1990 as something passed by Parliament cannot, in law, be against public policy.

I hope that this is all academic and that you have had an interesting but entirely pointless time reading this chapter so far but I have my nagging doubts. The law is *not* clear and conditional fees are deeply unpopular with the bar and apparently some members of the judiciary.

Clearly they are acceptable in legal aid cases and they are enforceable against *the client* because Parliament has said so (Section 58(3)) but that does not of itself abolish the indemnity principle.

The indemnity principle is in any event, causing very real practical problems in relation to two areas –

(a) Contingency Fees
(b) Green Forms

Contingency Fees

As we have seen contingency fees are allowed in non-contentious work which includes all Tribunals of first instance save the Lands Tribunal. Generally Tribunals deal with appeals against decisions of the State or its Agencies, *e.g.* VAT Tribunals, Social Security Tribunals etc. and there is normally no question of inter-partes costs ever being considered. However Industrial Tribunals are a major exception as their work is almost entirely concerned with resolving disputes between private citizens or companies, not disputes between citizens and the state.

Thus although the starting point in Industrial Tribunals is that costs will not be awarded there are exceptions and a considerable number of costs orders are made (See Chapter 19 *Industrial Tribunals* for the circumstances when costs are payable).

So you act for a client in an Industrial Tribunal on a contingency fee basis and win. Can you obtain costs from the other side? The answer appears to be "No".

In *Commissioners for Customs and Excise* v *Raz* Times Law Reports 5th December 1994) a tax consultant represented a client at a VAT Tribunal on the basis that his fees would be equal the costs recovered. It was held that there was nothing to indemnify and therefore no order for costs was made. As far as I am aware there has been no Industrial Tribunal or Employment Appeal Tribunal decision on this point but the implications of the Raz case are clear – if the client is not on a traditional "blank-cheque" arrangement neither he nor his lawyer can recover from the other side.

This is particularly unjust and damaging in Industrial Tribunals because Legal Aid is not available and contingency fees are the only way many clients can afford a lawyer. Costs are only awarded if a party has behaved unreasonably, vexatiously or frivolously or has been warned by the Tribunal at a pre-hearing review that his case has little prospect of success and he is therefore at risk of costs. Let us look at an example of how this rule can work. The facts of the case are the same but the ways the employers handle it are very different.

Example A

Having taken advantage of the Law Society rule change concerning the naming of solicitors' firms the innovative (but illiterate) firm of Suing R Us agree to undertake on a contingency fee basis Ms Fondled's sex discrimination case against her erstwhile employers the Accountants Messrs Gropers, who have not had the benefit of a name change. Messrs Gropers act responsibly and take and pay for legal advice, realise they have a weak case, apologise and settle the case for £6,000. Suing R Us take £2,000 as a fee, Ms Fondled gets an apology and £4,000 and everyone is happy.

Example B

The facts of the case are the same but Messrs Gropers refuse to take legal advice. Their written defence to the Tribunal is so weak that the Tribunal itself lists the case for a pre-hearing review and orders Messrs Gropers to pay the maximum deposit of £150 as a condition of continuing and warn them that if they lose, as they surely will, they will be liable for the costs of the Applicant, Ms Fondled.

Messrs Gropers handle the case themselves and behave disgracefully at the Tribunal and their conduct makes the case last three days. They lose. The Tribunal awards Ms Fondled £6,000. Her solicitors apply for costs on the four separate and justified grounds that the Respondents have behaved frivolously *and* vexatiously *and* unreasonably and in any event had been given a costs warning by another Tribunal at a pre-hearing review.

Mr Groper, having had a few beers at lunchtime, laughs and tells the Tribunal that they cannot award costs because the Applicant's solicitors were acting under a contingency fee agreement and whilst they are at it could he have back the £150 deposited as that was a deposit against costs and the Tribunal has no power to order costs because of the indemnity principle?

Well that's a very sensible law isn't it?

The Green Form Trap

A solicitor advises a client under a Green Form and does, say, 2 hours work for which he is entitled to remuneration at the current Green Form rate £44 per hour. The case is won and the solicitor submits details of his costs to the other side. Because of the indemnity principle he is only entitled to £44 per hour *from the other side* in respect of the Green form work as against the going rate of around £120 per hour.

Thus by advising the client under a Green Form the solicitor loses £76 per hour.

That was the decision in *Joyce* v *Kammac (1988) Limited* (1996 1 AER).

In spite of all the recent cases the Green Form Trap remains fully effective.

Because of the continuing relevance of the indemnity principle and its particular influence in conditional and contingency fees it is worth taking a look at the law and cases.

At common law it has historically been the case that contingency fees were unlawful on public policy grounds. Indeed until 1967:

- *maintenance* – the improper financial assistance by one person to another in prosecuting or defending proceedings in which the person rendering the assistance has no legitimate interest;

and

- *champerty*: aggravated maintenance whereby a third party provides assistance to a party in return for a promise of a share in the proceeds or subject matter of the action;

were *criminal* offences.

Thus no win no fee agreements were champertous and thus the solicitor committed a criminal offence, as well as a tortious act.

The Criminal Law Act 1967 abolished both the criminal offences and the torts of champerty and maintenance. However, that Act expressly preserved the invalidity of champertous agreements. Section 14(2) provided that:

> The abolition of criminal and civil liability under the law of England and Wales for maintenance and champerty shall not affect any rule of that law as to the cases in which a contract is to be treated as contrary to public policy or otherwise illegal.

Thus contingency fee agreements remained unlawful and unenforceable on public policy grounds.

As the Vice-Chancellor Sir Richard Scott said in his judgment in *Bevan Ashford* v *Geoff Yeandle (Contractors) Limited (in Liquidation)* 8 April 1998:

> There were many critics of this state of affairs. Contingency fee agreements had been for a long time not only permissible but the norm in the United States for the prosecution of speculative monetary claims, whether contractual or tortious. Contingency fee agreements were permissible in Scotland. The rising cost of litigation and its effect in depriving citizens who fall outside the financial limits of Legal Aid eligibility of access to the civil courts led to an increasing demand for some form of contingency fee agreements to be available for use in this country in civil litigation.

In 1990 Parliament passed the Courts and Legal Services Act which we have examined. As stated earlier in this chapter, it was apparent that this cast grave doubts on the rights of the Courts, the Law Society and the Bar to use "public policy" arguments to justify the ban on contingency fees.

Section 58(3) of the Act took conditional fee agreements out of the class of illegal and unenforceable champertous agreements.

Five years later the Order and Regulations were passed and, as we have seen, conditional fees began.

Outside those limited areas sanctioned by Parliament in the 1995 Statutory Instruments – that is personal injury, insolvency and European Human Rights Cases – the old law remained.

Not only did that old law render any contingency fee agreement unenforceable against one's own client but it prevented recovery of costs from the other side in any circumstances outside those three areas.

Thus it had been held in *Gundry* v *Sainsbury* (1910) 1 KB 645 that only costs actually incurred by the client could be recovered from the other side.

A significant exception, which continues to be very important, was made in *Adams* v *London Improved Limited* (1921) 1 KB 495 when it was held that a client who is indemnified in respect of his own costs by a trade union or an insurer *could* recover costs from the other side.

Generally, however, and in spite of Parliment's stated view in 1990, the Courts operated the rule extremely harshly. Thus in *Mainwaring* v *Goldtech* (*The Times,* 19th February 1991) a solicitor was ordered to pay the other side's costs personally when he had maintained an action for an impecunious party who could not meet a Judgment or pay the other side's costs and in *McFarlane* v *E E Caledonia Limited* (Times Law Reports 8 December 1994) a non-party, Quantum Claims Compensation Limited, was ordered to pay the costs of a champertous action.

However some senior Judges began to see it differently.

In *Tolstoy-Miloslavsky* v *Aldington* (Court of Appeal 13 December 1995) Lord Justice Rose said:

> It is in the public interest and it has always been recognised that it is proper for counsel and solicitors to act without fee. The access to justice which this can provide for example in cases outside the scope of legal aid confers a benefit on the public. Section 58 of the Courts and Legal Services Act which legitimises conditional fees inferentially demonstrates Parliament's recognition of this principle. For it would be very curious if a legal representative on a contingent fee and therefore with a financial interest in the outcome of litigation could resist an order for costs against himself but one acting for no fee could not.

In *Connelly* v *RTZ Corp plc* 24 July 1997 the House of Lords had to decide whether the case should be held in Namibia or England

and Wales and amongst the reasons for choosing England and Wales was the availability of conditional fee agreements.

So the tide began to turn but solicitors were still faced with the indemnity rule acting to prevent them recovering costs from the other side if there was no primary liability on the client to pay, win or lose. Thus in *British Waterways Board* v *Norman* [1993] (26 HLR 232) the solicitors agreed to act for an impecunious woman who brought a private prosecution under the Environmental Protection Act 1990. The firm told her "not to worry" if the court refused to make a costs order in her favour.

The court held that no costs would be ordered where there was an agreement *express or implied* that the solicitors would only look to the client for costs if the case succeeded.

Thus the long-standing practice of solicitors taking cases on a speculative basis was effectively ended.

In *Aratra Potato Company Limited* v *Taylor Joynson Garrett* (1995) 4 AllER 695 the firm offered a fee package whereby clients were given a discount of 20% for all lost cases. The firm's own client, who had been billed on that basis after substantial litigation work had been carried out, then sought to set aside the agreement and escape payment for *all* fees on the basis that the agreement was a contingency fee agreement not covered by the Courts and Legal Services Act 1990 and thus contrary to public policy and unenforceable. The High Court agreed and freed the client from payment of *all* fees although it did not actually order fees already paid to be returned.

On February 27th 1998 the Court of Appeal gave its judgment in *Thai Trading* v *Taylor*. The full judgment is at Appendix 24 of this book.

The Court ruled that the *British Waterways Board* v *Norman* and the *Aratra Potato* case were wrongly decided, and ruled that an agreement to act on a no win no fee basis in any litigation is lawful, enforceable against one's client *and* that costs could be recovered from the other side. The only restriction is that the solicitor cannot change a "success fee" for winning, that is cannot seek charge *over and above* his normal fees.

It should be noted that the principle that a party can only recover from the other side the costs that he is liable to pay his own solicitor remains intact. Thus if the letter of engagement states £100 per hour as the fee then that is the limit of recovery even if the local court allows £120 per hour.

Likewise the "Green Form Trap" is unaffected.

What *has* gone is the concept that the client had to have a real liability to his own solicitor, *win or lose,* before recovering costs on a win.

I have always said that "no win no fee" arrangements cannot, as a matter of logic, fall foul of the indemnity principle because there *is* a liability on the client's part to pay in the event of a *win* and that is the only event which will lead to costs being sought against the other side. It was the bar on contingency fees which caused the problem. Their apparent illegality on public policy grounds meant that in fact there was no liability on a client to pay his own solicitor even in the event of a win because the contract was unlawful and therefore unenforceable.

That is precisely what Lord Justice Millett decided in the *Thai Trading* case:

> In a judgment for which I should wish to express my respectful admiration the Judge pointed out that, if the law relating to the recovery of contingent fees be put on one side, the so-called indemnity principle did not avail the Plaintiffs. Even if there was an express agreement that Mr Taylor would be paid his profit costs only if Mrs Taylor won her case, she would still be entitled to be indemnified against a legal liability which had been incurred in the events which had happened. The fact that she would have incurred no liability in a different event which had not happened would not affect this.

The Court went on to say:

> There is nothing in the Solicitors Act 1974 which prohibits the charging of contingent fees. Section 59(2) merely provides that nothing in the Act shall give validity to arrangements of the kind there specified. It does not legitimize such arrangements if they are otherwise unlawful, but neither does it make them unlawful if they are otherwise lawful.

Thus the Court formed the view that the real question was whether there were now public policy reasons for preventing no win no fee agreements and came strongly to the view that it is positively *in the public interest* to have such arrangements.

After a very extensive review of the authorities the Court said:

> It is time to step back and consider the matter afresh in the light of modern conditions. I start with three propositions. First, if it is contrary to public policy for a lawyer to have a financial interest in the outcome of a suit this is because (and only because) of the temptations to which it exposes him. At best he may lose his professional objectivity; at worst he may be persuaded to attempt to pervert the course of justice. Secondly there is nothing improper in a lawyer acting in a case for a meritorious client who

to his knowledge cannot afford to pay his costs if the case is lost. Not only is this not improper; it is in accordance with current notions of the public interest that he should do so. Thirdly if the temptation to win at all costs is present at all it is present whether or not the lawyer has formally waived his fees if he loses. It arises from his knowledge that in practice he will not be paid unless he wins.

Accordingly, either it is improper for a solicitor to act in litigation for a meritorious client who cannot afford to pay him if he loses or it is not improper for a solicitor to agree to act on the basis that he is to be paid his ordinary costs if he wins but not if he loses. I have no hesitation in concluding that the second of these propositions represents the current state of the law.

I reach this conclusion for several reasons. In the first place, I do not understand why it is assumed that the effect of the arrangement being unlawful is that the solicitor is unable to recover his proper costs in any circumstances. Where the solicitor contracts for a reward over and above his proper fees if he wins, it may well be that the whole retainer is unlawful and the solicitor can recover nothing. But where he contracts for no more than his proper fees if he wins, this result does not follow. There is nothing unlawful in the retainer or in the client's obligation to pay the solicitor's proper costs if he wins the case. If there is anything unlawful it is in the waiver or reduction of the fees if he loses. On ordinary principles the result of holding this to be unlawful is that the client is liable for the solicitor's proper costs even if he loses the case. I regard *Aratra Potator Co. Ltd* v *Taylor* as wrongly decided.

In the second place, it is in my judgment fanciful to suppose that a solicitor will be tempted to compromise his professional integrity because he will be unable to recover his ordinary profit costs in a small case if the case is lost. Solicitors are accustomed to withstand far greater incentives to impropriety than this. The solicitor who acts for a multinational company in a heavy commercial action knows that if he loses the case his client may take his business elsewhere.

Current attitudes to these questions are exemplified by the passage into law of the Courts and Legal Services Act 1990. This shows that the fear that lawyers may be tempted by having a financial incentive in the outcome of litigation to act improperly is exaggerated, and that there is a countervailing public policy in making justice readily accessible to persons of modest means. Legislation was needed to authorise the increase in the lawyer's reward over and above his ordinary profit costs.

It by no means follows that it was needed to legitimise the long-standing practice of solicitors to act for meritorious clients without means, and it is in the public interest that they should continue to do so.

There is nothing unlawful in a solicitor acting for a party to litigation to agree to forego all or part of his fee if he loses, provided that he does not seek to recover more than his ordinary profit costs and disbursements if he wins.

Solicitors Practice Rules

In spite of the Court of Appeals' decision the Law Society has reminded Solicitors (*Law Society's Gazette* 25th March 1998) that Thai Trading agreements still amount to a contingency fee as defined in Practice Rule 8 of the Solicitors Practice Rules and solicitors taking on such cases are in breach of Practice Rule 8 even though the Court of Appeal has said that it is positively in the public interest to have lawyers acting in this way.

The Law Society has now re-examined this rule which, as Lord Justice Millett pointed out, is based on a perception of public policy which is now wrong. It is to be amended to allow contingency fee arrangements where permitted under statue or common law. (*Law Society's Gazette* 10th June 1998)

The case of *Bevan Ashford* v *Geoff Yeandle (Contractors) Limited (In Liquidation), The Times* 23 April 1998, is concerned with the lawfulness of a success fee in non-conditional fee cases, and not with the indemnity principle as such, and is discussed in detail in Chapter 2 "What Can I do?"

Disbursements And Cash-Flow

Disbursements And Cash-Flow

Introduction

One of the main disadvantages of working on a conditional fee basis in personal injury work compared with working under a Legal Aid certificate is the absence of payments on account of disbursements and, less importantly, payments on account of costs.

It always should be remembered that conditional fees are not an alternative to Legal Aid and in most cases where the client has a nil contribution the client will still be better getting Legal Aid.

However the Government's Consultation Paper *Access to Justice with Conditional Fees* (4th March 1998) proposes the abolition of Legal Aid in personal injury work (except medical negligence). Thus conditional fee clients generally represent extra work to the firm or are clients who would have been dealt with on a "speculative funding" basis previously where precisely the same problems arise.

Because the overwhelming majority of plaintiffs in personal injury actions are successful the risk to the solicitor's business is non-existent as conditional fees allow the solicitor to expand the work and charge an increased fee in 95% or so of cases that are successful. This more than makes up for the costs in the cases lost.

Thus conditional fee work in personal injury cases presents problems of *cash-flow* and not problems of *profitability*. This nevertheless is a serious problem. It is often said that most businesses that go under do so with a full order book.

Minimising Cash-Flow Problems

Disbursements

The best policy for a firm is to try and get the client to pay as many of the disbursements as possible as the case proceeds but for the firm to be prepared to pay the disbursements if a client cannot afford them.

If Legal Aid is abolished for personal injury work the position is likely to change as marketing will be targeted at everyone, including for example those on benefit who will have no possibility of being able to afford medical report fees *etc*. Until then assume that anyone who does not qualify for legal aid, even with a contribution, can afford to pay *something* towards the disbursements. It does not have to be "all or nothing". Solicitor and client can agree that the client will pay, say, half of the cost of disbursements.

This is not simply a cash-flow question – it also gives the client a financial interest in co-operating with the solicitor and pushing ahead with the case to recover the disbursements paid out, win or lose. Clients failing to co-operate with the solicitor represent a greater risk of the solicitor not getting paid than losing cases.

The initial disbursements in any case are predictable, for example:

- Police Report fee
- GP's Report fee
- Medical expert's fee
- Medical records fees

Monthly Payments

The client should be told in writing as early as possible about these disbursements, their value and when they are likely to need to be paid. This gives clients an opportunity to budget and if appropriate solicitors should offer to accept monthly payments beginning immediately to build up a fund to pay these disbursements; the client continuing the monthly payments until the disbursements have been paid for. This can appear a particularly attractive option to a client faced with deciding whether or not to accept an offer of Legal Aid with a high monthly contribution. Faced with the prospect of paying say £70 per month for the life of the case to the Legal Aid Board which will not be recovered in the event of defeat and indeed will lay him open to paying an identical sum to the other side, or paying say £30 per month for 18 months, knowing that it will be recovered win or lose, the client is likely to prefer the latter.

Credit Cards

Virtually everyone uses credit cards on a regular basis, particularly for more substantial purchases and yet few solicitors offer this facility to their clients. Credit card payments are treated as cash and can be drawn against immediately and typically the solicitor will pay 3–4% of the value to the credit card company.

Thus if the disbursements in a case are £500 and the client pays them all by credit card then it will cost the solicitor £20 since in effect receipts are £480 from the credit card company, but the experts will want paying their full fee of £500. However, including the success fee, the average profit costs charged on personal injury work should be at least £3,000 per case, until the introduction of the Woolf Report reforms, probably in October 1999, when this figure is likely to fall.

Thus it will be seen that if by operating user-friendly methods of paying for disbursements one extra case is brought into practice this covers the cost of 150 clients paying their disbursements by credit card.

The credit card facility is attractive to clients across the solicitor's practice and not just in conditional fee work or personal injury work.

Solicitor Funding the Disbursements

Let us again assume that the total disbursements in the case are £500 but this time the client can pay nothing towards them, either by monthly instalments or by credit card payments and thus this is the worst case scenario for the solicitor's cash-flow.

Provided proceedings are issued, the disbursements will be recovered: from the other side in the event of a win and the insurers in the event of a defeat. Thus the solicitor is *lending* the client the money and not *giving* the client the money, win or lose.

The disbursements should not be outstanding on average for more than six months and assuming the solicitor is paying around 10% interest the cost sustained is £25: £500 at 10% per annum = £50 divided by 2 = £25.

Thus by this method of funding each extra case attracted to the practice pays for 120 interest free loans to clients. To put it another way:

If you were allowed to, and there were no ethical or moral issues, would you pay £25 for the introduction of a case that you will ultimately bill at £3,000?

Charging Interest to Clients

This can be done but in view of the small amounts of interest involved I do not believe it worth setting up the systems and calculating the interest let alone risking the clients' goodwill.

Let us say you recover £5,000 for your client and of course you receive your costs from the other side. You charge the client £1,250 being the agreed maximum 25% of the damages and you then add on a bill for £25 interest. If I was a client I would have expected the solicitor to absorb that in the 25% of damages taken.

No win – no fee on disbursements

This is a more radical idea whereby the client pays absolutely nothing, so the solicitor pays the insurance premium and the disbursements as they are incurred. If the case is won then the solicitor recovers the disbursements, but not necessarily the insurance premium, from the other side. If the insurance premium is not recovered from the other side then it is taken out of the client's damages. (The Government's Consultation Paper *Access to Justice with Conditional Fees* proposes to make the insurance premium a recoverable disbursement in all cases.)

In addition in relation to a winning client the solicitor takes an extra fee, say £50, to cover such matters as interest and the risk of losing and thus funding the insurance premium. The losing client pays literally nothing at all and the solicitor recovers disbursements, but definitely not the insurance premium, from the insurers.

The benefit of this last system is that it is truly "no win – no fee" and can be advertised as such without qualification (see further Chapter 21 *Marketing*) and is likely to be very attractive to clients especially to those who currently qualify for free legal aid which is likely to be removed.

The disadvantages are that the clients, having literally nothing to pay, may present much weaker cases to the solicitor and may be less willing to accept the solicitors refusal to take the case on as the client has literally nothing to lose.

This further problem is unlikely to be a significant one as in spite of the widespread availability of initial free interviews we know that the vast majority of clients who have had an accident never take any, even free, legal advice and thus it is apparent that clients themselves filter out virtually all weak claims and indeed filter out most of the ones they are bound to win!

The other disadvantage of the scheme is that it is likely to be so popular that the solicitor will in virtually all cases be funding the disbursements, albeit making a further profit at the end of the day as £50 per case on the winners more than covers the losers. However it greatly exacerbates the cash-flow problem. Even for the smallest firm a well-run marketing and advertising campaign is likely to produce a hundred new cases in eighteen months. The good news is that that is about £300,000 worth of new work – the bad news is that it is also around £50,000 in disbursements that have to be found.

Experts

Negotiating Deferred Fees

One of the simplest ways of reducing cash-flow problems is to agree with experts that payment of their fees be deferred. Thus a typical arrangement may be that the expert is paid within six months of delivery of his invoice or 14 days of receipt by the solicitor of payment for that invoice, whichever is sooner. This gives the solicitor and/or the client, whoever is paying, a substantial period of credit and a sporting chance of actually concluding the case, thus obtaining payment from the other side, before the six months is up.

Some solicitors have negotiated credit periods of six months and some have reached agreement that the expert's fees will not be paid until the conclusion of the case. This latter option is becoming increasingly common. The Bond Solon Solicitors' Survey on Expert Witnesses (June 1998) shows that 34% of solicitors' Survey on Expert Witnesses (June 1998) shows that 34% of solicitors have instructed experts on a deferred fee basis.

A firm marketing conditional fee work will increase its caseload considerably. In the example I gave above the extra 100 cases in eighteen months results in £50,000 disbursements having to be found. Where do they go? Well mainly to the experts of course.

Thus solicitors are in strong bargaining positions with experts and should use that bargaining power. As the disbursements are effectively covered, either by winning or by the insurance policy in the event of losing, I concentrate on obtaining deferred payment rather than reducing the fees. This is far more attractive to the expert and it is the funding of the credit which is the problem for solicitors and not the actual level of disbursements. Not having to find £500 until the end of a case usually is better than having to find £400 straight away.

It is worth making the point to the experts that the money is absolutely safe and that neither the client nor the solicitor will end up paying it.

No Win – No Fee

I believe the day will come when experts will work on a no win – no fee basis in the same way as solicitors *i.e.* if a case is lost they charge nothing but if it is won they charge an enhanced fee. My post-bag shows a number of experts moving towards this system. The June 1998 Bond Solon Survey shows that 13% of solicitors have instructed experts on a no win – no fee basis and 50% of solicitors thought experts should be able to work in this way.

There are arguments for and against this development, the main one against being that experts should remain impartial and this will compromise their impartiality. However experts are already widely regarded as "hired guns". (see, for example, *The Woolf Report*). Mark Solon of Bond Solon shares this view.

Interestingly this has not happened in the United States where experts get paid in any event and do not generally work on a contingency fee basis. As one American Lawyer put it to me:

> You don't mess with the experts.

Indeed in the United States law report headnotes contain, as a matter of course, the names of the experts as well as the lawyers! Having said that, in certain States there are Bar-approved "ethical contingency fee programmes" so for example experts advertise to lawyers with the message

> "offers your client the option of fee for service or Bar-approved ethical contingency fee programs."

What a lot of experts *will* do already in this country is to offer a free or low-cost screening service to weed out, quickly and cheaply the weak cases.

This happens in the United States, where expert advertisements for "free case analysis" or "free initial case consultation" are common.

Another variation in the United States is the Expert Witness Consultants who will consider the case and put the lawyer in touch with an appropriate expert and then make an introduction charge if the lawyer instructs the expert. This has been taken a step further whereby some consultants will contact the appropriate experts to determine if the case has potential merit. If it does not, then no fee is paid. If it does have merit then an introduction fee is paid.

Another, possibly more questionable, practice in the United States is to prepare a report whereby a charge is only raised if it is favourable. This leads to such advertisements as:

GUARANTEED FAVOURABLE MEDICAL EXPERT OPINIONS

OR

YOU DON'T PAY A PENNY

The Future

The role of experts is likely to change and in particular their fees are likely to drop as a result of the changes proposed in the Woolf Report and to Legal Aid. A full discussion of these matters is beyond the scope of this book but suffice to say the days when an expert delivered an invoice and the tab was picked up by the Legal Aid Board are going for ever.

Once the solicitor has to directly fund the disbursements then things will change. The Bond Solon Expert Witness Survey 1997 showed that as at Autumn 1997 55 out of 800 respondents (9.3%) had actually worked on a contingency fee basis already: a figure that is bound to rise as Legal Aid is removed. 516 out of 595 (86.7%)

did Legal Aid work so a lot of experts are going to have to change or go hungry.

In any event the use of experts is likely to decline dramatically if the Woolf Report proposals are implemented in full. This too will have an impact on expert fees and terms on engagement.

One point should be noted concerning medical records fees. The cost of these adds up. Some orthopaedic surgeons pay these fees themselves and then include them in a single charge to the solicitor whereas others leave the solicitor to pay the individual charges.

Although the overall cost is higher, when the orthopaedic surgeon pays for everything it benefits the solicitor because payment of the fees records is deferred until payment of the orthopaedic surgeon's fee is due. Furthermore there is less chance of what can be numerous different charges being missed when the solicitor prepares the bill for the other side.

There are maximum fees for medical records under the Access to Medical Records Act and solicitors should make themselves familiar with these, and enforce them against doctors and Health Trusts.

Other Disbursements

As at the time of writing the police have not yet been privatised and thus fees for the Police Report and Court Fee will have to be paid as and when they due, *i.e.* payment cannot be deferred. Court fees are now a significant element of the costs of the case but there are exemptions for clients on certain benefits and the scope of those exemptions is likely to be increased. Thus where a client is in receipt of benefit the solicitor should find out if court fee exemption is available.

Counsel's Fees

I deal with these in Chapter 16

Work In Progress

Extra clients means extra files that need servicing and sooner or later that means extra staff and a larger salary bill. Typically you will not get paid for eighteen months to two years after the client first walks in the door.

Thus there will be cash-flow implications of carrying work in progress. However, this is a problem common to any expanding business and needs to be seen in that context. It is *not* a cash-flow problem caused by bad management, failure to bill on time, failure to collect bills etc. but by *expansion.*

If your firm has an existing personal injury practice there are almost bound to be a number of files which could be finished off with concentrated effort. It is probably that at any one time at least 10% of files in anyone's cabinet are capable of immediate settlement *i.e.* all the information has been gathered and the parties are close enough that a few phonecalls and some negotiations will settle the matter.

A concentrated effort on those files will pay a new solicitor's salary for a year. Get your new solicitor to concentrate on finishing those matters off and, somewhat bizarrely, you will find your cash-flow improves when you take on the new lawyer.

The Bank

Once the conditional fees and extra success fees start rolling in, the cash-flow problem largely takes care of itself. Not only is the firm generating extra profit but as a case closes borrowings for the disbursements are also paid off. Nevertheless there is likely to be a period when cash-flow is a problem and the answer is to talk to the bank.

The extent of the average solicitor's business and budget forecast is to notice when the overdraft is about to go over the limit and to pick up the phone to the bank manager. Curiously the banks are less than impressed by this method of running what can be a substantial business.

Conditional fees in personal injury cases represent a tremendous opportunity for solicitors. They are both profitable to the solicitor and extremely popular with clients. The financial implications are *cash-flow* and not *profitability* ones and these can be overcome by planning and budgeting and if necessary, borrowing.

The Law Society has reached an agreement with Guinness Mahon, a merchant bank, whereby solicitors can borrow to fund disbursements. The interest rate is not very attractive and the solicitor remains liable to the bank. There is little or no advantage as against firms borrowing from their own bank, save that it is a different source of money.

However if firms are having trouble borrowing from their own bank to finance disbursements in conditional fee work, that indicates underlying problems with the firm's profitability which will not be solved merely by going to another, probably more expensive, source of funding.

Solicitors with no underlying problems should not lose this opportunity because of the fear of the short-term effect on the overdraft.

Chapter 18

Counsel

In ordinary civil litigation cases Counsel's fees are regarded as a disbursement in the same way as a Court fee or medical report fee and thus a winning Plaintiff in a personal injury case recovers Counsel's fees as a disbursement on top of his own solicitor's fees. This is about to change and in effect Counsel's fees will become part of the overheads of running a solicitors office in the same way as costs draftsman's fees or accountant's fees are.

The Woolf Report treats Counsel's fees in the fast track procedure in that way and as the fast track is now to cover all claims up to £15,000 (plus straight-forward claims above that amount) this covers the vast majority of personal injury claims. As conditional fees are extended to other areas of civil litigation, this limit will also cover the vast majority of claims in those areas.

Under the Woolf Report fixed cost scheme in fast track cases a fixed advocacy fee will be paid to the advocate and a solicitor is not free to negotiate a low fee with a young barrister and pocket the rest. If Counsel is instructed, then the advocacy fee goes to counsel and the solicitor will receive nothing extra for instructing Counsel, attending conferences with Counsel or attending court on the trial of the matter.

If the solicitor undertakes the advocacy then obviously he or she gets the whole of that advocacy fee.

In block funded legal aid contracts the position will be the same, *i.e.* if the solicitor receives £100,000 per year to do all of the personal injury work in the town of Painsville and he pays out £20,000 in counsel's fees then he has the balance of £80,000. If he does all of the pleadings and advocacy himself then he retains the whole £100,000. Decisions on whether to instruct Counsel are a matter for each practice but clear arrangements should be made with the client as to what is to happen in the event of Counsel being instructed.

If the barrister is to be paid on an ordinary basis, that is not on a conditional fee basis, then his or her fees are payable win or lose.

In the event of winning there is little problem as most, if not all, of the barrister's fees will be recovered from the other side and normally a deal can be done with Counsel's Clerk to waive the rest.

Any shortfall would be small and should in my view be paid out of the solicitor's success fee unless the client has insisted on Counsel in which case the client should be liable for any shortfall.

The problem arises if the case is lost.

Again if the client has insisted on Counsel being instructed then the client should be responsible for all of the barrister's fees and this must be made clear at the beginning of the case before the issue of whether or not to instruct Counsel arises. Thus those firms of solicitors which generally carry out their own advocacy should explain this to their clients and explain that if they want a barrister instructed then they will be responsible for the barrister's fees.

What needs to be made absolutely clear is that Accident Line Protect Insurance does *not* cover counsel's fees and thus Accident Line Protect already regard Counsel's fees as part of the overheads of a solicitors practice and *not* disbursements. Thus if a case is lost then all of the other disbursements will be picked up by Accident Line Protect **but Counsel's fees will not.** It is crucial that this is made crystal clear to clients at the outset.

If the solicitors choose to instruct Counsel because they do not like, or do not feel competent enough to prepare pleadings, advices *etc.*, and to appear in court then in my view those fees should be borne by the solicitor. If a client comes to a solicitor on a "no win – no fee" basis then that's precisely what it should be unless the *client* insists on Counsel being instructed. In my experience this is very rare as clients prefer one person to be responsible for the case from "soup to nuts" *i.e.* from beginning to end.

In the vast majority of personal injury cases there will be no problems as the cases will be won, but the position will be different as conditional fee arrangements spread to other, riskier, areas.

An alternative is, of course, to instruct Counsel on a conditional fee basis but many at the Bar are hostile to conditional fees.

I understand their concerns in this area as they are likely to have a much higher percentage of doubtful cases amongst their workload. Whereas a solicitor will win around 95% of the personal injury cases in which he or she is instructed the percentage for Counsel is likely to be significantly lower and therefore there will be a much greater chance on any given case of them receiving no payment.

It would be helpful if the Bar gave detailed figures of precisely what percentage of cases are won, and at what stage, by barristers acting on behalf of plaintiffs in personal injury cases as then the Law

Society and the Bar Council might stand a chance of reaching an acceptable form of agreement.

I propose an alternative system. I am old enough to remember the old Legal Aid System in the Magistrates' Court which was that irrespective of who did the work the barrister and solicitor split the fee equally. Sometimes this worked to the solicitor's advantage and sometime to Counsel's advantage. For example where a solicitor had done a lot of work preparing a matter for trial but the client then pleaded guilty at court, the barrister got a good fee for relatively little work whereas if it was a "brief at court" the solicitor got half the fee for doing very little.

I am not recommending a return to what were often very poor instructions given by solicitors to Counsel but the principle of taking the rough with the smooth is a fair and workable one. Thus Counsel is instructed to advise on quantum and he advises that the appropriate figure is £20,000. Shortly after the matter settles for that sum and the solicitors success fee is £5,000. Solicitor and Counsel share this fee and thus Counsel receives £2,500, plus whatever can be got from the other side, for an advice on quantum.

Quite frequently Counsel will do very little work but receive a good fee. Take a more typical case where the quantum figure is £4,000 and therefore the success fee is £1,000 split between the barrister and solicitor, *i.e.* £500 each. That still represents a substantial fee for an advice on quantum.

Exactly the same principles apply to pleadings and in any case where Counsel has been instructed and the matter then settles the barrister is likely to do very well out of this system. It is of course unlikely that a barrister will do only a small amount of work in a *losing* case, by definition those cases are likely to go to trial and then be lost.

Obviously there will be cases where Counsel says "forget it" and the solicitor and client take that advice and the barrister receives no fee but has done little work. However the Bar's concern, which I fully understand, is the frequency with which they will go to trial, lose and get nothing for a great deal of work.

I believe that my proposal addresses this problem although it works in a rather different way.

Conditional fees for solicitors give them, in practice, a relatively small uplift but on virtually all of the cases. For the Bar they will get their uplift on significantly fewer cases but that uplift will be much greater. The Bar's hostility to conditional fees is a matter for them but they are now flying in the face of almost everyone including the last Lord Chancellor, the present Lord Chancellor, Sir Peter Middleton, The Consumers Association and most important of all the clients themselves.

My scheme also has the added benefit of simplicity for clients. They pay nothing if they lose and if they win they pay a maximum of 25% of the damages to the solicitor and it will be a matter of no concern to them as to how that success fee is split between Counsel and the solicitor.

The Law Society's Model Conditional Fee Agreement between solicitors and clients in personal injury matters deals with advocacy in the following terms:

6.   *Payment for Advocacy*
     The cost of advocacy and any other work by us, or by a solicitor agent on our behalf, forms part of our basic costs.

     Barristers who have a Conditional Fee Agreement with us
     If you win, their fee is our disbursement which can be covered from your opponent. You must pay the Barrister's uplift fee shown in the separate Conditional Fee Agreement we make with the Barrister. We will discuss the Barrister's uplift fee with you before we instruct him or her. If you lose, you pay nothing.

     Barristers who do not have a Conditional Fee Agreement with us
     If you lose and you have not been paying the Barrister's fees on account, we are liable to pay them. Because of this, we add an extra success fee if you win. This extra success fee is not added if you have been paying the Barrister's fees on account. If you win, you are liable to pay the Barrister's fees. See "Success Fee" in the Agreement.

     Other points concerning Barristers
     If you chose a Barrister we do not recommend, we may decide not to seek a conditional fee agreement with him or her. The points in the previous paragraph will then apply.
     If we ask a Barrister to provide advice or to draft documents, the fees will be treated as set out in this condition.

If you reject our advice to use a Barrister, you may not compel us to provide advocacy ourselves. Following our refusal to provide advocacy, we can end the agreement if you still reject our advice to use a Barrister.

It should be borne in mind that the total success fee cannot exceed 100% of the basic costs and thus if you insert that figure in the agreement then the figure for the extra success fee must be 0% as the total must not exceed 100%. As we have seen all of this is irrelevant as it will be the cap that bites and determines the total fund available to the solicitor and barrister by way of a success fee.

It should be noted that the restriction on increasing the solicitor's fees by no more than 100% does not apply to arrangements between solicitors and Counsel and thus Counsel can be "over" compensated as I have suggested in any individual case to make up for the fact that the Bar has a far higher percentage of losers (cases, that is, not barristers!)

Another benefit of the system I propose is that it will work in other areas of civil litigation where the result is far less predictable, that is where the Plaintiff success rate is far lower. At present a number of individual barristers, particularly in chambers outside London, are coming to individual arrangements with instructing solicitors in personal injury cases. A common arrangement is that the barrister will get no fee in the event of a defeat but will have his or her fee increased by 25% in the event of a win. Of course the basic Counsel's fee is likely to be recovered from the other side in the event of a win and therefore the extra cost to the solicitor is just the additional 25%.

If the solicitor caps his or her own success fee at 25% of damages, as virtually all solicitors do, then before the solicitor has to eat into basic costs to pay counsel's extra fee the barrister's *normal* fee must *exceed* the damages, which is extremely unlikely.

Example

	£
Award	10,000
Solicitor 25% share	2,500
Counsel's fee	10,000
Counsel's success fee (25%)	2,500

Result: All of solicitor's capped success fee goes to Counsel.

Solicitors may consider it worthwhile stipulating that Counsel's *success fee* shall never exceed the solicitor's own capped success fee thus ensuring that Counsel's success fee never eats into the solicitor's *basic costs* as opposed to the solicitor's success fee.

Solicitor and Counsel should in any event be clear at the outset as to who will do what work, *i.e.* will solicitor or counsel attend interlocutory hearings etc. If both the instructing solicitors and Counsel want to make conditional fees work then they will. If not then there is only going to be one loser and that is the Bar.

At Appendix 28 is the Second Model Agreement (April 1998) prepared by the Association of Personal Injury Lawyers and the Personal Injury Bar Association.

Industrial Tribunals

Industrial Tribunals

Introduction

Industrial tribunal work, including advocacy and all preparation and all connected matters are classed as *non-contentious business* and thus can be funded by way of *contingency* fee agreements.

Many solicitors still doubt that this is the case (see Chapter 2 *What Can I Do?* for a detailed examination of this topic). To reassure you I quote from the *Law Society's Gazette* 93/37 9th October 1996 "Question of Ethics" feature:

Q. "Can I do industrial tribunal work on a contingency fee basis?"

A. "Yes. The restrictions on contingency fees in practice rule 8 only apply to contentious matters. Proceedings before tribunals, other than the Lands Tribunal and the Employment Appeal Tribunal, are non-contentious and, therefore, the restrictions on contingency fees do not apply. You must, of course, ensure that your fees are fair and reasonable."

That, I hope, settles the matter.

There is little doubt that in the near future the majority of civil litigation will be dealt with under a fixed or no-costs regime with lawyers charging their own clients an extra fee for winning. Thus the methods of working in employment on a no win – no fee basis are very much more relevant to civil litigators than conditional fees in personal injury work. If you can operate a no win – no fee employment department profitably you should have little difficulty in dealing with all civil litigation profitably in a post Woolf world.

If you cannot do so then you are likely to have considerable problems from October 1999 onwards.

Appeals

Note that an appeal to the Employment Appeal Tribunal from the decision of an Industrial Tribunal *cannot* be dealt with under a Contingency Fee Agreement. However the proposed extension of *conditional* fees to all civil proceedings is likely to change this situation and it is possible that *contingency* fees will be available in Industrial Tribunals and *conditional* fees in the Employment Appeal Tribunal. A Thai Trading agreement whereby a solicitor agrees to charge his or her normal fee in the event of a win but nothing in the event of a defeat may already be used in the Employment Appeal Tribunal. No extra "success fee" may be charged for winning in a Thai Trading agreement.

At the end of this chapter is a Model Contingency Fee Agreement for use in Industrial Tribunal cases (at page 203).

Jurisdiction

The jurisdiction of Industrial Tribunals is enormous and new cases are running at around 100,000 per year representing a huge potential market for solicitors operating on a no win – no fee basis. Even this figure is likely to rise dramatically with the introduction of the Working Time Directive, the minimum wage and the Government's proposed reduction of the qualifying period for unfair dismissal from 2 years to 1 year. Legal Aid is not available although the Green Form scheme is available for advice *but not* advocacy. Since the abolition of the contributory Green Form Scheme few people now qualify. For those who do I set out later in this chapter details of how use of the Green Form can be combined with no win – no fee arrangements in Industrial Tribunal work. Note also that it is proposed to restrict Green Form work in *all* cases (except matrimonial) to between 100 and 200 firms nationwide. My clear advice is to get out of all Green Form work now.

Because of the non-availability of Legal Aid and the fact that by definition most potential Applicants have lost their job, relatively few Applicants to Industrial Tribunals are legally represented even though this is by far the most complex common area of law. Compare this with personal injury law, which is relatively straightforward and where liability is not normally in dispute, and you will realise that there is a great unmet demand for lawyers in employment work.

The reason that demand is unmet is because of costs. Contingency fee arrangements solve that problem. Competent employment lawyers operating on a no win – no fee basis are flooded with work. However employment work involves very different considerations from personal injury work which is where most no win – no fee firms will have tested the water.

The Applicant success rate is very much lower than in personal injury work. The success rate varies enormously depending upon the particular jurisdiction but taken overall it is around 50%[1].

Consequently risk assessment is very different (See Chapter 6 *Risk? What Risk?* for risk assessment in personal injury work. That chapter most definitely does *not* apply to employment law.)

Thus employment law is an interesting test area for other areas of civil litigation, such as contract, building disputes, *etc.* where the success rate is very much lower than in personal injury work. When conditional fees are extended to these, riskier, areas risk assessment becomes much more relevant.

Furthermore no costs are generally recoverable from the loser in Industrial Tribunal cases and thus it is a forerunner of Woolf Report fast-track cases where fixed, and often uneconomic, costs will be recoverable from the other side.

Efficiency

Well everybody believes in efficiency but of course under the blank-cheque system lawyers get paid more for being inefficient and running up the hours. No such considerations apply when no costs are to be recovered from the other side and when fees from one's own client are dependent upon the result and not time spent, which becomes wholly irrelevant.

Thus the magic formula is to spend the minimum time consistent with achieving the maximum damages. Both the solicitor and the client have identical interests. The solicitor who cuts corners and

---

1 The figures for 1995-1996 show the disposal of all Industrial Tribunal claims to be:

Settled through ACAS	30.6%
Withdrawn	36.5%
Dismissed at Tribunal	15.3%
Successful at Tribunal	13.9%

The source is April 1997's Labour Market Trends. The figures do not add up to 100% and it is not known how many of the withdrawn cases were withdrawn upon payment by the Respondent and it is not known how many of the ACAS settlements involved no payment. Clearly those settled through ACAS are likely to contain a very much higher percentage of cases where payment was made compared with the withdrawn cases.

50:50 is probably about right. Interestingly and significantly and in marked contrast to the view held by the public most Applicants at *Tribunals* lose.

jeopardises the outcome risks losing and getting no fee or under-settling and getting a lower fee. The inefficient slow-working solicitor gets no extra fee for the extra time spent.

Level of fee-earners

The talented and skilled lawyer will thus benefit. Because of this, no win – no fee work requires a high level of fee-earner in employment work, either a solicitor or an experienced and qualified legal executive with an extensive knowledge of employment law. The dabblers and the dawdlers are better off on the hourly-rate treadmill. It is the dynamic pro-active specialists who will succeed in contingency fee work in difficult and risky areas.

Having said that a lot of employment work involves small sums of money – often only £200 or so unpaid wages or unpaid holiday pay. Solicitors almost always turn such work away. In fact it is ideal work for a trainee solicitor or legal executive to cut their teeth on in terms of preparation and advocacy and learning to work other than by the hour. Moving up the scale settlements of £750 or so can provide good fees and can be easily handled by a trainee in her second year or a more experienced legal executive.

Generally though even routine employment work requires a knowledgeable lawyer.

Advocacy

Around one-third of Industrial Tribunal claims go to trial which is a far higher percentage than any other kind of ordinary civil work. It is a waste of time even thinking about doing employment work on a contingency fee basis unless you are prepared to do the advocacy in-house.

As no fees are recoverable from the other side you will have to fund the *whole* of Counsel's fees when you win. Assuming you have been lucky enough to find a barrister to appear on a no win – no fee basis he or she will understandably want an extra fee on winning to make up for the risk of losing and getting nothing.

Bang goes the fee. I am all for "no win – no fee" but a straight "no fee" attracts me less.

In any system where no, or only fixed costs, are recoverable from the other side contracting out the advocacy to Counsel makes no sense at all. You can get by without in-house advocates in areas of work which rarely go to trial, such as personal injury, but not in employment.

Standardisation

Standard letters, standard advices, computer databases of levels of awards, ready reckoners for basic awards and redundancy awards all improve the service to the client whilst lessening the time spent on the individual case.

As an example only there is at the end of this chapter at Addenda C and D ready reckoners for basic awards and redundancy awards and a guide as to how to use them. Thus this task is reduced to seconds and the client has a copy to take home rather than having to take a note. The detailed calculations took me hours and took hours to set up but time is then saved in every case for ever more.

Under the hourly rate system the lawyer who has never bothered to prepare such a table and calculates it each time (often wrongly in my experience) gets paid more than me. Contingency fees reverse this. In my firm we have a substantial number of such forms, ready reckoners *etc.* but that will be the subject matter of another book!

Likewise having a database of awards or settlements in discrimination cases improves the service to the client whilst minimising the time spent on each file. You should never settle any case in any area of law without keeping a record of the relevant facts and the award of settlement for future use. That is how experience, knowledge, judgement and speed are developed.

Properly done standardisation improves, not lessens, the quality of service to the client.

Risk

No win – no fee means that if you lose when acting for an Applicant there is no fee. However good a lawyer you are you will never win as high a percentage of say race discrimination cases as you will say unfair dismissal cases. Thus in assessing risk regard must be had to the *type* of Industrial Tribunal case being dealt with. I set out below a list, not exhaustive, of Industrial Tribunal jurisdictions and, where known the Applicant success rate and the median award. The success rate relates to Tribunal hearings *only* and not settled or withdrawn cases. Good as you may be you will not significantly shift these percentages. In other words out of every 100 potential race cases that get as far as you around 80 will be lost. What you *can* do by careful and skilful selection is to weed out some of the losers and thus increase the percentage of winners *that you take on*.

You cannot increase the base number of winners. Thus if out of a basket of 100 race cases 20 are winners you may, by selection, change that to 20 out of say 40. You will not increase your overall fees for that work but you will reduce the amount of work you have to do in order to win the 20 cases.

This is a crucial point as standardisation and efficiency mean that you can take more risks and win more cases, albeit a lower percentage. This is because if in fact you take on 40 and not 100 cases are bound to exclude some winners and therefore some fees. Too cautious an approach means a reduced caseload and reduced fees.

1995/96

Jurisdiction	Applicant Success Rate at Trial
Unfair Dismissal	38.00%
Redundancy	68.19%
Breach of Contract	58.79%
Race Discrimination	19.40%
Sex Discrimination	37.97%
Equal Pay	43.90%
Wages Act (now Part II Employment Right Act)	63.24%

(*Note:* The raw figures were taken from Labour Market Trends, April 1997. The percentage calculations are mine.)

As far as Disability Discrimination is concerned full figures are not yet available as the Act only came into effect on 2nd December 1996. However up to 1st November 1997, that is 11 months after it came into force, 924 Industrial Tribunal Applications had been issued under the Act giving a projected figure of almost exactly 1,000 case in the first year. 60% of these cases related to dismissal. Of these a total of 378 have been disposed of as follows:

	Number	%
Applicant successful at Tribunal	9	2.38
Respondent successful at Tribunal	41	10.85
Withdrawn or settled	328	86.77
	378	100.00
of those that went to trial the figures are:		
Applicant successful at Tribunal	9	18.00
Respondent successful at Tribunal	41	82.00
	50	100.00

This is almost exactly the same percentage as race discrimination. As at June 1998 new Disability cases are running at over 200 a month.

Reward

Because of the much higher risk of losing and the fact that costs are not recoverable from the other side even in the event of a win it is common to charge 33% of damages as a fee rather than the 25% which is standard in personal injury cases.

For the reasons set out in Chapter 3 *The Success Fee and the Cap – Myth and Reality* I advise that the 33% *includes* VAT giving a net rate of 28.05%. Thus

	£
Award	10,000.00
Net costs	2,808.51
VAT thereon	491.49
Total take	3,300.00

Percentage of what?

Industrial Tribunal awards are not split into general and special damages in the way that personal injury awards are although in certain types of case, such as discrimination, the effect is the same with an award for injury to feelings and an award representing actual loss. Settlements are nearly always expressed in global terms – it is rare for the constituent elements to be separated out.

Because of these factors, and the fact that generally no costs are recoverable from the other side I advise taking 33% of the whole award or settlement irrespective of how it is made up. The only exception is in relation to recoupable benefits which are paid back to the Department of Social Security and thus never seen by the client.

Recoupment only occurs when damages are awarded by an Industrial Tribunal. If settlement is agreed then, in contrast to personal injury cases, there is no recoupment. Even if liability is bitterly contested provided the parties agree the *amount of damages* there is no recoupment of benefit. If this proves impossible and there is recoupment then the Industrial Tribunal Office, in conjunction with the Department of Social Security, calculates the sum to be recouped and does this *after* the hearing and thus the winning Applicant has to wait to see what he or she will actually receive.

In any event Recoupment does *not* apply to discrimination cases.

1995-1996 median awards by Tribunals were:

£

Race Discrimination	2,714
Sex Discrimination	2,708
Unfair Dismissal	2,499

(*Source:* Labour Market Trends April 1997)

Non-financial awards

Tribunals sometimes make non-financial awards such as reinstatement (old job back) or re-engagement (returning to the same firm but in a different capacity). Such awards are very rare but *settlement* of cases on this basis is more common[2]. I advise valuing reinstatement or re-engagement as worth three months' net pay, so if you are working on a 33% contingency fee then the fee is one month's net pay. Often the agreed reinstatement or re-engagement is part of a wider financial settlement and I believe it is easier to gross it all up and take a third.

Other non-financial awards are rare but will become less rare as the disability discrimination case law builds up and orders are made to change work practices and to make alterations to buildings.

In Disability Discrimination Act cases the solicitor and client should establish at the outset what it is that the client wants and place an agreed value upon it. For example a client with impaired

---

2   Of the cases upheld at tribunal only 0.6% resulted in an order of re-instatement or re-engagement in 1995–6. (Source: Labour Market Trends April 1997).

vision may want alterations to a building made which will allow him or her to remain in employment. That needs to be valued and again I suggest that an appropriate value is three months' net pay so that the fee, inclusive of VAT, would be one month's net pay.

Often a good reference is important to a client and again that should be valued, perhaps at one month's net pay, with the solicitor receiving 33%.

Another way of valuing non-financial awards is to give them a specific value, say £3,000 for reinstatement or re-engagement and £1,000 for a reference with the solicitor taking 33%, rather than relating it to pay.

There are of course endless permutations but generally the simpler the better, especially from a marketing point of view. The important thing is that the solicitor and the client agree the value of non-financial awards *before* the work is begun.

What is the base-line?

Frequently employment clients come in having already received an offer of settlement but wanting to secure an increase. Clearly if a client has been offered £15,000 and the solicitor secures £21,000 but charges 33% of the whole lot the client is worse off than had he accepted the original offer! Thus I advise agreeing the baseline (which with a continuing benefits package, outplacement counselling etc is not always easy) and then charging 33% of the *extra money achieved*. Thus

	£
Offer	15,000
Solicitor's Settlement	21,000
Increase achieved	6,000
Fee (33% thereof)	1,980

Resources

I do not want to concentrate on the hours spent on a file because the whole benefit of no win – no fee is that working practices improve and lawyers become more efficient and give a far better service. However it is clear that some work will always involve more resources than other work. Employment law will rarely involve the use of direct financial resources as there are no disbursements but the time spent in a case *is* variable. For example a race discrimination case will normally involve more work than an unfair dismissal case with a much higher risk of losing and a very similar average award.

By way of example let us look at two baskets, each of 100 cases, all taken on by the solicitors. One is entirely unfair dismissal cases and one is entirely race discrimination cases. 33% of damages is charged in each case.

Unfair Dismissal

Average number of wins (38%)	38	
Median award		£2,499.00
Therefore total damages 38 x 2,499 =		£94,962.00
33% thereof		£31,337.46

Race Discrimination

Average number of wins (19.4%)	19.4	
Median award		£2,714.00
Therefore total damages 19 x 2,714 =		£52,651.60
33% thereof		£17,375.03

Thus in baskets of 100 cases, all taken on, the unfair dismissal basket will produce fees of £31,337.46 whereas the race discrimination basket will produce fees of £17,375.03 a ratio of 1.8 to 1.

However if we assume that on average a race case involves three times as much work as an unfair dismissal case then *for the same resources* the lawyer dealing with unfair dismissal cases will bill three times as much and thus the figures become:

Unfair dismissal £31,337.46 x 3 =	£94,012.38
Race	£17,375.03
a ratio of 5.4 to 1.	

This combining of the 3 R's – Risk Reward and Resources is likely to be the model formula for all civil work in the future.

(In reality an employment practice is much more profitable than this because of the number of termination settlements settled very quickly for little work and high rewards. The success rate *at*

Tribunal for breach of contract cases is 58.79% and for "Wages Act" claims it is 63.24% (*Source:* Labour Market Trends, April 1997).

Special Aspects

Restrictive Covenants

If the removal of the restrictive covenants is in issue and is important to the client then a value should be placed upon their removal. This will need to be judged in each case but if this removal is necessary to allow the client to continue working, or to set up in business then the value may be high – perhaps 6 months' net pay or £15,000 with the solicitor taking 33%.

The law of contract is beyond the scope of this book but remember that a finding of unfair constructive dismissal nearly always means that restrictive covenants will fall.

Of course if High Court or County Court proceedings are actually issued then it remains unlawful to work on a contingency or conditional fee basis in employment work, although this is expected to change in the very near future, but note the decision in *Thai Trading Co (a Firm)* v *Taylor, The Times* 6th March 1998, Court of Appeal, discussed elsewhere.

Breach of contract

Note that breach of contract claims in employment matters can be brought in the High Court, County Court or Industrial Tribunal although the maximum *award* that an Industrial Tribunal can make is £25,000. Contingency fees and conditional fees remain illegal in the High Court and County Court in breach of contract cases although this is expected to change soon, but note the effect of the *Thai Trading* case.

However the availability of contingency fee arrangements in Industrial Tribunals is only one of many factors to be taken into account in considering whether to bring a breach of contract claim in the Industrial Tribunal or the High/County Court.

At Addendum B of this chapter I set out a model letter to be sent to clients advising of the options and the consideration to be taken into account and I refer you to that letter for the necessary information.

Income Tax

Whether or not any settlement is subject to income tax will depend upon a number of factors.

The combined effect of Section 148 and 188 of the Income and Corporation Taxes Act 1988 is that the first £30,000 is tax-free *unless* settlement is made in accordance with a "pay in lieu" of notice clause in an employment contract in which case it is all taxable. (See *EMI Group Electronics Ltd* v *Coldicott (Inspector of Taxes)* Chancery Division, *The Times*, 14 November 1997).

Usually only the net sum, after tax, will be paid to the employee and that net sum is normally the one cited in any agreement or settlement and should form the basis of the pool for the solicitors 33% "take". Otherwise the client stands to lose 73% of the gross sum (40% tax and 33% solicitor's fees) or expressed another way 55% of the actual sum received will go in solicitor's fees. Thus, for example:

		£
Settlement		100,000
Tax		40,000
Net sum		60,000
Solicitors fee (33% of gross sum)		33,000
Balance to client		27,000
% of net sum to solicitor	55	
% of net sum to client	45	

That will not win many friends or new clients!

Costs

Costs are generally not payable in Industrial Tribunal cases but may be awarded in certain circumstances. Schedule 1 Rule 12 of The Industrial Tribunals (Constitution and Rules of Procedure) Regulations 1993 state in part:

> Costs
> 12.-(1)
>> Where, in the opinion of the tribunal, a party has in bringing or conducting the proceedings acted frivolously, vexatiously, abusively, disruptively or otherwise unreasonably, the tribunal may make -

(a) an order containing an award against that party in respect of the costs incurred by another party;

(b) an order that that party shall pay to the Secretary of State the whole, or any part, of any allowances (other than allowances paid to members of tribunals) paid by the Secretary of State under Paragraph 10 of Schedule 9 to the 1978 Act[3] to any person for the purposes of, or in connection with, his attendance at the tribunal.

I set out the whole Costs Rule at pages 210 of this chapter but two points should be noted. Firstly the client should be warned of this potential liability to costs and Paragraph 7 of the Model Contingency Fee Agreement does so. Secondly the question should be addressed of what happens to the costs awarded *to* one's winning client.

Again our model contingency fee agreement is clear:

"If we recover costs on your behalf they belong to us. In other words, if you win, you will pay us 33% of your damages whether or not we also recover any costs from your opponent."

Because of the indemnity rule there is a potential problem in recovering costs from your opponent when you are acting on a no win – no fee basis. (See Chapter 15 *The Indemnity Principle*) Realistically your opponent is unlikely to ask unless of course they have read this book.

Appeals

Appeals to the Employment Appeal Tribunal are classed as contentious business and therefore cannot be conducted on a no win – no fee basis. This prohibition applies whether you are acting for an appellant appealing against an Industrial Tribunal decision or a respondent resisting such an appeal and it applies to employers and employees alike. Note however the possibility of a Thai Trading agreement.

At the time of writing legal aid is still available for matters before the Employment Appeal Tribunal and it is available for appellants and respondents, employees and employers, but not of course for limited companies who can never get legal aid.

There is also a free non-means tested pro bono Duty Solicitor scheme in operation at the Employment Appeal Tribunal and this covers advice and also advocacy at the preliminary hearing stage.

---

3   Now Section 5(2) and (3) Industrial Tribunals Act 1996

The scheme was formerly known as the Employment Appeal Tribunal Advisory Service but is now known as the Employment Law Advisory Service. The author is a member of the scheme. Please contact him for further information.

The Green Form and Contingency Fees

Green Form clients may have their case prepared by a solicitor but then have to conduct the Tribunal hearing themselves or try and find the fee for the solicitor's advocacy. By definition someone in receipt of Green Form Legal Aid is unlikely to be able to afford this.

There is no objection to a "mix and match" approach whereby the matter is prepared under a Green Form but the advocacy is carried out under a contingency fee agreement. This limits the solicitor's exposure to carrying out unpaid work to the advocacy. The solicitor will still get paid for the preparation, win or lose.

It is unlawful to make a charge to a client in respect of work for which a Green Form was in existence. To avoid this pitfall it is suggested that the contingency fee for advocacy alone for a client assisted under a Green Form be:

> one-third less any sum to which the solicitor's legal advice and assistance charge attaches as a result of advice and assistance having been given under the Legal Aid Act 1988.

In such cases the solicitor claims from the Legal Aid Board in the usual way but this would be recouped out of the client's damages leaving the solicitor the balance of the one-third fee. The net effect is exactly the same, namely that the solicitor receives one-third of the damages.

Of course if the client loses then the solicitor does the advocacy for nothing but still receives the Green Form payment for preparation.

The big disadvantage for the solicitor is that if the case settles during the currency of a Green Form he or she only gets the Green Form rate – around £45 per hour – and not 33% of the damages. Obviously the client benefits from this.

If a further extension to a Green Form has been refused by the Legal Aid Board then it is permissible to move straight on to a contingency fee agreement and take 33% less any sum recouped by the Legal Aid Board *even if the case is settled prior to the hearing.*

Ethical problems arise for franchised solicitors who are themselves responsible for whether or not to grant an extension to themselves. There are guidelines about how many hours Green Form work may be done in each category of work and a solicitor could argue that once he or she is beyond these guidelines it is reasonable to refuse an extension and thus move on to a contingency fee agreement. However the precise point at which a case is settled will have a very significant effect on the solicitors and client's respective shares and a client may take some convincing that a franchised solicitor was justified in refusing herself an extension.

Example A
Green Form allowance 8 hours – £10,000 settlement – Case settled after 8 hours

Solicitor's fee (8 x £45)	340.00
Balance to client	9,660.00

Example B
Green Form allowance 8 hours – £10,000 settlement – Case settled after 8 hours 5 minutes

Solicitor's fee	3,333.33
Balance to client	6,666.67

Thus the 5 minutes have cost the client £2,993.33 being the difference between the net sum received by the client in the two examples.

You may think it better to recognise that no talented employment lawyer wishes to bill at £45 per hour, burn all of your Green Forms and tell the clients that they must go elsewhere if they want to sign a Green Form.

Few clients now qualify for Green Form Legal Advice so you may wish to keep a stock purely to see if the client qualifies on financial grounds. If not then you have no problem – if they do you may feel it proper to advise them of local employment specialists still doing Green Form work (if there are any).

Summary

Industrial Tribunal and employment work carried out on a Contingency Fee basis is very popular with clients and, properly marketed, will lead to a significant increase in work. It also provides a relatively quick turn round. There is minimal risk to the client, no need to insure against the other side's costs and rarely any disbursements. Thus cash-flow problems are minimised.

However the awards are relatively low and the risk of losing is high and employment is a difficult and complex, but growing, area of the law.

CONTINGENCY FEE AGREEMENT

This agreement is a legally binding contract between you and [   ] solicitors.

Agreement Date •••

We, the solicitors   **You, the client**

Messrs   •••

What is covered by this agreement

Your industrial tribunal claim relating to your employment with •••

What is not covered by this agreement

Any counterclaim against you
Any appeal you make or any appeal made by your opponent.

Paying Us

If you win the case you pay us 33% of your damages plus any disbursements. This figure includes vat at the standard rate, currently 17.5%.

If you lose the case you do not pay us anything, except disbursements.

N.B. Disbursements are payments we make on your behalf to others involved in the case. We will notify you of disbursements incurred as we go along. We would expect the only disbursements to be travelling and subsistence expenses incurred in attending the tribunal hearing.

If you end the agreement before the case is won or lost, you are liable to pay our costs at the rate of £170 per hour with letters and telephone calls charged at £17.00 each unless they last for ten minutes or longer in which case they will be charged at the appropriate proportion of the hourly rate. All of these figures attract VAT at the standard rate of 17.5%.

For what happens if we end the agreement before the case is won or lost, please refer to paragraph 5.

1. Our responsibilities

We must always act in your best interests in pursuing your claim for damages and obtaining for you the best possible results, subject to our duty to the tribunal; we must explain to you the risks and benefits of taking legal action; we must give you our best advice about whether to accept any offer of settlement.

2. Your responsibilities

You must give us clear instructions which allow us to do our work properly; you must not ask us to work in an improper or unreasonable way; you must not deliberately mislead us; you must co-operate with us when asked; you must go to the tribunal hearing when asked; you must pay for disbursements as the case goes on.

3. What happens if you win

If you win (which means that your case is decided in your favour whether by a tribunal or an agreement to pay you damages) you pay us 33% of any damages plus any disbursements. You agree that we may receive the damages your opponent has to pay. If your opponent refuses to accept our receipt, you will pay the cheque you receive into a joint bank account in your name and ours. Out of the money you agree to let us take 33% of the damages plus any outstanding disbursements. You take the rest.

If your opponent fails to pay any damages owed to you we have the right to take recovery action in your name to enforce a judgement, order or agreement. The costs of this action are payable by you to us in addition to 33% of the damages.

4. What happens if you lose

If you lose you do not have to pay us anything, except our disbursements.

5. What happens if the agreement ends before the case itself ends

You can end the agreement at any time. You are then liable to pay us our costs incurred up to the date you end the agreement calculated at the hourly rate, set out above under "Paying Us".

We can end the agreement if you do not keep to your responsibilities in paragraph 2. You are then liable to pay us our costs incurred up to the date the agreement ends calculated at the hourly rate.

We can end the agreement if we believe that you are unlikely to win and you disagree with us. You do not have to pay us anything.

We can end the agreement if you reject our opinion about making a settlement with your opponent. You are then liable to pay us our costs incurred up to the date the agreement ends calculated on the hourly rate (unless your damages are 20% more than the offer we advised you to accept in which case you do not have to pay us anything).

6. What happens after the agreement ends

After the agreement ends we will apply to have our name removed from the record of the tribunal proceedings in which we are acting. We have the right to preserve a lien over any property of yours in our possession unless any money owed to us under this agreement is paid in full. This means we can keep your papers until you pay us in full.

7. Costs

Industrial Tribunals have the power to award costs in limited circumstances. If we recover costs on your behalf they belong to us. In other words, if you win, you will pay us 33% of your damages whether or not we also recover any costs from your opponent.

If you lose and you are ordered to pay costs to your opponent, then those costs will be payable by you.

The 1993 Regulations in relation to costs in Industrial Tribunals state:-

> "*Where, in the opinion of the tribunal, a party has in bringing or conducting the proceedings acted frivolously, vexatiously, abusively, disruptively or otherwise unreasonably, the tribunal may make –*
>
> a.   *an order containing an award against that party in respect of the costs incurred by another party;*
>
> b   *an order that that party shall pay to the Secretary of State the whole, or any part of any allowances (other than allowances paid to members of tribunals) paid by the Secretary of State under *paragraph 10 of Schedule 9 to the Employment Protection (Consolidation) Act 1978 to any person for the purposes of or in connection with his attendance at the tribunal.*"

* Now Section 5(2) and (3) Industrial Tribunals Act 1996.

Signed for the solicitors

Signed by the client

Sample Letter

Ref

29th June 1998

Mr A Client
The Street
Town
County
Postcode

Dear Mr Client

Re: Employment Advice

I refer to our meeting and confirm that my firm will be pleased to act for you in relation to matters arising out of your employment which ended on [insert date].

As mentioned, any claim for unfair dismissal can only be brought in the Industrial Tribunal and the claim must be with the Tribunal within three months of your dismissal, ie it must actually be with the Tribunal by [enter date].

A breach of contract claim in relation to your notice pay can be brought in the High Court, County Court or Industrial Tribunal. The Industrial Tribunal claim must be brought within the same three months time limit as the unfair dismissal claim but you have six years to bring a breach of contract claim in the County or High Court.

I set out below the various factors to be taken into account in deciding whether to bring a claim in the High/County Court or Industrial Tribunal.

High/County Court

- Court Fee payable on issue of proceedings.
- Legal Aid available.
- Formal. Heard by a Judge.
- Interest payable at 8% from date debt due, ie [insert date].
- Majority of costs recoverable by the winning party.
- Majority of costs payable by the losing party.
- "No win – no fee" arrangements *not* available.
- Lengthy delays before hearing (approximately one year).
- Unlimited jurisdiction, ie no cash limit.
- Six years in which to bring a claim.
- Appeal direct to Court of Appeal.

Industrial Tribunal

- No fee payable on issue.
- No Legal Aid available.
- Interest only payable from date of *award* not date debt due.
- Less formal. Heard by a Chairman (equal to a Judge) and *lay* members.
- Relatively speedy (three to four months).
- Costs generally not recoverable by winning party.
- Costs generally not payable by losing party.
- "No win – no fee" arrangements *are* available.
- Jurisdiction limited to £25,000.
- Claim to be with Tribunal within three months.
- Appeal to Employment Appeal Tribunal the Court of Appeal ie extra layer of appeal.

The £25,000 awardable by an Industrial Tribunal is in addition to any compensation for unfair dismissal.

The maximum compensatory award for unfair dismissal is £12,000.00.

The basic award is calculated by reference to your age and length of service and in your case it would be [enter amount].

Thus the maximum that could be awarded by an Industrial Tribunal for your unfair dismissal claim is [enter amount] and for your breach of contract claim, [enter amount] giving a total of [enter amount].

If I acted for you under a Contingency Fee Agreement I would take 33% of any damages recovered.

As stated above we are not allowed to act on this basis in the County Court or High Court.

If your former employers institute injunction proceedings arising out of the restrictive covenants contained in your contract of employment you should contact me immediately, again this work cannot be done under a "no win – no fee" arrangement, if proceedings are actually issued.

All work carried out by me on your behalf will be charged at [enter hourly rate] per hour, with letters and telephone calls at [enter rate] each unless they last for ten minutes or longer in which case they will be charged at the appropriate proportion of the hourly rate. All of these figures attract VAT at the standard rate of 17.5%. We accept all major credit cards.

I look forward to hearing from you in due course but please bear in mind the strict Industrial Tribunal time limit mentioned above and if there is anything that was not made clear at our meeting or in this letter, please contact me.

Yours sincerely

Chart 1: Redundancy payment

Age (years)	2	3	4	5	6	7	8	9	10	11	12	13	14	15	16	17	18	19	20
20	1	1	1	1	–														
21	1	1½	1½	1½	1½	–													
22	1	1½	2	2	2	2	–												
23	1½	2	2½	3	3	3	3	–											
24	2	2½	3	3½	4	4	4	4	–										
25	2	3	3½	4	4½	5	5	5	5	–									
26	2	3	4	4½	5	5½	6	6	6	6	–								
27	2	3	4	5	5½	6	6½	7	7	7	7	–							
28	2	3	4	5	6	6½	7	7½	8	8	8	8	–						
29	2	3	4	5	6	7	7½	8	8½	9	9	9	9	–					
30	2	3	4	5	6	7	8	8½	9	9½	10	10	10	10	–				
31	2	3	4	5	6	7	8	9	9½	10	10½	11	11	11	11	–			
32	2	3	4	5	6	7	8	9	10	10½	11	11½	12	12	12	12	–		
33	2	3	4	5	6	7	8	9	10	11	11½	12	12½	13	13	13	13	–	
34	2	3	4	5	6	7	8	9	10	11	12	12½	13	13½	14	14	14	14	–
35	2	3	4	5	6	7	8	9	10	11	12	13	13½	14	14½	15	15	15	15
36	2	3	4	5	6	7	8	9	10	11	12	13	14	14½	15	15½	16	16	16
37	2	3	4	5	6	7	8	9	10	11	12	13	14	15	15½	16	16½	17	17
38	2	3	4	5	6	7	8	9	10	11	12	13	14	15	16	16½	17	17½	18
39	2	3	4	5	6	7	8	9	10	11	12	13	14	15	16	17	17½	18	18½
40	2	3	4	5	6	7	8	9	10	11	12	13	14	15	16	17	18	18½	19
41	2	3	4	5	6	7	8	9	10	11	12	13	14	15	16	17	18	19	19
42	2½	3½	4½	5½	6½	7½	8½	9½	10½	11½	12½	13½	14½	15½	16½	17½	18½	19½	20½
43	3	4	5	6	7	8	9	10	11	12	13	14	15	16	17	18	19	20	21
44	3	4½	5½	6½	7½	8½	9½	10½	11½	12½	13½	14½	15½	16½	17½	18½	19½	20½	21½
45	3	4½	6	7	8	9	10	11	12	13	14	15	16	17	18	19	20	21	22
46	3	4½	6	7½	8½	9½	10½	11½	12½	13½	14½	15½	16½	17½	18½	19½	20½	21½	22½
47	3	4½	6	7½	9	10	11	12	13	14	15	16	17	18	19	20	21	22	23
48	3	4½	6	7½	9	10½	11½	12½	13½	14½	15½	16½	17½	18½	19½	20½	21½	22½	23½
49	3	4½	6	7½	9	10½	12	13	14	15	16	17	18	19	20	21	22	23	24
50	3	4½	6	7½	9	10½	12	13½	14½	15½	16½	17½	18½	19½	20½	21½	22½	23½	24½
51	3	4½	6	7½	9	10½	12	13½	15	16	17	18	19	20	21	22	23	24	25
52	3	4½	6	7½	9	10½	12	13½	15	16½	17½	18½	19½	20½	21½	22½	23½	24½	25½
53	3	4½	6	7½	9	10½	12	13½	15	16½	18	19	20	21	22	23	24	25	26
54	3	4½	6	7½	9	10½	12	13½	15	16½	18	19½	20½	21½	22½	23½	24½	25½	26½
55	3	4½	6	7½	9	10½	12	13½	15	16½	18	19½	21	22	23	24	25	26	27
56	3	4½	6	7½	9	10½	12	13½	15	16½	18	19½	21	22½	23½	24½	25½	26½	27½
57	3	4½	6	7½	9	10½	12	13½	15	16½	18	19½	21	22½	24	25	26	27	28
58	3	4½	6	7½	9	10½	12	13½	15	16½	18	19½	21	22½	24	25½	26½	27½	28½
59	3	4½	6	7½	9	10½	12	13½	15	16½	18	19½	21	22½	24	25½	27	28	29
60	3	4½	6	7½	9	10½	12	13½	15	16½	18	19½	21	22½	24	25½	27	28½	29½
61	3	4½	6	7½	9	10½	12	13½	15	16½	18	19½	21	22½	24	25½	27	28½	30
62	3	4½	6	7½	9	10½	12	13½	15	16½	18	19½	21	22½	24	25½	27	28½	30
63	3	4½	6	7½	9	10½	12	13½	15	16½	18	19½	21	22½	24	25½	27	28½	30
64	3	4½	6	7½	9	10½	12	13½	15	16½	18	19½	21	22½	24	25½	27	28½	30

Take age at date of dismissal or redundancy and number of years' completed service. Read off multiplier and apply to *gross* weekly pay up to a maximum of £220 per week.

Chart 2: Redundancy payment

Age (years)	2	3	4	5	6	7	8	9	10	11	12	13	14	15	16	17	18	19	20
20	220	220	220	220															
21	220	330	330	330	330														
22	220	330	440	440	440	440													
23	330	440	550	660	660	660	660												
24	440	550	660	770	880	880	880	880											
25	440	660	770	880	990	1100	1100	1100	1100										
26	440	660	880	990	1100	1210	1320	1320	1320	1320									
27	440	660	880	1100	1210	1320	1430	1540	1540	1540	1540								
28	440	660	880	1100	1320	1430	1540	1650	1760	1760	1760	1760							
29	440	660	880	1100	1320	1540	1650	1760	1870	1980	1980	1980	1980						
30	440	660	880	1100	1320	1540	1760	1870	1980	2090	2200	2200	2200	2200					
31	440	660	880	1100	1320	1540	1760	1980	2090	2200	2420	2420	2420	2420	2420				
32	440	660	880	1100	1320	1540	1760	1980	2200	2420	2420	2530	2640	2640	2640	2640			
33	440	660	880	1100	1320	1540	1760	1980	2200	2420	2530	2640	2640	2860	2860	2860	2860		
34	440	660	880	1100	1320	1540	1760	1980	2200	2420	2640	2640	2860	2970	3080	3080	3080	3080	
35	440	660	880	1100	1320	1540	1760	1980	2200	2420	2640	2860	2970	3080	3190	3300	3300	3300	3300
36	440	660	880	1100	1320	1540	1760	1980	2200	2420	2640	2860	3080	3190	3300	3410	3520	3520	3520
37	440	660	880	1100	1320	1540	1760	1980	2200	2420	2640	2860	3080	3300	3410	3520	3630	3740	3740
38	440	660	880	1100	1320	1540	1760	1980	2200	2420	2640	2860	3080	3300	3520	3630	3740	3850	3960
39	440	660	880	1100	1320	1540	1760	1980	2200	2420	2640	2860	3080	3300	3520	3740	3850	3960	4070
40	440	660	880	1100	1320	1540	1760	1980	2200	2420	2640	2860	3080	3300	3520	3740	3960	4070	4180
41	440	660	880	1100	1320	1540	1760	1980	2200	2420	2640	2860	3080	3300	3520	3740	3960	4180	4290
42	550	770	990	1210	1430	1650	1870	2090	2420	2530	2640	2970	3190	3410	3630	3850	4070	4290	4510
43	660	880	1100	1320	1540	1760	1980	2200	2420	2640	2860	3080	3300	3520	3740	3960	4180	4400	4620
44	660	990	1210	1430	1650	1870	2090	2420	2530	2640	2970	3190	3410	3630	3850	4070	4290	4510	4730
45	660	990	1320	1540	1760	1980	2200	2420	2640	2860	3080	3300	3520	3740	3960	4180	4400	4410	4840
46	660	990	1320	1650	1870	2090	2420	2530	2640	2970	3190	3410	3630	3850	4070	4290	4510	4515	4950
47	660	990	1320	1650	1980	2200	2420	2640	2860	3080	3300	3520	3740	3960	4180	4400	4620	4620	5060
48	660	990	1320	1650	1980	2420	2530	2640	2970	3190	3410	3630	3850	4070	4290	4510	4730	4950	5170
49	660	990	1320	1650	1980	2420	2640	2860	3080	3300	3520	3740	3960	4180	4400	4620	4840	5060	5280
50	660	990	1320	1650	1980	2420	2640	2970	3190	3410	3630	3850	4070	4290	4510	4730	4950	5170	5390
51	660	990	1320	1650	1980	2420	2640	2970	3300	3520	3740	3960	4180	4400	4620	4840	5060	5390	5500
52	660	990	1320	1650	1980	2420	2640	2970	3300	3630	3850	4070	4290	4510	4840	4950	5170	5145	5610
53	660	990	1320	1650	1980	2420	2640	2970	3300	3630	3960	4180	4400	4620	4840	5060	5280	5500	5720
54	660	990	1320	1650	1980	2420	2640	2970	3300	3630	3960	4290	4510	4730	4950	5170	5390	5610	5830
55	660	990	1320	1650	1980	2420	2640	2970	3300	3630	3960	4290	4620	4840	5060	5280	5500	5720	5940
56	660	990	1320	1650	1980	2420	2640	2970	3300	3630	3960	4290	4620	4950	5170	5390	5610	5830	6050
57	660	990	1320	1650	1980	2420	2640	2970	3300	3630	3960	4290	4620	4950	5280	5500	5720	5940	6160
58	660	990	1320	1650	1980	2420	2640	2970	3300	3630	3960	4290	4620	4950	5280	5610	5830	6050	6270
59	660	990	1320	1650	1980	2420	2640	2970	3300	3630	3960	4290	4620	4950	5280	5610	5940	6160	6380
60	660	990	1320	1650	1980	2420	2640	2970	3300	3630	3960	4290	4620	4950	5280	5610	5940	6270	6490
61	660	990	1320	1650	1980	2420	2640	2970	3300	3630	3960	4290	4620	4950	5280	5610	5940	6270	6600
62	660	990	1320	1650	1980	2420	2640	2970	3300	3630	3960	4290	4620	4950	5280	5610	5940	6270	6600
63	660	990	1320	1650	1980	2420	2640	2970	3300	3630	3960	4290	4620	4950	5280	5610	5940	6270	6600
64	660	990	1320	1650	1980	2420	2640	2970	3300	3630	3960	4290	4620	4950	5280	5610	5940	6270	6600

Actual calculations using chart 1.

SCHEDULE 1, Rule 12 of The Industrial Tribunals (Constitution and Rules of Procedure) Regulations 1993

Costs

12 (1)Where, in the opinion of the tribunal, a party has in bringing or conducting the proceedings acted frivolously, vexatiously, abusively, disruptively or otherwise unreasonably, the tribunal may make –

   (a) an order containing an award against that party in respect of the costs incurred by another party;

   (b) an order that that party shall pay to the Secretary of State the whole, or any part, of any allowances (other than allowances paid to members of tribunals) paid by the Secretary of State under paragraph 10 of Schedule 9 to the 1978 Act to any person for the purposes of, or in connection with, his attendance at the tribunal.

(2) Paragraph (1) applies to a respondent who has not entered an appearance in relation to the conduct of any part in the proceedings which he has taken.

(3) An order containing an award against a party ("the first party" in respect of the costs incurred by another party ("the second party") shall be –

   (a) where the tribunal thinks fit, an order that the first party pay to the second party a specified sum not exceeding £500;

   (b) where those parties agree on a sum to be paid by the first party to the second party in respect of those costs, an order that the first party pay to the second party a specified sum, being the sum so agreed; or

   (c) in any other case, an order that the first party pay to the second party the whole or a specified part of the costs incurred by the second party as taxed (if not otherwise agreed).

(4) Where the tribunal has on the application of a party postponed the day or time fixed for or adjourned the hearing, the tribunal may make orders, of the kinds mentioned in paragraphs (1)(a) and (1)(b), against or, as the case may require, in favour of that party as respects any costs incurred or any allowances paid as a result of the postponement or adjournment.

(5) A tribunal shall make orders against a respondent of the kinds mentioned in paragraphs 1(a) and 1(b) as respects any costs or any allowances paid

as a result of the postponement or adjournment of a hearing where, on a complaint of unfair dismissal –

(a) the applicant has expressed a wish to be reinstated or re-engaged which has been communicated to the respondent at least 7 days before the hearing of the complaint, or

(b) the proceedings arise out of the respondent's failure to permit the applicant to return to work after an absence due to pregnancy or confinement,

and the postponement or adjournment has been caused by the respondent's failure, without a special reason, to adduce reasonable evidence as to the availability of the job from which the applicant was dismissed, or, as the case may be, which she held before her absence, or of comparable or suitable employment.

(b) Any costs required by an order under this rule to be taxed may be taxed in the county court according to such of the scales prescribed by the county court rules for proceedings in the county court as shall be directed by the order.

(7) Where –

(a) a party has been ordered under rule 7 to pay a deposit as a condition of being permitted to continue to participate in proceedings relating to a matter,

(b) in respect of that matter, the tribunal has found against that party in its decision, and

(c) there has been no award of costs made against that party arising out of the proceedings on the matter,

the tribunal shall consider whether to award costs against that party on the ground that he conducted the proceedings relating to the matter unreasonably in persisting in having the matter determined by a tribunal; but the tribunal shall not make an award of costs on that ground unless it has considered the document recording the order under rule 7 and is of the opinion that the reasons which caused the tribunal to find against the party in its decision were substantially the same as the reasons recorded in that document for considering that the contentions of the party had no reasonable prospect of success.

(8) Where an award of costs is made against a party who has had an order under rule 7 made against him (whether the award arises out of the proceedings relating to the matter in respect of which the order was made or out of proceedings relating to any other matter considered with that matter), his deposit shall be paid in part or full settlement of the award –

(a) where an award is made in favour of one party, to that party, and

(b) where awards are made in favour of more than one party, to all of them or any one or more of them as the tribunal thinks fit, and if to all or more than one, in such proportions as the tribunal considers appropriate,

and if the amount of the deposit exceeds the amount of the award of costs, the balance shall be refunded to the party who paid it.

Criminal Injuries Compensation Scheme

Criminal Injuries Compensation Scheme

Introduction

Criminal Injuries Compensation Authority (CICA) work is ideally suited to being funded by way of contingency fee agreements as there is no risk of paying costs in the event of an unsuccessful application. By the same token costs are not recoverable and thus the client has to fund the solicitor's fees and that is best done out of damages.

For solicitors there are minimal disbursements and thus there is no cash-flow problem. Although the risk of failing to get an award is much higher than in ordinary personal injury work, the amount of work that the solicitor needs to do is very much less. Furthermore as the scheme is now operated by reference to a tariff it is relatively easy to predict the level of award and the consequent solicitor's fee. Thus risk management is made easier.

Thus on the 3 R's test – Risk, Reward and Resources, CICA work scores reasonably on risk, reasonably on reward and very well on resources.

Another advantage ought to be that cases are concluded much more quickly than ordinary personal injury cases but unfortunately that is certainly not the position at present.

In this chapter I set out details of the way the scheme works and the tariffs and as an Addendum at page 235 in this chapter is a Model Contingency Fee Agreement for use in Criminal Injuries Compensation Authority claims.

The Scheme

The Criminal Injuries Compensation Act 1995 was introduced by the Home Secretary in response to the decision of the House of Lords on the 5th April 1995 in which they ruled that the original tariff scheme brought into effect on the 1st April 1994 had been unlawfully introduced. The tariff scheme was set up to replace the previous 1990 Criminal Injuries Compensation Scheme based on common law principles which had been in effect since 1964. The original tariff scheme introduced resulted in significantly lower awards to victims of crime and was successfully challenged by numerous trades unions and the TUC.

In its first year of operation the original tariff scheme was not any quicker than the common law scheme. Of the 66,387 cases lodged only 11,076 cases or 16.7% were determined compared with 70% of cases resolved in one year under the old scheme.

The new scheme came into force on the 1st April 1996. Guidelines are:

1. The Applicant must have been a victim of a crime of violence, and
2. physically and/or mentally injured as a result, and
3. have been in England, Scotland or Wales at the time when the injury was sustained, and
4. injured seriously enough to qualify for at least the minimum award available under the Scheme (£1,000).

A dependant or relative of a victim of a crime of violence where that victim has died, may also qualify for an award.

Furthermore unless there are good reasons the client must also have:

A. Reported the incident *personally* to the Police as soon as possible after it happened and
B. the application must be received within two years of the date of the incident causing the injury.

The application is investigated by the Authority who normally make enquiries of the Police, a Medical Authority and any other relevant bodies to enable the claim to be assessed.

It is the responsibility of a Claims Officer within the Authority to decide in accordance with the Scheme what award if any should be made and how it should be paid. In the first instance they will decide as to entitlement to an award under the scheme ie as to whether the client sustained the injuries as a direct result of a crime of violence and they will then refer to the tariff to see what award should be made. Once the initial application has been accepted it will be necessary to assess the seriousness of the injury and again it must qualify for an award of at least £1,000. The Claims Officer will then identify the tariff level into which the injury falls.

They may ask the applicant to attend at the hearing centre or be referred for an examination by a Doctor of their choice for which they will pay reasonable travelling expenses.

If the applicant has suffered more than one injury, he will receive the full award for the more serious injury, 10% of the tariff award for the second injury and 5% of the tariff award for third most serious injury, and so on. Example:

> Where the injuries are a depressed fracture of the skull (single tariff payment £6,000), loss of two front teeth (£2,000) and a broken nose (£1,500) the combined award would be £6,000 plus £200 plus £75 totalling £6,275.

The tariff includes an element of compensation for a degree of shock which an applicant in normal circumstances would experience as a result of the incident resulting in the injuries.

If the shock is such that it would attract an award from a higher tariff level than the injury itself then the award for shock will be paid rather than the award for the injury.

An award will be reduced by the full amount of any payment of compensation or damages received in respect of the same injuries (*i.e.* if the court or any other body makes an award in connection with this incident).

Compensation for Loss of Earnings

If the injury has caused the applicant to lose or is likely to cause them to lose earnings or incapacity for any longer than 28 full weeks then the applicant may be eligible for additional compensation. No compensation is payable for the first 28 full weeks of lost earnings or incapacity. Additional expenses may be considered but only if the Applicant has been incapacitated or is likely to incapacitated for longer than 28 full weeks and have incurred special expenses such as medical, dental, optical treatment.

An Applicant does not have to be employed to be considered for this element of damages.

Fatal Cases

Those eligible to apply are dependents or relatives which for the purposes of the scheme are husband or wife, unmarried but long term partner, parent, child or former husband or wife who was financially supported by the deceased.

Consideration of these applications for compensation in respect of any fatal case are subject to the same eligibility requirements under the scheme and will apply to the applicant and the deceased.

Any decision made by the Authority will be notified in writing and where an award has been reduced or withheld, written reasons will be given.

Re-opening of Cases

The Authority has the discretion to re-open a case after a final decision has been made if the medical condition caused by the original injury has deteriorated to such an extent that an injustice would occur or the condition was not known at the time of the original decision. Therefore the Authority may consider re-opening such cases where the injuries are now more serious and the applicant would therefore qualify for a higher award.

Medical evidence must be supplied in support of an application to re-open a case and if the application is made more than two years after the date of the final decision it will only be re-opened if the CICA is satisfied that it will not involve extensive enquiries.

If an applicant is not happy with any award made he or she must apply within 90 days setting out in writing the reasons why he or she does not agree with the decision. The case will then be considered afresh by a Claims Officer more senior to the one who made the original decision. Both eligibility and the amount of the award will be reviewed and a fresh decision, together with reasons, will be supplied.

If the Applicant then considers that there are further grounds for contesting the review he or she may apply to the Appeals Panel within 30 days of that decision, again supplying details in writing. The Appeals Panel will then consider whether an increase should be made or even whether to reduce or hold an award. A decision made by the panel, whether at an oral hearing or otherwise, is final.

The Authority does have power to consider applications submitted outside of the period of two years but it is for the applicant to show that there is a reasonable reason for the application not being brought before and that it would be an injustice not to allow it to proceed.

Minor injuries such as scratches or bruises alone will not qualify for an award but an Applicant who has suffered a combination of minor injuries such as grazing, cuts, lacerations, bruising, black eyes, bloody nose etc which caused him to visit his doctor for treatment at least twice and from which he did not recover for at least six weeks may qualify under the scheme.

To qualify for an award in respect of a mental injury alone the Authority must be satisfied that the applicant was put in reasonable fear of immediate physical harm to himself and that he either witnessed or was closely involved in the aftermath of an incident where a person with whom the Applicant had a close relationship of love and affection was physically injured.

In respect of eligibility and the question of whether the injury was directly attributable to a crime of violence there is no legal definition of the term "crime of violence" but this would usually involve a physical attack on a person for example assaults, wounding, sexual offences. However this is not always the case and the Authority takes great care when considering these applications. In some cases an extreme *threat* of violence may qualify and be considered a crime of violence.

An Applicant may still be eligible for compensation even if the injuries were caused by someone who could not be held responsible under criminal law because they were too young or were insane.

It is also possible to bring a claim under the scheme through injury suffered as a result of a crime of violence as a result of trespass on the railway. For example, an Applicant is employed by a railway company and was present and saw another person injured or killed as a result of trespassing on the railway, or discovered a body on or beside the track, or was involved in the immediate aftermath of the incident. The Applicant must of course sustain shock as a result of this to the extent that he qualifies for the minimum award.

Accidental injuries do not generally qualify but there are exceptions. For example an Applicant was injured whilst preventing an offence being committed by attempting to catch an offender or suspected offender or helping the police catch an offender will qualify.

In addition if an Applicant can show that he was taking an exceptional risk at the time the injury was sustained accidentally he may be able to claim. For example a Police Officer who tripped in the street in broad daylight when running to apprehend an offender would be unlikely to be compensated. Similarly climbing over a wall or fence would not normally be considered an exceptional risk. However an action which would not be considered to be an exceptional risk during the day may be so at night.

It is therefore necessary to look at the facts surrounding accidental injury and to see as to whether these circumstances constitute an exceptional risk.

Likely disqualifications

- For an award to be made the Applicant must inform the Police personally of the offence unless there is a good reason, although it is not necessary for the offender to be prosecuted. In any event an Applicant will be expected to have reported the matter as quickly as possible.
- It must again be noted that reports by friends or relatives or work mates will not be sufficient unless there is good reason. However there may be circumstances where an Applicant reports it to another acceptable body such as a hospital where he works.
- It is necessary to co-operate with the Police. Failure to provide a statement or attend court means the application may be rejected.
- The Applicant must co-operate with the CICA. Failure to do so may result in an application being rejected.
- The Authority will also look at conduct before, during or after the event, such as fighting or provocation and an award may be reduced or withheld if:
  - A. The injury was caused in a fight in which the Applicant voluntarily agreed to take part (the fact that he agreed to a fist fight and the other person drew a weapon will not make any difference), or
  - B. Without reasonable cause the Applicant struck the first blow regardless of the degree of retaliation thereafter, or
  - C. The incident formed part of a pattern of violence in which the Applicant was a voluntary participant, or
  - D. The Applicant was injured whilst attempting to obtain revenge against an assailant, or

E. The Applicant used offensive language or behaved in an aggressive or threatening manner which led to the attack which caused the injuries sustained.

The Authority also has the ability to withhold or reduce an award on the basis of the applicant's character as shown by his/her criminal convictions even though these may be unrelated to the incident in question.

It is not always necessary to obtain medical evidence in support of an application in the first instance. It is only necessary when the injuries are clearly very serious or the tariff scheme does not cater for the client's injuries. The board has the power to obtain its own medical evidence and this avoids the client incurring disbursements which they will have to pay for irrespective of the outcome.

Once an offer is received from the CICA you can see which tariff band it comes within and review the decision accordingly.

Bear in mind that if an award of £1,000 is made by the CICA which reflects level 1 disabling for six to thirteen weeks and the client has continuing symptoms or is out of that time span the solicitor can submit that the Applicant is entitled to an increased award and could then recommend obtaining medical evidence and incurring the cost thereof. In addition there is a risk factor when a CICA client comes in soon after the incident and is still recuperating. It is then difficult to say what the level of continued period of pain and suffering is likely to be and as to whether a report would be justified.

The sensible way to proceed is to lodge the application, allow the authority to carry out investigations and by the time that they come to make a decision or award or even consider getting their own medical evidence you will be further down the line and able to assess fully the recovery period concerned.

There are provisions for interim payments to be awarded pending a decision by the Home Secretary at the appropriate figure where it is not catered for by the tariff but this is likely to lead to substantial delay.

The number of applicants applying to the Authority in the last 5 years has been between 65,000 and 75,000 per annum.

Criminal Injuries Compensation (Overseas) Scheme

Note also the Ministry of Defence's Criminal Injuries Compensation (Overseas) Scheme which was introduced in 1980 to give injured members of the Services compensation equivalent to that available had they been the victim of a crime of violence in Great Britain.

The Scheme does not provide awards to those injured by acts of violence occurring "as a result of war operations or military activity by warring factions". Thus the Scheme does not cover members of peace-keeping forces such as British forces in Bosnia.

LEVELS OF COMPENSATION

Level 1	£1,000
Level 2	£1,250
Level 3	£1,500
Level 4	£1,750
Level 5	£2,000
Level 6	£2,500
Level 7	£3,000
Level 8	£3,500
Level 9	£4,000
Level 10	£5,000
Level 11	£6,000
Level 12	£7,500
Level 13	£10,000
Level 14	£12,500
Level 15	£15,000
Level 16	£17,500
Level 17	£20,000
Level 18	£25,000
Level 19	£30,000
Level 20	£40,000
Level 21	£50,000
Level 22	£75,000
Level 23	£100,000
Level 24	£175,000
Level 25	£250,000

TARIFF OF INJURIES

Description of Injury	Levels	Standard Amount £
Bodily functions: hemiplegia (paralysis of one side of the body)	21	50,000
Bodily functions: paraplegia (paralysis of the lower limbs)	24	175,000
Bodily functions: quadriplegia/tetraplegia (paralysis of all 4 limbs)	25	250,000
Brain damage: moderate impairment of social/intellectual functions	15	15,000
Brain damage: serious impairment of social/intellectual functions	20	40,000
Brain damage: permanent – extremely serious (no effective control of functions)	25	250,000
Burns: multiple first degree: covering at least 25% of body (for other burn injuries see under individual parts of the body)	19	30,000

Epilepsy: serious exacerbation of pre-existing condition	10	5,000
Epilepsy: fully controlled	12	7,500
Epilepsy: partially controlled	14	12,500
Epilepsy: uncontrolled	20	40,000
Fatal injury (one qualifying claimant)	13	10,000
Fatal injury (each qualifying claimant if more than one)	10	5,000
Head: burns: minor	3	1,500
Head: burns: moderate	9	4,000
Head: burns: severe	13	10,000
Head: ear: fractured mastoid	1	1,000
Head: ear: temporary partial deafness – lasting 6 to 13 weeks	1	1,000
Head: ear: temporary partial deafness – lasting more than 13 weeks	3	1,500
Head: ear: partial deafness (one ear) {remaining hearing socially useful	8	3,500
Head: ear: partial deafness (both ears) {with hearing aid if necessary	12	7,500
Head: ear: total deafness (one ear)	15	15,000
Head: ear: total deafness (both ears)	20	40,000
Head: ear: partial loss of ear(s)	9	4,000
Head: ear: loss of ear	13	10,000
Head: ear: loss of both ears	16	17,500
Head: ear: perforated ear drum	4	1,750
Head: ear: tinnitus (ringing noise in ears) – lasting 6–13 weeks	1	1,000
Head: ear: tinnitus – lasting more than 13 weeks	7	3,000
Head: ear: tinnitus – permanent (moderate)	12	7,500
Head: ear: tinnitus – permanent (very serious)	15	15,000
Head: eye: blow out fracture of orbit bone cavity containing eyeball	7	3,000
Head: eye: blurred or double vision – lasting 6–13 weeks	1	1,000
Head: eye: blurred or double vision – lasting more than 13 weeks	4	1,750
Head: eye: blurred or double vision – permanent	12	7,500
Head: eye: Cataracts one eye (requiring operation)	7	3,000

Head: eye: Cataracts both eyes (requiring operation)	12	7,500
Head: eye: Cataracts one eye (permanent/inoperable)	12	7,500
Head: eye: Cataracts both eyes (permanent/inoperable)	16	17,500
Head: eye: corneal abrasions	5	2,000
Head: eye: damage to iris resulting in hyphaema (bleeding in occular chamber)	6	2,500
Head: eye: damage to irises resulting in hyphaema (bleeding in occular chamber)	11	6,000
Head: eye: detatched retina	10	5,000
Head: eye: detatched retinas	14	12,500
Head: eye: degeneration of optic nerve	5	2,000
Head: eye: degeneration of optic nerves	10	5,000
Head: eye: dislocation of lens	10	5,000
Head: eye: dislocation of lenses	14	12,500
Head: eye: glaucoma	6	2,500
Head: eye: residual floaters	10	5,000
Head: eye: traumatic angle recession of eye	6	2,500
Head: eye: loss of one eye	18	25,000
Head: eye: loss of both eyes	23	100,000
Head: eye: loss of sight of one eye	17	20,000
Head: eye: loss of sight of both eyes	22	75,000
Head: eye: partial loss of vision – 6/9	12	7,500
Head: eye: partial loss of vision – 6/12	13	10,000
Head: eye: partial loss of vision – 6/24	14	12,500
Head: eye: partial loss of vision 6/36	15	15,000
Head: eye: partial loss of vision – 6/60	16	17,500
Head: face: burns – minor	5	2,000
Head: face: burns – moderate	10	5,000
Head: face: burns – severe	18	25,000
Head: face: scarring: minor disfigurement	3	1,500
Head: face: scarring: significant disfigurement	8	3,500
Head: face: scarring: serious disfigurement	12	7,500
Head: facial: dislocated jaw	5	2,000

Head: facial: permanently clicking jaw	10	5,000
Head: facial: fractured malar and/or zygomatic – cheek bones	5	2,000
Head: facial: fractured mandible and/or maxilla – jaw bones	7	3,000
Head: facial: multiple fractures to face	13	10,000
Head: facial: temporary numbness/loss of feeling, lasting 6–13 weeks	1	1,000
Head: facial: temporary numbness/loss of feeling (lasting more than 13 weeks) – recovery expected	3	1,500
Head: facial: permanent numbness/loss of feeling	9	4,000
Head: nose: deviated nasal septum	1	1,000
Head: nose: deviated nasal septum requiring septoplastomy	5	2,000
Head: nose: undisplaced fracture of nasal bones	1	1,000
Head: nose: displaced fracture of nasal bones	3	1,500
Head: nose: displaced fracture of nasal bones requiring manipulation	5	2,000
Head: nose: displaced fracture of nasal bones requiring rhinoplasty	5	2,000
Head: nose: displaced fracture of nasal bones requiring turbinectomy	5	2,000
Head: nose: partial loss (at least 10%)	9	4,000
Head: nose: loss of smell and/or taste (partial)	10	5,000
Head: nose: loss of smell or taste	13	10,000
Head: nose: loss of smell and taste	15	15,000
Head: scarring: visible, minor disfigurement	3	1,500
Head: scarring: significant disfigurement	7	3,000
Head: scarring: serious disfigurement	10	5,000
Head: skull: balance impaired – permanent	12	7,500
Head: skull: concussion (lasting at least one week)	3	1,500
Head: skull: simple fracture (no operation)	6	2,500
Head: skull: depressed fracture (no operation)	9	4,000
Head: skull: depressed fracture (requiring operation)	11	6,000
Head: skull: subdural haematoma – treated conservatively	9	4,000
Head: skull: subdural haematoma – requiring evacuation	12	7,500
Head: skull: brain haemorrhage (full recovery)	9	4,000

Head: skull: brain haemorrhage (residual minor impairment of social/intellectual functions)	12	7,500
Head: skull: stroke (full recovery)	10	5,000
Head: teeth: fractured/chipped tooth/teeth requiring treatment	1	1,000
Head: teeth: chipped front teeth requiring crown	1	1,000
Head: teeth: fractured tooth/teeth requiring crown	1	1,000
Head: teeth: fractured tooth/teeth requiring apicectomy (surgery to gum to reach root – root resection)	5	2,000
Head: teeth: damage to tooth/teeth requiring root–canal treatment	1	1,000
Head: teeth: loss of crowns	2	1,250
Head: teeth: loss of one front tooth	3	1,500
Head: teeth: loss of two or three front teeth	5	2,000
Head: teeth: loss of four or more front teeth	7	3,000
Head: teeth: loss of one tooth other than front	1	1,000
Head: teeth: loss of two or more teeth other than front	3	1,500
Head: teeth: slackening of teeth requiring dental treatment	1	1,000
Head: tongue: impaired speech: slight	5	2,000
Head: tongue: impaired speech: moderate	10	5,000
Head: tongue: impaired speech: serious	13	10,000
Head: tongue: impaired speech: severe	16	17,500
Head: tongue: loss of speech : permanent	19	30,000
Head: tongue: loss of tongue	20	40,000
Lower limbs: burns – minor	3	1,500
Lower limbs: burns – moderate	9	4,000
Lower limbs: burns – severe	13	10,000
Lower limbs: fractured ankle (full recovery)	7	3,000
Lower limbs: fractured ankle (with continuing disability)	10	5,000
Lower limbs: fractured ankles (full recovery)	12	7,500
Lower limbs: fractured ankles (with continuing disability)	13	10,000
Lower limbs: fractured femur – thigh bone (full recovery)	7	3,000
Lower limbs: fractured femur (with continuing disability)	10	5,000
Lower limbs: fractured femur – both legs (full recovery)	12	7,500

Lower limbs: fractured femur – both legs (with continuing disability)	13	10,000
Lower limbs: fractured fibula – slender bone from knee to ankle (full recovery)	7	3,000
Lower limbs: fractured fibula (with continuing disability)	10	5,000
Lower limbs: fractured fibula – both legs (full recovery)	12	7,500
Lower limbs: fractured fibula – both legs (with continuing disability)	13	10,000
Lower limbs: fractured great toe	6	2,500
Lower limbs: fractured great toe – both feet	10	5,000
Lower limbs: fractured phalanges – toes	3	1,500
Lower limbs: fractured heel bone (full recovery)	6	2,500
Lower limbs: fractured heel bone (with continuing disability)	10	5,000
Lower limbs: fractured heel bone – both feet (full recovery)	10	5,000
Lower limbs: fractured heel bone – both feet (with continuing disability)	13	10,000
Lower limbs: fractured patella – knee cap (full recovery)	12	7,500
Lower limbs: fractured patella (with continuing disability)	13	10,000
Lower limbs: fractured patella – both legs (full recovery)	15	15,000
Lower limbs: fractured patella – both legs (with continuing disability)	17	20,000
Lower limbs: dislocated patella – both legs (full recovery)	5	2,000
Lower limbs: dislocated patella – both legs (with continuing disability)	16	17,500
Lower limbs: arthroscopy (investigative surgery/repair to knees) – no fracture	5	2,000
Lower limbs: fractured metatarsal bones (full recovery)	6	2,500
Lower limbs: fractured metatarsal bones (with continuing disability)	12	7,500
Lower limbs: fractured metatarsal bones – both feet (full recovery)	10	5,000
Lower limbs: fractured metatarsal bones – both feet (continuing disability)	15	15,000
Lower limbs: fractured tarsal bones (full recovery)	6	2,500
Lower limbs: fractured tarsal bones (with continuing disability)	12	7,500
Lower limbs: fractured tarsal bones – both feet (full recovery)	10	5,000

Lower limbs: fractured tarsal bones – both feet (continuing disability)	10	5,000
Lower limbs: fractured tibia – shin bone (full recovery)	7	3,000
Lower limbs: fractured tibia (with continuing disability)	10	5,000
Lower limbs: fractured tibia – both legs (full recovery)	12	7,500
Lower limbs: fractured tibia – both legs (with continuing disability)	13	10,000
Lower limbs: paralysis of leg	18	25,000
Lower limbs: loss of leg below knee	19	30,000
Lower limbs: loss of leg above knee	20	40,000
Lower limbs: loss of both legs	23	100,000
Lower limbs: minor damage to tendon(s)/ligament(s) (full recovery)	1	1,000
Lower limbs: minor damage to tendon(s)/ligament(s) (with continuing disability)	7	3,000
Lower limbs: moderate damage to tendon(s)/ligament(s) (full recovery)	5	2,000
Lower limbs: moderate to tendon(s)/ligament(s) (with continuing disability)	10	5,000
Lower limbs: severe damage to tendon(s)/ligament(s) (full recovery)	7	3,000
Lower limbs: severe damage to tendon(s)/ligament(s) (with continuing disability)	12	7,500
Lower limbs: scarring: minor disfigurement	2	1,250
Lower limbs: scarring: significant disfigurement	4	1,750
Lower limbs: scarring: serious disfigurement	10	5,000
Lower limbs: sprained ankle – disabling for at least 6–13 weeks	1	1,000
Lower limbs: sprained ankle – disabling for more than 13 weeks	6	2,500
Lower limbs: sprained ankle-both feet-disabling for at least 6–13 weeks	5	2,000
Lower limbs: sprained ankle-both feet-disabling for more than 13 weeks	8	3,500
Pattern of severe abuse over a period exceeding 3 years	11	6,000
Repeated non-consensual vaginal and/or anal intercourse over a period up to 3 years	13	10,000

Repeated non-consensual vaginal and/or anal intercourse over a period exceeding 3 years	16	17,500

Sexual Assault (single incident – victim any age)

Minor indecent assault – non-penetrative indecent physical act over clothing	1	1,000
Serious indecent assault – non-penetrative indecent act under clothing	5	2,000
Severe indecent assault – indecent act involving digital, or other non-penile penetration, and/or oral/genital contact	7	3,000
Non-consensual vaginal and/or anal intercourse	12	7,500
Non-consensual vaginal and/or anal intercourse by two or more attackers	13	10,000
Non-consensual vaginal and/or anal intercourse with other serious bodily injuries	16	17,500

Shock

Disabling, but temporary mental anxiety, medically verified	1	1,000

Disabling mental disorder, confirmed by psychiatric diagnosis:

lasting up to 28 weeks	6	2,500
lasting over 28 weeks to one year	9	4,000
lasting over one year but not permanent	12	7,500
Permanently disabling mental disorder confirmed by psychiatric prognosis	17	20,000
Torso: back: fracture of vertebra (full recovery)	6	2,500
Torso: back: fracture of vertebra (continuing disability)	10	5,000
Torso: back: fracture of more than one vertebra (full recovery)	9	4,000
Torso: back: fracture of more than one vertebra (continuing disability)	12	7,500
Torso: back: prolapsed invertebral disc(s) – seriously disabling – not permanent	10	5,000
Torso: back: prolapsed invertebral disc(s) – seriously disabling – permanent	12	7,500
Torso: back: ruptured invertebral disc(s) requiring surgical removal	13	10,000
Torso: back: strained back – disabling for 6 – 13 weeks	1	1,000
Torso: back: strained back – disabling for more than 13 weeks	6	2,500
Torso: back: strained back – seriously disabling – not permanent	10	5,000

Torso: back: strained back – seriously disabling – permanent	12	7,500
Torso: burns: minor	3	1,500
Torso: burns: moderate	9	4,000
Torso: burns: severe	13	10,000
Torso: punctured lung	7	3,000
Torso: two punctured lungs	11	6,000
Torso: collapsed lung	8	3,500
Torso: two collapsed lungs	12	7,500
Torso: permanent and disabling damage to lungs from smoke inhalation	10	5,000
Torso: loss of spleen	9	4,000
Torso: damage to testes	4	1,750
Torso: dislocated hip (full recovery)	4	1,750
Torso: dislocated hip (continuing disability)	12	7,500
Torso: fractured hip	12	7,500
Torso: dislocated shoulder (full recovery)	4	1,750
Torso: dislocated shoulder (continuing disability)	10	5,000
Torso: fractured rib	1	1,000
Torso: fractured rib(s) (two or more)	3	1,500
Torso: fractured clavicle – collar bone	5	2,000
Torso: two fractured clavicles	10	5,000
Torso: fractured coccyx – tail bone	6	2,500
Torso: fractured pelvis	12	7,500
Torso: fractured scapula – shoulder blade	6	2,500
Torso: two fractured scapula	11	6,000
Torso: fractured sternum – breast bone	6	2,500
Torso: frozen shoulder	8	3,500
Torso: hernia	8	3,500
Torso: injury requiring laparotomy	8	3,500
Torso: injury to genitalia requiring medical treatment – no permanent damage	4	1,750
Torso: injury to genitalia requiring medical treatment – permanent damage	10	5,000
Torso: loss of fertility	21	50,000

Torso: loss of kidney	17	20,000
Torso: loss of testicle	10	5,000
Torso: scarring: minor disfigurement	2	1,250
Torso: scarring: significant disfigurement	6	2,500
Torso: scarring: serious disfigurement	10	5,000
Upper limbs: burns: minor	3	1,500
Upper limbs: burns: moderate	9	4,000
Upper limbs: burns: severe	13	10,000
Upper limbs: dislocated/fractured elbow (full recovery)	7	3,000
Upper limbs: dislocated/fractured elbow (continuing disability)	12	7,500
Upper limbs: two dislocated/fractured elbows (full recovery)	12	7,500
Upper limbs: two dislocated/fractured elbows (continuing disability)	13	10,000
Upper limbs: dislocated finger(s) or thumb – one hand (full recovery)	2	1,250
Upper limbs: dislocated finger(s) or thumb – one hand (continuing disability)	6	2,500
Upper limbs: dislocated finger(s) or thumb(s) – both hands (full recovery)	7	3,000
Upper limbs: dislocated finger(s) or thumb(s) – both hands (continuing disability)	12	7,500
Upper limbs: fractured finger(s) or thumb – one hand (full recovery)	3	1,500
Upper limbs: fractured finger(s) or thumb – one hand (continuing disability)	8	3,500
Upper limbs: fractured finger(s) or thumb – both hands (full recovery)	9	4,000
Upper limbs: fractured finger(s) or thumb both hands (continuing disability)	12	7,500
Upper limbs: fractured hand (full recovery)	5	2,000
Upper limbs: fractured hand (continuing disability)	10	5,000
Upper limbs: two fractured hands (full recovery)	8	3,500
Upper limbs: two fractured hands (continuing disability)	12	7,500
Upper limbs: fractured humerus – upper arm bone (full recovery)	7	3,000

Upper limbs: fractured humerus – upper arm bone (continuing disability)	10	5,000
Upper limbs: fractured humerus – both arms (full recovery)	12	7,500
Upper limbs: fractured humerus – both arms (continuing disability)	13	10,000
Upper limbs: fractured radius – smaller forearm bone (full recovery)	7	3,000
Upper limbs: fractured radius – (continuing disability)	10	5,000
Upper limbs: fractured radius – both arms (full recovery)	12	7,500
Upper limbs: fractured radius – both arms (continuing disability)	13	10,000
Upper limbs: fractured ulna – inner forearm bone (full recovery)	7	3,000
Upper limbs: fractured ulna – (continuing disability)	10	5,000
Upper limbs: fractured ulna – both arms (full recovery)	12	7,500
Upper limbs: fractured ulna – both arms (continuing disability)	13	10,000
Upper limbs: fractured wrist – including scaphoid fracture (full recovery)	7	3,000
Upper limbs: fractured wrist – including scaphoid fracture (continuing disability)	11	6,000
Upper limbs: two fractured wrists – including scaphoid fracture (full recovery)	11	6,000
Upper limbs: two fractured wrists – including scaphoid fracture (continuing disability)	13	10,000
Upper limbs: fractured wrist – colles type (full recovery)	9	4,000
Upper limbs: fractured wrist – colles type (continuing disability)	12	7,500
Upper limbs: two fractured wrists – colles type (full recovery)	12	7,500
Upper limbs: two fractured wrists – colles type (continuing disability)	13	10,000
Upper limbs: partial loss of finger (other than thumb/index) (one joint)	6	2,500
Upper limbs: partial loss of thumb or index finger (one joint)	9	4,000
Upper limbs: loss of one finger other than index	10	5,000
Upper limbs: loss of index finger	12	7,500
Upper limbs: loss of two or more fingers	13	10,000
Upper limbs: loss of thumb	15	15,000

Upper limbs: loss of hand	20	40,000
Upper limbs: loss of both hands	23	100,000
Upper limbs: loss of arm	20	40,000
Upper limbs: loss of both arms	23	100,000
Upper limbs: paralysis of arm	19	30,000
Upper limbs: paralysis of both arms	22	75,000
Upper limbs: permanently & seriously impaired grip – one arm	12	7,500
Upper limbs: permanently & seriously impaired grip – both arms	15	15,000
Upper limbs: scarring: minor disfigurement	2	1,250
Upper limbs: scarring: significant disfigurement	6	2,500
Upper limbs: scarring: serious disfigurement	9	4,000
Upper limbs: minor damage to tendon(s)/ligament(s) (full recovery)	1	1,000
Upper limbs: minor damage to tendon(s)/ligament(s) (with continuing disability)	7	3,000
Upper limbs: moderate damage to tendon(s)/ligament(s) (full recovery)	5	2,000
Upper limbs: moderate damage to tendon(s)/ligament(s)	10	5,000
Upper limbs: severely damaged tendon(s)/ligament(s) (full recovery)	7	3,000
Upper limbs: severely damaged tendon(s)/ligament(s) (permanent disability)	12	7,500
Upper limbs: sprained wrist – disabling for 6 – 13 weeks	1	1,000
Upper limbs: sprained wrist – disabling for more than 13 weeks	3	1,500
Upper limbs: two sprained wrists – disabling for 6 – 13 weeks	5	2,000
Upper limbs: two sprained wrists – disabling for more than 13 weeks	7	3,000

Notes to the Tariff

1. Minor injuries will only qualify for compensation where the applicant has sustained at least three separate injuries of the type illustrated below, at least one of which must still have had significant residual effects six weeks after the incident. The injuries must also have necessitated at least two visits to or by a medical practitioner within that six week period. Examples of qualifying injuries are:

   (a) grazing, cuts, lacerations (no permanent scarring)

   (b) severe and widespread bruising

   (c) severe soft tissue injury (no permanent disability)

   (d) black eye(s)

   (e) bloody nose

   (f) hair pulled from scalp

   (g) loss of fingernail

2. Shock or 'nervous shock' may be taken to include conditions attributed to post-traumatic stress disorder, depression and similar generic terms covering:-

   (a) such psychological symptoms as anxiety, tension, insomnia, irritability, loss of confidence, agoraphobia and pre-occupations with thoughts of guilt or self-harm; and

   (b) related physical symptoms such as alopecia, asthma, eczema, enuresis and psoriasis. Disability in this context will include impaired work (or school) performance, significant adverse effects on social relationships and sexual disfunction.

CONTINGENCY FEE AGREEMENT

This agreement is a legally binding contract between you and [   ] solicitors.

Agreement Date

We, the legal representative   **You, the client**

What is covered by this agreement

Your claim for compensation from the Criminal Injuries Compensation Authority (the "Authority") regarding personal injury and/or loss suffered on [   ]

What is not covered by this agreement

Any action you wish us to take in relation to a re-opening or review of the Authority's decision and any appeal against a decision made by the Authority on review.

Paying Us

If you are awarded compensation from the Authority you pay us a sum equivalent to 33% of that compensation plus any disbursements. This figure includes VAT at the rate (now 17½%) that applies when the work is done.

If you lose the case you do not pay us anything.

If you end the agreement before the Authority makes a decision with regard to whether or not to award you compensation, you are liable to pay our costs at the rate of £170 per hour with letters and telephone calls charged at £17 each unless they last for ten minutes or longer in which case they will be charged at the appropriate proportion of the hourly rate. All of these figures attract VAT at the rate (now 17½%) that applies when the work is done.

For what happens if we end the agreement before the Authority makes a decision with regard to whether or not to award you compensation, please refer to paragraph 5.

1 Our responsibilities

We must always act in your best interests in pursuing your claim for compensation and obtaining for you the best possible results, subject to our duty to the Authority.

2 Your responsibilities

You must give us clear instructions which allow us to do our work properly; you must not ask us to work in an improper or unreasonable way; you must not deliberately mislead us; you must co-operate with us when asked; you must pay for disbursements as the case goes on.

3 What happens if you win

If the Authority awards you compensation you pay us a sum equivalent to 33% of any compensation plus any disbursements. You agree that we may receive the compensation the Authority pays to you. If the Authority refuses to accept our receipt, you will pay the cheque you receive into a joint bank account in your name and ours. Out of the money you agree to let us take a sum equivalent to 33% of the damages plus any outstanding disbursements. You take the rest.

If the Authority fails to pay any compensation to you we have the right to take recovery action in your name to enforce a judgement, order or agreement. The costs of this action are payable by you to us in addition to a sum equivalent to 33% of the damages.

4 What happens if you lose

If you lose you do not have to pay us anything, except our disbursements.

5 What happens when the agreement ends before the case itself ends

You can end the agreement at any time. You are then liable to pay us our costs incurred up to the date you end the agreement calculated at the hourly rate.

We can end the agreement if you do not keep to your responsibilities in condition 2. You are then liable to pay us our costs incurred up to the date the agreement ends calculated at the hourly rate.

We can end the agreement if we believe that you are unlikely to obtain compensation from the Authority and you disagree with us. You do not have to pay us anything.

We can end the agreement if you reject our opinion about accepting compensation from the Authority. You are then liable to pay us our costs incurred up to the date the agreement ends calculated at the hourly rate.

6 What happens after the agreement ends

After the agreement ends we will inform the Authority that we are no longer acting as your representative. We have the right to preserve our lien over any property of yours in our possession unless any money owed to us under this agreement is paid in full.

Signed for the legal representative

Signed by the client

Marketing

Marketing

Marketing conditional and contingency fees involves the same principles as marketing any other aspect of a solicitor's practice. The subject of marketing as a whole is beyond the scope of this book but there are some matters particular to conditional and contingency fees which I deal with in this chapter.

Advertising generally is regulated by the Committee for Advertising Practice (CAP – how appropriate for Conditional Fees!) and also the Advertising Standards Authority (ASA). In the case of solicitors, but not outside competitors for legal business, advertising is also regulated by the Law Society.

"No Win – No Fee" in Conditional Fee Agreements

The phrase "No Win – No Fee" to describe conditional and contingency fee arrangements is acceptable, with qualifications, to both CAP and the Law Society.

If Client pays nothing

If the Solicitor *always* pays the insurance premium and *all* disbursements then the term "No Win – No Fee" may be used without qualification.

Client pays insurance only

If the client will not be required to pay for disbursements, but will have to pay the insurance premium then the expression "No Win – No Fee" should be qualified with details of the insurance premium. Thus in non-medical negligence personal injury matters the wording should be:

£95.68 insurance premium payable in road traffic matters, £161.20 in other cases.

This phrase may be asterisked to the foot of the advertisement or bracketed immediately below the wording "No Win – No Fee".

As we have seen in Chapter 5 *Costs Insurance: Accident Line Protect* there are many exclusions even within the field of personal injury to the types of cases that can be insured for the above premia. At present neither the CAP nor the Law Society require any exclusions, or even the fact that there *are* exclusions, to be stated.

As conditional fees are extended to all civil litigation the same principles are almost bound to apply, namely that if the solicitor pays the insurance premium and all disbursements then the phrase may be used without qualification but if the solicitor requires payment of the insurance premium then this must be mentioned in the advertisement.

It is *not* necessary to state the amount of the premium but the ordinary Accident Line Protect premia are relatively low and therefore attractive to mention.

This is *not* the case in medical negligence and will not necessarily be the case in all other civil work. Thus phrases such as:
"Subject to payment of insurance" or "Subject to a one-off insurance premium" *are* acceptable.

Phrases such as "cheap insurance" or "low-cost insurance" should be avoided. These are relative and subjective terms. £95.68 may seem cheap to a solicitor or a comfortably off client – it will certainly not seem so in the future to someone on benefit who wants a no win – no fee arrangement because Legal Aid has been withdrawn from personal injury work.

Client pays insurance and disbursements

Where the client has to fund the insurance premium and the disbursements the qualification should be "Some expenses may be payable" again either bracketed immediately below the wording "No Win – No Fee" or asterisked to the foot of the advertisement.

Such wording may be used even if the client is only liable to pay the insurance premium and the phrase "some expenses may be payable" is probably preferable to the insurance wording, which although exposing the client to less expenditure is rather clumsy now that Accident Line Protect have introduced different premia for different types of case.

Furthermore as conditional fees are extended to all other civil litigation there will be many different insurance policies issued and many different premia. A standard "some expenses may be payable" allows individual firms and the profession generally to get a simple message across in a simple way in all areas of work.

The permitted wording and its placement minimise the extent to which the powerful and attractive phrase "No Win – No Fee" is diluted. Asterisking to the bottom of the page is probably the most effective way of keeping clean the "No Win – No Fee" message.

The Choices

Thus the choices are:

NO WIN – NO FEE
(Some expenses may be payable)
or
NO WIN – NO FEE*
[advertisement]
*Some expenses may be payable

The above wording and methods satisfy both the Law Society and the Committee for Advertising Practice and any proposed alternative wording may be cleared direct with CAP's copy advice team on 0171 580 4100.

As a result of a decision by the Advertising Standards Authority, the insurance premium has been held not to be "a fee". Furthermore it was held the phrase "No Win – No Fee" did not imply that the offer was open to everyone. (*Law Society's Gazette* 10th July 1996)

The Cap

Provided you use the Underwood's method, see Chapter 3 *The Success Fee and the Cap – Myth and Reality, i.e.* cap *all* the fees to the client, that is basic costs *and* the success fee then the following phrase is acceptable:

MAXIMUM 25%* OF DAMAGES

---

* including VAT

If you intend to use the Law Society's Model Conditional Fee Agreement method, *i.e.* cap only the *success fee* then this needs to be stated, *e.g.*

MAXIMUM SUCCESS FEE – 25% OF DAMAGES

Even this may be held to be misleading as it does not make it clear that the client will have to pay solicitor's fees over and above the success fee and that this may wipe out the damages.

(For a full discussion of these matters see Chapter 3 *The Success Fee and the Cap – Myth and Reality*).

If Value Added Tax is to be charged *on top* of the 25% **this should be clearly stated**. If a client receives £10,000 damages and is charged a capped success fee of:

25%	£2,500.00
VAT thereon	£437.50
	£2,937.50

The client will, quite rightly, point out that that is a success fee of 29.375% and not 25%.

The current Law Society Model Conditional Fee Agreement provides for VAT to be added to the 25% cap giving an effective "take" from the client's damages of 29.375%.

My clear advice is that the cap should *include* VAT, *i.e.* that you take 25% including VAT. This is very much easier to market and it is fairer to the client and any changes in the rate of VAT do not affect the sum paid to the client. (To calculate the VAT contained within a gross sum divide the gross sum by 47 and multiply the rest by 7.)

Example

	£
Damages	10,000.00
Capped success fee including VAT =	2,500.00
2,500 ÷ 47 = 53.19	
53.19 X 7 = 372.34	
Therefore net costs (2,500 – 372.34) =	2,127.66
Thus costs	2,127.66
VAT thereon at 17.5%	372.34
	2,500.00

It will be seen that including the VAT in the 25% produces an actual cap of 21.28% net of VAT.

Note that even if VAT is included in the 25% cap this fact must be stated. This is because of Paragraph 5(a) of the Solicitors' Publicity Code:

> Any publicity as to charges or a basis of charging must be clearly expressed. It must be stated what services will be provided for those charges or on that basis of charging. Any circumstances in which the charges may be increased or the basis altered must be stated. It must be clear whether disbursements and VAT are included.

The rules concerning claiming expertise are exactly the same as any other type of work or method of funding. It is permissible to mention membership of any Law Society Panel. At present the relevant ones would be the Personal Injury Panel and the Medical Negligence Panel but this will change as conditional fees are extended. In insolvency advertisements mention of membership of the Insolvency Practitioners Association would be relevant. Beyond that the normal rules apply.

At Appendix 10 is the Solicitors' Publicity Code.

At Appendix 9 is the Law Society Guidance on the Application of Existing Rules and Principles of Professional Conduct to Conditional Fee Arrangements.

I have dealt with specific examples relating to Personal Injury cases because that is the major field where conditional fee agreements are already allowed and thus some "case law" has developed. The principle however will apply is exactly the same way to all other areas of *conditional* fees as their scope is extended.

Contingency Fees

Exactly the same principles apply but generally there will be no insurance premia payable as at present contingency fees are only permissible in non-contentious work where generally costs do *not* follow the event and thus there is no potential liability for the other side's costs.

Obviously if no insurance premium is payable the relevant wording can be omitted. Likewise if no expenses are payable – as will be the case generally in Industrial Tribunal cases – the advertisement need not contain any qualifying words thus leaving the "No Win – No Fee" tag clean.

It is for each firm to devise its own advertising campaign and that will depend upon the image the firm wishes to promote. However at the end of this chapter are some examples of my own firm's advertisements which, so far, have emerged unscathed by the Committee for Advertising Practice. (Some earlier ones were more controversial!). For my firm these advertisements have been very successful.

A Word of Warning

Some solicitors do not like conditional fees and they do not like the threat that they pose to their traditional inefficient expensive way of working. Some of these solicitors prefer to spend their time making complaints about advertisements rather than developing their practices and offering their services in a way that is attractive to their clients, that is the public. One major local Law Society apparently takes the same view.

In order that we may return these legal dinosaurs to their own little Jurassic Park I will give preliminary advice free of charge in relation to actual complaints about any actual advertisement. In any event I want to co-ordinate information on complaints and the firms making these complaints, and the attitude being taken by the Law Society.

Referral Agencies

Conditional fees are still not being widely offered by solicitors. Thus it is useful and profitable to ensure that everyone who does, or may, refer work to you is aware that you offer conditional fees as part of your company's service to its clients.

For example ensure that your local Citizens Advice Bureau is aware that you offer this service and *how it works*. Offer to train their advisers. Prepare a leaflet. Buy them a copy of this book! Keep referral agencies up to date with developments, including related topics, such as the withdrawal of legal aid or a toughening up of the merits test.

Clients

Write to all existing and past clients explaining that your firm now offers "no win – no fee" as part of its service. Explain the areas where this is allowed and how it works.

As conditional fees are extended to other areas write to your clients again. Keep repeating the message.

Consider targeting particular groups of clients. For example small businesses are likely to find conditional fees particularly attractive as it enables them to budget and to know their maximum liability: offer to address the local Chamber of Commerce. As conditional fees are extended to other areas and the Woolf Report fixed costs regime comes in much greater certainty is imported into the whole field of legal costs. Properly marketed this will lead to a major expansion of work for solicitors.

The Law Society commissioned Gallup to do an omnibus survey in March 1994. 3,000 people were interviewed but the figures were extrapolated up to the general population to produce the following results:

- 3.7 million accidents had occurred in the last 12 months
- 7 million had accidents in the previous 3 years. Of the 7 million:
- 3 million sought advice from their doctors
- 37% felt someone else was at fault
- 28% felt it was their own fault
- 12% felt it was shared fault
- 23% felt it was no-ones fault – (still a huge number who do not realise that they can pursue a claim)

Where advice was sought:

- 45% sought advice from their GPS
- 24% no advice was sought
- 13% other
- 12% sought advice from solicitors
- 5% sought advice from friends/families
- 6% sought advice from police
- 1% sought advice from CABx

- 21% stated they planned to pursue a claim
- 77% did not.

Of those who pursued a claim:

- 66% went through their solicitor
- 27% went through their insurance company
- 7% other
- 0% (less than 1%) went through a claims adjuster.

1998

NEW YEAR – NEW PROMISES
UNDERWOODS SOLICITORS
SETTING THE STANDARDS

Our promises to you:-

- **FREE first interview**
- **First appointment within 48 hours**
- **All calls answered promptly and returned within 24 hours**
- **Written reports on your matter at least once per month**
- **You will be seen on time for your appointment**

We also offer:-

- **Evening appointments**
- **No win – No Fee***
- **FREE Car parking**
- **Freephone telephone number and FREEPOST address**

Thank you to those people who returned our questionnaires.
We do listen and value your opinions!

UNDERWOODS SOLICITORS
SERVING ST ALBANS

•Where permitted by Parliament.
Some expenses may be payable. Insurance against paying costs is available. We will pay this if you cannot afford it.

Future Shock

Future Shock

Conditional Fees

Conditional Fees will be extended to all civil work save family work, probably with effect from Autumn 1998. In its consultation paper *Access to Justice with Conditional Fees* (Appendix 27 to this book) in March 1998, the Lord Chancellor's Department says at paragraph 2.7:

> The Government wishes, subject to this consultation, to allow conditional fee agreements to be entered into in *any* proceedings, save in the categories presently prescribed by statute, that is family and criminal cases.

It is likely that the regulations and orders covering the new fields where conditional fees will become available will follow the Conditional Fee Agreements Order 1995 and the Conditional Fees Agreements Regulations 1995 dealing with the existing areas of work, that is personal injury, insolvency and human rights.

However there are two significant proposed changes covering all conditional fee cases.

Insurance Premium

The Government proposes that any insurance premium paid to protect against meeting an opponents costs should be recoverable against the losing party as a disbursement. This would of course make acting on a conditional fee basis more attractive although its effect may not be as significant as first appears.

In cases where the plaintiff has a strong chance of winning, such as personal injury cases, the insurance premium is modest precisely because the risk of losing, and therefore the insurers' exposure, is low. Thus lawyers and clients need little extra incentive to take on these cases.

The problem comes when the insurance premium is high and of course the reason it is high is because of the high risks and higher level of costs as already seen in medical negligence cases.

The Government's proposal would of course assist a *winning* party but the whole point of taking out insurance is that at that stage the party is unsure as to whether or not they will win. Thus the high cost of insurance premia in difficult areas is likely to remain a deterrent to plaintiffs and their lawyers, even if they become recoverable in the event of a win.

Nevertheless this proposal is welcomed.

The Success Fee

A more controversial and significant proposal is that the winning party's success fee should be recoverable from the losing side. Thus in personal injury cases, where the imposition of the cap normally determines the success fee, the losing defendant will be liable to pay the plaintiff's solicitor 25% of the damages on top of the ordinary inter-partes costs, which in the vast majority of cases are likely from October 1999 to be fixed costs under the Woolf Report.

The Government itself in its proposals recognises that this is likely to create satellite litigation.

This proposal is, in my view, unwise. Not only is it unfair on defendants that they should have to pay a very significant extra fee dependant upon what method of funding the plaintiff uses but it will inevitably create satellite litigation.

One of the joys of the Woolf Report is that there will be no arguments about costs, which will be fixed, and a defendant will be obliged to accompany the damages cheque with a costs cheque in the fixed sum.

Thus although the fixed costs on average will be lower than costs at present, solicitors will be spared the significant costs incurred in instructing costs draftsmen and dealing with court taxation of inter-partes costs. This benefit will be lost if there are arguments, as there are bound to be, between plaintiff's lawyers and defendants over the success fee.

Furthermore it is bound to lead to increased success fees. The 25% voluntary cap has become almost standard and many firms utilise the Underwoods method and cap *all* charges to their client at 25%. Solicitors will have no incentive to do this if the success fee is to be paid by a losing party. Rather it will be in the solicitor's interest to be pitch the success fee as high as possible but settle for what they can get from the other side and not bother to bill their own clients or to agree a fixed sum with the client irrespective of the costs recovered from the other side.

This will put us straight back into the "speculative funding" system which operated for decades before the introduction of conditional fees.

The Government's proposals seemed to be based on a mis-understanding of the existing situation as at paragraph 2.14 the consultation paper says:

> It seems wrong that a successful party who without a conditional fee agreement might not have been able to bring their case is unable to recover all the lawyers costs that they have incurred.

Well the system of inter-partes costs and taxation has always meant that a winning party has to bear some of their own costs and further more the whole point of the Woolf Report is to limit the exposure of the losing party to pay the winning party's costs.

Furthermore the Government proposes to raise the Small Claims limit to £5,000 which will mean that most people in most cases will have to pay *all* of their own lawyer's fees even if they win.

This proposal is in direct contrast to the whole tone of the Woolf Report and it is hard to see how the Woolf Report fast track fixed costs system can be introduced alongside a system where plaintiff lawyers can recover the success fee in conditional fee cases.

Peter Hurst, the Chief Taxing Master takes the same view:

> There is a far better argument for recovering the insurance premium than there is for recovering a success fee.
>
> (*New Law Journal* 20 March 1998)

Legal Aid

There are three distinct and separate threats to Legal Aid work:

- that Legal Aid will be abolished completely for certain types of work;
- that the terms on which Legal Aid will be available will make it unobtainable and/or unacceptable to most clients;
- that block contracts, fundholding and restricting Legal Aid work to Panel Members will make Legal Aid literally unavailable as far as most firms of solicitors are concerned

and deeply unattractive to many of the firms who would qualify for Legal Aid work.

The Lord Chancellor's Department Consultation Paper *Access to Justice with Conditional Fees* March 1998 is in fact mainly concerned with the withdrawal or reduction of Legal Aid and only a relatively small part deals with conditional fees.

This is a very important document as it sets out the Government's proposals in relation to both Legal Aid and Conditional Fees and the whole document is attached at Appendix 27.

The Government view of Legal Aid and its proposals to reduce the budget closely follow those contained in the previous Government's White Paper on Legal Aid entitled

> *Striking the Balance – the Future of Legal Aid in England and Wales* (HMSO CM 3503)

presented to Parliament in June 1996.

The closing date for responses to the consultation paper was 30th April 1998 and at the time of writing (June 1998) no announcement has been made concerning the results of that consultation process.

Abolition of Legal Aid

In the consultation paper the Government proposes *removing entirely from the scope of Legal Aid* all money or damages claims. It proposes the immediate abolition of Legal Aid in the following areas:

- Personal Injury cases except Medical Negligence;
- disputes about inheritance under a will or an intestacy;
- matters affecting the administration of a trust or the position of a trustee;
- matters relating to the position of directors of companies, restoring a company to the Register or dealing with the position of minority shareholders;
- matters affecting partnerships;
- matters before the Lands Tribunal;
- cases between landowners over a disputed boundary of adjacent property;
- cases pursued in the course of a business.

(paragraphs 3.23 and 3.24)

The Government calculates that these immediate changes will lead to 60% of money or damages claims being removed form the scope of Legal Aid. These changes do not require legislation and are likely to be implemented by early 1999.

Deferred Abolition of Legal Aid in the Remaining Areas

The Government proposes the abolition of Legal Aid in all other money or damages claims, including medical negligence, but recognises that there will need to be a transitional period of a "few years" to allow conditional fees and associated insurance products to develop. *(paragraph 3.27)*

Thus the Government's clear proposal is to abolish Legal Aid entirely in all money or damages claims over the next few years with the categories listed above being excluded immediately. It is anticipated that the proposal to remove Legal Aid in this second group of cases, and the transitional arrangements relating thereto will be contained in the Modernisation of Justice Bill expected to be presented to Parliament in late 1998. However there is now speculation that this Bill, which will also introduce the Woolf Report reforms, will be deferred until 1999.

Medical Negligence

Legal Aid will remain available in medical negligence cases but only for the "next few years" and only a very small number of firms will be able to undertake such work.

At paragraphs 3.18 and 3.19 the Government states

> We propose to limit the right of choice of solicitor who may undertake medical negligence cases under Legal Aid.
>
> In future, the Legal Aid Board should provide assistance in these cases through contracts under Part IV of the Legal Aid Act 1988. Contracts would be given only to solicitors who have shown that they have sufficient competence in this area. Competence might be demonstrated by membership of the Law Society's Medical Negligence Panel, or of some other panel (for example, that maintained by the Association for Victims of Medical Negligence), or by some other objectively verifiable criteria.

High Cost Cases

The Government is considering a temporary special Legal Aid scheme for high costs cases but this would be limited to cases where the Plaintiff's **costs** are likely to exceed £100,000.

This applies to so few cases and affects so few clients and so few firms of solicitors that it is not worth considering in detail but the fund should be in place by early 1999.

Block Contracting

In those limited areas where Legal Aid will remain it will be restricted to those solicitors who have contracts with the Legal Aid Board. This is another cost-cutting, and therefore fee-reducing, exercise. At *paragraph 1.7* the consultation paper reads:

> Contracting will allow the Government to get the most for the money that is spent and to spend it on those cases which most need it.

In any event who on earth in their right mind is going to apply for a contract to do Legal Aid work in an area where the Government has openly said it intends to abolish *completely* in "the next few years"? (Well lots of you actually but don't say I did not warn you!)

Toughening of Merits Test

The Consultation Paper says that it intends to "remove weak cases from the Legal Aid system by toughening the legal merits test so that only cases with a strong prospect of success are supported with taxpayers money." *(paragraph 1.7)* It says that "too many weak cases are granted legal aid. The hopes of litigants are unrealistically raised, and the opposing party is exposed to unnecessary costs which they cannot recover."

Still want to apply for your Legal Aid Franchise?

Community Legal Service

Well I have publicly supported this idea for 23 years so I am not about to start criticising it now. (See page 283, Report of the 74th Annual Conference of the Labour Party, Blackpool 1975 – when I was just 19 years old!)

However it does mean that what limited public money is made available for legal services will not all end up in private practice and indeed why should it? Solicitors in private practice are likely to see an ever decreasing percentage of their fees being recovered from the State.

The Consultation Paper states:

> The Community Legal Service will vary from area to area according to local needs. The principle will be to provide effective mechanisms to enable the socially excluded and economically disadvantaged to enforce the legal rights which substantially influence their lives, such as housing, welfare, consumer and employment rights.

Miscellaneous

Housing Claims

The Government proposes, *at paragraph 3.12*, that some form of public money remain available for both parties in housing matters although no details are given as to the operation of any such scheme.

It is likely that housing claims will be one of the main areas of work of the Community Legal Services.

Judicial Review

The Government states that it believes it right to ensure that the poor are also able to exercise the right of challenges through judicial review, and that legal aid should remain available for those who qualify.

In spite of this assurance, the position is likely to worsen for such cases as the toughening of the merits test will hit judicial review cases particularly hard.

Victims of Public Authorities

The consultation paper states:

similar special considerations apply where a person claims that he is the victim of some action of the authorities, for example, the police. The Government believes that assistance must continue to be available, for the present, to allow those who qualify for legal aid to bring claims of this kind.

Contracted Legal Aid

It is now clear that legal aid will remain available in certain areas for a few years but, as has long been proposed, only those solicitors holding contracts with the Legal Aid Board will be able to carry out such work.

In "Reforming the civil advice and assistance scheme – exclusive contracting – the way forward" (April 1998) the Legal Aid Board proposes that, apart from family matters, between 100 and 200 Green Form contracts will cover the entire country by the end of 1999. That works out at one firm per 500,000 of the population on the basis of 100. Thus, excluding family work, just *one* firm in say, Liverpool, or Manchester or Leeds or Newcastle or Plymouth or Bristol will be allowed to do *any* Green Form work. This document, according to Steve Orchard, Chief Executive of the LAB (equivalent to Captain of the Titanic) will be the foundation for all future legal aid contracting.

Excluding the areas of family law and criminal law where there is no immediate proposal to abolish or restrict legal aid, will legal aid work be worth doing?

It is important to realise that cash controlled fixed costs do *not* mean fixed fees per case as already exists in criminal and some other types of work. It is not a "swings and roundabouts" approach that rewards efficient firms who can do the same job in less time. Far from it. Fixed costs means that a firm will get the contract to do all of the legal aid work in one town in one category for three years at a price of say £50,000 per annum, subject to a minimum caseload. Thus there will be a little incentive for a firm to market itself, develop a reputation and expand because no more fees will be forthcoming in the three year period. The object will be to do as little work as possible whilst satisfying the criteria.

The carrot of an improved new contract at the end of the three year period is a particularly mouldy one. The firm will be heavily dependent upon Legal Aid and other methods of funding, such as conditional fees will, of necessity have been developed and concentrated on by competitors. If you lose your contract you stand to lose much of your business just as cleaning companies do when they lose a contract to clean a County's schools or a Trust's hospitals. What happens there is that most of the staff simply transfer to the new contractor.

Is that the way you want to build up your practice?

Remember too that this is a cost-cutting exercise – it does not pretend to be anything else. It is the whole basis of the proposal. It is your costs that will be cut.

Furthermore solicitors operating under a fixed price contract will be under enormous pressure to offer a second rate service, particularly when it comes to experts' reports. Who is going to get the better, more expensive report, the contract solicitor who has to pay it out of his own budget or the conditional fee solicitor whose client is insured for it?

True in most cases both will get it back from the Defendant's insurers at the end of the day but every time you fail to do so it is £500 or so *out of profit costs.*

The contract solicitor needs to have a far sharper risk-assessment procedure than a conditional fee solicitor. The risk of losing some cases is part of the conditional fee deal and it is compensated by the extra fee – the success fee – and extra clients. Contract Legal Aid work has all the risks of conditional fees and none of the benefits.

In conditional fee work if you lose you get nothing. At present if the client is legally aided you get £65 per hour. In the future every loss including disbursements is simply paid for out of your contract fee, *i.e.* out of your own money. With the best will in the world this is bound to lead to legal aid clients getting a second class service.

Example

You have two clients with identical circumstances and cases: Linda Appleby (LA) chooses Legal Aid whereas Charlie Farthing (CF) chooses a Conditional Fee Agreement.

Matters proceed. You have used up most of your Legal Aid budget. Employment Consultant's reports are required. You can get by without them but the case will be less well presented and the damages lower. This was recognised by solicitors' firms taking part in the Green Form Block Contract Pilot, in a Briefing Note (page 129 of documentation in Law Society Conference of 29 April 1998: *Contracting Services – The Future of Legal Aid?*)

> Firms were concerned that there would be a conflict of interest with their clients in that firms may be reluctant to spend money on disbursements for fear of running out of contract money before the end of the contract.

Charlie Farthing presents no problem. You obtain an Employment Consultant's report, the cost of which you recover if you win and is insured if you lose.

What about legally-aided Linda Appleby?

Supposing you had had a Legal Aid contract in early 1997 when court fees were increased massively. Where would the extra come from? You.

There is a further major objection to Legal Aid contracts. They will take away your independence and your client's independence.

"Loser pays" – but for how much longer?

The need for costs insurance is primarily caused by the rule that an unsuccessful party in a legal action pays the other side's costs and the successful party recovers part of his or her costs, a concept generally known amongst lawyers as "costs following the event". The justification is that a party put to the expense of engaging lawyers should not be out of pocket if the court finds that they are in the right.

In reality the rule now operates in an almost arbitrary manner due to the large number of exceptions. Personal injury work is one area where the rule still applies, but in the majority of other cases it does not now apply. With the likelihood that conditional fees will be introduced for all civil work thought needs to be given now to the future.

The Future

Operating successfully, and profitably under Woolf involves many of the same consideration and changes required to operate conditional fees successfully.

Costs are directly related to the damages recovered and to the stage of proceedings reached, *not* the number of hours racked up.

Efficient solicitors who make good use of information technology, precedent letters and documents and standard procedures will profit.

Cases will be dealt with more quickly and with less work. Removal of the twin obstacles of cost and delay will encourage far more clients to instruct solicitors. Indeed this is an inherent and interesting dilemma of the Woolf Report. Entitled *Access to Justice* it seeks in part to remove cases from the court system but recognises that improving access to justice will increase work for solicitors by providing them with more clients. These are not necessarily incompatible aims and The Woolf Report recognises that defendants must no longer be allowed to delay matters for tactical reasons.

All of this is good news for personal injury solicitors. Some commentators believe that the Woolf Report fails to take proper heed of conditional fees. I believe the opposite is true. The whole fast-track procedure can only work in the context of conditional fees.

Super Future Shock 2010
– A Law Odyssey

Betty Green is injured in a road traffic accident. As the airbag is activated so the emergency services are automatically alerted by satellite and an immediate record is made of the speed at the time of collision, the position of the vehicles and pedestrians, the weather conditions, temperatures, road conditions and all other information relevant to the accident which has of course been recorded on video cameras.

Both parties' insurers are automatically notified by the vehicle.

Betty Green is injured and attends the automated Medical Report Centre (MedCent) which she accesses by way of credit card. She follows the instructions throughout the automated process and at the end of it is presented with a detailed medical report.

Betty Green goes home and reads and considers the report.

She accesses the internet and pays a further fee to CompAssess and electronically sends the report to CompAssess.

CompAssess is the automated government system which lists generals damages for every conceivable injury and was originally based on a greatly expanded Judicial Studies Board Guidelines and Criminal Injuries Compensation Authority Tariff.

Betty Green's report is automatically read and considered by CompAssess which within minutes provided her with a detailed advice on quantum with supporting cases and CompAssess Guidelines.

CompAssess also carries out a full interest calculation.

All major insurers have agreed to accept the reports of the MedCent and the findings of CompAssess and thus Betty Green electronically sends the report and CompAssess' statement to the other side's insurers and two minutes later Betty Green receives electronic confirmation that 10,000 euros have been transferred to her account.

The money will come in useful as Betty Green is unemployed having been recently made redundant from her post as a Personal Injury Solicitor.

THE END

JUNE 1998

Courts and Legal Services Act 1990, s.58

Conditional Fee Agreements

58–(1) In this section "a conditional fee agreement" means an agreement in writing between a person providing advocacy or litigation services and his client which –

    (a)   does not relate to proceedings of a kind mentioned in subsection (10);

    (b)   provides for that person's fees and expenses, or any part of them, to be payable only in specified circumstances;

    (c)   complies with such requirements (if any) as may be prescribed by the Lord Chancellor; and

    (d)   is not a contentious business agreement (as defined by section 59 of the Solicitors Act 1974)[1]

(2) Where a conditional fee agreement provides for the amount of any fees to which it applies to be increased, in specified circumstances, above the amount which would be payable if it were not a conditional fee agreement, it shall specify the percentage by which that amount is to be increased.

(3) Subject to subsection (6), a conditional fee agreement which relates to specified proceedings shall not be unenforceable by reason only of its being a conditional fee agreement.

(4) In this section "specified proceedings" means proceedings of a description specified by order made by the Lord Chancellor for the purposes of subsection (3).

(5) Any such order shall prescribe the maximum percentage for each description of specified proceedings.

(6) An agreement which falls within subsection (2) shall be unenforceable if, at the time when it is entered into, the percentage specified in the agreement exceeds the prescribed maximum permitted percentage for each description of proceedings to which it relates.

(7) Before making any order under this section the Lord Chancellor shall consult the designated judges, the General Council of the Bar, the Law Society and such other authorised bodies (if any) as he considers appropriate.

---

1   1974 C.47

(8) Where a party to any proceedings has entered into a conditional fee agreement and a costs order is made in those proceedings in his favour, the costs payable to him shall not include any element which takes account of any percentage increase payable under the agreement.

(9) Rules of court may make provision with respect to the taxing of any costs which include fees payable under a conditional fee agreement.

(10) The proceedings mentioned in subsection (1)(a) are any criminal proceedings and any proceedings under –

    (a)   the Matrimonial Causes Act 1973[2];
    (b)   the Domestic Violence and Matrimonial Proceedings Act 1976[3];
    (c)   the Adoption Act 1976[4];
    (d)   the Domestic Proceedings and Magistrates' Courts Act 1978[5];
    (e)   sections 1 and 9 of the Matrimonial Homes Act 1983[6];
    (f)   Part III of the Matrimonial and Family Proceedings Act 1984[7];
    (g)   Parts I, II or IV of the Children Act 1989[8]; or
    (h)   the inherent jurisdiction of the High Court in relation to children.

2 1973 c.18
3 1976 c.50
4 1976 c.36
5 1978 c.22
6 1983 c.19
7 1984 c.42
8 1989 c.41

Conditional Fee Agreements Order 1998 (S.I. 1998 no. 1860)

The Lord Chancellor, in exercise of the powers conferred on him by sections 58(4) and (5) of the Courts and Legal Services Act 1990 [1990 c.41], having consulted in accordance with section 58(7) of that Act, makes the following Order, a draft of which has been laid before and approved by resolution of each House of Parliament:

Citation and commencement and interpretation

1. (1) This Order may be cited as the Conditional Fee Agreements Order 1998 and shall come into force on the day after the day on which it is made.
   (2) In this Order "the Act" means the Courts and Legal Services Act 1990.

Revocation of 1995 Order

2. The Conditional Fee Agreements Order 1995 [S.I. 1995/1674] is revoked.

Specified proceedings

3. (1) All proceedings are proceedings specified for the purposes of section 58(3) of the Act (conditional fee agreements in respect of specified proceedings not to be unenforceable).
   (2) Proceedings specified in paragraph (1) shall be specified proceedings notwithstanding that they are concluded without the commencement of court proceedings.

Maximum permitted percentage increase on fees

4. For the purposes of section 58(5) of the Act the maximum permitted percentage by which fees may be increased in respect of any proceedings designated by article 3 as proceedings specified for purposes of section 58(3) of the Act is 100%.

Explanatory Note

(This note is not part of the Order)

Section 58 of the Courts and Legal Services Act 1990 provides that a conditional fee agreement which relates to specified proceedings shall not be unenforceable by reason only of its being a conditional fee agreement. Section 58(1)(a) excludes agreements in respect of criminal proceedings and specified family proceedings from the scope of section 58. This Order replaces the Conditional Fee Agreements Order 1995, which specified a limited number of categories of proceedings, and specifies instead all proceedings (within the scope of section 58(7)) without any exceptions.

The Order also specifies (as did the 1995 Order) that the maximum percentage by which fees may be increased in respect of the specified proceedings is 100%.

August 1998

Statutory Instruments

1995 No. 1675
LEGAL SERVICES
THE CONDITIONAL FEE AGREEMENTS REGULATIONS 1995

Made	4th July 1995
Coming into force	5th July 1995

Whereas a draft of the above Regulations has been laid before and approved by resolution of each House of Parliament:

Now, therefore, the Lord Chancellor, in exercise of the powers conferred on him by sections 58(1) and 119 of the Courts and Legal Services Act 1990(1990 c.41. section 119 is an interpretation provision and is cited because of the meaning assigned to the word "prescribed"), hereby makes the following Regulations:-

Citation, commencement and interpretation

1. (1) These Regulations may be cited as the Conditional Fee Agreements Regulations 1995 and shall come into force on the day after the day on which they are made.
   (2) In these Regulations –
   "agreement" in relation to an agreement between a legal representative and an additional legal representative, includes a retainer;
   "legal aid" means representation under Part IV of the Legal Aid Act 1988(1988 c.34);
   "legal representative" means a person providing advocacy or litigation services.

Agreements to comply with prescribed requirements

2. An agreement shall not be a conditional fee agreement unless it complies with the requirements of the following regulations.

Requirements of an agreement

3. An agreement shall state –
   (a) the particular proceedings or parts of them to which it relates (including whether it relates to any counterclaim, appeal or proceedings to enforce a judgment or order);

(b)   the circumstances in which the legal representative's fees and expenses or part of them are payable;

(c)   what, if any, payment is due –
    (i)   upon partial failure of the specified circumstances to occur;
    (ii)   irrespective of the specified circumstances occurring; and
    (iii)   upon termination of the agreement for any reason;

(d)   the amount payable in accordance with sub-paragraphs (b) or (c) above or the method to be used to calculate the amount payable; and in particular whether or not the amount payable is limited by reference to the amount of any damages which may be recovered on behalf of the client.

Additional requirements

4.   (1)   The agreement shall also state that, immediately before it was entered into, the legal representative drew the client's attention to the matters specified in paragraph (2).

   (2)   The matters are –
    (a)   whether the client might be entitled to legal aid in respect of the proceedings to which the agreement relates, the conditions upon which legal aid is available and the application of those conditions to the client in respect of the proceedings;
    (b)   the circumstances in which the client may be liable to pay the fees and expenses of the legal representative in accordance with the agreement;
    (c)   the circumstances in which the client may be liable to pay the costs of any other party to the proceedings; and
    (d)   the circumstances in which the client may seek taxation of the fees and expenses of the legal representative and the procedure for so doing.

Application of regulation 4

5.   Regulation 4 shall not apply to an agreement between a legal representative and an additional legal representative.

Form of agreement

6.   An agreement shall be in writing and, except in the case of an agreement between a legal representative and an additional legal representative, shall be signed by the client and the legal representative.

Amendment of agreement

7.   Where it is proposed to extend the agreement to cover further proceedings or parts of them regulations 3 to 6 shall apply to the agreement as extended.

Dated 4th July 1995   *MacKay of Clashfern.C.*

EXPLANATORY NOTE

(This note is not part of the Regulations)

These Regulations prescribe the requirements with which an agreement between a client and his legal representative must comply so as to enable it to be a conditional fee agreement under section 58 of the Courts and Legal Services Act 1990.

The Regulations are also applied with modifications to an agreement between a legal representative and additional representative, eg solicitor and counsel

Civil Procedure Rules Part 48.9

Part 48.9 Conditional Fees

(1) This rule applies to every assessment (whether by the summary or detailed procedure) of a solicitor's bill to his client where the solicitor and the client have entered into a conditional fee agreement as defined in section 58 of the Courts and Legal Services Act 1990.

(2) In this rule –

'the base costs' means the costs other than a percentage increase;

'percentage increase' means a percentage increase pursuant to a conditional fee agreement entered into between the solicitor and his client or between counsel and the solicitor, or counsel and the client; and

'costs' includes all fees, charges, disbursements and other expenses charged by the solicitor or counsel under the conditional fee agreement in question.

(3) On an assessment to which this rule applies, the client may apply for assessment of the base costs or of a percentage increase or of both.

(4) Where the client applied for assessment of the base costs, the base costs are to be assessed in accordance with rule 48.8(2) as if the solicitor and his client had not entered into a conditional fee agreement.

(5) Where the client applies for assessment of a percentage increase, the court may reduce the percentage increase where it considers it to be disproportionate having regard to all relevant factors as they reasonably appeared to the solicitor or counsel when the conditional fee agreement was entered into.

(6) The court will not vary a percentage increase where the client is a child or patient, except in accordance with paragraph (5).

Civil Procedure Rules – Practice Direction Re Conditional Fees

Part 48.9 Conditional Fees

2.13 (1) A Client who has entered into a conditional fee agreement with a solicitor may apply for assessment of the base costs (which is carried out in accordance with Rule 48.8(2) as if there was no conditional fee agreement) or for assessment of the percentage increase (success fee) or both.

(2) Where the court is to assess the percentage increase, proportionality is relevant and the court will have regard to all the relevant factors as they appeared to the solicitor or counsel when the conditional fee agreement was entered into.

2.14 Where the client applies to the court to reduce the percentage increase which the solicitor has charged the client under the conditional fee agreement, the client must set out in writing in his application:

(a) the reason why the percentage increase should be reduced; and

(b) what the percentage increase should be.

2.15 The factors relevant to assessing the percentage increase include:

(a) the risk that the circumstances in which the fees or expenses would be payable might not occur;

(b) the disadvantages relating to the absence of payment on account;

(c) whether the amount which might be payable under the conditional fee agreement is limited to a certain proportion of any damages recovered by the client;

(d) whether there is a conditional fee agreement between the solicitor and counsel;

(e) the solicitor's liability for any disbursements.

2.16 When the court is considering the factors to be taken into account, it will have regard to the circumstances as they reasonably appeared to the solicitor or counsel when the conditional fee agreement was entered into or at the time of any variation of the agreement.

Section 27,
Access to Justice Act 1999

Conditional Fee Agreements

27. – (1) For section 58 of the Courts and Legal Services Act 1990 substitute-

"**Conditional fee agreements.**

58. – (1)   A conditional fee agreement which satisfies all of the conditions applicable to it by virtue of this section shall not be unenforceable by reason only of its being a conditional fee agreement; but (subject to subsection (5)) any other conditional fee agreement shall be unenforceable.

(2)   For the purposes of this section and section 58A-

(a)   a conditional fee agreement is an agreement with a person providing advocacy or litigation services which provides for his fees and expenses, or any part of them, to be payable only in specified circumstances; and

(b)   a conditional fee agreement provides for a success fee if it provides for the amount of any fees to which it applies to be increased, in specified circumstances, above the amount which would be payable if it were not payable only in specified circumstances.

(3)   The following conditions are applicable to every conditional fee agreement-

(a)   it must be in writing;

(b)   it must not relate to proceedings which cannot be the subject of an enforceable conditional fee agreement; and

(c)   it must comply with such requirements (if any) as may be prescribed by the Lord Chancellor.

(4)   The following further conditions are applicable to a conditional fee agreement which provides for a success fee-

(a)   it must relate to proceedings of a description specified by order made by the Lord Chancellor;

(b)   it must state the percentage by which the amount of the fees which would be payable if it were not a conditional fee agreement is to be increased; and

(c) that percentage must not exceed the percentage specified in relation to the description of proceedings to which the agreement relates by order made by the Lord Chancellor.

(5) If a conditional fee agreement is an agreement to which section 57 of the Solicitors Act 1974 (non-contentious business agreements between solicitor and client) applies, subsection (1) shall not make it unenforceable.

Conditional fee agreements: supplementary.

58A. –

(1) The proceedings which cannot be the subject of an enforceable conditional fee agreement are-

(a) criminal proceedings; and
(b) family proceedings, apart from proceedings under section 82 of the Environmental Protection Act 1990.

(2) In subsection (1) "family proceedings" means proceedings under any one or more of the following-

(a) the Matrimonial Causes Act 1973;
(b) the Adoption Act 1976;
(c) the Domestic Proceedings and Magistrates' Courts Act 1978;
(d) Part III of the Matrimonial and Family Proceedings Act 1984;
(e) Parts I, II and IV of the Children Act 1989;
(f) Part IV of the Family Law Act 1996; and
(g) the inherent jurisdiction of the High Court in relation to children.

(3) The requirements which the Lord Chancellor may prescribe under section 58(3)(c)-

(a) include requirements for the person providing advocacy or litigation services to have provided prescribed information before the agreement is made; and
(b) may be different for different descriptions of conditional fee agreements (and, in particular, may be different for those which provide for a success fee and those which do not).

(4) In section 58 and this section (and in the definitions of "advocacy services" and "litigation services" as they apply for their purposes) "proceedings" includes any sort of proceedings for resolving disputes (and not just proceedings in a court), whether commenced or contemplated.

(5) Before making an order under section 58(4), the Lord Chancellor shall consult-

     (a) the designated judges;

     (b) the General Council of the Bar;

     (c) the Law Society; and

     (d) such other bodies as he considers appropriate.

(6) A costs order made in any proceedings may, subject in the case of court proceedings to rules of court, include provision requiring the payment of any fees payable under a conditional fee agreement which provides for a success fee.

(7) Rules of court may make provision with respect to the assessment of any costs which include fees payable under a conditional fee agreement (including one which provides for a success fee)."

(2) In section 120(4) of the Courts and Legal Services Act 1990 (orders and regulations subject to affirmative procedure), for "58," substitute "58(4),".

Section 28,
Access to Justice Act 1999

Litigation funding agreements

28. In the Courts and Legal Services Act 1990, after section 58A (inserted by section 27 above) insert-

"Litigation funding agreements.

58B. –
(1) A litigation funding agreement which satisfies all of the conditions applicable to it by virtue of this section shall not be unenforceable by reason only of its being a litigation funding agreement.

(2) For the purposes of this section a litigation funding agreement is an agreement under which-

   (a) a person ("the funder") agrees to fund (in whole or in part) the provision of advocacy or litigation services (by someone other than the funder) to another person ("the litigant"); and
   (b) the litigant agrees to pay a sum to the funder in specified circumstances.

(3) The following conditions are applicable to a litigation funding agreement-

   (a) the funder must be a person, or person of a description, prescribed by the Lord Chancellor;
   (b) the agreement must be in writing;
   (c) the agreement must not relate to proceedings which by virtue of section 58A(1) and (2) cannot be the subject of an enforceable conditional fee agreement or to proceedings of any such description as may be prescribed by the Lord Chancellor;
   (d) the agreement must comply with such requirements (if any) as may be so prescribed;
   (e) the sum to be paid by the litigant must consist of any costs payable to him in respect of the proceedings to which the agreement relates together with an amount calculated by reference to the funder's anticipated expenditure in funding the provision of the services; and
   (f) that amount must not exceed such percentage of that anticipated expenditure as may be prescribed by the Lord Chancellor in

278 No Win, No Fee

relation to proceedings of the description to which the agreement relates.

(4) Regulations under subsection (3)(a) may require a person to be approved by the Lord Chancellor or by a prescribed person.

(5) The requirements which the Lord Chancellor may prescribe under subsection (3)(d)-

  (a) include requirements for the funder to have provided prescribed information to the litigant before the agreement is made; and
  (b) may be different for different descriptions of litigation funding agreements.

(6) In this section (and in the definitions of "advocacy services" and "litigation services" as they apply for its purposes) "proceedings" includes any sort of proceedings for resolving disputes (and not just proceedings in a court), whether commenced or contemplated.

(7) Before making regulations under this section, the Lord Chancellor shall consult-

  (a) the designated judges;
  (b) the General Council of the Bar;
  (c) the Law Society; and
  (d) such other bodies as he considers appropriate.

(8) A costs order made in any proceedings may, subject in the case of court proceedings to rules of court, include provision requiring the payment of any amount payable under a litigation funding agreement.

(9) Rules of court may make provision with respect to the assessment of any costs which include fees payable under a litigation funding agreement."

Section 29,
Access to Justice Act 1999

Recovery of insurance premiums by way of costs

29. Where in any proceedings a costs order is made in favour of any party who has taken out an insurance policy against the risk of incurring a liability in those proceedings, the costs payable to him may, subject in the case of court proceedings to rules of court, include costs in respect of the premium of the policy.

Annex 14F
The Law Society's Guide to the Professional Conduct of Solicitors

Guidance – Conditional Fee Agreements

Introduction

1. The Conditional Fee Agreements Regulations (see Annex 14B, p292 in the Guide) came into force on 5th July 1995, as did the Conditional Fee Agreements Order. The order has now been replaced by the Conditional Fee Agreements Order 1998 (see Annex 14C, p294 in the Guide). The effect of the new order and regulations together with the recent amendment made to rule 8 of the Solicitors' Practice Rules 1990 (**14.03**, p.278 in the Guide) is to permit solicitors to enter into conditional fee agreements ('no win, no fee') in respect of all proceedings, except family and criminal matters and all non-contentious matters.

2. The Council has considered whether any new practice rule or formal guidance is required in respect of conditional fee agreements. The Council is of the view that this is not necessary at this stage as, together with the regulations, existing rules and guidance deal adequately with the issues likely to arise. This note draws attention to the relevant provisions. The Council will keep the matter under review and, if experience of the operation of conditional fee agreements indicates that new issues are arising that should be addressed through rules or guidance, appropriate measures will be brought forward.

Specimen Agreement

3. The Society has produced an example of a conditional fee agreement which solicitors may choose to adapt as appropriate. It is emphasised that the form of agreement is not mandatory but it is intended to be of help to solicitors in producing a form of agreement which is appropriate to particular circumstances, including the requirements of an individual case.

Making an Effective Agreement

4. The Regulations prescribe matters which solicitors must deal with before entering a conditional fee agreement, as well as certain minimum requirements of the agreement itself:

   (A) *Requirements preliminary to an agreement*
       Before any agreement is entered into, the solicitor shall draw to the client's attention each of the following matters:
       (a) whether the client might be entitled to legal aid in respect of the proceedings to which the agreement relates, the conditions upon which legal aid is available and the application of those conditions to the client in respect of the proceedings;
       (b) the circumstances in which the client may be liable to pay the fees and expenses of the solicitor in accordance with the agreement;
       (c) the circumstances in which the client may be liable to pay the costs of any other party to the proceedings; and
       (d) the circumstances in which the client may seek taxation of the fees and expenses of the legal representative and the procedure for so doing.

   (B) *Requirements of an agreement*
       Any agreement shall state:
       (a) the particular proceedings or parts of them to which it relates (including whether it relates to any counterclaim, appeal or proceedings to enforce a judgment or order);
       (b) the circumstances in which the legal representative's fees and expenses or part of them are payable;
       (c) what, if any, payment is due:
           (i) upon partial failure of the specified circumstances to occur;
           (ii) irrespective of the specified circumstances occurring; and
           (iii) upon termination of the agreement for any reason;
       (d) the amount payable in accordance with sub-paragraphs (b) or (c) above or the method to be used to calculate the amount payable; and in particular whether or not the amount payable is limited by reference to the amount of any damages which may be recovered on behalf of the client.

   (C) *Form of agreement*
       Any agreement shall be in writing and shall be signed by the client and the solicitor.

5. Solicitors are reminded that practice rule 8 disapplies the prohibition on conditional fees only when the agreement allows for a contingency fee that is permitted under statute or by the common law. An attempt to make a conditional fee agreement, which fails because the regulations or law have not been complied with, would put the solicitor in breach of rule 8, and might be rendered unenforceable by reason of public policy. A solicitor will

not be able to recover costs under an unenforceable agreement; thus particular care should be taken to ensure that any agreement conforms strictly to the Regulations.

Conduct Issues

6. In addition to rule 8 itself, a number of the provisions contained in the Guide may be applied in relation to issues of professional conduct which arise in respect of conditional fee agreements. The essential starting point is rule 1 of the Solicitors' Practice Rules (see 1.01, p.1, in the Guide).

7. The general principles enshrined in practice rule 1 are reinforced by and elaborated upon in a number of principles contained in the Guide which are relevant to conditional fee agreements. Practice rule 15 (see 13.01, p.265 in the Guide) and the Solicitors' Costs Information and Client Care Code are also of particular importance.

The Solicitors' Costs Information and Client Care Code

8. The Solicitors' Costs Information and Client Care code (see 13.02, p.266 in the Guide) requires solicitors to give clients detailed advance information on costs, so that clients receive all the information needed to understand and make informed decisions as to agreements on costs. The code applies to conditional fees as it applies to any other basis of charging.

9. Solicitors are reminded that a breach of the code could lead to a finding that the solicitor has provided inadequate professional services (IPS) or, in a serious or persistent case, a finding of professional misconduct. See also 5.01, p160 in the Guide, regarding the availability of legal aid. Unreasonable failure to advise a client properly on some matters, particularly as to costs in litigation or the availability of legal aid, may well also give rise to a claim in negligence.

10. The Office for the Supervision of Solicitors treat a material breach of the code as *prima facie* evidence of IPS. Therefore, in the event of a complaint, the burden will be upon the solicitor to establish that the client was given full information about the risks and costs issues.

Taking Unfair Advantage

11. In accordance with 11.01, p.222 in the Guide: 'It is fundamental to the relationship which exists between solicitor and client that a solicitor should be able to give impartial and frank advice to the client, free from any external or adverse pressures or interests which would destroy or weaken the solicitor's professional independence, the fiduciary relationship with the client or the client's freedom of choice.'

12. Because of the fiduciary relationship which exists between solicitor and client, the solicitor must not take advantage of the client (see also 12.09, p.248 and 15.04, pp.316 in the Guide). In considering, therefore, whether a conditional fee arrangement would be appropriate in the circumstances of

any particular case, a solicitor should take care to ensure that his or her own financial interests are not placed above the general interests of the client.

13. Whilst a solicitor is generally free to decide whether to accept instructions from any particular client and the terms upon which instructions will be accepted (12.01, p.244 in the Guide), it is important that all the options available to the client for financing the proceedings should be explained and discussed, including the availability of legal aid. As with all litigation, the client's potential exposure to pay another party's costs should also be explained and discussed. The code in paragraph 3(c) provides that the information in paragraph 4 (advance costs) and 5 (additional information for particular clients) should be given at the outset and at appropriate stages throughout the matter, as do the regulations themselves. In particular, paragraph 4(j)(ii) requires that the solicitor should consider whether the client's liaibility for the costs may be covered by insurance; in this context such insurance may include 'after the event' insurance. Paragraph 4(j) requires the solicitor to discuss with clients how legal charges and disbursements are to be met; in this context an explanation may be appropriate of how a conditional fee agreement differs from the more usual basis of charging, where the client bears the risk of failure.

Fair and Reasonable Terms

14. Should the client opt to proceed on a conditional fee basis, the contents of the agreement should be clearly explained and care must be taken to ensure that the terms are fair and reasonable in the circumstances. Any attempt to take unfair advantage of the client by overcharging for work done or to be done (contrary to 14.12, p.282 in the Guide) raises an issue of conduct for the solicitor, quite apart from the remedies available to the client in relation to taxation. The taxation (now assessment) rules are in Part 47 of the Civil Procedure Rules.

Client's Risk

15. Paragraph 6(b) of the code provides that in all matters a solicitor should consider with clients whether the likely outcome will justify the expense or risk involved in relation to the matter. Specifically, the client must fully understand the nature and extent of his or her risk in relation to costs, including the costs of his or her opponent, in accordance with paragraphs 5(b) and (c) of the code.

16. Solicitors may wish the agreement to provide for a cap on the success fee for the benefit of the client to limit the possibility of the client suffering a net financial loss, even where successful in the proceedings, and the model agreement contains a suggested provision. The regulations require that the agreement must state whether or not such a provision applies.

Solicitor's Risk

17. An important issue which arises is that of the percentage 'uplift' applicable. Solicitors may well not wish to apply the same uplift to all cases, or to all elements within an individual case. The principles applicable on taxation in relation to the uplift relate the risk to the individual case. In considering what uplift to stipulate in any particular case, solicitors will wish to take into account the degree of risk of the case being lost and the cost of funding the litigation over a period of time. Paragraph 4(k) of the code, and **14.12** (see 14 above) are also relevant. The financial risk assumed by the solicitor may be a factor in deciding on the appropriate uplift, but in determining this the solicitor 'must not take unfair advantage of the client by overcharging for work to be done' (**14.12**, p.282), 'should discuss with the client whether the likely outcome in a matter will justify the expense involved' (see paragraph 4(k) of the code), and 'must not abuse his or her position to exploit a client by taking advantage of a client's inexperience... want of... business experience' (see **12.09** note 1, p.248).

Advising on Settlement

18. In advising client on matters of settlement, solicitors are reminded of the principles referred to in **11–12** above. Solicitors should always consider their overriding duty to act in the best interests of the client in achieving a suitable settlement *for the client* irrespective of the solicitor's own interest in receiving early payment of costs in accordance with the agreement.

Publicity

19. Although conditional fee agreements have commonly been referred to in the media as 'no win, no fee' agreements, solicitors are reminded of the provisions of the Solicitors' Publicity Code (Annex 11A, p.229 in the Guide). Paragraph 5(a) of the code specifically requires any publicity as to charges or a basis of charging to be clearly expressed, and under paragraph 10(c) of the code publicity must not be inaccurate or misleading in any way. Further, paragraph 5(c) of the code restricts advertising that a service is 'free' of charge where the conditions which are attached to that service effectively mean that the client will be required to make some payment in respect of the service.

20. Advertisements which purport to offer a solicitor's services on the basis that the client is, for example, able to litigate 'at no financial risk' would be misleading.

January 1996, updated February 1999

Solicitors' Publicity Code 1990

(with consolidated amendments to 3 March 1999)

Code dated 18th July 1990 promulgated by the Council of the Law Society with the concurrence of the Master of the Rolls under Rule 2 of the Solicitors' Practice Rules 1990, regulating the publicity of solicitors and recognised bodies in England and Wales or overseas, and the publicity of registered foreign lawyers practising in England and Wales.

1. General principles

    (a) *Compliance with professional obligations*
    Nothing in this code shall be construed as authorising any breach of the Solicitors' Practice Rules, and in particular Rule 1 thereof, or any other professional obligation or requirement.

    (b) *Publicity in bad taste*
    Solicitors shall not publicise their practices in any manner which may reasonably be regarded as being in bad taste.

    (c) *Misleading or inaccurate publicity*
    Publicity must not be inaccurate or misleading in any way.

    (d) *Statutory requirements*
    As a matter of professional conduct the publicity of a solicitor must comply with the general law. Solicitors are reminded, *inter alia*, of the requirements of:

    (i) any regulations made under the Consumer Credit Act 1974 concerning the content of advertisements;

    (ia) sections 20 and 21 of the Consumer Protection Act 1987 concerning misleading price indications;

    (ii) the Business Names Act 1985 concerning lists of partners and an address for service on stationery, etc.; and

    (iii) Chapter 1 of Part XI of the Companies Act 1985 concerning the appearance of the company name and other particulars on stationery, etc.

    (e) [repealed]

    (f) *Solicitors' responsibility for publicity*
    It is the responsibility of solicitors to ensure that all their publicity, and all publicity for their services which is conducted by other persons, complies with the provisions of this code. The responsibility cannot be

delegated. Where solicitors become aware of any impropriety in any publicity appearing on their behalf, they must use their best endeavours to have the publicity rectified or withdrawn as appropriate.

2. Contents of publicity – general

   (a) *Solicitor to be identified*
       Every advertisement by a solicitor must bear the solicitor's name or firm name (subject to paragraph 10 below on flag advertising).

   (b) *Claims to specialisation or particular expertise*
       It is not improper for a claim to be made that a solicitor (or a registered foreign lawyer) is a specialist, or an expert, in a particular field provided that such a claim can be justified.

   (c) *Success rate*
       No publicity may refer to a solicitor's success rate (or that of a registered foreign lawyer practising with the solicitor).

   (d) *Comparisons and criticisms*
       No publicity may make direct comparison or criticism in relation to the charges or quality of service of any other identifiable solicitor. However, a solicitor may participate in the preparation of a *bona fide* survey of legal services conducted by a third party which may make comparisons between the charges of or quality of service provided by different solicitors.

   (e) *The Law Society's coat of arms*
       The armorial bearings of the Law Society may not appear in a solicitor's publicity.

   (f) *Legal aid logo*
       Solicitors willing to undertake legal aid cases may use the legal aid logo in their publicity, but the logo must not be altered in any way. (Photographic copies of the logo can be obtained from the Legal Aid Board.)

3. Unsolicited visits and telephone calls

   Solicitors may not publicise their practices or properties for sale or to let by means of unsolicited visits or telephone calls except:
   (i)   by means of a telephone call to a current or former client; or
   (ii) by means of a visit or telephone call to another solicitor or to an existing or potential professional connection; or
   (iii) by means of a visit or telephone call made to publicise a specific commercial property or properties the solicitor has for sale or to let.

4. Naming clients

   Solicitors may name or identify their clients in advertisements for their practices or in the public media, or supply information about their clients to publishers of directories, provided that:
   (i)   the client gives consent which, in the case of advertisements and directories, shall be in writing; and

(ii)   any such naming or identification of a client is not likely to prejudice the client's interests.

5.   **Statements as to charges**

(a)   *Clarity*
Any publicity as to charges or a basis of charging must be clearly expressed. It must be stated what services will be provided for those charges or on that basis of charging. Any circumstances in which the charges may be increased or the basis altered must be stated. It must be clear whether disbursements and VAT are included.

(b)   *Fee from or upwards of a figure*
It is prohibited to state a fee as being from or upwards of a certain figure.

(c)   *Service free of charge*
Publicity may state that a particular service of a solicitor is free of charge, but this must not be conditional on the solicitor or any other person being given any other instructions, or receiving any commission or other benefit, in connection with that or any other matter.

(d)   *Composite fees*
Solicitors may quote a composite fee for two or more separate services offered, but
(i)   the solicitor must if required quote separate fees for the individual services; and
(ii)   the solicitor must if required carry out any one only of those services on the basis of the separate fee quoted; and
(iii)   except in relation to a composite fee for property selling and conveyancing services, the separate fees quoted may not total more than the composite fee.

(e)   *Commissions from third parties*
In publicity for conveyancing or other services of a solicitor, fees must not be quoted which are intended to be net fees, i.e. fees which are reduced by the availability of any commission (such as that on an endowment policy). Any fee quoted in such circumstances must be the gross fee, although there is no objection to mentioning that the availability for the benefit of the client of a commission may reduce the net cost of the transaction to the client; provided that, where such mention is made in connection with mortgages, there must be no implication that endowment mortgages are appropriate in all circumstances, and there must be included an indication of the solicitor's willingness to advise as to the appropriate type of mortgage for the client's circumstances.

(f)   *Fees for conveyancing services*
In publicity which includes references to charges for conveyancing services, regard must be had to paragraph 1(c) above (misleading or inaccurate publicity) and paragraph 5(a) above (clarity in statements as to charges).

The following are examples of publicity which would breach these provisions:

(i) publicity which includes an estimated fee pitched at an unrealistically low level, if the solicitor then charges higher or additional fees;

(ii) publicity which refers to an estimated or fixed fee plus disbursements, if the solicitor then charges as disbursements expenses which are in the nature of overheads such as normal postage and telephone calls, *unless* the publicity explicitly states that such charges will be made;

(iii) publicity which includes an estimated or fixed fee for conveyancing services, if the solicitor then mades an additional charge for work on a related mortgage loan or repayment, including work done for a lender, *unless* the publicity makes it clear that any such additional charge may be payable (e.g. by use of a formula like "excluding VAT, disbursements, mortgage related charges and fees for work done for a lender").

6. **Description of a multi-national practice**

In the case of a practice which has at least one registered foreign lawyer as a partner (or director, registered member or beneficial shareowner), a description of the firm appearing on any letterhead (or fax heading, or heading used for bills) of an English or Welsh office of the practice must, if the description includes the word "solicitor(s)", also include:

(i) Words denoting the countries or jurisdictions of qualification of the foreign lawyer partners (or directors, registered members and beneficial owners) and their professional qualifications; or

(ii) the words "registered foreign lawyer(s)";

and the categories of lawyer must appear in order, with the largest group of partners (or directors, registered members and beneficial shareowners) placed first. There must be no breach of paragraph (14(b) below on the use of the word "lawyer(s)".

7. **Naming and describing partners and staff**

(a) *Provisions applying to all practices*

(i) A member of staff (including a partner or director) other than a solicitor who holds a current practising certificate may only be named in a practitioner's publicity, including stationery, if the status of that person is unambiguously stated.

(ii) The term "legal executive" may only be used in a practitioner's publicity, including stationery, to refer to a Fellow of the Institute of Legal Executives; and "trainee solicitor" to refer to a person training as a solicitor under a training contract registered with the Law Society.

(iii) Practitioners are reminded of the danger of inadvertently holding out persons as partners in a firm by inclusion of both partners' and non-partners' names in a list. The status of non-partners must be indicated for avoidance of doubt whenever a situation of inadvertent holding out might otherwise arise.

(iv) The following terms, used alone or in combination, will be deemed to indicate that a person is a solicitor holding a current practising certificate, unless it is made clear that the person is not so qualified:

(A) associate;

(B) assistant;

(C) consultant.

(v) The following terms, used alone or in combination, will be deemed to indicate that a person is not a solicitor holding a current practising certificate, unless a contrary indication appears:

(A) executive;

(B) clerk;

(C) manager;

(D) secretary;

(E) paralegal.

(vi) The appearance against a person's name of an indication that he or she is qualified in a jurisdiction other than England and Wales, or the title licensed conveyancer, or registered foreign lawyer, or the title of any other profession, will be deemed to indicate that the person is not a solicitor holding a current practising certificate, unless a contrary indication appears. (See also paragraph 14(b) below on the use of the word "lawyer(s)".)

(b) *Additional provisions applying to multi-national practices*

(i) In the case of a practice which has at least one registered foreign lawyer as a partner, director, registered member or beneficial owner of a share, the notepaper of an English or Welsh office of the practice must contain either:

(A) a list of the partners or directors; or

(B) a statement that a list of the partners or directors and their professional qualifications is open to inspection at that office (see also paragraph 1(d)(ii) above, the Business Names Act 1985 and Rule 23 of the Solicitors' Incorporated Practice Rules).

(ii) Any such list, as well as a list of the partners or directors in any other publicity conducted in England and Wales, must indicate the countries or jurisdictions of qualification of the partners or directors and their professional qualifications.

(iii) Any letterhead (or fax heading, or heading used for bills) of an English or Welsh office of the practice must bear either:

(A) a description of the firm which includes the word "solicitor(s)" and complies with paragraph 6 above; or

(B) a firm name which includes the word "Solicitor(s)" and complies with note (iv) to Practice Rule 11 (names used by a firm); or

    (C) a list of the partners (or directors) which indicates their countries or jurisdictions of qualification and their professional qualifications as required by sub-paragraph (b)(ii) above; or

    (D) a statement that the partners (or directors) are solicitors and others, described in a way, and in an order, which would comply with paragraph 6 above.

   (iv) For the purpose of sub-paragraphs (b)(ii) and (iii) above:

    (A) there must be no breach of the principle set out in paragraph 14(b) below on the use of the word "lawyer(s)"; and

    (B) the word "solicitor(s)" is sufficient in itself to indicate that a solicitor's jurisdiction of qualification is England and Wales.

8. Directory headings

A firm may have an entry or advertisement in a directory or listing under any appropriate heading provided that either:

(i) the word "solicitor(s)"; or

(ii) as an additional option in the case of a directory referring wholly or mainly to practice outside England and Wales, the word "lawyer(s)" (but see paragraph 14(b) below);

appears *either* in the heading of the directory or listing *or* in a name or description of the practice appearing in the entry or advertisement itself.

9. Subsidiary practising style

[Repealed]

10. Flag advertising

(a) For the purpose of this paragraph, "flag advertising" means advertising conducted by or on behalf of solicitors under the logo of or in the name of a grouping or association including one or more firms of solicitors (or recognised bodies or multi-national partnerships) but without naming the firm or firms whose services are being advertised.

(b) Any flag advertising must include the word "solicitor(s)" (or, as an additional option in the case of publicity conducted outside England and Wales, the word "lawyer(s)") and an address at which the names of all the firms involved are available. For the use of the word "lawyer(s)" see paragraph 14(b) below.

(c) Notwithstanding anything in this paragraph, notepaper used on legal professional business must include the name of the firm concerned and not merely the name of the grouping or association.

11. Addresses to the court

It is not proper for solicitors to distribute to the press, radio or television copies of a speech or address to any court, tribunal or inquiry, except at the time and place of the hearing to persons attending the hearing to report the proceedings.

12. **Professional stationery**

   (a) *Application of the code to stationery*
   The provisions of this code apply to a solicitor's letterhead and matter similarly forming part of a solicitor's professional stationery.

   (b) *Practising address on stationery*
   Any stationery used by solicitors for their professional work must include a practising address and not merely a box number. Where a facsimile transmission is being sent, the front sheet should contain the solicitor's address if this is not contained in some other part of the transmission.

   (c) *Use of client's or employer's stationery and client's or employer's name on solicitor's stationery*
   Solicitors may use for their professional work the stationery of, or stationery including the name of, a client or non-solicitor employer, provided that:
      (i) either the letterhead or the signature makes it clear that the stationery is being used by a solicitor on legal professional business and that the solicitor is responsible for the contents of the letter; and
      (ii) the stationery is being used for the business of that client or non-solicitor employer or for third parties in circumstances permitted by Practice Rule 4.

   (d) *Stationery of a recognised body*
   The professional stationery of a recognised body and of a partnership which includes a recognised body as a partner must comply with the Solicitors' Incorporated Practice Rules from time to time in force.

13. **Professional announcements, advertisements for staff, etc.**

   Any professional announcement, advertisement for staff, advertisement offering agency services, or any other like advertisement by a solicitor (including any advertisement in the Law Society's *Gazette*) must comply with the provisions of this code.

14. **International aspects of publicity**

   (a) No publicity for a solicitor's practice may be conducted in a jurisdiction other than England and Wales in any manner that would contravene either (i) the provisions of this code or (ii) any restrictions in force in that other jurisdiction concerning lawyers' publicity. For the purposes of this paragraph publicity shall be deemed to be conducted in the jurisdiction in which it is received. However, publicity shall not be regarded as being conducted in a jurisdiction in which such publicity would be improper if it is conducted for the purpose of reaching persons in a jurisdiction or jurisdictions where such publicity is permitted and its receipt in the former jurisdiction is incidental.

(b) Whether in England and Wales or in any other jurisdiction, a solicitor's advertising (including stationery – see paragraph 16(ii) below) must not, except in the expression "registered foreign lawyer(s)", use the word "lawyer(s)" to refer to a person's qualification in a member state of the European Community unless the qualification is that of a "lawyer" as defined in the 1977 Lawyers' Services Directive as from time to time amended.

15. Institutional publicity

(a) *Institutional publicity by the Law Society*
This code does not apply to publicity by the Law Society, or any body established under the control of the Law Society, concerning the services of solicitors in general or any class or group of solicitors.

(b) *Institutional publicity by local law societies*
This code does not apply to publicity by a local law society concerning the services of solicitors in general.

(c) *Publicity naming solicitors*
Where any publicity referred to in (a) and (b) above names individual solicitors or firms, such publicity must comply with this code as if the publication were by individual solicitors.

16. Interpretation

In this code:

(i) All references to individual practice rules are references to the Solicitors' Practice Rules 1990 and all words have the meanings assigned to them in Rule 18 of those rules; and

(ii) "advertisement" and "advertising", except where the context otherwise requires, refer to any form of advertisement and include *inter alia* brochures, directory entries, stationery, and press releases promoting a solicitor's practice; but exclude press releases prepared on behalf of a client.

17. Commencement

This code will come into force on 1 September 1990.

Note: Breaches of the Publicity Code

Where contravention of this code is not serious, the Council encourages local law societies to bring breaches to the attention of the solicitors concerned. Serious or persistent cases should be reported to the Office for the Supervision of Solicitors.

Practice Rule 1 (basic principles)

'A solicitor shall not do anything in the course of practicing as a solicitor, or permit another person to do anything on his or her behalf, which compromises or impairs or is likely to compromise or impair any of the following:

(a) the solicitor's independence or integrity;

(b) a person's freedom to instruct a solicitor or his or her choice;

(c) the solicitor's duty to act in the best interests of the client;

(d) the good repute of the solicitor or of the solicitors' profession;

(e) the solicitor's proper standard of work;

(f) the solicitor's duty to the Court.'

Solicitors' Practice Rules 1990, rule 1.

Rule 8 (Contingency Fees)

(1) A solicitor who is retained or employed to prosecute or defend any action, suit or other contentious proceeding shall not enter into any arrangement to receive a contingency fee in respect of that proceeding, save one permitted under statute or by the common law.

(2) Paragraph (1) of this rule shall not apply to an arrangement in respect of an action, suit or other contentious proceeding in any country other than England and Wales to the extent that a local lawyer would be permitted to receive a contingency fee in respect of that proceeding.

Rule 18 (Application and Interpretation)

(2) *(Interpretation)*

(c)   "contingency fee" means any sum (whether fixed, or calculated either as a percentage of the proceeds or otherwise howsoever) payable only in the event of success in the prosecution or defence of any action, suit or other contentious proceeding;

14.04 Contingency Fees – additional guidance

1. A contingency fee is any sum (whether fixed, or calculated either as a percentage of the proceeds or otherwise howsoever) payable only in the event of success in the prosecution or defence of any action, suit or other contentious proceeding. The fact that an agreement further stipulates a minimum fee in any case, win or lose, will not prevent it from being an arrangement for a contingency fee. See rule 18(2)(a)–(c) of the Solicitors' Practice Rules 1990 (Annex 1A at p.29).

2. Rule 8 came into force on 7th January 1999. It allows a contingency fee to the extent that it is permitted by the common law. It seems, at present, that the decision in *Thai Trading Co (a firm)* v *Taylor* [1998] 2 WLR 893 represents the common law. This case permits a solicitor to seek no more than ordinary profit costs in a winning case, and less (but not necessarily nothing) if the case is lost. Other cases currently before the courts or awaiting appeal may change the position.

3. It is anticipated that the Access to Justice Bill will put those contingency fee arrangements that are now permitted by common law on a similar statutory basis to conditional fee agreements, but this is unlikely to become law before the end of 1999. Any solicitor proposing to enter into a contingency fee arrangement must, therefore, satisfy himself or herself as to the current position at law. Any solicitor who is in doubt as to the legal position may contact the Practice Advice Service for guidance (see p.xv for contact details).

4. The reference in rule 8 to a contingency fee arrangement permitted by statute refers to a conditional fee agreement which complies with the Conditional Fee Agreements Order 1998 (see 14.05 below and Annex 14C, p.294).

5. Prior to the conclusion of a matter (contentious or non-contentious) a solicitor should not agree with a client to acquire an interest in the publication rights with respect to that matter (see 15.04 note 2, p.317).

6. A solicitor may enter into an agreement to be paid on a commission basis to recover debts due to a client, provided that the agreement is limited to debts which are recovered without the institution of legal proceedings or forms a legally binding contingency fee agreement.

7. Section 59(2) of the Solicitors Act 1974 (contentious business agreements) provides *inter alia* that nothing in the Act shall give validity to a contingency fee agreement (see Annex 14A at p.285). For conditional fee agreements see 14.05 below.

14.05 Conditional Fee Agreements – additional guidance

1. Under practice rule 8 solicitors may enter into conditional fee agreements in relation to all proceedings except criminal proceedings and specified family proceedings. See section 58 of the Courts and Legal Services Act 1990 and the Conditional Fee Agreements Order 1998 (S.I. 1998 no. 1860).

2. Solicitors may not enter into conditional fee agreements where the client has legal aid. Where legal aid is granted in respect of proceedings to which a conditional fee agreement relates, that agreement cannot apply to costs incurred whilst the client is in receipt of legal aid.

3. The maximum percentage by which fees may be increased in respect of the proceedings which are the subject of the conditional fee agreement is 100%.

4. The Conditional Fee Agreements Regulations 1995 prescribe matters which solicitors must deal with before entering into a conditional fee agreement and set out certain minimum requirements of the agreement itself (see Annex 14B, p.292). The regulations also apply which modifications to an agreement between solicitors and barristers.

5. See Annex 14F (p.303) for a statement of the application of the rules and principles of professional conduct to conditional fee agreements.

6. Copies of the Society's model agreement for use in personal injury cases, leaflets for clients and *Conditional Fees – A Survival Guide* by Bawdon and Napier may be ordered from Marston Book Services (see p.xv for contact details).

LAW SOCIETY'S MODEL CONDITIONAL FEE AGREEMENT

The agreement is a binding legal contract between you and your solicitor/s. Before you sign, please read everything carefully. Please also read 'Conditional Fees Explained', a Law Society Leaflet we have given you.

An explanation of words like 'our disbursements', 'basic costs', 'win', and 'lose', is in condition 3 of the Law Society Conditions which you should read carefully.

Agreement date

[   ]

I/We, the solicitor/s

[

                                  ]

You, the client

[

                                  ]

What is covered by the agreement

* Your claim against [   ] for damages for personal injury suffered on
  [   ].
* Any appeal by your opponent.

What is not covered by the agreement

* Any counterclaim against you.
* Any appeal you make.

Paying us

Whatever happens you have to pay our disbursements. In addition:

If you win your claim, you pay our basic charges and a success fee. You may be able to recover our disbursements, basic costs, success fee and insurance premium from your opponent. Please see conditions 4 and 6.

If you receive interim damages, we may require you to pay our disbursements and a reasonable amount for our future disbursements.

If you receive provisional damages, we will be entitled to payment of your basic charges and success fee at that point. However, we may agree to delay payment of all or part of the success fee.

If you lose, you pay your opponent's charges and disbursements. For full details, see conditions 3(k) and 5.

If you win but on the way lose an interim hearing, you may be required to pay your opponent's charges of that hearing. Please see conditions 3(i) and 5.

If you end the agreement before you win or lose, you pay our basic charges. If you go on to win, you pay a success fee. For full details, see condition 7(b).

If we end the agreement before you win or lose, see condition 7(c).

Basic charges

These are for work done from now until this agreement ends.

How we calculate our basic charges

These are calculated for each hour engaged on your matter [from now until the review date on [   ]]. Routine letters and telephone calls will be charged as units of one tenth of an hour. Other letters and telephone calls will be charged on a time basis. The hourly rates are:

- Solicitors with over four years' experience after qualification £[   ]
- Other solicitors and legal executives and other staff of equivalent experience £[   ]
- Trainee solicitors and other staff of equivalent experience £[   ]

[We will review the hourly rate on the review date and on each anniversary of the review date. We will not increase the rate by more than the rise in the Retail Prices Index and will notify you of the increased rate in writing.]

Success fee

This is [   ]% of the basic charges

Value added tax

We add VAT, at the rate (now [   ]%) that applies when the work is done, to the total of the basic charges and success fee.

Cap on success fee

The total (including VAT) of our success fee and any barrister's success fee (see condition 6) will be capped at not more than 25% of your damages. For this calculation, we exclude any money your opponent pays to the DSS as recoverable state benefits.

To the extent that a success fee is recovered from your opponent, this paragraph does not apply.

Other points

Immediately before you signed this agreement, we explained the following to you:

Legal aid

- Whether you can get legal aid for your claim for damages.
- Under what conditions you can get legal aid.
- How those conditions apply to your claim for damages.

Charges and disbursements

- When and how you may have to pay our disbursements and charges.
- When and how you may have to pay the disbursements and charges of your opponent.
- When and how you can get our bills checked ('assessed') by a court.

Law Society Conditions

- That the attached Law Society Conditions are part of this agreement.
- How they operate.
- Any amendments or additions to them that apply to you.
- That you should also read them carefully.

Signatures

Signed by the solicitor/s

Signed by the client

This Agreement complies with the Conditional Fee Agreements Regulations 1995 (S.I. 1995 No. 1675).

LAW SOCIETY CONDITIONS

1 **Our responsibilities**

We must:

- always act in your best interests subject to our duty to the court;
- explain to you the risks and benefits of taking legal action;
- give you our best advice about whether to accept any offer of settlement;
- at the outset, give you the best information possible about the likely costs of your claim for damages.

2 **Your responsibilities**

You must:

- give us instructions that allow us to do our work properly;
- not ask us to work in an improper or unreasonable way;
- not deliberately mislead us;
- co-operate with us;
- go to any medical or expert examination or court hearing;

3   Explanation of words used

(a) *Advocacy*

Appearing for you at court hearings.

(b) *Basic charges*

Our charges for the legal work we do on your claim for damages.

(c) *Cap*

The limit on the amount of your damages that can be taken as success fees.

(d) *Claim*

Your claim is your demand for damages for personal injury whether or not court proceedings are issued.

(e) *Counterclaim*

A claim that your opponent makes against you in response to your claim.

(f) *Damages*

Money that you win whether by a court decision or settlement.

(g) *Our disbursements*

Payments we make on your behalf such as:

- court fees;
- experts' fees;
- accident report fees;
- travelling expenses.

(h) *Interim damages*

Money that a court says your opponent must pay or your opponent agrees to pay while waiting for a settlement or the court's final decision.

(i) *Interim hearing*

A court hearing which is not final.

(j) *Lien*

Our right to keep all papers, documents, money or other property held on your behalf until all money due to us is paid. A lien may be applied after the agreement ends.

(k) *Lose*

The court has dismissed your proceedings or you have stopped them on our advice.

(l)   Part 36 offers or payments

It may be that your opponent makes a Part 36 offer or payment which you reject and, on our advice, your claim for damages goes ahead to trial where you recover damages that are less than that offer or payment. If so, we will not add our success fee to the basic charges for the work done after we received notice of the offer or payment.

(m) Provisional damages

Money that a court says your opponent must pay or your opponent agrees to pay, on the basis that you will be able to go back to court at a future date for further damages if:

- you develop a serious disease; or
- your condition deteriorates;

in a way which has been proven or admitted to be linked to your personal injury claim.

(n)   Success fee

The percentage of basic charges that we add to your bill if you win your claim for damages. It cannot be more than 100% of the basic costs. It is paid out of your damages.

The percentage reflects:

- the fact that if you lose, we will not earn anything;
- the fact that if you win, we will not be paid our basic charges until the end of your claim;
- our arrangements with you about payment of disbursements.

The total of our success fee and any barrister's success fee (see condition 6) is capped – it will not be more than 25% of your damages. For this calculation we include VAT and exclude any money your opponent pays to the DSS as recoverable state benefits you receive.

(o)   Win

Your claim for damages is finally decided in your favour, whether by a court decision or an agreement to pay you damages. 'Finally' means that your opponent:

- is not allowed to appeal against the court decision; or
- has not appealed in time; or
- has lost any appeal.

4   **What happens if you win?**

If you win:-

- You are then liable to pay all our basic charges and success fee (please see condition 3(n)).
- Normally, you will be able to recover part or all of our basic charges and disbursements from your opponent.

- If you and your opponent cannot agree the amount, the court will decide how much you can recover. If the amount agreed or allowed by the court does not cover all our basic charges and disbursements, you pay the difference.
- If your opponent is on legal aid, we are unlikely to get any money from him or her. (So if this happens, you have to pay.)

You, not your opponent, pay our success fee.

You agree to pay into a designated account any cheque received by you or by us from your opponent and made payable to you. Out of the money, you agree to let us take the balance of the basic charges; success fee; remaining disbursements; and VAT. You take the rest.

We are allowed to keep any interest your opponent pays on the charges.

Payment for advocacy is explained in condition 6.

If your opponent fails to pay

If your opponent does not pay any damages or charges owed to you, we have the right to take recovery action in your name to enforce a judgment, order or agreement. The costs of this action become part of the basic costs.

5   **What happens if you lose?**

If you lose, you do not have to pay any of the basic charges or success fee. You do have to pay:

- us for our disbursements;
- your opponent's legal costs and disbursements.

If you are insured against payment of these amounts by your insurance policy, we will make a claim on your behalf and receive any resulting payment in your name. We will give you a statement of account for all money received and paid out.

If your opponent pays the charges of any hearing, they belong to us.

Payment for advocacy is dealt with in condition 6.

6   **Payment for advocacy**

The cost of advocacy and any other work by us, or by any solicitor agent on our behalf, forms part of our basic charges.

Barristers who have a conditional fee agreement with us

If you win, their fee can be recovered from your opponent. You must pay the barrister's success fee shown in the separate conditional fee agreement we make with the barrister. We will discuss the barrister's uplift fee with you before we instruct him or her. If you lose, you pay nothing.

Barristers who do not have a conditional fee agreement with us

If you choose a barrister then you will pay their fee if you lose your case

7. **What happens when the agreement ends before your claim for damages itself ends?**

(a) Legal aid

The agreement automatically ends if you get a legal aid certificate. Our basic costs up to that time, and a success fee, will only be payable to us if you win your claim for damages. You must pay our disbursements whether you win or lose (but see 'Accident Line Protect' below). If you ask another legal firm to act for you after you get legal aid, we may ask that firm to preserve our lien before handing over any documents on the case.

(b) Paying us if you end the agreement

You can end the agreement at any time. We then have the right to decide whether you must:

*   pay the basic costs and our disbursements including barrister's fees when we ask for them; or
*   pay the basic costs, our disbursements including barrister's fees and success fee if you go on to win your claim for damages.

(c) Paying us if we end the agreement

(i)   We can end the agreement if you do not keep to your responsibilities in condition 2. We then have the right to decide whether you must:

*   pay the basic charges and disbursements including barrister's fees when we ask for them; or
*   pay the basic charges, our disbursements including barrister's fees and success fees if you go on to win your claim for damages.

(ii) We can end the agreement if we believe you are unlikely to win but you disagree with us. If this happens, you will only have to pay our disbursements including barrister's fees.

(iii) We can end the agreement if you reject our opinion about making a settlement with your opponent. You must then:

*   pay the basic charges and our disbursements including barrister's fees;
*   pay the success fee if you go on to win the case (unless your damages or settlement are at least 20% more than the offer we advised you to accept).

If you ask us to get a second opinion from a specialist legal representative outside our firm, we will do so. You pay the cost of a second opinion.

(iv) We can end this agreement if you do not pay your insurance premium when asked to do so.

(d) Death

This agreement automatically ends if you die before your claim for damages is concluded. We will be entitled to recover our basic charges up to the date of your death from your estate.

Should your personal representatives wish to continue your claim for damages, we may offer them a new conditional fee agreement, as long as they agree to pay the success fee on our basic charges from the beginning of the agreement with you.

8   **What happens after the agreement ends**

After the agreement ends, we will apply to have our name removed from the record of any court proceedings in which we are acting unless you have legal aid and ask us to work for you.

We have the right to preserve our lien unless another solicitor working for you undertakes to pay us what we are owed including a success fee if you win.

EXPLANATORY NOTES

* **For Accident Line Protect cases, you need to insert the following clause on page 3 of the agreement beneath the paragraph headed "Cap on Success Fee":-**

"Accident Line Protect insurance (ALP)

Accident Line Protect is an insurance policy only made available to you by solicitors who have joined the Accident Line Protect scheme.

You agree to pay a premium of £[   ] for Accident Line Protect Insurance when you sign this agreement. We undertake to send this to the Broker on your behalf. If you lose after proceedings have been issued, Accident Line Protect will cover our disbursements and your opponent's charges and disbursements. It will not cover fees to your barristers or advocates. The maximum cover is £100,000.

If this agreement ends before your claim for damages ends, Accident Line Protect ends automatically. If this agreement has ended because you have got legal aid, your Accident Line Protect cover remains in force as regards your opponent's charges and our disbursements incurred up to the date this agreement ends."

* The model agreement has been drafted to include VAT in the cap. If you wish to provide that VAT is not included in the cap, you will need to alter the wording in the following paragraphs:-

  * Page 3, paragraph 2 headed "Cap on Success Fee" – in the first line, delete the word "including" and substitute the word "excluding"
  * Page 7, paragraph 3(n) headed "Success fee" – in the last sentence, delete the words "we include VAT" and substitute the words "we exclude VAT".

Contingency Fee Agreement for Criminal Injuries Compensation Authority Claims

This agreement is a legally binding contract between you and [   ] solicitors.

Agreement Date

We, the legal representative   You, the client

What is covered by this agreement

Your claim for compensation from the Criminal Injuries Compensation Authority (the "Authority") regarding personal injury and/or loss suffered on [   ]

What is not covered by this agreement

Any action you wish us to take in relation to a re-opening or review of the Authority's decision and any appeal against a decision made by the Authority on review.

Paying Us

If you are awarded compensation from the Authority you pay us 33% of that compensation plus any disbursements. This figure includes VAT at the rate (now $17^{1}/_{2}$%) that applies when the work is done.

If you lose the case you do not pay us anything.

If you end the agreement before the Authority makes a decision with regard to whether or not to award you compensation, you are liable to pay our costs at the rate of £170 per hour with letters and telephone calls charged at £17 each unless they last for ten minutes or longer in which case they will be charged at the appropriate proportion of the hourly rate. All of these figures attract VAT at the rate (now 17$\frac{1}{2}$ %) that applies when the work is done.

For what happens if we end the agreement before the Authority makes a decision with regard to whether or not to award you compensation, please refer to paragraph 5.

1. **Our responsibilities**

   We must always act in your best interests in pursuing your claim for compensation and obtaining for you the best possible results, subject to our duty to the Authority.

2. **Your responsibilities**

   You must give us clear instructions which allow us to do our work properly; you must not ask us to work in an improper or unreasonable way; you must not deliberately mislead us; you must co-operate with us when asked; you must pay for disbursements as the case goes on.

3. **What happens if you win**

   If the Authority awards you compensation you pay us 33% of any compensation plus any disbursements. You agree that we may receive the compensation the Authority pays to you. If the Authority refuses to accept our receipt, you will pay the cheque you receive into a joint bank account in your name and ours. Out of the money you agree to let us take 33% of the damages plus any outstanding disbursements. You take the rest.

   If the Authority fails to pay any compensation to you we have the right to take recovery action in your name to enforce a judgement, order or agreement. The costs of this action are payable by you to us in addition to 33% of the damages.

4. **What happens if you lose**

   If you lose you do not have to pay us anything, except our disbursements.

5. **What happens when the agreement ends before the case itself ends**

   You can end the agreement at any time. You are then liable to pay us our costs incurred up to the date you end the agreement calculated at the hourly rate.

   We can end the agreement if you do not keep to your responsibilities in condition 2. You are then liable to pay us our costs incurred up to the date the agreement ends calculated at the hourly rate.

We can end the agreement if we believe that you are unlikely to obtain compensation from the Authority and you disagree with us. You do not have to pay us anything.

We can end the agreement if you reject our opinion about accepting compensation from the Authority. You are then liable to pay us our costs incurred up to the date the agreement ends calculated at the hourly rate.

6. **What happens after the agreement ends**

After the agreement ends we will inform the Authority that we are no longer acting as your representative. We have the right to preserve our lien over any property of yours in our possession unless any money owed to us under this agreement is paid in full.

Signed for the legal representative

Signed by the client

Contingency Fee Agreement for Employment Tribunal Claims

This agreement is a legally binding contract between you and   solicitors.

Agreement Date	[Agreement date]
We, the solicitors	[Solicitors name and address]
You, the client	[Client's name and address]

What is covered by this agreement

Your Employment Tribunal claim(s) relating to your employment with [Employer's name].

What is not covered by this agreement

Any counterclaim against you.
Any appeal you make or any appeal made by your opponent.
Any reference to the European Court of Justice.
Representation by a barrister at the hearing.

Paying Us

If you win the case you pay us a third of the money we recover. This figure includes VAT at the standard rate, currently 17.5%. You also pay us disbursements.

If you lose the case you do not pay us anything, except disbursements.

Disbursements are payments we make on your behalf to others involved in the case. We will notify you of disbursements incurred as we go along. We would expect the only disbursements to be travelling and subsistence expenses incurred in attending the tribunal hearing.

If you end the agreement before the case is won or lost, you are liable to pay our costs at the rate of £190 per hour with letters and telephone calls charged at £19 each unless they last for ten minutes or longer in which case they will be charged at the appropriate proportion of the hourly rate. All of these figures attract VAT at the standard rate of 17.5%.

For what happens if we end the agreement before the case is won or lost, please refer to paragraph 5.

Non-monetary benefits

We, the solicitors and you the client agree that if we succeed in obtaining your re-employment with your opponent then in addition to any other monies payable to us under this agreement we shall be entitled to a sum equivalent to one month's net pay calculated by reference to the pay at which you are re-employed.

1. **Our responsibilities**

    We must always act in your best interests in pursuing your claim for damages and obtaining for you the best possible results, subject to our duty to the tribunal; we must explain to you the risks and benefits of taking legal action; we must give you our best advice about whether to accept any offer of settlement.

2. **Your responsibilities**

    You must give us clear instructions which allow us to do our work properly; you must not ask us to work in an improper or unreasonable way; you must not deliberately mislead us; you must co-operate with us when asked; you must go to the tribunal hearing when asked; you must pay for disbursements as the case goes on.

3. **What happens if you win**

    If you win (which means that your case is decided in your favour whether by a tribunal or an agreement to pay you money or by a payment from the Secretary of State or your opponent's receivers, trustees in bankruptcy or administrators or under a Voluntary Arrangement under the Insolvency Act 1986) you pay us our share of any money and our share of the value of any non-cash benefits plus any disbursements. You agree that we may receive the money your opponent has to pay. If your opponent refuses to accept our receipt, you will pay the cheque you receive into a joint bank account in your name and ours. Out of the money you agree to let us take our share of the money and our share of the value of the non-cash benefits plus any outstanding disbursements. You take the rest.

If your opponent fails to pay any damages owed to you we have the right to take recovery action in your name to enforce a judgement, order or agreement including the right to apply to the Secretary of State. The costs of this action are payable by you to us in addition to a third of the money.

4. **What happens if you lose**

   If you lose you do not have to pay us anything, except our disbursements.

5. **What happens if the agreement ends before the case itself ends**

   You can end the agreement at any time. You are then liable to pay us our costs incurred up to the date you end the agreement calculated at the hourly rate, set out above under "Paying Us".

   We can end the agreement if you do not keep to your responsibilities in paragraph 2. You are then liable to pay us our costs incurred up to the date the agreement ends calculated at the hourly rate.

   We can end the agreement if we believe that you are unlikely to win and you disagree with us. You do not have to pay us anything.

   We can end the agreement if you reject our opinion about making a settlement with your opponent. You are then liable to pay us our costs incurred up to the date the agreement ends calculated on the hourly rate (unless your damages are 20% more than the offer we advised you to accept in which case you do not have to pay us anything).

6. **What happens after the agreement ends**

   After the agreement ends we will apply to have our name removed from the record of the tribunal proceedings in which we are acting. We have the right to preserve a lien over any property of yours in our possession unless any money owed to us under this agreement is paid in full. This means we can keep your papers until you pay us in full.

7. **Costs**

   Employment Tribunals have the power to award costs in limited circumstances. If we recover costs on your behalf they belong to us. In other words, if you win, you will pay us one third of your damages whether or not we also recover any costs from your opponent.

   If you lose and you are ordered to pay costs to your opponent, then those costs will be payable by you.

   The 1993 Regulations in relation to costs in Employment Tribunals state:-

   "Where, in the opinion of the tribunal, a party has in bringing or conducting the proceedings acted frivolously, vexatiously, abusively, disruptively or otherwise unreasonably, the tribunal may make –

   a.   *an order containing an award against that party in respect of the costs incurred by another party;*

b   an order that that party shall pay to the Secretary of State the whole,
    or any part of any allowances (other than allowances paid to members
    of tribunals) paid by the Secretary of State under *paragraph 10 of
    Schedule 9 to the Employment Protection (Consolidation) Act 1978 to
    any person for the purposes of or in connection with his attendance at
    the tribunal."

*Now Section 5(2) and (3) Industrial Tribunals Act 1996.

This Agreement is a Non-Contentious Business Agreement within the meaning
of section 57 of the Solicitors Act 1974.

Signed for the solicitors

Signed by the client

© Kerry Underwood 1999.

Contingency Fee Agreement

For Small Track Claims

This agreement is a legally binding contract between you and   Solicitors.

Agreement Date

We, the legal representative   **You, the client**

What is covered by this agreement

Your county court claim relating to your action against
Any enforcement proceedings

What is not covered by this agreement

Any counterclaim against you
Any appeal you make or any appeal made by your opponent.

Paying Us

If you win the case you pay us [   ] of your damages plus any disbursements. This figure includes VAT at the standard rate, currently 17.5%.

We will pay the disbursements on your behalf as the case proceeds. If you win we will recover them from you. If you lose we will not recover them from you.

NB Disbursements are payments we make on your behalf to others involved in the case. We will notify you of disbursements incurred as we go along. We would expect the only disbursements to be travelling and subsistence expenses incurred in attending the arbitration hearing and the cost of a medical report.

If you end the agreement before the case is won or lost, you are liable to pay our costs at the rate of £190 per hour with letters and telephone calls charged at £19 each unless they last for ten minutes or longer in which case they will be charged at the appropriate proportion of the hourly rate. All of these figures attract VAT at the standard rate of 17.5%.

For what happens if we end the agreement before the case is won or lost, please refer to paragraph 5.

1. **Our responsibilities**

    We must always act in your best interests in pursuing your claim for damages and obtaining for you the best possible results, subject to our duty to the court; we must explain to you the risks and benefits of taking legal action; we must give you our best advice about whether to accept any offer of settlement.

2. **Your responsibilities**

    You must give us clear instructions which allow us to do our work properly; you must not ask us to work in an improper or unreasonable way; you must not deliberately mislead us; you must co-operate with us when asked; you must go to the arbitration hearing when asked; you must pay for disbursements as the case goes on.

3. **What happens if you win**

    If you win (which means that your case is decided in your favour whether by a court or an agreement to pay you damages) you pay us [   ] of any damages plus any disbursements. You agree that we may receive the damages your opponent has to pay. If your opponent refuses to accept our receipt, you will pay the cheque you receive into a joint bank account in your name and ours. Out of the money you agree to let us take [   ] of the damages plus any outstanding disbursements. You take the rest.

    If your opponent fails to pay any damages owed to you we have the right to take recovery action in your name to enforce a judgement, order or agreement. The costs of this action are payable by you to us in addition to [   ] of the damages.

4. **What happens if you lose**

    If you lose you do not have to pay us anything.

5. **What happens when the agreement ends before the case itself ends**

    You can end the agreement at any time. You are then liable to pay us our costs incurred up to the date you end the agreement calculated at the hourly rate.

    We can end the agreement if you do not keep to your responsibilities in condition 2. You are then liable to pay us our costs incurred up to the date the agreement ends calculated at the hourly rate.

We can end the agreement if we believe that you are unlikely to win and you disagree with us. You do not have to pay us anything.

We can end the agreement if you reject our opinion about making a settlement with your opponent. You are then liable to pay us our costs incurred up to the date the agreement ends calculated on the hourly rate (unless your damages are 20% more than the offer we advised you to accept in which case you do not have to pay us anything).

6. **What happens after the agreement ends**

After the agreement ends we will apply to have our name removed from the record of the court proceedings in which we are acting. We have the right to preserve our lien over any property of yours in our possession unless any money owed to us under this agreement is paid in full.

7. **Costs**

County Courts have the power to award costs in limited circumstances. If we recover costs on your behalf they belong to us. In other words, if you win, you will pay us [   ] of your damages whether or not we also recover any costs from your opponent.

If you lose and you are ordered to pay costs to your opponent, then those costs will be payable by you.

The Civil Procedure Rules 1998, Part 27.14 states

(2) *The Court may not order a party to pay a sum to another party in respect of that other party's costs except-*
   (a) *the fixed costs payable under Part 45 attributable to issuing the claim;*
   (b) *in proceedings which included a claim for an injunction or an order for specific performance a sum not exceeding the amount specified in the relevant practice direction for legal advice and assistance relating to that claim;*
   (c) *costs assessed by the summary procedure in relation to an appeal under rule 27.12; and*
   (d) *such further costs as the court may assess by the summary procedure and order to be paid by a party who had behaved unreasonably.*

Signed for the legal representative

Signed by the client

Personal Injury Conditional Fees Explained

1. What are
conditional fees?

Conditional fees are a new way to pay for the services of a solicitor in certain types of cases. This leaflet deals with personal injury cases.

If you choose a Conditional Fee Agreement the money you will have to pay your solicitor depends on whether you win or lose your case.

IF YOU WIN:

You can receive from your opponent

- damages
- money to pay for all or some of your solicitor's basic costs, VAT and expenses (expenses are also known as "disbursements")

You pay

- your solicitor's basic costs and expenses
- a success fee to your solicitor

IF YOU LOSE:

You pay

- your solicitor's expenses
- your opponent's legal costs

(but see section 4 – Insurance cover – Accident Line Protect)

2. Some Terms
Explained

"basic costs" – refer to the normal charges of a solicitor worked out on an hourly rate basis

"success fee" – is a percentage (up to a maximum 100%) of your solicitor's basic costs added to your bill

"disbursements" – are your solicitor's expenses which may include court fees; experts' fees; accident report fees; official search fees; travelling expenses and in some cases barrister's fees

3. Other ways
to pay

You should discuss with your solicitor other ways to pay for legal help. Ask your solicitor how likely you are to win. That helps you to decide which way to pay for your case.

LEGAL AID

You should ask your solicitor:

- whether you are entitled to legal aid
- if you are, what contributions you will have to pay (if any)
- what difference having legal aid would make if you win or lose your case

PAYING YOUR SOLICITOR PRIVATELY

You should ask your solicitor how much you would have to pay if you did not have a Conditional Fee Agreement. And ask what would happen about payment if you won or if you lost your case.

THE LAW SOCIETY

THE LAW SOCIETY

4. Insurance cover
Accident Line Protect

Solicitors who are members of the Law Society's Accident Line Scheme can arrange this insurance for you. It can provide cover up to £100,000 for a premium of £85. The policy covers you for your opponent's legal costs and for the expenses for reports etc obtained for you by your solicitor (but not barrister's fees) in the event of you losing your case. You should discuss the scope of this insurance cover and other insurance policies which may be available with your solicitor.

◆ ask for the leaflet on "Accident Line Protect"

◆ make sure you understand what the policy provides

◆ discuss what you may have to pay out if you are not covered

5. The conditional
fee agreement

If you decide to go ahead, you will be required to sign a written agreement. This sets out all the terms of the contract between yourself and your solicitor. For example, it will say what happens if you or your solicitor want to end the agreement.

The Law Society has published a model Conditional Fee Agreement. Your solicitor does not have to use this. But any other agreement must cover the same issues. You should discuss the agreement with your solicitor to make sure you know what is expected of you and your solicitor.

All agreements must say whether there is a limit on the success fee (see Section 2 – Some Terms Explained). For example, the Law Society agreement says that the success fee cannot be more than 25% of the damages you receive. Your solicitor must discuss this with you.

THE LAW SOCIETY

6. What to ask
your solicitor

Before you sign a Conditional Fee Agreement you will want to know whether it is right for you. Here are some questions which you should ask your solicitor.

◆ What other means of paying are available to me? ☐

◆ Am I eligible for legal aid? ☐

◆ Can I get insurance cover against having to pay the other side's costs if I lose? ☐

◆ How good are my chances of winning my case? ☐

◆ Is it likely that my opponent can or will pay even if I win? ☐

◆ What damages would I be likely to receive? ☐

◆ What is the effect of winning on any DSS payments I may be receiving? ☐

◆ How is the "success fee" worked out? ☐

◆ What do "success" and "win" mean? ☐

◆ What are solicitors' basic costs and who pays these? ☐

◆ What expenses might I be required to pay and when? ☐

◆ What happens if I need a barrister? ☐

◆ How will I be kept informed about the progress of my case? ☐

THE LAW SOCIETY

Initial letter to client

Please ask for
<Name>

1999

[Name of Recipient]
[Address]
[Town]
[County]
[Postcode]

Dear [Salutation]

Re: Your Personal Injury Claim

This firm is prepared to deal with this mater on a Conditional Fee basis – often known as the "no win – no fee" scheme.

What this means is that if you do not win your case then there is no fee, but if you do win then the firm's normal fees will be doubled which will then be £ [   ] hour plus VAT.

However, I will guarantee that the fee charged to you, including VAT, will not exceed 25% of any damages recovered on your behalf. In view of the level of fees and the amount of work to be done I would expect the fee charged to you to be 25% of your damages.

In simple terms, if I recover £4,000 on your behalf then you would get £3,000 and I would get £1,000. This also applies to Special Damages as well as General Damages.

In addition I would keep any costs recovered from the other side and I would return to you any disbursements paid, e.g. for medical reports etc.

The potential problem with this scheme is that if you lose then although you would owe this firm nothing, you would be responsible for the other side's costs. However, we can insure against this prosect for a one-off payment of £ [   ]. It is a condition of this firm taking your case on a "no win – no fee" basis that I take out this insurance on your behalf.

I confirm that apart from the insurance premium, the only payments which you will be asked to make in respect of your case will be "disbursements" which I have to pay out on your behalf.

Examples of disbursements are:-

- Fee for obtaining medical records;
- Fee for medical expert report;
- Court Fees;
- Fee for a police accident report;
- Fee for a non-medical expert report

If you win your claim then you will recover most, if not all, of those payments except the insurance premium. If you lose the case, then you will be repaid those disbursements under the terms of the Accident Line Protect insurance policy, provided that court proceedings have been issued. Please arrange payment of the disbursements before I have to pay them out. I will provide you with invoices where possible. If you have any difficulty in paying the disbursements, please contact me to discuss the matter. We accept all major credit cards.

I went through the approximate level of disbursements you will have to pay at our meeting. Please contact me if you require any further information.

I enclose two signed copies of the Conditional Fee Agreement. If you are happy with the same as drafted, please sign both copies and retain one copy for your records. Please return the other copy to me.

I am bound to advise you at this stage that you are entitled to have this firm's costs checked by the Court after the case is over and this procedure is known as assessment. I enclose a separate advice sheet concerning this procedure.

I have of course advised you in detail concerning Legal Aid and I enclose a separate letter concerning this together with two leaflets published by the Legal Aid Board. If there is anything you wish to discuss concerning the availability of Legal Aid, please contact me. This firm does do Legal Aid work and would be prepared to act for you under a Legal Aid Certificate.

If you prefer you may pay this firm's private charging rate which is £[   ] per hour plus VAT with letters and telephone calls charged at £[   ] each plus VAT. If you win your case I would expect to recover disbursements plus approximately 60% of your costs. However, if you lose the case you will be responsible for the other side's costs. If you wish to consider instructing this firm on a private fee paying basis please contact me.

You may have legal expenses insurance which covers your claim. If so, we will be pleased to act under the terms of that insurance.

If there is anything in this letter you wish to discuss, please telephone me as it is particularly important that you understand fully what is involved in a Conditional Fee Agreement.

Yours sincerely,

Name

Company

Client Letter of Acceptance

[Name]
[Address]
[Town]
[County]
[Postcode]

1999

[Firm Name]
[Address]
[Town]
[County]
[Postcode]

I confirm my acceptance of the sum of £[amount of damages] in full and final settlement of my claim arising out of injuries suffered by me on [date of injury].

I understand that by accepting this sum I am concluding the matter and will be unable to make any further claim.

I also authorise you to deduct the sum of £[25%] being one quarter of my damages in accordance with the Conditional Fee Agreement between us and I understand that these charges are in addition to any costs and disbursements recovered from the [ins company] and I understand that the disbursements paid by me will be refunded to me.

_____

Signed [Name]

_____

Dated

Client Letter of Authority

[Name]
[Address]
[Town]
[County]
[Postcode]

[To Whom]

I [Name] authorise and request you to make my damages cheque payable to my solicitors:

Messrs [Solicitor's Firm Name]
[Address]
[Town]
[County]
[Postcode]

_____

Signed [Name]

_____

Dated

Letter to Client Advising of Payment into Court

1999

[Name of Recipient]
[Address]
[Town]
[County]
[Postcode]

Dear [Salutation]

Re: Your Accident

I have today received notification that the defendant has paid [£   ] into court.

You have 21 days from the date of receipt by me of that notice to decide whether or not to accept the money paid into court. Thus you must make your decision by [   ] at the latest.

If you accept the money paid in then the defendant's insurers will pay your costs in the usual way just as if the matter had been settled on the basis of payment to you of [£   ].

In accordance with the Conditional Fee Agreement that we have entered into my firm will charge a success fee but this will not exceed 25% of the damages, ie a maximum of [£   ] and thus you will receive [£   ].

If you do not accept the payment-in then the case continues in the usual way and the Judge who tries the matter will not be aware of the fact that there has been a payment-in, let alone the amount.

If the amount awarded by the Judge is [£   ] or less then you will be ordered to pay the other side's costs from the date of the payment-in but in fact those will be met by the insurers [   ] and thus your damages will be preserved in tact as far as the other side's costs are concerned. In accordance with the Conditional Fee Agreement I will make no charge for work done after the payment-in in those circumstances.

I value the claim as worth at least [£   ] and therefore I advise you [not to accept the payment-in]/[as I value the claim at only [£   ] my advice is that you should accept the payment-in]/[although I value your claim at [£   ] which is only [£   ] more than the amount paid in I do not advise you to accept the risk of proceeding and therefore my advice is that you should accept the payment in.]

[Additional wording only to be used when advising rejection of payment-in]

[If I turn out to be wrong in my advice and you fail to beat the payment-in at court then my firm will make up the difference by reducing our success fee. Thus if the Judge awards you £1,000 less than the sum now paid into court I will reduce my success fee by that sum and thus you will receive exactly the same in your hand as if you had accepted the payment-in].

As the amount paid in is [£[A]   ] the Judge will therefore have to award less than [£[A minus 25%]] for you to lose out. I believe that is very unlikely.

I appreciate that the rules relating to payments into court are complicated and I suggest you telephone me to discuss the matter or make an appointment to see me. In view of the time limit please do this as quickly as possible.

I look forward to hearing from you.

Yours sincerely

Note: This letter is very much clearer when the actually sum paid into court is inserted.

Letter to Client Confirming Acceptance of Damages

1999

[Name of Recipient]
[Address]
[Town]
[County]
[Postcode]

Dear [Salutation]

Re: Your Personal Injury Claim

I refer to my telephone conversation earlier today and confirm that I have written to the defendant's insurers accepting the sum of [£   ] inclusive of general and special damages with general damages being valued at [£   ] and special damages at[£   ].

In accordance with the terms of the conditional fee agreement signed by us I am entitled to charge 25% of the total of [£   ] but I do not propose making any charge in relation to the special damages element of [£   ]. Thus I am restricting my firm's charges to you of 25% of the general damages figure of [£   ] and that gives a total of [£   ] including VAT.

I enclose my firm's bill in that sum. Please sign the enclosed authority to [   ] instructing them to make the damages cheque payable to this firm. I will then deduct the sum of [£   ].

You have paid a total of [£   ] disbursements on the [   ] and this sum will be refunded to you once I receive the same from the defendant's insurers.

The overall effect is that from this case you will receive [£   ] plus the return of the disbursements paid by you.

As advised all along the insurance premium of [£   ] paid to Accident Line Protect is not recoverable.

Finally you will recall that the Conditional Fee Agreement, as well as restricting my firm's costs chargeable to you to 25% of the damages, also restricted my firm's additional costs for acting under a conditional fee agreement to 100% of our normal costs, ie double our normal costs.

In fact the figure charged to you works out as a success fee of [%] because of the imposition of the 25% cap.

I appreciate that the calculations are somewhat complicated and if there is anything you wish to discuss, please telephone me.

Kind regards

Yours sincerely

CFA Analysis Form

CLIENT   :

CASE CLOSURE NO   :

DATE OF ACCIDENT   :

DATE OF CFA   :

INSURANCE CERTIFICATE NO   :

ESTIMATE OF DAMAGES GIVEN   :

ACTUAL   :

VARIANCE   :

REASON FOR VARIANCE   :

PROCEEDINGS EVER ISSUED ?   :

SOURCE   :

FEE EARNER   :

DATE DAMAGES CHEQUE RECEIVED   :

COSTS (*ALL* FIGURES *NET* OF VAT)

(A) FULL SOLICITOR AND OWN CLIENT COSTS :

(B) PROFIT COSTS FROM OTHER SIDE   :

(C) FEE CHARGED TO CLIENT   :

(D) BALANCE OF A MINUS B   :

(E) ACTUAL SUCCESS FEE (C MINUS D)   :

(F) SUCCESS FEE IN CFA (%)   :

(G) ACTUAL SUCCESS FEE (%) (E as a % OF A) :

COMMENTS

Analysis of Conditional Fee Agreements

Of Completed Analysis Forms – case finished

Won	59
Withdraw	3
Lost	0
Total	62

Of the first 50 signed Conditional Fee Agents

Won	37
Liability Admitted	3
Liability Disputed	8*
Withdrawn	2
Total	50

*of which 8 have proceedings issued and 1 is pending trial

Average Success Fee (capped at 25% including VAT)	£832.53 plus VAT £145.69 £978.22

IN THE SUPREME COURT OF JUDICATURE   CCRTF 97/0880 CMS2
COURT OF APPEAL (CIVIL DIVISION)
ON APPEAL FROM THE READING COUNTY COURT
(His Honour Judge Hague)

Royal Courts of Justice,
Strand, London WC2

Friday, 27th February 1998

Before:

LORD JUSTICE KENNEDY
LORD JUSTICE MILLETT and
LORD JUSTICE HUTCHISON

THAI TRADING (A FIRM)   Plaintiffs/Respondents

−v−

MRS MARGERY TAYLOR   Defendant

and

MR WILFRID DAVID TAYLOR   Appellant/Appellant
(of Taylors Solicitors, Caversham)

DR J WILLIAMS (instructed by Messrs Taylors of Caversham, Reading) appeared on behalf of the Appellant.
THE RESPONDENT PLAINTIFFS MR A BEARD and MR T BEARD (assisted by MR HEAVER, their McKenzie Friend) appeared in person.

JUDGMENT
(As approved by the Court)

(Crown Copyright)

Friday, 27th February 1988

LORD JUSTICE MILLETT:

In June 1991 Mrs Taylor ordered a four-poster Thai carved bed from the Plaintiffs for the price of £2,500. She paid a deposit of £1,500. The bed was delivered, but it did not match Mrs Taylor's expectations. She rejected it and refused to pay anything more. The Plaintiffs brought proceedings in the Reading County court for the unpaid balance of the purchase price and Mrs Taylor counterclaimed for the return of the money she had paid.

The case was a small, run-of-the-mill county court case and should have been disposed of speedily and with relatively little expense. Unfortunately it had a protracted history and involved a number of court appearances, with the result that the present appeal, which relates to Mrs Taylor's costs, is concerned with a sum which is out of all proportion to the amount originally in issue.

Mrs Taylor won her case. The Plaintiffs' action was dismissed and Mrs Taylor obtained judgment on her counterclaim. The Plaintiffs were ordered to pay Mrs Taylor's costs up to 22nd March 1993 and from 25th January 1994 with no order as to costs for the intervening period. This reflected the fact that Mrs Taylor had eventually succeeded on a point not taken before the District Judge.

In the course of taxation the Plaintiffs challenged the amount claimed to be due from them. Mrs Taylor had paid the disbursements out of her own money and the Plaintiffs did not dispute their liability for these. But they disputed any further liability on the ground that Mrs Taylor was not legally liable to pay her solicitor his profit costs. It is a well settled principle that a successful party who has been awarded his costs can recover by way of indemnity only the costs which he is legally liable to pay to his own solicitor or in the case of disbursements to third parties. The principle was established in *Gundry* v *Sainsbury* (1910) 1 KB 645, where the successful party was unable to obtain an order for costs because his solicitor had agreed to act for him without reward.

The circumstances which give rise to the allegation that Mrs Taylor was not legally liable to pay her solicitor's profit costs are as follows. Mrs Taylor's husband is a solicitor practising under the firm name of Taylors. He is a sole practitioner. Mrs Taylor works for the firm as an accounts clerk. She naturally employed the firm to act for her in the proceedings brought against her, and it represented her throughout the course of the litigation.

Mrs Taylor deposed in an affidavit as follows:

> There was no agreement either expressly or by implication between myself and my husband, acting as my solicitor, that he would not render bills to me. Upon the recovery of costs awarded to me they will be dealt with in the same way as with any client recovering costs following litigation and a bill will be raised covering these costs.

The Judge (His Honour Judge Nigel Hague QC) accepted Mrs Taylor's evidence that there was no express agreement between her and her husband in regard to her costs, but he found that there was an understanding that she would not pay anything if she lost.

He said:

> ... the commonsense of the matter points strongly to the conclusion that Taylors would only be paid by Mrs Taylor if and to the extent that she won the litigation and could recover the costs from the Plaintiffs. I cannot believe that Taylors intended or expected to be paid if she lost. The notions that in those circumstances Taylors would have billed Mrs Taylor and that she would have paid such a bill (whether out of her own earnings or savings or out of money provided by her husband), thereby increasing Mr Taylor's profits and his income tax liability, are to my mind fanciful...

> For those reasons, although I reject the Plaintiffs' first contention that Mrs Taylor was under no obligation to pay Taylors in any circumstances, I accept their second contention. I find that there was an understanding between Taylors and Mrs Taylor that she would not be liable to them for any profit costs except in the event of success in the litigation and an order for costs in her favour, when she would be liable for their normal profit costs.

There is no appeal from this finding, which was based on inference from the primary facts. In my opinion the facts did not warrant the inference that there was any understanding as to Mrs Taylor's legal liability in respect of costs. To my mind the only legitimate inference was that, while Mrs Taylor's legal liability for costs was not affected, save in unforeseen circumstances neither party expected Mr Taylor to demand payment or enforce her liability unless she won her case and to the extent that she recovered costs from the Plaintiffs.

In a Judgment for which I should wish to express my respectful admiration the Judge pointed out that, if the law relating to the recovery of contingent fees be put on one side, the so-called indemnity principle did not avail the Plaintiffs. Even if there was an express agreement that Mr Taylor would be paid his profit costs only if Mrs Taylor won her case, she would still be entitled to be indemnified against a legal liability which had been incurred in the events which had happened. The fact that she would have incurred no liability in a different event which had not happened would not affect this.

Had he felt free to do so, the Judge would have held that the agreement between Mrs Taylor and her husband which he had found was entered into was a valid and enforceable agreement. But he reluctantly concluded that he was bound by authority, in particular the decisions of the Divisional Court in *British Waterways Board v Norman* (1993) 22 HLR 232 and of Garland J in *Aratra Potato Co Ltd v Taylor Johnson Garrett* [1995] 4 All ER 695, to hold that the agreement, being an agreement for a contingent fee, was contrary to public policy and so void. Those decisions also showed that the consequence was that there was no legal liability on Mrs Taylor to pay Taylors' profit costs, and hence by virtue of the indemnity principle no liability on the Plaintiffs to pay such costs.

The Judge felt the injustice of the result which he was constrained by authority to reach. He subjected the two decisions to which I have referred to respectful criticism, but rightly held that he was bound by them. We are not so bound, and are free to examine the underlying principles afresh.

Mrs Taylor has appealed the Judge's decision, but has no financial interest in the result of the appeal. Accordingly Mr Taylor has been joined as an additional party to the appeal and argument has been presented on his behalf.

The Solicitors Act 1974

It should be observed at the outset that there is nothing in the Solicitors Act 1974 which prohibits the charging of contingent fees. Section 59(2) merely provides that nothing in the Act shall give validity to arrangements of the kind there specified. It does not legitimise such arrangements if they are otherwise unlawful, but neither does it make them unlawful if they are otherwise lawful.

The Solicitors Practice Rules 1987 by contrast provide that a solicitor engaged in any contentious business shall not enter into any arrangement to receive a contingency fee, that is to say a fee payable only in the event of success in the proceeding. There is now an exception for conditional fee agreements which satisfy the requirements of the Courts and Legal Services Act 1990. Except as there provided, therefore, it is unprofessional conduct for a solicitor to enter into any agreement even for his normal fee where this is dependent on achieving a successful result in litigation. The Plaintiffs placed much reliance on this. But the fact that a professional rule prohibits a particular practice does not of itself make the practice contrary to law: see *Picton Jones & Co.* v *Arcadia Developments Ltd.* [1989] 1 EGLR 42. Moreover, the Solicitors Rules are based on a perception of public policy derived from judicial decisions the correctness of which is in question in this appeal.

Maintenance and champerty

The law governing contingent fees outside the scope of the Courts and Legal Services Act 1990 is derived from the public policy relating to champerty and maintenance. Until 1967 these were both criminal and tortious. Following the recommendation of the Law Commission, the Criminal Law Act 1967 provided that they should no longer be either criminal or tortious. Section 14(2) of the Act, however, preserved the rule of the common law that they are contrary to public policy.

Maintenance was described by Lord Denning MR in *Re Trepca Mines* (No. 2) [1963] 1 Ch. 199, 219 as improperly stirring up litigation and strife by giving aid to one party to bring or defend a claim without just cause or excuse.

Champerty was described by Scrutton LJ in *Ellis* v *Torrington* [1920] 1 KB 399, 412 as

... only a particular form of maintenance where the person who maintains takes as a reward a share in the property recovered.

This last formulation does not assume that the maintenance is unlawful. There can be no champerty if there is no maintenance; but there can still be champerty even if the maintenance is not unlawful. The public policy which informs the two doctrines is different and allows for different exceptions. In examining the present scope of the doctrine, it must be remembered that public policy is not static. In recent times the roles of maintenance and champerty have been progressively redefined and narrowed in scope. The current position is stated by the decision of the House of Lords in *Giles* v *Thompson* [1994] 1 AC 142, 161.

Maintenance

The policy underlying the law of maintenance was described by Fletcher-Moulton LJ in *British Cash and Parcel Conveyors Ltd* v *Lamson Store Service Co. Ltd.* [1908] 1 KB 1006 at 1015 in terms which were approved by Lord Mustill in *Giles* v *Thompson* as follows:

It is directed against wanton and officious intermeddling with the disputes of others in which the [maintainer] has no interest whatever, and where the assistance he renders to one or the other party is without justification or excuse.

The language and the policy which it describes are redolent of the ethos of an earlier age when litigation was regarded as an evil and recourse to law was discouraged. It rings oddly in our ears today when access to justice is regarded as a fundamental human right which ought to be readily available to all.

But even in former times maintenance was permissible when the maintainer had a legitimate interest in the outcome of the suit. This was not confined to cases where he had a financial or commercial interest in the result. It extended to other cases where social, family or other ties justified the maintainer in supporting the litigation. In *Neville* v *London Express Newspaper Ltd.* [1919] AC 368 at p. 389 Lord Haldane said:

Such an interest is held to be possessed when in litigation a master assists his servant, or a servant his master, or help is given to an heir, or a near relative, or to a poor man out of charity, to maintain a right which he might otherwise lose.

In *Bradlaugh* v *Newdegate* (1883) 11 QBD 1 at p. 11 Lord Coleridge CJ spoke of

... the interest which consanguinity or affinity to the suitor give to the man who aids him, or the interest which arises from the connection of the parties, e.g. as master and servant...

In *Condliffe* v *Hislop* [1996] 1 WLR 753 this Court held that it was not unlawful for a mother to provide limited funds to finance her bankrupt son's action for defamation.

In the present case the Plaintiffs do not contend that Mr Taylor was guilty of unlawfully maintaining his wife's suit. He was doubly justified in doing so; the suitor was both his wife and his employee.

Champerty

In *Giles* v *Thompson* Lord Mustill cited with approval Fletcher-Moulton LJ's description of maintenance to which I have already referred, and added:

> This was a description of maintenance. For champerty there must be added the notion of a division of the spoils.

The public policy which underlies the doctrine of champerty was described by Lord Denning MR *in Re Trepca Mines Ltd. (No. 2)* at pp. 219–20:

> The reason why the common law condemns champerty is because of the abuses to which it may give rise. The common law fears that the champertous maintainer might be tempted, for his own personal gain, to inflame the damages, to suppress evidence, or even to suborn witnesses.

Describing champerty as "a particularly obnoxious form of maintenance" in *Trendtex Trading* v *Credit Suisse* [1980] 1 QB 629, 654, Lord Denning reserved his particular condemnation for the lawyer who charged a contingency fee, that is to say, a fee which would be payable only if his client was successful. He said:

> [Champerty] exists when the maintainer seeks to make a profit out of another man's action – by taking the proceeds of it, or a part of them, for himself. Modern public policy condemns champerty in a lawyer whenever he seeks to recover – not only his proper costs – but also a portion of the damages for himself; *or when he conducts a case on the basis that he is to be paid if he wins but not if he loses* (my emphasis).

Lord Denning was there repeating what he had said in *Wallersteiner* v *Moir* (No. 2) [1975] 1 QB 373 at p. 393:

> English law has never sanctioned an agreement by which a lawyer is remunerated on the basis of a "contingency fee", that is that he gets paid the fee if he wins, but not if he loses. Such an agreement was illegal on the ground that it was the offence of champerty...

Lord Denning was prepared nevertheless to authorise the plaintiff in a derivative action to enter into a contingency fee agreement, but the other members of the court (Buckley and Scarman LJJ) thought otherwise. It is, however, clear from the judgments of the majority that they did not have in mind the charging of normal fees contingent on success in the action. Thus Buckley LJ said at p. 402:

> Under a contingency fee agreement the remuneration payable by the client to his lawyer in the event of his success must be higher than it would be if the lawyer were entitled to be remunerated, win or lose: the contingency fee must contain an element of compensation for the risk of having done the work for nothing. It would, it seems to me, be unfair to the opponent of a contingency fee litigant if he were at risk of being ordered to pay higher costs to his opponent in the event of the latter's success in the action than would be the case if there were no contingency fee agreement.

It is understandable that a contingency fee which entitles the solicitor to a reward over and above his ordinary profit costs if he wins should be condemned as tending to corrupt the administration of justice. There is no reason to suppose that Lord Denning in *Trendtex Trading* v *Credit Suisse* or and of the members of the court in *Wallersteiner* v *Moir* had in mind a contingency fee which entitles the solicitor to no more than his ordinary profit costs if he wins. These are subject to taxation and their only vice is that they are more than he will receive if he loses. Such a fee cannot sensibly be described as a "division of the spoils". The solicitor cannot obtain more than he would without the arrangement and risks obtaining less. On the principle that "the worker is worthy of his hire" I would regard the solicitor who enters into such an arrangement, not as charging a fee if he wins, but rather as agreeing to forego his fee if he loses. I question whether this should be regarded as contrary to public policy today, if indeed it ever was.

In *British Waterways Board* v *Norman* the solicitors knew that their client was on income support, advised her to bring a private prosecution without suggesting to her that she would have to pay anything towards the costs, and only expected to be paid by her if she was successful and an order for costs was made against the Board. It never occurred to the client that she would have to pay any costs out of her own pocket. The Divisional Court held that the only possible conclusion from these facts was that there was an understanding amounting in law to a contract that the client would not be liable for their costs if she lost the case. This was in the face of evidence which the magistrates accepted that there was no contractual arrangement with the client that the solicitors would not collect costs from her if the case was lost, that there was no question of a contingency fee, and no agreement express or implied that the solicitors would only be paid if successful. I doubt that the Divisional court was correct to conclude that there was only one possible interpretation of the facts. It is not uncommon for solicitors to take on a case for an impecunious client with a meritorious case, knowing that there is no realistic prospect of recovering their costs from the client if the case is lost, without thereby waiving their legal right to their fees in that event. As every debt collector knows, what is legally recoverable and what is recoverable in practice are not the same.

The Divisional Court followed Lord Denning's indication of the width of the doctrine in *Trendtex Trading* v *Credit Suisse*. McCowan LJ explained the rationale at p. 242 as follows:

> To put it in a nutshell, once a lawyer has a personal interest in litigation, his or her objectivity may be affected.

Tuckey J said that if it was made clear that the client was liable for costs irrespective of the outcome of the proceedings, there could be no objection to the solicitor agreeing that such liability need not be discharged until the outcome of the proceedings was known. At that stage, *provided it had not formed the basis of any prior agreement with the client,* the solicitor could properly forego his right to be paid to the extent that any of the costs were not recovered from the other party to the proceedings. In the present case the Judge described this conclusion as most unsatisfactory. He pointed out, justifiably in my opinion, that it elevates form above substance, and invites solicitors to produce documents evidencing an agreement which both parties know would not be enforced. I agree with the Judge's comment that the need for solicitors to engage in a subterfuge of this kind in order to recover their costs in the event of a successful outcome to the litigation shows that the underlying reasoning is unsound.

In *Aratra Potato Co. Ltd* v *Taylor Johnson Garrett* [1995] 4 All ER 695 the absurdities to which such reasoning is capable of leading were dramatically exposed. Solicitors were engaged on a retainer which included a term that there would be a 20% reduction from solicitor/client costs for any lost cases. Garland J held that it was champertous and contrary to public policy for solicitors to agree a differential fee dependent on the outcome of litigation; that the entire retainer was unlawful; and accordingly the solicitors could not recover their outstanding fees for work done irrespective of the outcome of the cases and with or without the reduction. The fact that the solicitors were seeking to recover no more (and in respect of lost cases less) than their ordinary profit costs made no difference.

If this is the law then something has gone badly wrong. It is time to step back and consider the matter afresh in the light of modern conditions. I start with three propositions. First, if it is contrary to public policy for a lawyer to have a financial interest in the outcome of a suit this is because (and only because) of the temptations to which it exposes him. At best he may lose his professional objectivity; at worst he may be persuaded to attempt to pervert the course of justice. Secondly, there is nothing improper in a lawyer acting in a case for a meritorious client who to his knowledge cannot afford to pay his costs if the case is lost: see *Singh* v *Observer Ltd.* (Note) [1989] 3 All ER 777; *A Ltd* v *B Ltd* [1996] Ch.D. 665. Not only is this not improper; it is in accordance with current notions of the public interest that he should do so. Thirdly, if the temptation to win at all costs is present at all, it is present whether or not the lawyer has formally waived his fees if he loses. It arises from his knowledge that in practice he will not be paid unless he wins. In my judgment the reasoning in the *British Waterways Board* v *Norman* is unsound.

Accordingly, either it is improper for a solicitor to act in litigation for a meritorious client who cannot afford to pay him if he loses, or it is not improper for a solicitor to agree to act on the basis that he is to be paid his ordinary costs if he wins but not if he loses. I have no hesitation in concluding that the second of these propositions represents the current state of the law.

I reach this conclusion for several reasons. In the first place, I do not understand why it is assumed that the effect of the arrangement being unlawful is that the solicitor is unable to recover his proper costs in any circumstances. Where the solicitor contracts for a reward over and above his proper fees if he wins, it may well be that the whole retainer is unlawful and the solicitor can recover nothing. But where he contracts for no more than his proper fees if he wins, this result does not follow. There is nothing unlawful in the retainer or in the client's obligation to pay the solicitor's proper costs if he wins the case. If there is anything unlawful, it is in the waiver or reduction of the fees if he loses. On ordinary principles the result of holding this to be unlawful is that the client is liable for the solicitor's proper costs even if he loses the case. I regard *Aratra Potato Co. Ltd.* v *Taylor* as wrongly decided.

In the second place, it is in my judgment fanciful to suppose that a solicitor will be tempted to compromise his professional integrity because he will be unable to recover his ordinary profit costs in a small case if the case is lost. Solicitors are accustomed to withstand far greater incentives to impropriety than this. The solicitor who acts for a multinational company in a heavy commercial action knows that if he loses the case his client may take his business elsewhere. In the present case, Mr Taylor had more at stake than his profit costs if he lost. His client was his wife; desire for domestic harmony alone must have provided a powerful incentive to win.

Current attitudes to these questions are exemplified by the passage into law of the Courts and Legal Services Act 1990. This shows that the fear that lawyers may be tempted by having a financial incentive in the outcome of litigation to act improperly is exaggerated, and that there is a countervailing public policy in making justice readily accessible to persons of modest means. Legislation was needed to authorise the increase in the lawyer's reward over and above his ordinary profit costs.

It by no means follows that it was needed to legitimise the long-standing practice of solicitors to act for meritorious clients without means, and it is in the public interest that they should continue to do so. I observe that the author of *Cook on Costs* (2d. Ed) at p. 341 expresses his doubt that it is now against public policy for a solicitor to agree with a client that he will not charge a fee unless a particular result is achieved. I agree with him and would hold that it is not.

Conclusion

In my judgment there is nothing unlawful in a solicitor acting for a party to litigation to agree to forego all or part of his fee if he loses, provided that he does not seek to recover more than his ordinary profit costs and disbursements if he wins. I would accordingly overrule the decisions in *British Waterways Board* v *Norman* and *Aratra Potato Co. Ltd.* v *Taylor Johnson Garrett* and allow the appeal.

LORD JUSTICE HUTCHISON: I agree that this appeal should be allowed for the reasons that Lord Justice Millett has given, with which I am in complete agreement.

LORD JUSTICE KENNEDY: I also agree.

Order: appeal allowed with costs.

Court of Protection Master's Direction 1/95 Conditional Fees

Solicitors are now permitted to ask for costs on a contingency basis in personal injury cases. They are referred to as "conditional fees". If solicitors wish to enter into an agreement with a patient to charge conditional fees, the question should be referred to the Master. Most personal injury litigation involving patients is likely to continue to be conducted with the help of legal aid but conditional fee agreements will no doubt be sought in some cases.

Briefly, a conditional fee agreement is likely to promise the solicitor that if the litigation is successful, the solicitor will recover from the patient his or her conventional ("basic") costs and disbursements plus a success fee of up to 100% of basic costs, or of 25% of the damages recovered, whichever is less. Basic costs and disbursements, but not the success fee, will remain due from the losing defendants to the patient.

If the patient loses the case, the defendants' costs are likely to have to be paid by the patient. This can be insured against and will involve a one-off premium, probably not more than £200.

Further directions may be issued as the practice and procedure on this subject develop.

Mrs A B Macfarlane

Master

14th July 1995

Section 30,
Access to Justice Act 1999

Recovery where body undertakes to meet costs liabilities

30. –

(1) This section applies where a body of a prescribed description undertakes to meet (in accordance with arrangements satisfying prescribed conditions) liabilities which members of the body or other persons who are parties to proceedings may incur to pay the costs of other parties to the proceedings.

(2) If in any of the proceedings a costs order is made in favour of any of the members or other persons, the costs payable to him may, subject to subsection (3) and (in the case of court proceedings) to rules of court, include an additional amount in respect of any provision made by or on behalf of the body in connection with the proceedings against the risk of having to meet such liabilities.

(3) But the additional amount shall not exceed a sum determined in a prescribed manner; and there may, in particular, be prescribed as a manner of determination one which takes into account the likely cost to the member or other person of the premium of an insurance policy against the risk of incurring a liability to pay the costs of other parties to the proceedings.

(4) In this section "prescribed" means prescribed by regulations made by the Lord Chancellor by statutory instrument; and a statutory instrument containing such regulations shall be subject to annulment in pursuance of a resolution of either House of Parliament.

(5) Regulations under subsection (1) may, in particular, prescribe as a description of body one which is for the time being approved by the Lord Chancellor or by a prescribed person.

Section 31,
Access to Justice Act 1999

Rules as to costs

31. In section 51 of the Supreme Court Act 1981 (costs), in subsection (2) (rules regulating matters relating to costs), insert at the end "or for securing that the amount awarded to a party in respect of the costs to be paid by him to such representatives is not limited to what would have been payable by him to them if he had not been awarded costs."

Summary of Terms of Engagement on a Conditional Fee Basis

Counsel:

Solicitor:

Client:

Re:

Solicitor/Client CFA
date:

Success fee:

Solicitor's normal   £
charging rate (before
success fee) per hour:

Counsel's normal   – Advisory work and drafting: £--- per hour
charging rate (before   – Court appearances
success fee):   (A)   **Fast track cases**

Such sum as is prescribed by Part 46.2 Civil
Procedure Rules 1998, currently

Value of the Claim	*Amount of fast track trial costs which the court may award*
Up to £3,000	£350
More than £3,000 but not more than £10,000	£500
More than £10,000	£750

          (B)   **Multi-track cases**

              (1)   *Brief fee – trial*

For a trial estimated at up to 2 days:
£---; three days to five days: £---; five to

eight days: £---, eight to 12 days: £---;
13 to 20 days: £---.

(2) *Brief fee – interim hearings*
For an interim hearing estimated up to one hour, £---, one hour to half a day £---, half a day to one day £---, over one day will be charged as if it was a trial.

Solicitor's signature:

Counsel's signature:

Date of this Agreement:

SOLICITOR/COUNSEL CONDITIONAL FEE AGREEMENT

The Nature of the Agreement

1   In this agreement 'Counsel' means   ; 'the solicitor' means   ; 'the Client' means

2.   This agreement which is not a contract enforceable by law forms the basis on which instructions are accepted by Counsel from the solicitor to act on a conditional fee basis for the Client in his/her claim against   ('the Opponent') for   until

(1)   the claim is won, lost or otherwise concluded or

(2)   this agreement is terminated.

3.   This agreement relates to issues of

(1)   jurisdiction;

(2)   breach of duty;

(3)   causation;

(4)   damages;

(5)   limitation.

4.   It covers any proceedings to enforce a judgment or order and it covers any appeal made by the Opponent but it does not cover any appeal made by the Client, and it does not cover any counterclaim.

5.   Counsel has been provided with:

(1)   a copy of the conditional fee agreement between the solicitor and the Client,

(2) a copy of the insurance policy indemnifying the client or a written explanation of why there is no insurance in place or a self-insurance declaration within the meaning of Section 30 Access to Justice Act 1999.

(3) all relevant papers and risk assessment material.

6. The solicitor confirms that the Client or any Litigation Friend has consented to the terms and conditions set out in this agreement insofar as they relate to the Client.

Obligations of Counsel

7. Counsel agrees to act diligently on all proper instructions from the solicitor subject to paragraph 8.

8. Counsel is not bound to accept instructions

(1) to appear at any interim hearing;

(2) to draft documents or advise if a barrister of similar seniority would not ordinarily be instructed to do so if not instructed on a conditional fee basis;

(3) outside the scope of this agreement.

Obligations of the Solicitor

9. The solicitor agrees:

(1) promptly to copy this agreement to the Client/Litigation Friend.,

(2) to act diligently in all dealings with Counsel and the prosecution of the claim, including delivering, within a reasonable time, papers requested by Counsel.

(3) promptly to bring to Counsel's attention:
   (a) any priority or equivalent report to insurers.
   (b) any Part 36 offer to settle;
   (c) any Part 36 payment into court;
   (d) any evidence information or communication which may materially affect the merits of any issue in the case;

(4) promptly to communicate to the Client any advice by Counsel:
   (a) to make, accept or reject any Part 36 offer;
   (b) to accept or reject any Part 36 payment in;
   (c) to incur, or not to incur, expenditure in obtaining evidence or preparing the case.,
   (d) to instruct Leading Counsel or a more senior or specialised barrister;
   (e) that the case is likely to be lost;

(f) that damages and cost recoverable on success make it unreasonable or uneconomic for the action to proceed;

(5) promptly to inform Counsel of any listing for trial or other hearing for which Counsel is to be instructed,

(6) to deliver the brief for trial not less than one working week before trial,

(7) following termination of this agreement promptly to inform Counsel of any development which may affect his entitlement to any fees.

Termination of the agreement by Counsel

10. Counsel may terminate the agreement, provided he does so promptly in writing to the Solicitor, if

(1) the solicitor is in breach of any obligation in paragraph 10,

(2) the solicitor, Client or Litigation Friend rejects Counsel's advice in any respect set out in paragraph 9(5),

(3) Counsel is informed or discovers the existence of any set-off or counterclaim which materially affects the likelihood of success and/or the amount of financial recovery in the event of success;

(4) information has been falsified or knowingly withheld by the solicitor, Client or Next Friend, of which Counsel was not aware and which he could not reasonably have anticipated, which materially affects the merits of any substantial issue in the case.

Termination of the agreement by the solicitor

11. The solicitor may terminate the agreement at any time on the instructions of the Client or any Litigation Friend.

Automatic termination of the agreement

12. This agreement shall automatically terminate if:

(1) Counsel accepts a full-time judicial appointment;

(2) the solicitor's agreement with the Client is terminated;

(3) legal aid is granted to the Client;

(4) the Client dies.

Client becoming under a disability

13. If the Client at any time becomes under a disability then the solicitor will

    (1)   consent to a novation of his conditional fee agreement with the Client to the Litigation Friend and

    (2)   where appropriate, apply to the court to obtain its consent to acting under a conditional fee agreement with the Litigation Friend.

Thereafter, the Litigation Friend shall, for the purposes of this agreement, be treated as if he/she was and has always been the Client.

Counsel's normal fees

14. (1)   Counsel's fees upon which a success fee will be calculated (the normal fees) will be as follows: -

    –   **Advisory work and drafting**
        In accordance with Counsel's hourly rate obtaining for such work in this field currently £--- per hour.

    –   **Court appearances**
       (A) **Fast track cases**
           Such sum as is prescribed by Part 46.2 Civil Procedure Rules 1998, currently

Value of the Claim	*Amount of fast track trial costs which the court may award*
Up to £3,000	£350
More than £3,000 but not more than £10,000	£500
More than £10,000	£750

       (B) **Multi-track cases**
         (1) *Brief fee – trial*
            For a trial estimated at up to 2 days: £---; three days to five days: £---; five to eight days: £---; eight to 12 days: £---; 13 to 20 days: £---.
         (2) *Brief fee – interim hearings*
            For an interim hearing estimated up to one hour, £---, one hour to half a day £---, half a day to one day £---, over one day will be charged as if it was a trial.

Counsel's success fee

15. (1)   The rate of Counsel's success fee will be 100% of Counsel's normal fees;

(2) the success fees payable to the Solicitor and Counsel (inclusive of VAT) will be capped so that their aggregate shall not exceed [%] of the aggregate of damages and interest awarded or agreed, whether recovered or not;

(3) the success fees of the Solicitor and of Counsel shall be aggregated and divided equally between them;

(4) in the event that the normal fees of the Solicitor and/or Counsel are reduced by agreement with the Client's opponent or his opponent's Solicitors or by party and party assessment, that part of the normal fees not recovered from the opponent and charged to the client, together with the success fees of the Solicitor and Counsel (inclusive of VAT), will be capped so that their aggregate shall not exceed [%] of the aggregate of damages and interest awarded or agreed, whether recovered or not;

(5) for the purposes of such calculation damages will be net of any benefits deductible under the Social Security (Recovery of Benefits) Act 1997;

Counsel's expenses

16. Expenses shall only be payable insofar as they are recovered from the opponent, and shall attract no success fee and shall comprise reasonable travel and accommodation expenses.

Counsel's entitlement to fees if the agreement is not terminated

17. (1) 'Success' means the same as 'win' in the Conditional Fee Agreement between the solicitor and the Client.

(2) Subject to paragraphs 18, 20 & 21 hereof, in the event of success the Solicitor will pay Counsel his normal and success fees.

18. If the amount of damages and interest awarded by the court is less than a Part 36 payment into Court or an effective Part 36 offer then:

(1) if Counsel advised its rejection he is entitled to normal and success fees for work up to receipt of the notice of payment into Court or offer but no fees thereafter;

(2) if Counsel advised its acceptance he is entitled to normal and success fees for all work done.

19. If the case is lost or on Counsel's advice ends without success, then Counsel is not entitled to any fees or expenses.

Counsel's entitlement to fees on termination of the agreement

20. (1) If this agreement is terminated by Counsel under paragraph 10 (save as a result of advice given under Clause 9(5)(f) or by the solicitor under paragraph 10 hereof, then Counsel, provided he does so promptly in writing, may elect either

      (a) to receive payment of normal fees without a success fee which the solicitor shall pay not later than three months after termination or

      (b) to await the outcome of the case and receive payment of normal and success fees if it ends in success.

    (2) If the agreement terminates automatically under paragraph 12 or by Counsel as a result of advice given under clause 9(5)(f), Counsel will await the outcome of the case and receive payment of normal and success fees if it ends in success.

23. If the Client or any Litigation friend wishes to challenge:

     (1) the entitlement to fees of Counsel or the level of such fees following termination of the agreement or

     (2) any refusal by Counsel after signing this agreement to accept instructions, the Solicitor must make such challenge in accordance with the provisions of paragraphs 14 and 15 of the Terms of Work upon which barristers offer their services to solicitors (Annexe D to the Code of Conduct of the Bar of England and Wales).

Return of work

22. If Counsel in accordance with the Bar's Code of Conduct is obliged to return any brief or instructions in this case to another barrister, then

     (1) Counsel will use his best endeavours to ensure that an appropriate barrister agrees to act for the Client on the same terms as this agreement,

     (2) If Counsel is unable to secure an appropriate replacement barrister to act for the Client on the same terms as this agreement Counsel will be responsible or any additional fee incurred by the Solicitor or Client;

     (3) subject to paragraph 22(4) hereof, if the case ends in success, Counsel's fees for work done shall be due and paid on the conditional fee basis contained in this agreement whether or not the replacement barrister acts on a conditional fee basis, but

     (4) if the Solicitor or Client rejects any advice by the replacement barrister of the type described in paragraph 9(5) hereof, the Solicitor

shall immediately notify Counsel whose fees shall be paid as set out in paragraph 20(1) hereof.

Assessment and payment of fees

23. The Solicitor shall pay Counsel interest that has accrued on Counsel's outstanding fees, insofar as it has been recovered from the Opponent.

24. (1) The Solicitor will inform Counsel in good time of the date, place and time of any assessment the Client has taken out pursuant to Part 47 Civil Procedure Rules 1998 and unless Counsel is present or represented at the assessment will place Counsel's written representations before the assessing officer.

    (2) If Counsel's fees are reduced on a solicitor and own client assessment then
    (a) the Solicitor will inform Counsel within seven days;
    (b) subject to any appeal, Counsel will accept such fees as are allowed on that assessment and will repay forthwith to the Solicitor any excess previously paid.

Dated ....

Signed by Counsel or by his
clerk with Counsel's authority ....

Signed by the Solicitor ....

© Kerry Underwood 1999.

The Law Society's Personal Injury Panel

Selection Criteria

3.1 Eligibility

(i) Those eligible to join the Panel
Solicitors and current Fellows of the Institute of Legal Executives, who have passed the Institute's Civil Litigation and Tort papers. Applications from Fellows who qualified before these papers existed will be considered on their individual merits.

(ii) Practising Certificates
All solicitor applicants must hold a current practising certificate.

(iii) Minimum qualification period
Solicitor applicants must have been admitted to the Roll for at least three years. Fellows must have at least three years experience after achieving Fellowship of the Institute and must currently be Fellows of the Institute.

Applicants with less than three years post qualification experience may be considered under exceptional circumstances (e.g. those who have transferred jurisdiction, or from the Bar or who were FILEX and then became solicitors).

3.2 Experience

(i) An applicant will be expected to have carried out or directly and actively supervised:
(a) at least 60 personal injury instructions in the five years prior to the application or
(b) at least 36 personal injury instructions in the three years prior to the application
(c) in either case, no more than half of the instructions should be in medical negligence cases.

(ii) An applicant will be expected to have carried out or directly and actively supervised:
(a) at least one personal injury case where the award or settlement was approved by the Court because the plaintiff was under a disability, for example a child.

(b) at least ten cases set down for trial, of which at least two must have involved a dispute over liability.

(iii) Applicants who are unable to comply fully with the experience criteria, detailed above, may still be admitted to the Panel if they are able to demonstrate a suitable level of experience. For example, it may be that the applicant:

(a) has been concerned with catastrophic injury cases which has limited the number of cases they have been able to deal with.

(b) spends 100% of their time on civil litigation of which personal injury litigation is a part.

(c) has not set down 10 personal injury cases for trial but has set down many other cases for trial (see paragraph 3.2(iv)).

(iv) Applicants should normally be able to demonstrate that they have set down at least 10 cases for trial during their practising career. Where applicants cannot demonstrate that they have set down 10 personal injury cases they should provide details of other civil cases which they have set down for trial.

3.3 Training

(i) An applicant will be required to provide details of training courses attended over the past three years. This information is required to aid the assessment of borderline applicants and decide other measures to be used in determining the application.

(ii) The Society may require an applicant to attend a relevant training course as a condition of acceptance to the Panel.

(iii) For reselection purposes; Panel members will be expected to have undertaken appropriate training courses to update their knowledge and be in a position (e.g. by training records) to demonstrate this.

Conditional Fee Agreement

FOR NON-PERSONAL INJURY MONEY CLAIMS

The agreement is a legally binding contract between you and your Solicitor. For an explanation of words like 'Disbursements', 'Basic Costs', 'win', and 'lose', see clause 3.

Agreement date   [Agreement date]

We, the Solicitor

You, the client   [Client's name and address]

What is covered by the agreement
Your claim for [Claim]
against [Defendant]

What is not covered by the agreement
Any counterclaim against you.
Any appeal you make
Any appeal made by your opponent

1. **We must**

   * always act in your best interests in pursuing your claim for damages and obtaining for you the best possible result, subject to our duty to the court and the terms of any Insurance;
   * explain to you the risks and benefits of taking legal action;
   * give you our best advice about whether to accept any offer of settlement;
   * at the outset, give you the best information possible about the likely costs of your case.

2. **You must**

   * give us a complete and truthful account of the facts of the case and all relevant documentary or other evidence in your possession.

* give instructions that allow us to do our work properly;
* not ask us to work in an improper or unreasonable way;
* not deliberately mislead us;
* cooperate with us when asked;
* go to any expert examination or court hearing when asked;
* pay for disbursements as the case goes on.
* comply at all times with the requirements of the Insurance

3. **Explanation of words used**

Administration Fee	A fee charged by any insurer or proposed insurer to consider whether to insure against legal costs if the case is lost.
Advocacy	Appearing for you at court hearings.
Basic Costs	Our costs for legal work. Basic costs are worked out in line with our hourly rate of [ ] plus VAT. The hourly rate is the same as would be charged if the work was not done under a conditional fee agreement.
Case	Your claim for damages described above.
Damages	Money that a court says you or your opponent must pay (or money that you or your opponent agree to pay) in settlement of the case.
Disbursements	Payments we make on your behalf to others involved in the case.
Insurance	The policy of insurance entered into by you and us with the Insurer to cover legal costs if the case is lost. We recommend that you have insurance in place immediately.
Interim damages	Money that a court says your opponent must pay while waiting for a settlement or the courts final decision. Out of this money we may require you to pay our remaining disbursements and a reasonable amount for our future disbursements.
Lien	Our right to keep all papers, documents, money or other property held on your behalf until all money due to us is paid. A lien may be applied after the agreement ends.
Lose	The court has dismissed your proceedings or you have stopped them on our advice.

Opponent	The party or parties from whom you are claiming damages in the case.
Success Fee	percent of Basic Costs. The Success Fee is added to your bill if you win the case. It is paid out of your damages.
	The total of our Success Fee (see condition 6) is capped – it will not be more than [%] of the damages recovered and includes VAT.
Payment into court	It may be that your opponent makes a payment into court which you reject and, on our advice, the case goes ahead to trial where you recover damages that are less than the Payment into Court. If so, you do not have to pay any of the basic costs for the work done after we receive notice of the payment in.
Win	The case is finally decided in your favour, whether by a court decision or an agreement to pay you damages. 'Finally' means that your opponent: • is not allowed to appeal against the court decision; or • has not appealed in time.

4. **What happens if you win?**

If you win, you are liable to pay our disbursements, the Insurance premium and administration fee (if you have not already paid these), our Basic Costs and the Success Fee. Normally, however, you will be able to recover part of our disbursements and Basic Costs from your opponent. The court will decide how much you can recover if you and your opponent cannot agree the amount. If the amount agreed or allowed by the court does not cover all our work, you pay the difference. If your opponent is on legal aid, we are unlikely to get any money from him or her; so, if this happens, you have to pay the whole amount of our Basic Costs. **You, not your opponent, pay our Success Fee.**

You agree that we may receive the damages and costs your opponent has to pay. If your opponent refuses to accept our receipt, you will pay the cheque you receive from your opponent into a joint bank account in your name and ours. Out of the money, you agree to let us take the balance of the Basic Costs; Success Fee; remaining disbursements; and VAT. You take the rest.

We are allowed to keep any interest your opponent pays on the costs.

Payment for barristers is explained in clause 6.

If your opponent does not pay any damages or costs owed to you, we have the right to take recovery action in your name to enforce a judgment, order or agreement. The costs of this action become part of the Basic Costs.

5. **What happens if you lose?**

If you lose, you do not have to pay any of the Basic Costs or Success Fee.

You do have to pay:-

* us for our disbursements;
* your opponent's legal costs and disbursements;
* any damages awarded or agreed against you if your opponent succeeds in any claim against you;
* the administration fee unless it has already been paid or we have agreed otherwise
* the Insurance premium unless it has already been paid or unless the Insurance provides for non-payment of the premium in the event losing the case.

Payment for barristers is dealt with in clause 6.

If the agreement is covered by Insurance, we will make a claim on your behalf and receive any resulting payment in your name. We will give you a statement of account for all money received and paid out.

If your opponent pays you the costs of any hearing, they belong to us.

6. **Payment for advocacy**

The cost of advocacy forms part of our Basic Costs.

For a Barristers who have a conditional fee agreement with us, if you win, their fee is our disbursement which can be recovered from your opponent. You must pay the barrister's uplift fee shown in the separate conditional fee agreement we make with the barrister. We will discuss the barrister's uplift fee with you before we instruct him or her. If you lose, you pay nothing.

If you choose a barrister we do not recommend, we may decide not to seek a conditional fee agreement with him or her and their fee is a disbursement.

The total of the success fee and the barrister's uplift fee will not exceed [cfa % rate] of the damages.

If you reject our advice to use a barrister, you may not compel us to provide advocacy ourselves. Following our refusal to provide advocacy, we can end the agreement if you still reject our advice to use a barrister.

7. **What happens when the agreement ends before the case itself ends ?**

If this agreement ends for whatever reason the Insurance ends automatically. If the agreement has ended because you have got legal aid, any Insurance cover remains in force as regards your opponent's costs and our disbursements incurred up to the date the agreement ends. If it ends for any other reason you are liable for your opponents costs and our disbursements.

You can end the agreement at any time but cover under Insurance will end automatically if you do. We then have the right to decide whether you must:

- pay the Basic Costs, and our disbursements, when we ask for them; or
- pay the Basic Costs and our disbursements and, if you go on to win the case, the Success Fee .

We can end the agreement if you do not keep to your responsibilities in clause 2. We then have the right to decide whether you must:

- pay the Basic Costs, and our disbursements, when we ask for them; or
- pay the Basic Costs and our disbursements and, if you go on to win the case, the Success Fee .

We can end the agreement if we believe you are unlikely to win but you disagree with us. If this happens, you will only have to pay our disbursements if these have not already been paid by you.

We can end the agreement if you reject our opinion about making a settlement with your opponent. You must then:

- pay the Basic Costs, and our disbursements, if these have not already been paid by you and
- pay the Success Fee if you go on to win the case (unless your damages or settlement are at least 20% more than the offer we advised you to accept).

If you ask us to get a second opinion from a specialist legal representative outside our firm, we will do so. You pay the cost of a second opinion.

8. **What happens after the agreement ends**

After the agreement ends, we will apply to have our name removed from the record of any court proceedings in which we are acting unless you have legal aid and ask us to work for you. We have the right to preserve our lien unless another solicitor working for you undertakes to pay us what we are owed including a Success Fee if you win.

Immediately before you signed the agreement, we explained the following points to you.

Legal aid
- Whether you can get legal aid for this case.
- Under what conditions you can get legal aid.
- How those conditions apply to this case.

Costs and disbursements
- In what circumstances you may have to pay our disbursements and costs.
- In what circumstances you may have to pay the disbursements and costs of your opponent.
- In what circumstances you can get our bills checked by a court (known as 'Detailed Assessment'), and how to do so.

Special Conditions

This agreement is a legally binding contract between you and   solicitors. It covers all work we do from the date you sign the agreement.

Signed for the Solicitors

Signed by the client

Conditional Fees: Sharing the Risks of Litigation

September 1999

- **HOW TO RESPOND**

- **SUMMARY**

  - Conditional Fee Regulations
  - Conditional Fees and Litigation Funding

PART ONE

- **Conditional Fee Agreements**

  - Background
  - History
  - Speculative Agreements
  - Access to Justice Act

- **Recovering the Success Fee**

  - Recovery of Costs
  - The Success Fee
  - Recovery of the Insurance Premium

PART TWO

New Regulations

  - Current Regulations
  - New Regulations
  - CFAs for Children and Patients
  - CFAs where no uplift will be charged.
  - Litigation Funding Agreements and Membership Organisations

CONCLUSION – comments are requested on:

- Conditional Fee Agreements
- Insurance premiums
- New Regulations

HOW TO RESPOND

Comments on the paper should be sent to the following address by 26 November 1999:

Ms Helen Williams
Lord Chancellor's Department
3rd Floor, Selborne House
Victoria Street
London SW1E 6QW

Unless you ask the Department to keep your name or the contents of your response confidential, your name and the general contents of your response may be made public, in response to questions under the Open Government initiative. Please ensure your response is marked clearly, if you wish your response or your name to be kept confidential. Confidential responses will be included in any statistical summary of numbers of comments received and views expressed.

Additional copies of this paper are available from Melissa Rippin at the above address (0171–210 8774).

SUMMARY

1. In the Government's consultation paper 'Access to Justice with Conditional Fees', issued in March 1998, it was proposed that, as part of the Government's commitment to making conditional fee agreements (CFAs) work, the success fee in a CFA, and any insurance premium paid to protect against meeting a party's own and their opponent's costs, should be recoverable from the losing opponent. Responses to the consultation paper informed the Government's decision to accept these proposals and the Access to Justice Act 1999 (the Act) has provided, amongst other things, the vehicle to do so.

2. However, the Act only provides the legislative framework. The detail of the changes to conditional fees will be provided through secondary legislation, while the operation of the recoverability of the success fee and insurance premium will be informed by Rules of Court and Practice Directions. Both elements require consultation with affected parties.

3. The aim of this paper is twofold: to seek views on the practical operation of recoverability; and to seek views on the contents of the statutory

instruments, and any Rules of Court, which are a necessary consequence of the changes to conditional fee agreements brought about by the Act.

4. It is proposed that:

Success Fee

- The other party should receive immediate notification of the existence of the CFA and whether a success fee is being claimed, but not the level of that fee.

- Both the client and the losing opponent should be able to challenge the success fee through an assessment by the courts.

- The recoverability of the success fee should not be retrospective but should apply only to CFAs which are entered into, and/or in respect of proceedings commenced, after the relevant section of the Act comes into force.

Insurance premium

- The other party should receive immediate notification of the existence of the policy.

- Both the client and the losing opponent should be able to challenge the level of the insurance premium through an assessment by the courts.

- The recoverability of the insurance premium should not be retrospective but should apply only to policies signed after the coming into force of the relevant section of the Act.

5. Comments are also requested on:

- what (if any) sanctions would be appropriate if a party failed to disclose that they were funding their case under a CFA;

- whether the legal representative should be required to produce written reasons for the level of uplift charged when the terms of the CFA are agreed;

- the stage at which these reasons should be disclosed to the court;

- whether a mechanism should be developed for settling disputes over the assessment of success fees in cases settled pre issue;

- what form that mechanism should take;

- the stage at which the court should receive information about the existence of an insurance policy.

Conditional Fee Regulations

6. The paper also addresses the question of whether the rules which have governed conditional fee agreements to date require amendment in the light of the experience of operating CFAs, and the consequence of the changes brought about by the Act. In particular the paper questions

whether greater clarification is required in the area of the information provided to, and knowledge required of, litigation friends when entering into a CFA on behalf of a child or patient.

7. Comments are therefore particularly requested on:

   - whether the solicitor should be under an obligation to explain the agreement to the client in addition to providing written information.

   - whether the solicitor should be required to discuss with the client the desirability of insurance cover in a CFA, to cover the client's own costs liability and their potential liability for their opponent's costs.

   - whether the solicitor should be under an obligation to advise on the relative advantages and disadvantages of the available insurance funding products and to explain in detail what cover, etc. the recommended products provide.

   - whether the maximum % allowable as a success fee should remain at 100%.

   - whether there should be provision that, where the court considered the success fee to be excessive and not to be met in whole by the unsuccessful opponent, the client should not be responsible for meeting the difference between the success fee claimed and the amount recovered.

   - whether additional information should be provided to the litigation friend.

   - whether that information should be in writing and supplemented by an oral explanation of the consequences.

   - whether the current regulations are sufficient to ensure clarity in the operation of CFAs.

   - whether the proceedings in which no success fee can be claimed should be limited to proceedings under s.82 of the Environmental Protection Act 1990 (as proposed).

   - what factors should inform the Lord Chancellor when prescribing membership organisations for the purposes of s.30 of the Access to Justice Act 1999.

   - the mechanism for determining the level of the 'self insurance' premium under s.30 of the Access to Justice Act 1999.

8. Given the likely impact of the proposals on the solicitor and client relationship, the Lord Chancellor will wish to consider all relevant issues before coming to a conclusion on their implementation.

Conditional Fees and Litigation Funding

9. The Legal Aid Board's consultation paper on the Funding Code (end note 1) introduced the concept of litigation funding, whereby the Legal Services Commission would provide a partial funding of proceedings in cases which are otherwise funded through private arrangements such as CFAs. The partial funding would be of particular relevance where the investigative or overall costs stretched a firm's resources. Responses to that consultation indicated support for the concept of litigation support and the Board has been developing proposals for the way in which litigation funding will interact with CFAs. The Board will publish its Report and revised Code later this Autumn which will include proposals for litigation funding.

PART ONE

Conditional Fee Agreements

Background

1. Conditional fees are defined in s.58 of the Courts and Legal Services Act 1990 as amended by s.27(1) of the Access to Justice Act 1999. A conditional fee agreement is 'an agreement …which provides for … fees and expenses, or any part of them, to be payable only in specified circumstances'.

2. Traditionally CFAs, also known as 'no win no fee', have allowed solicitors to agree to take a case in the understanding that, if the case is lost, they will not charge their clients for all or any of the work undertaken. In agreeing to this the client also agrees that if the case is successful, the solicitor can charge a success fee on top of the normal fees, to compensate for the risk the solicitor has run of not being paid all or some of the fees. That success fee is calculated as a percentage of the normal fees and the level at which the success fee is set will reflect the risk involved. That said, it is not a requirement of a CFA that a success fee must be charged.

3. The no fee element relates to the solicitor's fees alone and does not cover the ancillary expenses of the case, such as expert reports, and may not cover counsel's fees. However, the solicitor may agree to fund these costs as part of the agreement or may arrange financial cover for his client. Alternatively, a CFA can be entered into between a solicitor and counsel or, in very limited circumstances, between client and counsel. Insurance policies are also available which provide cover for the solicitor's fee and/or for the opponent's costs should the case be unsuccessful. The premium paid for insurance cover is determined by the provider and will be dependent on a number of factors, including the strength of the case, the likely quantum, and the legal representative's experience of undertaking such cases. Premiums may range from £100 to many millions depending on the case insured.

History

4. Conditional fee agreements were introduced by the Courts and Legal Services Act 1990 (end note 2) which made provision for agreements in which it was explicit that part or all of the legal representative's fees were payable only in the event of success. The definition of CFAs in s.58 of that Act excludes criminal and most family proceedings and is limited to agreements specified by Order by the Lord Chancellor, which comply with requirements prescribed by the Lord Chancellor in regulations. The Order also specifies the maximum percentage by which normal fees may be increased in the event of a successful outcome.

5. The first Order was brought into force on 5 July 1995 (end note 3). This limited conditional fee agreements to personal injury cases, insolvency cases and cases before the European Court of Human Rights. From that date it was lawful, in those limited cases, for a legal representative to enter into an agreement with his client whereby costs would be recoverable from the client only in certain circumstances and where the normal costs could be increased by a percentage uplift of not more than 100% should those circumstances occur. Regulations specifying the information which a conditional fee agreement must contain and which must be brought to the client's attention were also brought into force at that time (end note 4). In July 1998 the range of proceedings was extended as far as possible under the 1990 Act to all civil proceedings, other than family cases (end note 5). There has been an increasing use of conditional fee agreements with very few complaints about the way in which they have operated. The evidence also points to the increasing use of CFAs in areas such as defamation. Many of these cases would probably not have been brought but for the existence of conditional fees.

6. Since their introduction in 1995, the Law Society has produced guidance for solicitors about the use of conditional fee agreements and a model agreement for use between clients and solicitors. It has also advised solicitors to apply a voluntary limit of 25% on the proportion of damages which a success fee should represent. The guidance and model agreement are currently under review.

Speculative Agreements

7. While the extension of conditional fee agreements to all civil business has provided access to justice for individuals who may not have otherwise litigated, the definition of a conditional fee agreement is limited and does not encompass all situations where a legal representative agrees to act for his client at different rates to that which he will seek to recover from his client's opponent.

8. Two recent decisions have tested the way in which alternative agreements for funding cases are viewed, *Thai Trading Co. (A Firm)* v *Taylor* (1998) 3 All ER 65 and *Bevan Ashford* v *Geoff Yeandle (Contractors) Ltd* (1998) 3 All ER 238. In the former case the Court of Appeal held that there were

no longer public policy grounds to prevent legal representatives agreeing to work for less than their normal fees in the event that they were unsuccessful, provided they did not seek to recover more than their normal fees if they were successful. In *Bevan Ashford* the Vice Chancellor held that where a person uses an alternative remedy to court proceedings in a class of proceedings where conditional fee agreements are lawful in the courts, and that all the relevant provisions relating to the form and content of the agreement as prescribed by the relevant regulations (the Conditional Fees Regulations 1995) were complied with, there were no public policy grounds for holding the agreement unlawful. On the contrary, it would be of benefit for clients to have access to these agreements to enable them to use alternative dispute mechanisms.

9. The Lord Chancellor considered that it was in the public interest that the position regarding Thai Trading and Bevan Ashford type agreements should be clear. He therefore took the opportunity of the Access to Justice Bill to take these judgments into statute law rather than leaving the matter to the common law. This has been done by making all agreements to work for less than normal fees subject to s.58 of the Courts and Legal Services Act. This will secure the greater certainty that statute law provides, and will ensure that such agreements can be properly regulated, for example by requiring solicitors to give relevant information to potential clients.

Access to Justice Act

10. The Access to Justice Act received Royal Assent on 27 July 1999. The relevant sections relating to conditional fee agreements and insurance premiums are sections 27 to 31 (annex C). Section 27 replaces s.58 of the Courts and Legal Services Act 1990 and provides a clearer definition of conditional fee agreements. It also makes the winning party's success fee potentially recoverable from the other side. Section 27 also amends s. 58 of the Courts and Legal Services Act to allow cases to be brought using a CFA under s.82 of the Environmental Protection Act, although these are criminal cases. Section 28 allows a party to be funded by a Trade Union, or other prescribed group, and Section 30 provides for such a group which took responsibility for a party's liabilities to recover from the opponent a sum in recognition of this liability. Section 29 makes the costs of the winning party's after the event insurance premium recoverable from the other side. Section 31 is the enabling provision which provides the Lord Chancellor with the power to amend the indemnity principle which underlies costs. Any amendment of the indemnity principle will be effected through Rules of Court, on which consultation has recently taken place.

11. Regulations will prescribe the requirements with which all CFAs must comply. In addition, the powers in s.27 of the Act will allow the Lord Chancellor to prescribe different requirements for different types of agreement or classes of case and to define which CFAs will be eligible to incur a success fee and which will not. The power to specify proceedings by order is not confined to court proceedings, but extends to other

methods of dispute resolution, thereby incorporating the result of Bevan Ashford into proceedings. A CFA which complies with these requirements shall not be unenforceable by reason of its being a CFA, unless it relates to criminal proceedings, family proceedings, or proceedings which have not been specified. Where the CFA relates to such proceedings, or does not comply with the requirements in the regulations, the Act explicitly provides that the agreement is unenforceable. The success fee is enforceable only where the agreement complies with the prescribed requirements; relates to specified proceedings; and the percentage increase does not exceed that set out in the order specifying the proceedings.

Recovering the Success Fee

Recovery of Costs

12. The liability for meeting the costs of a solicitor in an action rests with the solicitor's client. The giving of instructions by a client to a solicitor constitutes the creation of a contract between that client and solicitor, and creates the solicitor's right to be paid his costs for pursuing a case, together with any disbursements incurred.

13. Where a party is successful in an action, the general rule is that the unsuccessful party will be ordered to pay the costs of the successful party. The level of those costs, and the extent to which all or part of the costs are to be met by the unsuccessful party, will be assessed (formerly taxed) by the court. This is known as the assessment of costs between the parties. In assessing the costs payable, the court will allow a reasonable amount in respect of all costs reasonably incurred and any doubts about those costs will be resolved in the favour of the unsuccessful party. From 26 April, the court has had to consider whether the costs being claimed are proportionate, amongst other things, to the issues at stake and the complexity of the case (see Rules 1.1(2)(c) and 44.5(1) of the Civil Procedure Rules 1998).

14. The courts have the discretion to disallow all or part of the costs incurred by the successful party, dependent on the circumstances of the case and its conduct. This may occur where a solicitor or client undertakes steps in proceedings which are not reasonable. In such circumstances the court will not order the unsuccessful party to meet those costs and hence the costs allowed 'between the parties' will be lower than the amount for which the successful party is liable to his solicitor. Any difference between a 'between the parties' costs order and the clients' liability to their own solicitor must be resolved between them, either through the solicitor reducing the costs claimed, or through the client agreeing to meet the difference. Where they cannot agree, an assessment of the solicitor's own client costs will take place.

The Success Fee

15. Currently any success fee in a CFA is not recoverable. Section 27 of the Act amends s. 58 of the Courts and Legal Services Act to provide that a success fee due under a CFA is to be treated as part of the costs recoverable under an order for costs. The change ensures that there will be no ambiguity about whether the costs are recoverable, while retaining the courts' general discretion as to the award of costs and determination of the amount of costs.

16. The earlier consultation attracted mixed views about the disclosure of the level of the success fee to the other side. Some consultees felt that early disclosure of the existence of a CFA and the level of success fee could lead to an early settlement, and would give the opponent some certainty about their potential liability for costs. However, concern was also expressed that disclosure of the success fee could put the opponent at an advantage, since the level of the success fee claimed might divulge too much information about the relative strength of case. The Government accepts these concerns, but believes that, on balance, the opponent should have some indication that they may be liable to pay an uplift on the other party's costs. It is therefore proposed that:

> The other party should receive immediate notification of the existence of the CFA and whether a success fee is being claimed, but not the level of that fee.

17. This requirement could be included in the relevant protocol. Views are invited as to what sanctions might be appropriate if a party did not abide by the terms of that protocol, and failed to inform the other side of the existence of the CFA.

> *Q1. What (if any) sanctions would be appropriate if a party failed to disclose that they were funding their case under a CFA?*

18. Section 48.9(5) of the Civil Procedure Rules provides that the court may reduce the amount of success fee claimed, where it considers it to be disproportionate, having regard to all relevant factors as they reasonably appeared to the solicitor or counsel when the CFA was entered into. Some respondents to the earlier consultation were concerned that the opponent, with the benefit of hindsight, could argue that the level of the success fee was disproportionate to the risk of the case, and that this would encourage satellite litigation as to the appropriateness of the level of the fee. The nature of a conditional fee is such that the legal representative may well have set the success fee at the beginning of the cases when the information is necessarily incomplete. One option to resolve this would be to require the legal representative to set down in writing the risk analysis and reasons for the uplift claimed when the terms of the CFA are agreed, and to produce further written reasons if the uplift claimed was changed during the course of the case. This document could then be disclosed to the court at the end of the case, or at any prior stage, if the level of success fee was in dispute. This would provide the court with information with which to

judge whether the success fee was fair and reasonable, while reducing the negative effect of hindsight.

> *Q.2 Should the legal representative be required to produce written reasons for the level of uplift charged when the terms of the CFA are agreed?*
>
> *Q.3 At what stage should this be disclosed to the court?*

19. A corollary of the ability to recover the success fee is the ability of the paying party to object to the level of that fee. The current costs rules provide that where a party does not agree with all or part of the costs being claimed, a detailed assessment of those costs will take place. This applies to both the costs to be met by the unsuccessful opponent and the costs for which the solicitor's own client is liable. Just as a court may conclude that it is not reasonable for the unsuccessful party to meet all of the cost claimed, so might a court conclude that it is not reasonable that a client should meet all of his solicitor's costs.

20. The level of the success fee will be open to assessment, and where a court concludes that the level of the fee is unreasonable, then the fee may be reduced accordingly. This will ensure that the unsuccessful opponent is protected from unrealistic success fees. However, the Government recognises that a significant proportion of litigants have little or no experience of litigation with which to judge whether the success fee proposed is reasonable and an equivalent protection from unreasonable success fees is desirable. It is therefore proposed that:

> **Both the client and the losing opponent should be able to challenge the success fee through an assessment by the courts.**

21. In making the success fee recoverable, consideration has to be given to the effective date from which a paying party will be liable to pay the success fee. Consideration was given to making the success fee recoverable for all those CFAs in place on the day on which the relevant section of the Act comes into force. However, this would place an undue burden on the unsuccessful opponent, who would be faced with a liability which was not anticipated and which may, in differing circumstances, have acted as a factor in determining how the case was conducted. An alternative is to make the success fee recoverable for that portion of the costs which relate to the period after the relevant section comes into effect. However, this would require the parties and the court to make additional detailed financial calculations. It would also introduce the possibility of rear loading of costs in the run up to the implementation date to ensure that the maximum possible success fee was allowed. To ensure a clear commencement date from the introduction of recoverability of the success fee, it is proposed that:

> **The recoverability of the success fee should not be retrospective but should apply only to CFAs which are entered into, and/or in respect of proceedings commenced, after the relevant section of the Act comes into force.**

22. The Government recognises that the proposals set out above relate solely to those cases which proceed to trial. The new Civil Procedure Rules relating to the Fast Track and the use of pre–action protocols in personal injury cases will increase the number of cases settling before the issue of proceedings. All settlements, whether reached through the Part 36 mechanism or otherwise, are made with an eye to what a court would order. However, the extent to which a particular settlement or offer does so is for the parties and will depend on the strength of the case and the parties' desire to avoid litigation.

23. Nothing in the Act or the Civil Procedure Rules prevents a party from offering an amount which reflects a success fee (if it is known), or the recipient of the offer from stipulating for it to be covered. That said, there is concern that the inability to compel the inclusion of the success fee element will result in parties being discouraged from accepting offers and instead proceeding to trial, with the unstated sole aim of recovering the success fee as part of the costs order. However, this is a risk with all cases where the parties cannot agree on the level of costs to be paid, and it is questionable whether it would be right to develop a special mechanism for CFAs which does not apply to other costs. In this context, views are invited on the following:

> *Q.4 Should a mechanism be developed for settling disputes over the assessment of success fees in cases settled pre issue?*
> *Q.5 What form should that mechanism take?*

Recovery of the Insurance Premium

24. Section 29 of the Act provides that any insurance premium paid to insure against the risk of incurring a liability in those proceedings may be claimed as a disbursement on taxation. While this clause ensures that this disbursement may be claimed, the court retains the discretion whether to allow the disbursement and at what level, applying the normal tests on assessment.

25. The proposal to make clear that the insurance premium is recoverable attracted considerable support although there were concerns that this might lead to an overall increase in premiums. There were similar concerns that, although an opponent should be aware of their potential liability for an insurance premium, information about the amount of premium could disclose views on the strength of the case. It is therefore proposed that:

> **The other party should receive immediate notification of an insurance policy covering the CFA, but not the price of that policy, or its coverage.**

26. As with success fees, the Government is concerned to ensure that the assessment of whether an insurance premium is reasonable should not be distorted by hindsight. The court will need to decide whether the level of cover was fair and reasonable when the policy was taken up, and may therefore need information about the level of the insurance premium, the extent of cover and the date when the policy was signed.

Q.6 When should the court receive this information?

27. It is not proposed that solicitors are required to seek the cheapest insurance policies, since this is not a requirement when procuring other forms of disbursement, such as expert reports. However, the court will wish to consider whether the cover purchased was appropriate and proportionate to the case being assessed. Where the court is of the opinion that it is not, it will be free to assess the premium accordingly, whether in the context of 'own client' assessment or 'between the parties' assessment. If it is reasonable that the unsuccessful opponent is protected from unreasonable insurance premiums, then it is also reasonable that the solicitor's own client should receive this protection. It is therefore proposed that:

> Both the client and the losing opponent should be able to challenge the level of the insurance premium through an assessment by the courts.

28. It is also proposed that:

> The recoverability of the insurance premium should not be retrospective but should apply only to policies entered into after the coming into force of the relevant section of the Act.

PART TWO

New Regulations

Current Regulations

29. Section 58 of the Courts and Legal Services Act defines a CFA as an agreement which provides for the payment of a legal representative's fees and expenses conditional upon a specified event occurring. A CFA must comply with any requirements prescribed by the Lord Chancellor in regulations, and the Lord Chancellor may prescribe different requirements in respect of particular agreements or classes of case. The Conditional Fee Agreements Order 1998 (which revoked the 1995 Order) specifies the proceedings in which a CFA can be made and the maximum permitted percentage by which fees may be increased (100%). The Conditional Fee Agreements Regulations 1995 prescribe the requirements with which an agreement between a client and his legal representative must comply.

30. A conditional fee agreement must be in writing and must:

- describe the particular proceedings to which it relates;
- the circumstances in which the fees and expenses are payable;
- the circumstances for payment should other circumstances occur.

31. The Regulations also require that the legal representative draw the client's attention to the matters below:

- whether the client might instead be entitled to legal aid and the conditions which apply to legal aid;

- the circumstances in which the client may be liable to pay the fees and expenses of the legal representative;
- the liability for the costs of the other party;
- the operation of the assessment of costs.

New Regulations

32. The conditional fee Regulations have now been in place for four years, albeit initially to a restricted extent, and practitioners will have experienced their operation at a practical level. Since the Access to Justice Act has introduced new provisions on CFAs, it is an opportune time to consider whether the existing Regulations would benefit from amendment.

33. The Regulations governing CFAs seek to ensure that the client is given sufficient information to understand what a CFA is; what the implications are for the client in entering into a CFA, both if they are successful or unsuccessful; the alternatives ways of financing the action other than through a CFA; and the client's ability to seek an assessment of their solicitor's fees. These requirements remain valid.

> **It is proposed that the current requirements relating to the detail to be included in a CFA (paragraph 30 above) should be replicated, as should the requirements relating to the information to be provided to the client (paragraph 31 above).**

34. However, the preliminary results of independent research into clients' experience of conditional fees indicates that although clients are provided with information on the way in which CFAs operate, that information is not necessarily understood. To some extent this lack of understanding may be a result of the trust placed members of a profession which underlies the solicitor/client relationship and the consequent lack of a desire on the client's part to question the solicitor's recommendation. However, it may also be true that, to an extent, this lack of knowledge results from the way in which the information is provided and the client's inexperience of the legal process. Solicitors may well provide written information on CFAs, but this is not necessarily supplemented by an explanation of their effect, with the opportunity to ask questions of the solicitor. This problem is not novel in that it must be open to question how far, for example, clients have ever understood the operation of the indemnity principle and its implication for costs liability or other technical aspects of the rules governing litigation. Nonetheless, transparency is highly desirable in all aspects of litigation and should be addressed whenever it arises.

> *Q.7 Should the solicitor be under an obligation to explain the agreement to the client in addition to providing written information?*

35. The Solicitors' Costs Information and Client Care Code 1999 regulates the information solicitors provide to their clients. Parts 4(ii) and (iii) of that code relate to the discussions which should take place on the use of insurance to cover the client's own costs liability and their liability for their

opponent's costs. Whilst anecdotal evidence suggests that solicitors are discussing the use of insurance cover in CFAs, there is no requirement in the CFA regulations that such information should be provided.

> *Q.8   Should the solicitor be required to discuss with the client the desirability of insurance cover in a CFA, to cover the client's own costs liability and their potential liability for their opponent's costs?*

36. It is also clear that clients can be confused by the way in which the CFA and any insurance and/or funding products interact and about the relative advantages and disadvantages of such products. In particular a client may be unsure about the role of the insurance policy and the extent to which it protects against the liability for those costs not covered by the CFA.

> *Q.9   Should the solicitor be under an obligation to advise on the relative advantages and disadvantages of the available insurance funding products and to explain in detail what cover, etc. the recommended products provide?*

37. Comments are also requested on the continuing suitability of the 100% cap on the success fee. It could be argued that the cap is unnecessary since the opponent will be able to challenge the level of the success fee. Given that many opponents, particularly in personal injury cases, will be repeat players such as insurance companies, they can be expected to be active in challenging unreasonable success fees. The operation of the 100% cap places a limit on what risks solicitors may feel able to accept and removal of the cap should see an increase in the availability of CFAs.

> *Q.10   Should the maximum success fee remain at 100%?*

38. That said, it is arguable that the cap does offer protection to clients who technically may be liable for the difference between the amount of any success fee recovered from unsuccessful opponents and that agreed with their solicitors, if higher. However, it is doubtful whether a court would order a client to pay such an excess having decided that it was unreasonable to order the losing opponent to do so on the basis it was excessive.

> *Q.11   Should there be provision that, where the court considered the success fee to be excessive and not to be met in whole by the unsuccessful opponent, the client should not be responsible for meeting the difference between the success fee claimed and the amount recovered?*

CFAs for Children and Patients

39. The Government believes that, in principle, children or patients (end note 6) should be able to use conditional fee agreements. Litigation friends or guardians ad litem currently need to consider how best to retain the services of a legal representative to represent the child, whether a case is funded through private resources or legal aid. The Government does

recognise, however, that it is important that the person who, on behalf of the child, enters into an agreement about the way legal representatives are paid and opponent's costs, is fully informed about all options for funding cases and the consequences of particular options, not least the success fee.

40. Whilst the Government believes this can be provided for by effective regulations, any regulations should ensure that clients are given the information they need to understand what is happening generally and what the implications are for entering into the agreement. The provisions of the current regulations are set out at paragraphs 30 and 31.

> *Q.12 To what extent are the current regulations sufficient to ensure that litigation friends are fully informed of the implications of CFAs?*
>
> *Q.13 Are the circumstances of litigation friends such that specific regulations are necessary?*
>
> *Q.14 Should the information be provided in writing and supplemented by an oral explanation of the consequences?*

41. In posing these questions the Government is aware of the detail of the Solicitor's Costs Information and Client Care Code 1999.

CFAs where no uplift will be charged.

42. The decision in *Thai Trading* (c.f. paragraph 8) had the effect that housing disrepair cases under s.82 of the Environmental Protection Act 1990 (EPA) could be brought on a speculative basis. Section 82 allows people aggrieved by a statutory nuisance to seek an order for that nuisance to be put right. These cases are heard in a magistrates' court and are technically criminal cases, but they are brought to enforce a civil right. In the light of representations from housing support groups, the Government agreed to maintain the present position whereby Thai Trading style agreements are available for proceedings under s.82 of the EPA. Currently, proceedings brought under s.82 of the EPA do not attract a success fee. The Government does not intend that this position should change. It is therefore proposed that:

Proceedings under s.82 of the EPA will not attract a success fee.

43. The ability to specify in regulations whether a success fee is allowable or not in specific categories of case is not limited to proceedings under s.82 of the EPA.

> *Q.15 Are there other specific categories of case where the charging of an uplift is unacceptable and a success fee should not be allowed?*

Litigation Funding Agreements and Membership Organisations

44. The consultation paper Access to Justice with Conditional Fees, recognised and welcomed the fact that there are many membership organisations, such as Trade Unions, which provide legal services to their members as a benefit of membership. Members who have a sufficiently strong case may

use legal representatives retained by the membership organisation, often at no cost additional to their membership subscription. In addition, the organisations usually undertake to indemnify their members against any liability for their opponents' costs, should their claims be unsuccessful. More recently, Trade Unions have begun opening up their legal services to wider groups, such as families of members. The Government has welcomed these developments and was aware of the concerns of membership organisations that they should not be prevented from providing the fullest legal assistance to their members and families because the nature of their schemes did not sit easily with the legislative constraints of conditional fees.

45. For example, a current obstacle in developing these arrangements more fully lies in an organisation's ability to recover any success fee or insurance element in the cost of funding cases. Whilst any membership organisation can take out insurance policies for each member assisted, and, if successful, recover the premium in costs from the other side, in practice this does not occur. Membership organisations are nearly always sufficiently large that, rather than incurring the costs of commercial insurance premiums (which includes the administrative costs of the insurer in providing the policy and an element of profit), they meet the costs directly in the cases that their members lose. In essence, they 'self insure'.

46. To allow membership organisations to recover that element of 'self insurance' in successful cases, the Act provides that regulated prescribed bodies can recover a sum towards the provision made to protect the member against the risk of having to meet an opponent's costs and their own disbursements. The section also allows for regulations prescribing the maximum amount that can be recovered in this way. In particular it provides that the way the recoverable sum is to be determined may be prescribed so that it may take into account the costs of commercial insurance.

47. The detail of the provisions in the Act applies to bodies of a prescribed description who undertake to meet liabilities of members or other persons who are parties to proceedings. Although most organisations which use this provision will be membership organisations, it is recognised that other organisations or bodies may offer similar services without requiring those they assist to be members of the organisation. Moreover, if membership organisations make their legal services available to non–members (such as the case of Unions extending services to member's families) it is important that those individuals are included in the new arrangements. The Act therefore states that such funding bodies are of a description "prescribed by regulations made by the Lord Chancellor...".

> *Q.16 What factors should inform the Lord Chancellor in prescribing such bodies?*

48. In addition to the mechanism for authorising funders, the Act provides that regulations may prescribe the maximum amount which can be recovered as a 'self insurance' element and may also prescribe the way that

sum is to be determined. Whilst the Government does not seek to impose a fixed sum for the 'self insurance' element, it does wish to ensure that all parties to proceedings are clear how any sum for self insurance has been calculated. It also wishes to ensure that those who are liable to pay the sum do not find themselves facing a sum which is greater than the costs of a commercial insurance policy. One solution could be to prescribe that:

(a) The level of the 'self insurance' premium should be no more than an equivalent commercial premium minus a fixed % to represent a commercial firm's profit level; and

(b) The organisation must demonstrate that the level of the 'self insurance' premium has been calculated with reference to the above, to the satisfaction of the court.

Q.17 Is the mechanism proposed above sufficient?
Q.18 At what level should the % reduction be set?

49. These changes will allow membership organisations to continue to offer their services as effectively as possible without requiring them to develop artificial mechanisms to take full advantage of the changes made to the CFA legislation. It should also protect the unsuccessful opponent from unreasonable levels of 'self insurance'.

CONCLUSION

Comments are requested on:

Conditional Fee Agreements

The proposals that:

- The other party should receive immediate notification of the existence of the CFA and whether a success fee is being claimed, but not the level of that fee.
- Both the client and the losing opponent should be able to challenge the success fee through an assessment by the courts.
- The recoverability of the success fee should not be retrospective but should apply only to CFAs which are entered into, and/or in respect of proceedings commenced, after the relevant section of the Act comes into force.

And on the following Questions:

Q.1   What (if any) sanctions would be appropriate if a party failed to disclose that they were funding their case under a CFA?

Q.2   Should the legal representative be required to produce written reasons for the level of uplift charged when the terms of the CFA are agreed?

Q.3   At what stage should this be disclosed to the court?

Q.4   Should a mechanism be developed for settling disputes over the assessment of success fees in cases settled pre issue?

Q.5   What form should that mechanism take?

Insurance premiums

The proposals that:

- The other party should receive immediate notification that an insurance policy covers the CFA but not the costs of that policy, or its coverage.
- The recoverability of the insurance premium will not be retrospective but will date from the point at which the policy was entered into, after the commencement of the relevant section of the Act.
- Both the client and the losing opponent should be able to challenge the level of the insurance premium through an assessment by the courts.

And on the following Question:

Q.6   When should the court receive information about the level of the insurance premium, its coverage and the date when the policy was signed?

New Regulations

The proposal that:

- The current requirements relating to the detail to be included in a CFA should be replicated, as should the requirements relating to the information to be provided to the client.

And on the following Questions:

Q.7   Should the solicitor be under an obligation to explain the agreement to the client in addition to providing written information?

Q.8   Should the solicitor be required to discuss with the client the desirability of insurance cover in a CFA, to cover the client's own costs liability and their potential liability for their opponent's costs?

Q.9   Should the solicitor be under an obligation to advise on the relative advantages and disadvantages of the available insurance funding products and to explain in detail what cover, etc. the recommended products provide?

Q.10 Should the maximum success fee remain at 100%?

Q.11 Should there be provision that, where the court considered the success fee to be excessive and not to be met in whole by the unsuccessful opponent, the client should not be responsible for meeting the difference between the success fee claimed and the amount recovered?

Q.12 To what extent are the current regulations sufficient to ensure that litigation friends are fully informed of the implications of CFAs?

Q.13 Are the circumstances of litigation friends such that specific regulations are necessary?

Q.14 Should the information be provided in writing and supplemented by an oral explanation of the consequences?

Q.15 Are there other specific categories of case where the charging of a success fee is unacceptable and a success fee should not be allowed?

Q.16 What factors should inform the Lord Chancellor in prescribing a funder?

Q.17 Is the mechanism for assessing the 'self insurance' element sufficient?

Q.18 At what level should the % reduction be set?

The Lord Chancellor believes that the approach canvassed above would offer a procedure which provides the court with sufficient information to assess whether the conditional fee and insurance premium was reasonable, without providing the opposing party with any privileged information, and would remove the distorting influence of hindsight.

However, the Lord Chancellor is aware that the approach canvassed may bring with it difficult issues which will requires resolution. In particular he recognises that issues raised may have consequences for the practitioner in the field and therefore welcomes comments on the issues raised in this paper.

End Notes:

1. The Funding Code, a new approach to funding civil cases. LAB 1999

2. Section 58 of the Courts and Legal Services Act 1990

3. The Conditional Fee Agreements Order 1995

4. The Conditional Fee Agreements Regulations 1995 (Annex A)

5. The Conditional Fee Agreements Order 1998 (Annex B)

6. Part 21.1(2) of the Civil Practice Rules states

    " 'child' means a person under 18; and

    'patient' means a person who by reason of metal disorder within the meaning of the Mental Health Act 1983 is incapable of managing his own affairs."

Pre-issue Contingency Fee Agreement

This agreement is a legally binding contract between you and Underwoods solicitors. It will take effect from the Agreement Date below and stay in force until it is terminated by you or by us or the case is concluded or court proceedings are issued – whichever of these events takes place first. **If this Agreement ends because court proceedings are issued it will cease to have any effect and will be replaced by the Conditional Fee Agreement between you and Underwoods of the same date.**

Agreement Date:

We, the solicitors: Kerry Underwood and Robert Males Trading as Underwoods, 1 Holywell Hill, St Albans, Hertfordshire, AL1 1ER

You, the client:

1. **What is covered by this agreement**

    Your claim against   ("your opponent") up to but not including the issue of court proceedings.

2. **What is not covered by this agreement**

    Any counterclaim against you.
    Any costs incurred after court proceedings are issued.

3. **Paying Us**

   If you recover money from your opponent, you pay us 25% of that plus any disbursements. This figure includes VAT at the standard rate, currently 17.5%.

   If you recover nothing from your opponent you do not pay us anything, except disbursements.

   NB. Disbursements are payment we make on your behalf to others involved in the case. We will notify you of disbursements incurred as we go along.

   If you end the agreement before any money is recovered, you are liable to pay our costs at the rate of £190 per hour with letters and telephone calls charged at £19.00 each unless they last for ten minutes or longer in which case they will be charged at the appropriate proportion of the hourly rate. All of these figures attract VAT at the standard rate of 17.5%.

   For what happens if we end the agreement before any money is recovered, please refer to paragraph 9.

   For what happens if court proceedings are issued, please refer to paragraph 10.

4. **Our responsibilities**

   We must always act in your best interests in pursuing your claim for damages and obtaining for you the best possible results, subject to our duty to the court; we must explain to you the risks and benefits of taking legal action; we must give you our best advice about whether to accept any offer of settlement.

5. **Your responsibilities**

   You must give us clear instructions which allow us to do our work properly; you must not ask us to work in an improper or unreasonable way; you must not deliberately mislead us; you must co-operate with us when asked; and you must pay for disbursements as the case goes on.

6. **What happens if you win**

   If you recover money from your opponent, you pay us 25% of any damages plus any disbursements. You agree that we may receive the money which your opponent pays. If your opponent refuses to accept our receipt, you will pay the cheque you receive into a joint bank account in your name and ours. Out of the money you agree to let us take 25% of the damages plus any outstanding disbursements. You take the rest.

   If your opponent fails to pay any money he has agreed to pay you in settlement of your claim, we have the right to take recovery action in your name to enforce the agreement. The costs of this action are payable by you to us in addition to 25% of the damages.

7. **What happens if you recover no money**

   If you recover no money you do not have to pay us anything, except our disbursements.

8. **What happens if you end this agreement**

   You can end the agreement at any time. If you terminate our retainer you will be deemed to have ended this agreement. You are then liable to pay us our costs incurred up to the date you end the agreement calculated at the hourly rate, set out above under "Paying Us". If you subsequently accept an offer made to you before the agreement end, or an offer which is not 20% greater than any offer which has been made, when the agreement ends, you will also pay us 25% of the damages (less such sum you have already paid to us by way of costs).

9. **What happens if we end this agreement**

   We can end the agreement if you do not keep to your responsibilitites in paragraph 5. You are then liable to pay us our costs incurred up to the date the agreement ends calculated at the hourly rate.

   We can end the agreement if we believe that you are unlikely to win and you disagree with us. You do not have to pay us anything.

   We can end the agreement if you reject our opinion about making a settlement with your opponent. You are then liable to pay us our costs incurred up to the date the agreement ends calculated on the hourly rate, plus any disbursements, but if you go on to recover damages 20% more than the offer we advised you to accept we will refund the costs you have paid us (but not the disbursements).

10. **What happens if this agreement ends because court proceedings are issued**

    The agreement ceases to have any effect and is replaced by your conditional fee agreement with us of the same date which then applies to all the work done from the date of both agreements.

11. **What happens after the agreement ends**

    We will have the right to preserve a lien over any property of your in our possession unless any money owed to us under this agreement is paid in full. This means we can keep your papers until you pay us in full.

12. **Costs**

    If we recover costs on your behalf they belong to us. In other words, if you win, you will pay us 25% of your damages whether or not we also recover any costs from your opponent.

Signed for the Solicitors..

Signed by the client ....

Index

Revised reprint (RR pages) follow the Tables at the front of the book.